THE
JEWISH TRAVELLERS
IN THE
TWELFTH CENTURY

Yosef Levanon

University Press
of America™

Library of Congress Catalog Card Number: 80-5521

For my dear parents,

Rachel and Eliezer Bayaz,

with love and respect.

TABLE OF CONTENTS

TABLE OF CONTENTS (Cont'd)

PREFACE

The twelfth century occupies a unique place in
Jewish Medieval history since it was a century of
turning points for the Jews both in Europe and in
the Orient. Although ultimately it was not until
the beginning of the thirteenth century that the
personal relationships between Jews and Christians
took a new turn, nonetheless, the three widespread
crusades of 1096, 1147, and 1189 ushered in an era
of suffering for the Jewish people.

Previous persecutions had been temporary and
were usually initiated by a leader of the state.
In contrast, the persecutions beginning with the
crusade of 1096 promulgated generations of hatred
against the Jews. These persecutions left unfor-
gettable memories in the Jewish mind, creating a
twelfth-century Jewish heroism, a willingness to
die for the "Sanctification of the Name." This dark
period, when the gap widened between the Jews and
the Christian society around them, is recorded in
the elegies and lamentations, the literary productions of the age.

In addition, the history of the Jews in Moslem
countries, especially Spain during the twelfth century, is an era of degeneration for Judaism: persecutions, forced conversions, and refugees on the
roads marked the closing of the golden age of Spanish Jewry and the destruction of Jewish life in
Moslem Spain. The crusading movement and the persecutions of the Almohades and the Almoravids con-
fronted Jewish leaders with the question of the
future of their nation.

The Jews, witnessing a great struggle over the
Holy Land, interpreted the events around them in
terms of the Messianic expectations of the time.
The rise and fall of a series of false Messiahs
both in the West and in the Orient confirmed the
Jewish inner turmoil. Since the Holy Land had been
historically promised to them by God, the Jews were
also very certain that the awaited Messiah would

return them there. This conviction was confirmed
by the Crusaders' increasing inability to maintain
their position in the Holy Land.

It is necessary here to point out the demogra-
phical factor of the Jewish population in the
twelfth century and the place of importance of these
Jewish centres. Previous to the twelfth century,
the majority of the Jewish population was concentrated in the old centres of the Orient, especially
in Babylonia, where there was intellectual leadership. It became increasingly clear, however, that
this period tolled the death knell for that leadership. Although in Babylonia itself there was a
temporary revival of the autonomous Jewish institutions, including the Exilarchate and the Academies,
one can feel the approaching end of this once
strong community. Soon the Mongol invaders would
put an end to the Abbasside caliphate and with it
would come the end of Jewish life there. Both numerically and intellectually, the centre of Jewish
life shifted from the Orient to Europe, where the
twelfth-century Renaissance was just beginning.

During this century of upheaval and persecution, three Jewish travellers fortunately left
accounts of their itineraries. They are Rabbi
Benjamin of Tudela, Rabbi Petachia of Regensburg,
and Rabbi Jacob ben Nathaniel ha-Cohen. Since
Rabbi Benjamin's account is the most detailed, historians pinpoint his travelogue as the most historically important.

The purpose of this book is to use the material left by these three Jewish travellers to analyze the changing Jewish world of the twelfth century. The author proposes to deal with the following subjects:

1) What were the links between the travellogue literature and the restless historial period?
Was the twelfth-century traveller incidental to the
time or a product of that era's Jewish state of
affairs? What were the goals of the travellers?
Can one consider them pilgrims on their way to the

Holy Land, merchants, or even rich tourists?

2) In the light of the crusading movement, it is important to analyze the place the Holy Land occupies within the travelogue literature. What was the concept of the Promised Land in the thoughts of the Jewish traveller of the time? What was the destiny and future of the Terra Sancta over which West and East fought? Was it true that the Promised Land was destined to remain in ruins forever? To whom had the Land been promised? In the second half of the twelfth century the crusaders were losing power and the Moslems were gaining strength, but was it true that Islam was going to become the owner of the Holy Land? Thus, the Holy Land question as it is reflected within the accounts is basic.

3) In the atmosphere of the crusading movement, a time of persecutions and forced conversion, the sanctification of the name of God through death and of the Hasidic movement, one is faced with the idea of a Messiah and the concept of redemption. It is quite important to explore how the complicated problem of exile and redemption were reflected in the travellers' thoughts.

4) Another important subject concerns the Jewish communities in the areas covered by the travellers. How ere they described economically, intellectually and politically within the accounts of the itineraries? It would be interesting to determine whether the decline of Jewish life in the Orient and its ascendance in the West can be detected within these accounts.

It is hoped that through this investigation of the travel accounts of Rabbi Benjamin, Rabbi Petachia and Rabbi Jacob ben Nathaniel in the twelfth century, a more meaningful view of Jewish history will be gained.

CHAPTER I

HISTORICAL BACKGROUND

The Twelfth Century and the Situation

of the Jews in Europe

The twelfth century, as a century of crusades, was a turning point in terms of Jewish emotions. The relationship between the Jews and their neighbours at that time seems to have deteriorated. One could say that Jews living in that period discerned the future historical impact of the crusades,[1] which were firmly imprinted on the historic consciousness of the Jews. While Dinur and others[2] think that the persecutions which accompanied the crusades caused the entire Jewish nation to reflect on their future, these reflections were, in fact, limited.

Before the crusades the Jews of Germany had dwelt in peace. They were able to own land and were not despised by the Gentiles. Afterwards, the atmosphere changed.[3] In an historical sense, the results of these persecutions differed from the results of previous attacks. Since the area of the massacres was so large, the echo which accompanied them was very great.[4] Undoubtedly, the Tatna'v (1096) massacres were the first of those which included, geographically speaking, a large inhabited Jewish area of Western and Central Europe. According to the author of the Hagezerot Hayesanot (Old Persecutions), the crusaders intended to exterminate the entire Jewish population of the area.[5] This account agrees with the chronicler Joseph ha-Cohen, who states that the crusaders killed the "Jews that happened to be in the placed in which they passed."[6] Other eyewitness reports and traditions confirm this. The picture is the same everywhere, as persecutions ranged all along the route from Normandy to Jerusalem. Because of the

suddenness and intensity of the persecutions, many
details of the attacks were remembered by subsequent generations.[7]

These persecutions differed from previous ones
in the intensity of religious zeal and social dis-
satisfaction. These factors encouraged the attacks
on the Jews, in which different social classes participated.[8] The call to redeem the holy sepulchre[9]
was connected with an emphasis on acquiring wealth
from conquered countries. Pope Urban II binds together the two elements of materialistic benefits
and religious enthusiasm:

> This land in which you live, surrounded
> on one side by the sea and on the other side
> by mountain peaks, can scarcely contain so
> many of you. It does not abound in wealth:
> indeed, it scarcely provides enough food for
> those who cultivate it. Because of this you
> murder and devour one another, you wage wars,
> and you frequently wound and kill one an-
> other. . . Begin the journey to the Holy
> Sepulcher: conquer that land . . . the land
> which was given by God to the children of
> Israel and which, as the Scripture says,
> 'is all milk and honey.'
> Jerusalem is the navel of the world, a
> land which is more fruitful than any other,
> a land which is like another paradise of
> delights... It begs increasingly that you
> will come to its aid. It looks for help
> from you, especially, because, as we have
> said, God has bestowed glory in arms upon
> you more than on any other nation. Under-
> take this journey, therefore, for the re-
> mission of your sins, with the assurance of
> glory which cannot fade in the kingdom of
> heaven.[10]

The combination of religious fervour and a
desire for wealth is especially noticeable in the
crusade of the peasants, who heeded the call of
the Pope and Peter the Hermit.[11] For the poor,
the crusade also meant obtaining freedom from

2

feudal rulers.[12] The mobs and their leaders considered attacks on the Jews as the first fulfil-
ment of their vows, and saw the confiscated property as a proper first payment. The religious element and the spontaneous reaction is also described
by Albert of Aachen.[13]

The fact that all social levels of Christian
society took part in the persecution[14] shows how
isolated the Jews were. The cruelty of the movement is characterized by the language it used,
speaking of revenge against the "enemies of God."
The author of the Old Persecutions reports:

> Whenever upon their way they came into
> cities in which Jews had their dwellings,
> each said to the other 'Here we are setting
> out on so long a journey toward the grave
> of the Lord and meaning to be revenged upon
> the Ishmaelites; and behold, in our very
> midst dwell the Jews who hung Him innocent
> upon the Cross and slew Him. Let us be up
> and take the revenge ourselves first upon
> them: Let us stamp them out from among
> the people's that the name of Israel be no
> more remembered: Or else let them become
> even as ourselves and accept our faith.'[15]

An easy way for a Jew to be saved was to forsake
his religion and accept Christianity.[16] The emotional descriptions given by the Church concerning
the sufferings of Christians at the hands of the
infidels[17] helped prepare the Christians to carry
out cruel deeds against the Jews.[18] Even the
Christian chroniclers tell us how cruelly the Jews
were murdered.[19]

The poetry of twelfth-century Franco-German
Jewry everywhere exhibits a spirit of martyrdom.
Hymns lamenting the downfall of communities were
sung in the synagogues, and many elegies were
written by eminent rabbis. These poems helped give
the Jews a sense of the anger and sorrow which had
been experienced.[20] The recorders of the persecutions gave a vivid picture of the cruelty of the

3

crusaders and how merciless they were.

Sanctification of the name of God became a no-
ble ideal and was real to the Jews of those generations. Entire families committed suicide to avoid
forced baptism. The Jews considered themselves to
be "a chosen generation" destined by God to sancti-
fy His name by death. R. Solomon ben Simon, a contemporary chronicler, gave the following account of
the martyrdom in Mainz:

> On the third day of Sivan, at one time the
> holy day of cleansing for Israel ... the pure
> and holy souls of the community of Mainz were
> exalted and deemed worthy of joining God....
> The villain Emicho, the enemy of the Jews,
> along with his detachment, arrived at noon,
> and the townsmen opened the gates for him.
> The enemies of God said one to another, 'Look,
> the gates are open; now let us avenge the
> blood of the crucified....' When the sons of
> the holy covenant became aware that their
> fate was sealed, all of them, old and young,
> girls, children, man and maidservants—
> mourned their lives and justified God's judge-
> ment. They said to one another 'Let us be
> strong, in order to endure what the holy
> faith imposes on us.... Blessed is the one
> who perishes in behalf of the One and Eternal
> .... The enemies are approaching. Let us
> sacrifice ourselves for God as soon as pos-
> sible. Whoever has a knife, let him examine
> it, if it has a chipped spot, and then let
> him cut our throats in the Name of the Eter-
> nal One— and then let him cut his own throat,
> or stick it into his belly....' Men killed
> their wives and children. A tender mother
> killed her beloved child. Girls, brides,
> bridegrooms looked through the windows, and
> cried, 'Lord, see what we are doing in behalf
> of your Holy Name!' ... Everyone brought a
> sacrifice, and himself turned into a sacri-
> fice.... All of them immolated themselves in
> behalf of the great and awesome Name. Who-
> ever heard or witnessed the like of it? Has

4

there, since the time of Adam, ever been such an akeda, 1100 sacrifices in one day?[21]

The biblical story of Abraham, who was willing to sacrifice his only son, became very meaningful in this period. In turn, the courage of the Franco-German communities became a significant symbol for later generations. They were able to transfer to their descendants the belief that Israel was a nation of God, and that their generation was a chosen one.

All in all a "special climate" coloured the period between the first crusade (1095-96) and the crusade directed against the Albigensian movement of the south of France (1208-13).[22] This climate was produced by a combination of religious fanaticism and an unrestrained desire for wealth. The major factors which contributed to the shattering of Jewish life were the basic insecurity of Jewish life and property, as well as the danger of false accusations which could lead to martydom and forced conversions. There is a great deal of evidence of the lack of security from both Jewish and non-Jewish sources.[23] The best proof is found in the letters of protection given to Jews by the popes of this period.[24] From these letters it is apparent that robbery and murder of Jews, as well as digging up corpses and charging Jews for their reburial, were common occurrences.

It is not accidental that immediately following the first phase of the crusader movement accusations against Jews became frequent. The year 1171 marked the beginng of an era of "blood accusations," where Jews were accused of poisoning rivers, wells and of ritual murder. This period had a lasting effect on the Jews, who became humble and suspicious. They kept their distance from their Christian neighbours, for an emotional and psychological barrier was erected between them.[25]

Every city produced its own accusations. The author of the Old Persecutions is conscious of these accusations as he reports:

...and so happened on the Tenth of Iyyar on
Sunday they played a trick.... They took an
animal corpse that had been buried thirty
days, they carried it into the city and declared: 'See what Jews did to one of us,
they took one gentile and drowned him and
poured that water in our wells in order to
kill us!' When everybody heard that...they
said: 'This is the time to take revenge of
our crucified, whom their ancestors had
killed! Now, none of them will be saved,
even the babies....'[26]

Here is another sample accusation:

Now will we say something of what befell in
King Stephen's time. In his time the Jews
of Norwich bought a Christian child before
Easter and tortured him with all the tor-
tures wherewith our Lord was tortured, and
on Long Friday hanged him on a road in
hatred of our Lord, and afterwards buried
him. They thought it would be concealed,
but our Lord showed that he was a holy
martyr. And the monks took him and buried
him honourably in the monastery, and through
our Lord he makes wonderful and manifold
miracles and he is— Saint William.[27]

The inevitable punishment for the entire Jewish
community was expected and planned for in advance.

Each new crusade brought with it new massacres, and the extent of the disaster depended on
local conditions. During the second crusade (1147)
the persecutions were mainly in France and
Germany; in the third (1189) in England and
Germany; in the fourth (1202) Germany, France and
England; during the crusade against the Albigenses
(1208-13) they took place in the north and south
of France. While the social elements of the Christian Society who participated and the means Jews
used to defend themselves varied from one area to
the next, a common effect of the persecutions is
noticeable: there were signs of deterioration of

6

the general condition of the Jews.[28]

A system for expelling Jews crystallized first
in France. The expulsions were accompanied by
forced conversions and confiscation of property.
Rigord, who began his chronicle <u>Gesta Philippi
Augusti</u> about 1186, reports:

> In the year of our Lord's Incarnation 1182,
> in the month of April,...an edict went
> forth from the most serene King, Philip
> Augustus, that all the Jews of his kingdom
> should be prepared to go forth by the com-
> ing feast of St. John the Baptist. And
> then the King gave them leave to sell each
> his movable goods before the time fixed,
> that is, the feast of St. John the Baptist.
> But their real estate, that is, houses,
> fields, vineyards, barns, winepresses, and
> such alike, he reserved for himself and his
> successors, the kings of the French.[29]

Finally the doctrine of persecuting Jews became
the official policy of the Church. Pope Innocent
III, in his letter to the Count of Nevers, January
17, 1208, says:

> The Lord made Cain a wanderer and a fugi-
> tive over the earth, but set a mark upon
> him, making his head to shake, lest any
> finding him should slay him; thus the Jews,
> against whom the blood of Jesus Christ
> calls out, although they ought not be
> killed, lest the Christian people forget
> the Divine Law, yet as wanderers ought
> they to remain upon the earth, until their
> countenance be filled with shame and they
> seek the name of Jesus Christ, the Lord.
> That is why blasphemers of the Christian
> name ought not to be aided by Christian
> princes to oppress the servants of the
> Lord, but ought rather be forced into the
> servitude of which they made themselves
> deserving when they raised sacrilegious
> hands against Him who had come to confer

7

true liberty upon them, thus calling down
His blood upon themselves and upon their
children....[30]

The Fourth Lateran Council (1215) formulated
the attitude towards the Jews into an organized
theory, which in practice was to keep the Jews in
Christian lands miserable, humble and feeling in-
ferior.[31] The literary evidence from that generation expresses the emotions of the Jews.[32]

The condition of the Jews declined in Moslem
lands as well after 1096.[33] No matter how they
differed in political and social order in the
twelfth century, Moslem Spain and Christian Europe
shared one common trait, for in both places refu-
fees could be seen on the highways. Religious motives propelled major movements in both areas, for
while the crusaders proceeded to Asia, the zealots
of Islam invaded Spain to establish their purified
religion.[34] Thus Moslem Spain was continuously at
war against the fanatic Almoravids and Almohades
in the twelfth century. The spirit of the times
manifested itself in both Christian and Moslem
movements. One reads about the desire of the leaders to purify the religion and to exterminate those
who disagreed with them.[35] This was a restless and
unstable society, fearing its rulers and waiting
for the appropriate time to get rid of them.

A new element in history of Jews in Moslem
areas was the forced conversions to Islam. The
situation deteriorated when the fanatic Almohades
appeared from Africa. They destroyed Jewish settlements in North Africa and southern Spain, and
caused the beginning of forced conversions. The
extent of the calamity caused by the Almohades in
Spain is expressed in a poetic lament of Abraham
ibn Ezra.[36]

All of this influenced the decline and destruction of the Jewish communities in those areas.
Thus, "that is how the Jewish center removed in
Spain: from the south to the north, from the Moslem principalities to the Christian— to Castilla,

8

Aragonia and Navarres."[37] Abraham ibn Daud, the
Jewish chronicler, an eyewitness to these events,
wrote:

> ...Some yielded to the sons of Edom, so that
> the Christians could get them out of the
> Moslem country. Others departed, naked and
> barefooted, stubbing their toes along the
> dark hills, and their children cried for
> bread in vain.... However, He who prepares
> the remedy before the illness sets in, im-
> pelled King Alfonso VII to appoint the dig-
> nitary Rabbi Judah ibn Ezra, as head of
> Calatrava, that had become a refuge through
> which the exiles had passed. Rabbi Judah
> freed the captives, fed the hungry, pro-
> vided water for the thirsty, clothed the
> naked and cared for all the needy until
> they reached the district of Toledo.[38]

Bearing in mind the above, it is not difficult to understand the rise at that time of a new
movement in Franco-German Jewry, the pietist movement. German Jews, already inclined towards great
piety, became yet more devout because of their
sufferings. A moralizing literature (mussar) emerged which reflected their views and beliefs. The
Book of the Devout (Sefer Hasidim)[39] became the
most popular of this genre of books. Echoes of
the Crusades were heard in its advice and directions. The book contains elements of mysticism
and superstitions.[40] In a period saturated with
religiosity, messianic expectations and meditations
about redemption are to be expected. Dinur may be
right[41] in that this messianism is found in an
imaginary world, and that its dreams and expectations are out of touch with reality.[42] Nevertheless, those dreams are real to the dreamers. For
the Jews of the period all of the signs of the end
of days were present: political disintegration,
wars and religious struggles, and invasions of
foreign people (Seljuks, Crusaders).

There is a special significance to this last
point. The new invasions raised in the Jewish

9

imagination the possibility of the existence of
free Jewish tribes in an unknown land. The appearance of such tribes would mark the beginning of the
redemption. Is it possible that the travellers
made an effort to obtain information concerning
these Jewish tribes?

The crusade movement created a new tension between East and West, between Islam and Christendom.
The Jews were affected. In many forms, Jewish
thought in this period was a direct response to the
challenge of the times.[43] Nevertheless, one should
keep in mind that though the crusades revealed the
physical danger in which the Jewish communities
stood, a more serious deterioration of the Jewish
situation did not occur until the thirteenth century. The crusades apparently did not play the de-
cisive role in the evolution of the condition of
the Jews in Europe. They were only one element,
albeit a significant one, in a larger and more com-
plex context.

Footnotes

[1] B.Z. Dinur, Israel in Diaspora (Israel Ba-
gola), 5 vols., 2d ed. (Tel Aviv, 1961-65, (2)I,
28: A. Haberman, A Book of Pogroms of Germany and
France: Memoires of Eyewitnesses in the Period of
the Crusades and Chosen Piyutim (Jerusalem, 1946),
p. 53; A. Neubauer and M. Stern (eds.), Quellen
zur Geschichte der Juden in Deutschland, 2 vols.
(Berlin, 1892), II, 25.

[2] Dinur, Israel in Diaspora (2)I, 1; S.W.
Baron, Social and Religious History of the Jews,
8 vols. and index vol. (Philadelphia, 1952-60),
IV, 89; H. Liebeschütz, "The Crusading Movement in
its Bearing on the Christian Attitude Towards
Jewry," J.J.S, X (1959), 110.

[3] H. Graetz, History of the Jews, 5 vols.
(Philadelphia, 1891-1898),III, 297; L. Dasberg,
Untersuchungen über die Entwertung des Judenstatus
im XI. Jahrhundert (Paris, 1965), p. 185.

[4]Dinur, Israel in Diaspora (2)I, 42; R.
Gedaliah ibn Yihiah, Chain of Tradition (Venetia,
1587), pp. 2-3.

[5]Haberman, p. 94; Neubauer and Stern, II, 48.

[6]Joseph ha-Cohen, Emek Ha-Backha (Valley of
Tears), ed. M. Letteris (Vienna, 1852), p. 14.

[7]Dinur, Israel in Diaspora (2)I, 1.

[8]Ibid., 2; Liebeschütz, 109.

[9]Dana C. Munro, "The Speech of Pope Urban II
at Clermont, 1085," AHR, XI (1905-6), 239.

[10]Robert the Monk, Historia Hierosolimitana, I,
1-3, RHC, HOcc, III, 729-30. Trans. James A.
Brundage, Crusades, A Documentary Survey (Wisconsin,
1962), p. 19.

[11]F. Duncalf, "The Peasants' Crusade," AHR,
XXVI (1920-21), 442; Liebeschütz, 109; N. Golb,
"New Light on the Persecution of French Jews at the
Time of the First Crusade," P.A.A.J.R., XXXIV
(1966), 23-34.

[12]J. Prawer, A History of the Latin Kingdom of
Jerusalem, 2 vols. (Jerusalem, 1963), I. 59.

[13]Dinur, Israel in Diaspora (2)I, 12; Albert
of Aachen, I, 2; RHC, HOcc, IV, 272.

[14]Dinur, Israel in Diaspora (2)I, 15; Haberman,
p. 94; Neubauer and Stern, II, 48.

[15]Dinur, Israel in Diaspora (2)I, 14; Haberman,
p. 93; Neubauer and Stern, II, 47; S. Schiffman,
"Heinrich IV und die Bischöfe in ihrem Verhalten
zu den deutschen Juden zur Zeit des ersten Kreuz-
zuges," Zeitschrift fur die Geschichte der Juden
in Deutschland, III (1931), 42, n. 13.

[16]See Solomon ben Simon's report, Neubauer and
Stern, II, 26; Schiffmann, 244-245.

[17]William of Tyre, History of Deeds Done Beyond the Sea, ed. E.A. Babcock and A.C. Krey, 2 vols. (New York, 1943), I, 88-92; Fulcher of Chartres, RHC, HOcc, I, 3.

[18]Dinur, Israel in Diaspora (2)I, 3.

[19]Albert of Aachen, RHC, HOcc, IV, 293. William of Tyre reports: "and so happened that those who had to go on their way in fear of God and to turn their hearts to God's commandments and to keep the evangelical discipline, turned instead to insanity. Also they slaughtered cruelly the Jews they found in the states and in the cities who were not expecting such things and did not plan cautiously. Especially large was the slaughter in the cities of Cologne and Mainz." William of Tyre, I, 113.

[20]Neubauer and Stern, II, 27, 28, 29, 40, 45, 46. Also see Schiffmann, 243-251.

[21]Dinur, Israel in Diaspora (2)I, 4.

[22]Ibid., 23; Neubauer and Stern, II, 6-8.

[23]Dinur, Israel in Diaspora (2)I, 128; Neubauer and Stern, II, 66.

[24]Migne, Patrologiae cursus completus, Series latina, CCXXI vols. (Paris, 1844-1864), CC. Col. 1339, No. 243; J. Aronius, Regesten zur Geschichte der Juden im fränkischen und deutschen Reiche bis zum Jahre 1273 (Berlin, 1902), No. 313a; the repetition of the bull Constitutio pro Judeis by Eugene III (1145-1153), Alexander III (1159-1181), Clement III (1187-1191), Coelestine III (1191-1198) and, reissued by Innocent III on Sept. 15, 1199 is explained by J. Régné, Etude sur la condition des Juifs de Narbonne du Ve au XIVe siècle (Narbonne, 1912), p. 30.

[25]Neubauer and Stern, II, 49, 66, 69; G. Kisch, The Jews in Medieval Germany (Chicago,

1949), p. 338; E.L. Dietrich, "Das Judentum im Zeitalter der Kreuzzüge," Saeculum, III (1952), 95, 126-127; Dasberg, p. 193.

[26] Habermann, p. 95; Neubauer and Stern, II, 49.

[27] J. Jacobs, The Jews of Angevin England (London, 1893), p. 19. Full English translation may be found in J.R. Marcus, The Jew in the Medieval World (Cincinnati, 1938), pp. 121-26 and on pp. 127-30 there is an account of the blood accusation of 1171.

[28] Dinur, Israel in Diaspora (2)I, 58; D. Berger, "The Attitude of St. Bernard of Clairvaux toward the Jews," P.A.A.J.R., XL (1972), 89, 101, 103, 105, 107-108.

[29] J.R. Marcus, The Jew in the Medieval World, p. 26; see also M. Pfaff, "Die soziale Stellung des Judentums in der Auseinandersetzung zwischen Kaiser und Kirche vom 3. bis zum 4. Laterankonzil 1179-1215," Vierteljahrschrift fur Sozial- und Wirtschaftsgeschichte, LII (1965), 200-201. It should be noted that the royal decree expelled Jews from the royal domain. The reign of Philip Augustus saw the status of the Jews more clearly defined and enforced (G.I. Langmuir, "Judei Nostri and the beginning of Capetian legislation," Traditio, XVI [1960], 214). It should be kept in mind that because of the limited effective royal power in France, up to the end of the 12th century, there was no central authority to protect the Jews (Langmuir, 206). The struggle between the magnates, and the royal power continued even beyond the 12th century. Therefore the effectiveness of the expulsion order could not be very harsh. As to the extensive discussion of the development of the control of the Frency Jewry, see Langmuir, 203-239. While Langmuir claims that the accession of Philip Augustus marked the end of a long period of security and royal generosity (ibid., 209), a slightly different picture of Northern French Jewry is given by R. Chazan who states that the available sources for the twelfth

and thirteenth centuries reflect a "striking level of security," R. Chazan, "Jewish Settlement in Northern France, 1096-1306," R.E.J., CXXVIII (1969), 43; R. Chazan, "The Bray Incident of 1192," P.A.A.J.R., XXXVII (1969), 5-6, 14; R. Chazan, Medieval Jewry in Northern France (Baltimore, 1973), pp. 26-29, 36, 38, 68, 134.

[30]S. Grayzel, The Church and the Jews in the XIII Century (New York, 1966), p. 127. See also the letter (July 15, 1205) to the Archbishop of Sens and Bishop of Paris, ibid., p. 115.

[31]During the thirteenth century the papacy became very strong (A.L. Smith, Church and State in the Middle Ages [Oxford, 1913], p. 6). However, for the Jews the thirteenth century marked the commencement of the most unfortunate period of their history (Grayzel, The Church and the Jews in the XIII Century, p. 3). In the Fourth Lateran Council (1215) the church's attitude towards the Jews was crystallized in a thoroughgoing theory of persecutions. It became the policy of the church to reduce the Jews in Christian lands to a lowly and miserable condition, and the Fourth Lateran Council made it the duty of the church and its leaders to enforce such a policy. Thus we read, "The order is given them to let the Jews wear clothes by which they might be distinguished from Christians,..." (Innocent III to the Archibishops and Bishops of France, 1215-1216; Migne, CCXVI, 994). Thus Innocent III effectively placed the Jews outside of Christian society. The church attacked the very foundations of the economic, political and social life of the Jews, and the reason for this activity was said to be a concern for the individual Christian (J.D. Mansi, et al., Sacrorum conciliorum nova et amplissima collectio, LIII vols. [Paris, 1901-1927], XXII, 1054-55). The Fourth Lateran Council decreed: (1) To outlaw Jewish money lending at excessive rates of interest, to save the individual Christian from ruin at the hands of the Jews involved in lending of money (Mansi, XXII, 1054-55); (2) the prohibition of commercial relations with the Jews (Mansi,

14

XXII, 1055); (3) the wearing of a badge (Mansi,
XXII, 1055); (4) that the Jews cannot be seen in
public on Christian holidays (Mansi, XXII, 1055);
(5) a prohibition against nominating Jews to public
positions (Mansi, XXII, 1058); (6) to make sure
that Jews who accepted Christianity would not ad-
here to their former religion (Mansi, XXII, 1058).

[32]Solomon ben R. Abraham in his hymn "Living
God," S. Berenfeld (ed.), Book of Tears, 2 vols.
(Berlin, 1924-26), I, 269.

[33]Dinur, Israel in Diaspora (2)I, 304.

[34]Ibid., 312.

[35]Ibid.

[36]In his elegy "Aha Jarad Ali Sfarad," Dinur,
Israel in Diaspora (2)I, 319.

[37]S.M. Dubnov, The History of the Jews, 5 vols.
(New York, 1968), II, 731.

[38]Sefer Haqabbalah, ed. G.D. Cohen (Philadelphia, 1967), pp. 97-98; A. Neubauer (ed.), Medieval Jewish Chronicles, 2 vols. (Oxford, 1887-95),
I, 79-80.

[39]Sefer Hasidim (The Book of the Devout), ed.
Reuven Margalioth (Jersualem, 1970), passim.

[40]Dietrich, 128; G. Scholem, "Jüdische Mystik
in Westeuropa im 12. und 13. Jahrhundert," Miscellanea Medievalia IV: Das Judentum im Mittelalter
(Berlin, 1966), pp. 41, 45.

[41]Dinur, Israel in Diaspora (2)III, 358.

[42]Ibid., 361.

[43]Baron, Social and Religious History of the
Jews, IV, 91.

15

CHAPTER II

BIOGRAPHICAL ELEMENTS OF OUR TRAVELLERS

Benjamin of Tudela

We know very little about the author of this
extremely important itinerary.[1] During his travels
he does not talk about himself which makes it difficult to know him better. All that is known about
the traveller is based on the Preface,[2] which neces-
sitates its being quoted here:

> This is the book of travels, which was com-
> piled by Rabbi Benjamin, the son of Jonah, of
> the land of Navarre,— his reponse be in Para-
> dise.
>   The said Rabbi Benjamin set forth from
> Tudela, his native city, and passed through
> many remote countries, as is related in his
> book. In every place which he entered, he
> made a record of all that he saw, or was told
> of by trustworthy persons— matters not pre-
> viously heard of in the land of Sepharad.
> Also he mentions some of the sages and illus-
> trious men residing in each place. He
> brought this book with him on his return to
> the country of Castile, in the year 4933
> (C.E. 1173). The said Rabbi Benjamin is a
> wise and understanding man, learned in the
> Law and the Halacha, and wherever we have
> tested his statements we have found them ac-
> curate, true to fact and consistent; for he
> is a trustworthy man.[3]

One must realize that the author of the Preface to the itinerary reminds the reader that the
information which Benjamin of Tudela brought with
him was hitherto unknown in Spain. His contemporaries were ready to listen and question him
about what he saw and heard. We can detect the
excitement that this itinerary must have aroused

16

through the words of the unknown author in his Preface when he reports on the newness of his information.

We also learn from the Preface that Rabbi Benjamin was knowledgeable in both Jewish Law and Halacha. Further proof of his education is in the very title "Rabbi."[4] The author emphasizes the fact that despite criticism, R. Benjamin's account was later proven to be true, accurate and consistent, for "in every place which he entered, he made a record of all that he saw, or was told of by trustworthy persons...."

In general, it may be said that Benjamin possessed a clear insight into the conditions and the history of the countries in which he travelled. It is probable that he travelled as a merchant,[5] and his history of commerce will always be looked upon as one of the earliest and most valued sources on the subject.[6]

From the itinerary itself we find further verification of his reliability. He supplies us with valuable details on various subjects, both Jewish and non-Jewish,[7] such as commerce, religion, and customs. There is no general account of the Mediterranean world or of the Middle East in this period which approaches that of Benjamin of Tudela in importance, whether for Jewish or for general history. He indicates the distances between the various towns he visited, tells who stood at the head of the Jewish communities and who were the most notable scholars.[8] He notes economic conditions, describing the activity of merchants from various lands in Barcelona, Montpellier, Alexandria, and speaks frequently of the occupations of the Jews. In this type of account there is really little opportunity for the traveller to reveal his halachic knowledge. However, according to Baron he did reveal an amazing awareness of sociological factors of the time.[9]

He was deeply interested in Jewish scholarship, and his account of the intellectual life in

17

Provence and Baghdad is of major importance, as is
his characterization of the organization of synagogue life in Egypt. The various religious sects
that were present also attracted his attention.
His descriptions of non-Jewish life are vivid as
well. He speaks of the continual fighting at Genoa
and Pisa, the seaports from which the Crusaders departed in Southern Italy. He reveals the weaknesses of the Byzantine Empire, and his account of the
Assassins and of the Ghuzz Turks are primary historical sources.[10] R. Benjamin is said to be the
first European of modern times to mention China by
its present name.[11]

        It is important, however, to remember that R.
Benjamin's chief interest was undoubtedly the conditions of the Jews of the countries that he visited. His account, which furnishes us with reli-
able details, is considered to be a source of primary importance for the history of the Jews in the
twelfth century. With the sole exception of the
Sefer Haqabbala, written about the same time by
Abraham ibn-Daud of Toledo,[12] there is no work
which compares with Benjamin's in value on these
subjects. His statistical data give us the first
accurate account of the density of the Jewish population in certain areas.[13]

        His journey took him from Tudela by way of
Saragossa and Tarragona to Barcelona, and thence
via Gerona into Provence. From Marseilles he went
by sea to Genoa, and through Pisa to Rome. From
Rome he went southward. He departed at Otranto,
sailing by way of Corfu to Arta, and then into
Greece. He seems to have spent a considerable
amount of time in Constantinople. From here he
went by sea through the Aegean Archipelago to
Cyrpus. He then crossed onto the mainland, making
his way southward via Antioch, Sidon, Tyre, and
Acre into the Holy Land. He travelled throughout
the Holy Land. On leaving Tiberias, he travelled
north to Damascus, and from there through Aleppo
and Mosul to Baghdad. He probably travelled
widely in Mesopotamia and Persia. Although it is
not likely that he was in China, India or Ceylon,

he does record some details of these countries, probably from hearsay.[14]

His own personal account is resumed in Egypt. From Egypt he re-embarked for Sicily and from there he probably made his way back to Spain by sea. He ends with an inaccurate picture of Jewish life in northern France and Germany, again presumably based on hearsay.[15] He re-entered Spain through Castile.[16]

According to all we have said up to this point there is no reason for surprise that scholars hold a very high opinion of Benjamin of Tudela.[17] Those personal qualifications found in the Preface— a "man of truth," "consistent," "a trustworthy person"— were emphasized in the very earliest known manuscript of the itinerary, which is in the British Museum. Baron notes that the conclusion arrived at by the author in his Preface bears the stamp of official action. Those who had "tested his statements" and "found them accurate" must have been persons of some authority. The description of Benjamin as a learned man in Rabbinic Judaism may have been challenged by later writers. These critics pointed to weaknesses in Benjamin's Hebrew style; however, these doubts were laid to rest by later writers.[18]

Benjamin's trustworthiness is emphasized by Borchardt who says that R. Benjamin, as he appears from the Preface to his itinerary, was regarded by his contemporaries as highly trustworthy. After considerable geographical research, he found this verdict constantly confirmed[19] and feels all the inaccuracies with which Benjamin has been charged are due to our own faulty interpretation. He confirmed his opinion by comparing Benjamin's account of the Lateran sculptures with that of Magister Gregorius, finding them to be the same.[20]

The details which have been mentioned above suffice to give us an idea of the rich content of Benjamin's account. Although his accounts are not entirely free from fiction, the narrative is

written in both a clear and concise manner.[21] He
is described by Purchas, who published an English
translation of his itinerary in 1625, as being
"reckoned one of the greatest travellers that ever
lived."[22] He is also described as the greatest
medieval Jewish traveller.[23] It has been said that
"whatever his intentions may have been, we owe
Benjamin no small debt of gratitude for handing to
posterity records that form a unique contribution
to our knowledge of geography and ethnology in the
Middle Ages."[24] Pinkerton is one of very few scholars who thinks that Benjamin of Tudela was a credulous man; nevertheless, he adds: "...yet there is
something surely due to him for the lights he has
communicated to the world."[25]

    Benjamin brought with him notes he had made
during his travels[26] ("...he made a record of all
that he saw, or was told....") and the details were
later compiled— as the Preface states— from these
notes. Some scholars doubt that Benjamin's itinerary was issued during his own lifetime, because
when the author of the Preface refers to this
evaluation of Benjamin's itinerary he continually
uses the past tense, saying for example, "wherever
we have tested" or "we have found."[27] However, for
Baron, there is no question that the evaluation was
issued during his lifetime. Even the "nishmato
'eden"— ("...his repose be in Paradise")— is only
a subsequent addition to answer later critics.[28]

    The unknown author of the Preface probably
compiled the account for Banjamin from those notes,
retaining the traveller's own words but omitting
much.[29] Benjamin, for instance, claims to have
noted everything that he saw and all that he heard
and his notes may have contained the names of his
informants, but in the itinerary as we have it today, according to W. Bacher, only Abraham the Pious
is mentioned by name.[30] W. Bacher did not realize[31] that there is one more informant mentioned
by name in the itinerary. He is R. Moses who gave
the information concerning the expedition of
Sinjar.[32]

20

Another fact which may be noted from the Preface is that "He brought this book with him on his return to the country of Castile, in the year 4933."[33] Accordingly, we know the year he returned to Spain, but we do not know the exact year he left Spain to begin his journey. Therefore, it is unclear and still controversial as to how many years R. Benjamin actually spent on his travels.

According to Adler[34] and Beazley,[35] the length of time he journeyed can be approximated. Adler continues by saying that very early in his journey, Benjamin visited Rome, where he found R. Jechiel, an official of the Pope Alexander.[36] According to Adler, that could be only Alexander III. Frederick Barbarossa supported the antipope Victor IV, and therefore Alexander had to leave Rome soon after his election in 1159 but before his consecration.[37] He returned to settle permanently in Rome in November 23, 1165, but was forced to leave again in 1167. Therefore, Adler assumes Benjamin must have been in Rome between the end of 1165 and 1167.[38]

Adler continues to say that Benjamin found in Cairo that the Fatimite Caliph was the recognized ruler.[39] This was El-'Adid, who died September 13, 1171. He was the last of the Fatimite dynasty.[40] A short time before his death, Saladin had become the ruler of Egypt[41] and had ordered the Khotba to be read[42] in the name of the Abbaside Caliph, el-Mostadi of Baghdad.[43] Thus, Benjamin's absence from Europe must be placed between 1166-1171.[44]

On his return, Benjamin passed through Sicily. At this time, the island was no longer governed by viceroy.[45] William II (the Good) came of proper age in 1169 to become king and Benjamin's visit here took place immediately afterwards, in 1170. Adler sees all the information presented in the itinerary as consistent with the view that R. Benjamin did in fact come to Sicily in the year 1170.[46]

21

Rabbi Petachia of Regensburg

We know even less about Petachia. His itinerary, described as a "Sivuv ha-Olam" or "world tour," does not furnish us any clear picture concerning his life.

R. Petachia, son of R. Jacob, the brother of the Tosaphist, R. Isaac Halavan, and of R. Nachman of Ratisbon,[47] was born in the first half of the twelfth century.[48] His permanent home appears to have been in Ratisbon (Regensburg), although he also resided in Prague. He set out on his "world tour" at the time that Benjamin of Tudela had already completed his own,[49] and their accounts complement each other in depicting the Jewish world of the twelfth century.[50]

Since R. Petachia's residence was on the eastern European border, it was inevitable that he would choose a route different from that of Benjamin of Tudela. From Prague he went to Poland, Kiev, and then across the Dnieper to the Crimea; from here to the Caucasus, and finally to Mesopotamia and Syria. In Mesopotamia and Syria he discovered established Jewish communities, in Mosul, Baghdad and Damascus, which he described in detail. Petachia visited Palestine, but found few Jews there. R. Petachia's itinerary is especially important geographically and historically because it can be used to verify Benjamin's itinerary. Simultaneously, the Holy Land became better known as a result of the "Sivuv."[51] Petachia's reference to the Karaites in Crimea[52] was the only source of information about this Jewish sect until his time. They were again forgotten until the beginning of the eighteenth century.[53]

It is impossible to state the exact time that Petachia set out on his travels, but when he came to Damascus he states: "This is a large city; the King of Egypt rules over it."[54] Thus, Petachia must have been there after Nureddin died in 1174[55] when Saladin captured Damascus and became the ruler

22

of the country.[56] At the same time the Crusaders were still in Jerusalem, as evidenced by Petachia's statement: "There is also a beautiful place which the Ishmaelites built in ancient times when Jerusalem was still in the hands of the Ishmaelites."[57] This indicates that the Rabbi arrived in Jerusalem before October 2, 1187, when the city came under the rule of Islam once again.[58] Accordingly, we are able to limit the period in which Petachia was on his travels between November 1174 and 1185.[59]

Grünhut[60] states that R. Petachia provides us with further clues to establish the time of his visit in the Orient. We know, Grünhut says, that Maimonides effected a change in the way the Eighteen Benedictions were to be recited. Following this change, the congregation participated, silently saying the prayer. This change was accepted in Egypt, as well as in Palestine, Syria and Babylonia. R. Petachia states clearly in his itinerary that in Babylona "...someone recites the prayer of Baruch Sheamar with a loud voice, another rises and recites all the praises and in this he is joined by the whole congregation, his voice, however, being heard above them all...and then goes on with the other prayer."[61] In participating silently "...with the other prayers" they probably followed Maimonides, Grünhut concludes.[62]

Furthermore, R. Petachia states in his itinerary that while he was in Baghdad he saw ambassadord from the Kings of Meshech requesting teachers and "Every disciple of the wise who is poor goes there to teach them the Law and Babylonian Talmud. From the land of Egypt the disciples go there to teach them."[63] Why the disciples in Egypt went to teach we do not know, as R. Petachia states that a request was sent only to Baghdad. Grünhut assumes that the same request for teachers was made of Maimonides in Egypt as of R. Samuel B. Ali in Baghdad. Since R. Petachia did not know about this request from Egypt and, since Maimonides was then already well known, this episode could not have happened later than 1177. Grünhut concludes,[64] therefore, that R. Petachia came to

the Orient after 1177. While we do not know how
long R. Petachia spent journeying between Prague
and Babylonia, in Grünhut's opinion[65] R.
Petachia came to Babylonia about 1179-80, thus probably beginning his journey from Prague shortly before
1178.

In his account there is no information on his
travels before he reached the Crimea, and very little on Crimea and Tartary. The entire account is
devoted to his travels in Babylonia, Syria and
Palestine, with special emphasis on Babylonia.
This fact brought some scholars to believe that
Petachia's aim in his journey was to go to Babylonia as a messenger of the German Jews in order
to seek a refuge there for his persecuted brethren
in Europe.[66]

According to his account, Petachia was a rich
man:[67]

> R. Petachia fell sick at Nineveh, and
> the King's Physicians said that he would
> not live. It is the custom there that
> when a Jew on his travels dies the Sultan
> takes half of his property; and because
> R. Petachia was dressed in beautiful
> clothes, they thought that he was rich;
> therefore, the scribes of the Sultan came
> thither to take possession of his pro-
> perty should he die. But R. Petachia gave
> directions, sick as he was, to carry him
> over the river Tigris.[68]

R. Petachia communicated extensively with the
Gaon— the head of the academy— in Babylonia, and
the Gaon gave him a letter of recommendation in
which he states: "Rabbi Samuel, the head of the
academy, gave Rabbi Petachia a document with his
seal, directing that he should have safe conduct
whithersoever he should go, and that he should be
shown the graves of the disciples of the wise and
of the righteous."[69] This shows R. Petachia as a
man of influence not only because he was a Jew
coming from a far-off land, but because he was, in

24

fact, rich and honoured. He was evidently a man
of wealth and his liberal backsheesh[70] enabled him
to enter tombs wich were closed even to non-Jews
who could not afford so much.[71]

Because he makes no mention of how he returned
home, it is probable that R. Petachia travelled by
sea to Greece and from there he continued to
Prague.[72]

R. Petachia did not write the itinerary himself. His notes of the journey were collected by
Judah b. Samuel Hasid. Because there are inter-
ruptions and dispersed paragraphs in the collection of the notes, it can be assumed that some of
the notes had been lost.[73] Not all the notes
brought by R. Petachia found their place in the
account: "He named all the cities, and stated how
many days it took him to travel from city to city.
However, there is no occasion to write it down."[74]
Furthermore, several episodes were not included in
their entirety in the account. For example, R.
Judah Hasid did not report in its entirety the
astrologer's conversation with R. Petachia in
Nineveh.[75] Also when R. Petachia describes the
grave of Ezekiel, he states:

> The head of the academy wrote down for
> the rabbi the names of the Amoraim buried
> there. Rabbi Petachia, however, forgot
> the list (and left it) in Bohemia, for he
> came from Bohemia hither.[76]

From what is said in the itinerary "...Rabbi
Judah the Pious would not write it down lest he
should be suspected of being a believer in the
words of Rabbi Solomon,"[77] it can be implied that
R. Judah the Pious began writing the itinerary but
a third person took over.[78] It can be concluded
that Rabbi Petachia brought his written notes and
some oral additions to R. Judah the Pious with the
intention of having him arrange the material.
However, R. Judah the Pious handed the material
with some additional notes, to a third unknown
writer, who is responsible for the account as it
is today.[79]

25

It is at the same time true that this third
unknown writer did not arrange the material well,
since the account suffers from chronological dis-
organization. For example, the stories on Jerusalem are not in chronological sequence. The
account of Jerusalem beginning on pages 88-89,[80]
is interrupted by the account on the Dead Sea, Hebron, Machpelah cave[81] and then is resumed.[82] Furthermore, after first relating the account on
Damascus[83] he then describes the Holy Land,[84] inter-
rupting this description with reference to the
synagogue, which Elisha built in Damascus— "...it
is large and divine service is performed in it,"[85]
and then continues with the Holy Land description.[86]
Finally, at the end of the account, there are reports concerning different geographical locations
which should be placed in the middle of the itinerary. For example, after the reports on Greece, he
refers to Babylonia:

> In Greece the Jews are subject to great
> oppression. ...There are so many congre-
> gations in Greece....In the village of Usha
> is buried Jonah, son of Amittai; in that of
> Bosra, of Babylon, is buried Ezra, the
> scribe. Rabbi Chana, the Baghdadi, who is
> mentioned in the Talmud, was of Baghdad,
> the great city mentioned before. At Babylon
> there are no stones, but everything is of
> brick.[87]

In summary, R. Petachia made notes of his experience during his journey. Possibly he himself
was not methodical.[88] However, the contents of his
book were not written by Petachia but by others who
followed but abbreviated his report.[89] Apparently
the book was written by several people, one of whom
was Judah B. Samuel Hasid of Regensburg.[90]

One very important difference exists between
the biography of Benjamin of Tudela and that of
Petachia which merits more attention. Benjamin of
Tudela is from Spain, and being a part of the intellectual environment in Spain, had a wider education
in Jewish life and world affairs. He is the

inheritor of the Golden Age in Spain[91]—and this
intellectual background is reflected in his itinerary. On the other hand, Petachia's "world tour"
also reflected the intellectual environment of
which he was a part, Germany. The Jews of Germany
did not study secular sciences.[92] Furthermore,
there were no signs of secular study developing.[93]
Their entire intellectual endeavours were directed
at Talmudical study, with religious moral feelings
finding their satisfaction either in Aggada and
Midrash or in mystic literature.

Keeping in mind this intellectual environment,
we are now able to understand Petachia and his ability as a traveller. Petachia was far less concerned with factual details than Benjamin of Tudela.
Thus, he merely quotes the biblical number of six
hundred thousand Jewish inhabitants when giving the
Jewish population of Babylonia, Persia, and Cush.[94]
These and many other exaggerations "merely reflected the tremendous impression made by the Near
Eastern civilization on this visitor from a backward country."[95] Petachia was also amazed by the
generally high level of education among Babylonian
Jews: "There is no one so ignorant in the whole
of Babylon, Assyria, Media, and Persia, but knows
the twenty-four books, punctuation, grammar, the
superfluous and omitted letters,..."[96] Coming from
Central Europe with the extensive emphasis on Talmudic learning, he was impressed by such competence
in biblical learning. He unquestionably accepts
all the popular legends as facts. He believes in
the miracles at the holy graves—two of which are
the graves of the prophet Ezekiel near Baghdad and
the grave of Ezra the Scribe near Shoshan. Generally speaking, Petachia's full attention centers
around the graves of the famous men—rather than
the culture in Palestine and Babylonia. Believing
in demons and the power of the supernatural, he
reported that Jews in Byzantium could conjure
demons to serve them. Furthermore, his account is
not only less accurate but much less attractive
than that of Benjamin of Tudela.[97]

Grünhut[98] correctly states that Benjamin and
Petachia are different in their characters. Benjamin knew Arabic while Petachia probably did not;
Benjamin offers a lot of information, and in many
cases he adds small details, while Petachia does
not often express his observations. Only at Babylonia does he show his ability to give a detailed
picture. While Benjamin notices that in Hillah
there are Jews and he gives their number and some
other details,[99] R. Petachia makes no mention of
Hillah. Likewise, Benjamin gives the number of
the Jews in Hamath,[100] while R. Petachia, who visited there, does not even mention the Jewish community. R. Benjamin notes the distances between
the towns he visits, but R. Petachia is silent on
that point, too.

Thus, we find Petachia a German Jew, naive
and unquestioning, devoted to God and Jewish life.
Even his language, compared with that of Benjamin
of Tudela, is awkward.[101]

Rabbi Jacob Ben R. Nathaniel ha-Cohen

What do we know about this traveller? No
more than his name and his father's name. Here
is how his account begins: "Account of the journeys to places in the Holy Land and the tombs
there of the righteous, composed by R. Jacob ben
R. Nathaniel ha Cohen when he entered the Holy
Land."[102] In addition he reveals to us his religious status in the Jewish community: he was a
Cohen (Priest). As a Cohen he had some other religious duties from which other Jews who do not
belong to the status of Cohanim were exempt.

At the end of the account, the traveller says:
"As I have been privileged to write about the Holy
Land, so may I be privileged to go there and die
there. Here end the words of me, Jacob ha Cohen,
of all the sights I saw in the Holy Land."[103]
This means that he wrote his account after he returned to his own country, because he wished to

"...be privileged to go there and die there."

In the entire itinerary—which is a short account of his journey to the east and is only known from the unique Ms. at the Cambridge University Library[104]—he does not mention the name of his mother country. It is important, of course, to know the geographical area from which Jacob ben Nathaniel ha-Cohen comes in order to have a better understanding of him. E.N. Adler[105] proposed that he is a European Jewish pilgrim without giving any specific country nor the reasons for this statement. What makes him a "European" we do not know. If we carefully examine the account, we are able to ascertain a few facts which will lead us to the country from which our traveller came.

His language is very unclear. Grünhut says: "...the writer himself was not well enough familiar with our holy language and his language is tedious and requires studying."[106] This unfamiliarity with the language seems to indicate a lack of education. Grünhut states that "the Spanish Jews as well as the French improved their language and made an effort to speak clearly...."[107] On the other hand, the traveller's lack of education presents the possibility that he was neither a Spanish, French nor an Italian Jew.[108]

Because some German expressions are contained in the account, the scholars believe that R. Jacob ben R. Nathaniel had a knowledge of German. For example, he uses the term "keneged" followed by a number[109] which indicates that the number is approximate rather than exact. The origin of this expression is in the German word "gegen."[110] If we also remember that Petachia of Regensburg wrote in a dull style,[111] we can then conclude that R. Jacob ben R. Nathaniel ha-Cohen came from Germany.[112] Eisenstein generally agrees that the language used by R. Jacob helps to identify him as a German Jew, although Jacob describes Joshua as "our master,"[113] a title used by the Arabs but borrowed and used by the Jews.[114]

29

In addition, there is, the author believes, one more point to be considered. Our pilgrim, rather than "a traveller"—reminds us of Petachia's account rather than that of Benjamin's. As a matter of fact, there is no similarity between the itinerary of Benjamin of Tudela and this short account of R. Jacob ben R. Nathaniel ha-Cohen. His interest and his scope of description is extremely limited as exemplified by the fact that he emphasizes the tombs and graves of the righteous fathers, and it seems that the main purpose of his journey was similar to that of a typical pilgrim of the Middle Ages. Through his short account, we have a picture of a very naive, devoted Jew, venerating graves and tombs, and his scope of knowledge seems to be very limited. His tedious language and his limited interest and purpose reminds us of the historical background of German Jews in the twelfth century—one of whom was Petachia. This substantiates the fact that R. Jacob ben R. Nathaniel ha-Cohen was indeed a German Jew.

The short account does not mention when Jacob set out on his journey. Steinschneider assigns it to between the thirteenth and fifteenth centuries.[115] Grünhut places it in the middle of the thirteenth century.[116] Grünhut expounds the following reasons for this decision. First, our traveller, at the beginning of his account says:

> In Jerusalem are the Tower of David and the Temple and the Sanctuary, and the western wall...and below Mount Olivet, opposite the tower, is a tower upon a tower, and it is (?) cubits high, and no road passes it, and the waters of Siloam are over against Zion and Jerusalem.[117]

Undoubtedly, says Grünhut, this tower has been built by the Crusaders,[118] before the Mongols invaded the area and, probably, also destroyed the tower.[119] Second, we find in the account itself as stated by Jacob: "In Hebron, I, Jacob, entered in the guise of a Gentile into the cave which is the cave of Machpelah,"[120] and the term Jacob uses

30

" הגוים " ("in the guise of a Gentile") is an expression designating the Christian pilgrim among
the European Jews.[121] This suggests that the Crusaders were still the rulers of Hebron where the
famous cave is located. This fact is consistent
with that given by Petachia and Benjamin—that in
their time, it was still possible to enter the cave,
since entrance to the cave was prohibited by the
Moslems after the conquest by Saladin in 1187.[122]

It is clear that Jacob ben Nathaniel ha-Cohen
was in the Holy Land while the Crusaders were still
there. Since Grünhut failed to take into account
the 1187 conquest by Saladin, in placing the date
of the journey in the middle of the thirteenth century, he is incorrect.[123] Furthermore, Jacob
states in the account:

> When a knight from Provence came and saw
> that the uncircumcised lit many lights upon
> the grave, he asked who is this one, and
> they answered, it is a righteous Jew.... He
> said to them, 'Why do you thus in honour of
> a Jew?' and took a stone and threw it on the
> ground.... He was on horseback....[124]

This can refer only to the time when the Crusaders
were still ruling before 1187. Thus, Jacob's journey can be set within the period either before or
after that of Benjamin's and Petachia's.[125]

The account, which was written by Jacob himself after he had returned to his country, is not
organized.[126] The description is not systematic
as exemplified by the fact that he describes one
place, depicts another, and then continues with the
original description. Since the accounts do not
follow chronologically, it is possible that Jabob
intended first to give a general description of his
journey and planned to add the details at a later
time,[127] though the details are also disorganized.

We can add here that Jacob ben R. Nathaniel
ha-Cohen might have had some difficulties on his
journey, because he states early in his account:

31

"I, Jacob, the son of R. Nathaniel ha-Cohen, journeyed with much difficulty, but God helped me to
enter the Holy Land,..."[128]   However, he fails to
explain the exact nature of his difficulties. On
the other hand, it is possible that the Hebrew
word "Tarahti" (טרחתי) does not have the meaning
of obstacles and difficulties as translated by E.N.
Adler. A Journey to the Holy Land in the twelfth
century by a pious German Jew is in itself an effort without any obstacles necessarily being incurred. Furthermore, the help of God in such an effort was needed at any time.

     Jacob ben Nathaniel was in Egypt, too. How-
ever, he starts his description in Hebron and continues north although he refers to places located
south of Hebron. From his description one can conclude that he travelled to Hebron from Egypt by way
of the Sinai Desert,[129] and from Hebron to Meron in
the North of the Holy Land, by way of Jerusalem,
Shechem and Tiberias.

     In spite of all we have said, his account is
important because it contains legends, customs and
traditions that are not known from any other
source.[130]

     To summarize, Petachia's near contemporary
Jacob ben Nathaniel ha-Cohen left behind a brief
account of his pilgrimage through the Holy Land,
with a few remarks, about Egypt. This type of pilgrimage, once characteristic of medieval Christians, was to be carried on by later Jewish pilgrims. "But it contributed little," as Baron says,
"to the general geographic information available to
educated Western Jews."[131] As Baron says,[132] no
Idrisis or Yaquts arose among the Jews to further
analyse the accounts in terms of their geographical
significance, both human and physical. The only
geographical significance derived from these accounts was in terms of astronomy rather than a true
geography.[133]

     Our travellers' accounts, though popular as
light reading, stimulated the imagination of the

western Jews, and kept alive their hope to return
to the Holy Land.[134]

Footnotes

[1]Benjamin's name is not mentioned by Isaac
Israeli who compiled a history of Jews in Spain
after Abraham ibn Daud. But he is mentioned in
the book of Sefer Iuchasin. He is mentioned only
in passing by Isaac Abravanel. M. Carmoly, Notice
Historique sur Benjamin de Tudèle, Nouvelle Edition Suivie de l'Examen géographique de ses Voyages, par J. Lelewel (Bruxelles et Leipzig, 1852),
pp. 6-7.
    Another traveller, Isaac ben Joseph ibn
Chelo (1334), also refers to him when he mentions
the Western Wall: "The Jews report thither to say
their prayers, as Rabbi Benjamin has already related." Isaac ben Joseph ibn Chelo, The Roads from
Jerusalem, ed. E.N. Adler, Jewish Travellers (New
York, 1966), p. 131.

[2]This Preface is of practically the same age
as the narrative it introduces, but by another
hand. Benjamin of Tudela, Sefer Masa'ot, ed. and
trans. A. Asher, 2 vols. (Berlin, 1840), II. 1.
    How long after the journey were the travel
notes compiled—we do not know.

[3]Benjamin of Tudela, The Itinerary of Benjamin
of Tudela, ed. M.N. Adler (Oxford, 1907), pp. 1-2.

[4]There is no authority for this except that
the conventional abbreviation "R" is added to his
name in the Hebrew sources.

[5]Sir R. Beazley, The Dawn of Modern Geography,
3 vols. (London, 1897-1906), II, 227. "It is fairly certain that Benjamin was not only a Rabbi but a
merchant."

[6]Benjamin of Tudela, Sefer Masa'ot, ed. Asher,

33

II, Introduction, ix.

[7]Petachia of Regensburg, Sivuv ha-Rav Rabi Petachia (The Itinerary of R. Petachia), ed. L. Grünhut (Jerusalem, 1905), Part II, Introduction, p. xiii.

[8]Ibid.

[9]Baron, Social and Religious History of the Jews, VI, 223.

[10]J. Pinkerton, Voyages and Travels, 17 vols. (London, 1811), VII, 3.

[11]Jewish Travellers, ed. E.N. Adler (New York, 1966), Introduction, p. xv.

[12]Abraham ibn Daud, Sefer Ha-Qabbalah, ed. Gerson D. Cohen (Philadelphia, 1967).

[13]The Itinerary of Petachia, ed. Grünhut, Part II, Introduction, pp. xii-xiii; see Chapter IV in the book.

[14]Beazley, II, 227.

[15]Ibid., 253.

[16]The Itinerary of Benjamin of Tudela, ed. M.N. Adler, p. 1; Carmoly, p. 9.

[17]Dubnov, History of the Jews, II, 747; Travel and Travellers of the Middle Ages, ed. A.P. Newton (New York, 1950), p. 105; Beazley states: "A new chapter of medieval travel begins with Rabbi Benjamin of Tudela. His records are the earliest important contributions of the Hebrew race to geography. They also mark a distinct advance in the movement from West to East, whose outlook now began to reach beyond the Euphrates to Central and further Asia." (Beazley, II, 218.)

[18]Baron, Social and Religious History of the Jews, VI, 223.

34

[19]P. Borchardt, "Benjamin of Tudela," E.J. (Berlin, 1929), IV, 130.

[20]Borchardt, "The Sculpture in Front of the Lateran as Described by B. of Tudela and Magister Gregorius," Journal of Roman Studies, XXVI (1936), 68-70.

[21]The Itinerary of Petachia, ed. Grünhut, Part II, Introduction, p. xiii.

[22]Jewish Travellers, ed. E.N. Adler, Introduction, p. xv.

[23]Ibid., p. 38.

[24]The Itinerary of Benjamin of Tudela, ed. M.N. Adler, Introduction, p. xiii.

[25]Pinkerton, VII, 20.

[26]The Itinerary of Benjamin of Tudela, ed. M.N. Adler, p. 1.

[27]Ibid.

[28]Carmoly quotes from Zacut's Sefer Iuchasin: "Que R. Benjamin le voyageur, ce grand luminaire, dont la clarté a éclairé tout Israël, est mort l'an 933 (1173). Il y a ici une double erreur." (Abraham ibn Zacut, Sefer Iuchasin [Amsterdam, 1717], p. 99.)
Carmoly then states: "d'abord l'éloge brillant de Zacut ne se rapporte pas à Benjamin, mais à Maimonïde..., puis la date de 933 est une faute d'impression, au lieu de 938 (1178),... A cette faute...il faut en ajouter une autre plus grave qui appartient au premier éditeur de ce livre précieux. Samuel Schalom, le corrupteur de l'oeuvre d'Abraham Zacut, a également falsifié ce passage. Voici comment s'exprime l'auteur lui-même dans son livre inédit.... 'R. Benjamin de Navarre, qui a parcouru le monde, a composé le livre des Voyages en l'an 938 (1178). Il avait vu à cette époque à

Posquière en Franch, Rabad...."

Having refuted Zacut's statement, Carmoly
concludes that, "Il resulte de ce passage que Benjamin était de Navarre, qu'il n'est pas mort en
938 (1178), mais qu'il a composé dans cette annee
la relation des ses voyages. Le célèbre Isaac
Abravanel confirme ce premier fait en remarquant
que Benjamin de Tudèle revint seulement de ses
voyages en 1173, mais sans nous dire toutefois qu'
il avait composé sa relation cinq ans plus tard,
en 1178.... Voici les propres paroles de ce grand
écrivain: 'On trouve ceci dans de Livre des Voyages, composé par le docte R. Benjamin, qui, sorti
de la ville de Tudèle du royaume de Navarre, est
allé dans un grand nombre de pays éloignés et a
consigné par écrit toutes les choses remarquables
qu'il avait vues jusqu'à son retour en Espagne,
l'an 4933 de la création." (Carmoly, pp. 7-8.)

[29] Benjamin of Tudela, Sefer Masa'ot, ed.
Asher, II, xvi-xvii.

[30] The Itinerary of Benjamin of Tudela, ed.
M.N. Adler, p. 25: "These things were told me by
the said Rabbi Abraham."

[31] Bacher, "Benjamin of Tudela," J.E., III, 34.

[32] The Itinerary of Benjamin of Tudela, ed.
M.N. Adler, p. 62: "This same R. Moses told me
all these things."

[33] Ibid., p. 1.

[34] Ibid., n. 2.

[35] Beazley, II, 225.

[36] The Itinerary of Benjamin of Tudela, ed.
M.N. Adler, pp. 5-6.

[37] Carmoly, p. 8.

[38] Beazley, II, 231, n. 1. According to C.C.
Roth, between November 1165 and July 1167,

"Benjamin of Tudela: The Last Stage," _Annuario di Studi Ebraici_ (1968-69), p. 47.

[39]Beazley, II, 261; _The Itinerary of Benjamin of Tudela_, ed. M.N. Adler, p. 71.

[40]Stanley Lane Poole, _A History of Egypt_ (London, 1936), p. 193.

[41]_Ibid._, p. 194

[42]_Ibid._, p. 193, Sept. 10, 1171.

[43]Behâ-Ed-Dîn, "The Life of Saladin," _Palestine Pilgrims' Text Society_, XIII (London, 1897), 61.

[44]For different opinions, see Benjamin of Tudela, _Sefer Masa'ot_, ed. Asher, II, 224-25; Beazley, 264, n. 1; Carmoly, p. 8; Dubnov, II, 756; Röhricht, _Bibliotheca Geographica Palaestinae_ (Jerusalem, 1963), p. 37.

[45]_The Itinerary of Benjamin of Tudela_, ed. M.N. Adler, p. 79: "Ships overlaid with silver and gold are there, belonging to the King, who takes pleasure trips in them with his women."

[46]_Ibid._, p. 3, n. 4; p. 9, n. 2; p. 15, n. 4; p. 61, n.1.

[47]_The Itinerary of Petachia_, ed. Grünhut, p. 1.

[48]_Jewish Travellers_, ed. E.N. Adler, p. 64.

[49]According to Eisenstein, his travels were only ten or fifteen years after those of Benjamin of Tudela (J.D. Eisenstein [ed.], _Ozar Masa'ot_ [Tel-Avid, 1969], p. 46).

[50]A. Ya'ari, _Travels to Palestine_ (Tel-Aviv, 1946), p. 50.

[51]_The Itinerary of Petachia_, ed. Grünhut, Part II, Foreword.

[52]The Itinerary of Petachia, ed. E.N. Adler, Jewish Travellers, p. 66.

[53]Eisenstein, p. 46.

[54]The Itinerary of Petachia, ed. E.N. Adler, Jewish Travellers, p. 85.

[55]Eisenstein, p. 46.

[56]J. Prawer, A History of the Latin Kingdom of Jerusalem, 2 vols. (Jerusalem, 1963), I, 438.

[57]The Itinerary of Petachia, ed. E.N. Adler, Jewish Travellers, p. 88.

[58]Prawer, A History of the Latin Kingdom of Jerusalem, I, 557; Beazley, II, 266.

[59]Eisenstein, p. 46; Baron, Social and Religious History of the Jews, VI, 436, n. 91; see also Röhricht, Bibliotheca, p. 40.

[60]The Itinerary of Petachia, ed. Grunuut, p. 45, n. 144, and Part II, pp. x-xi.

[61]Ibid., p. 24; The Itinerary of Petachia, ed. E.N. Adler, Jewish Travellers, p. 82.

[62]The Itinerary of Petachia, ed. Grünhut, p. 44, ns. 133, 134, 135.

[63]Ibid., p. 25; The Itinerary of Petachia, ed. E.N. Adler, Jewish Travellers, p. 83.

[64]The Itinerary of Petachia, ed. Grünhut, Part II, p. xi.

[65]Ibid., pp. xi-xii.

[66]For example, ibid., Part II, pp. vii-x; Ya'ari, Travels to Palestine, p. 48. We will return to this subject in Chapter III in the book.

[67] Ya'ari, _Travels to Palestine_, p. 49; Baron, _Social and Religious History of the Jews_, VI, 436, n. 91.

[68] _The Itinerary of Petachia_, ed. E.N. Adler, _Jewish Travellers_, p. 68. Baron states that under these circumstances, Petachia's account cannot be critically analyzed as is that of Benjamin (Baron, _Social and Religious History of the Jews_, VI, 436, n. 91).

[69] _The Itinerary of Petachia_, ed. E.N. Adler, _Jewish Travellers_, p. 73.

[70] Bribe.

[71] _The Itinerary of Petachia_, ed. E.N. Adler, _Jewish Travellers_, p. 89.

[72] Ya'ari, _Travels to Palestine_, p. 49.

[73] Eisenstein, p. 46.

[74] _The Itinerary of Petachia_, ed. E.N. Adler, _Jewish Travellers_, p. 85.

[75] Ibid.; see further on in the book.

[76] Ibid., p. 78.

[77] Ibid., pp. 68-69.

[78] Grünhut says that from what we find in the account (pp. 68-69), "R. Judah the Pious would not write it down lest he should be suspected of being a believer in the words of Rabbi Solomon," therefore R. Judah is not the editor of the Itinerary because it is not probable that he would write of himself as "pious" (_The Itinerary of Petachia_, ed. Grünhut, p. 40, n. 45).

[79] Eisenstein, p. 46; Baron, _Social and Religious History of the Jews_, VI, 436, n. 91.

[80] Jewish Travellers, ed. E.N. Adler, pp. 88-89.

[81] Ibid., pp. 89-90.

[82] Ibid., p. 90.

[83] Ibid., pp. 85-86.

[84] Ibid., pp. 86-87, 88-90.

[85] Ibid., p. 90.

[86] Ibid., pp. 90-91.

[87] Ibid., p. 91.

[88] Baron, Social and Religious History of the Jews, VI, 436, n. 91.

[89] The Itinerary of Petachia, ed. Grunhut, Part II, pp. v, vi, xii; Beazley, II, 265.

[90] Grünhut believes that it is possible that R. Judah the Pious from Regensburg, and R.J. ha-Laban and R. Nachman—Petachia's brothers—were the three who arranged and edited the material. If that is correct, Grünhut is surprised that the material needed three eminent people, and furthermore, they were not living in the same place. (R.J. ha-Laban resided in Prague, and the other two lived in Regensburg.) This is one of the reasons why Steinschneider considered Judah the Pious as the only editor. Grünhut continues to say that probably the fragmentary character of the material confused those people. In addition, R. Petachia added some oral information and it is possible that R. Judah the Pious was the last man who edited Sivuv (The Itinerary of Petachia, ed. Grünhut, Part II, Introduction, pp. vi-vii).

[91] Dubnov, II, 726.

[92] Natural science, philosophy, "grammar" as it was used in the Middle Ages.

[93] Graetz, History of the Jews, III, 421.

[94] The Itinerary of Petachia, ed. E.N. Adler, Jewish Travellers, p. 71.

[95] Baron, Social and Religious History of the Jews, VI, 224.

[96] The Itinerary of Petachia, ed. E.N. Adler, Jewish Travellers, pp. 69-70.

[97] Jewish Travellers, ed. E.N. Adler, Introduction, p. xvi; Beazley, II, 265.

[98] The Itinerary of Petachia, ed. Grünhut, Part II, pp. xii-xiii.

[99] The Itinerary of Benjamin of Tudela, ed. M.N. Adler, pp. 43, 46.

[100] Ibid., pp. 31-32.

[101] Ya'ari, Travels to Palestine, p. 50.

[102] The Itinerary of Rabbi Jacob ben R. Nathaniel ha-Cohen, ed. E.N. Adler, Jewish Travellers, (New York, 1966), p. 92.

[103] Ibid., p. 99.

[104] Grünhut edited the itinerary as an appendix to his edition of Petachia's, Introduction, p. 1.

[105] Jewish Travellers, ed. E.N. Adler, p. 92.

[106] The Itinerary of Jacob ben Nathaniel ha-Cohen, ed. Grünhut, Introduction, p. 1.

[107] Ibid., p. 2.

[108] Ya'ari, Travels to Palestine, p. 56.

[109] The Itinerary of Jacob ben Nathaniel ha-Cohen, ed. Grünhut, p. 14.

[110]Ya'ari, Travels to Palestine, p. 56; The Itinerary of Jacob ben Nathaniel ha-Cohen, ed. Grünhut, p. 14, n. 1, and Introduction, pp. 2-3. "ונחמי טבריה כנגד ד' מרחצאות על שפת ים כנרת מתוק כדבש" "The hot springs of Tiberias consist of some form of baths on the shore of the Lake, and the waters taste sweet as honey,..." (Jewish Travellers, ed. E.N. Adler, p. 96).

[111]The Itinerary of Petachia, ed. Grünhut, Introduction, p. 2.

[112]Ibid., pp. 2-3; Ya'ari, Travels to Palestine, p. 56.

[113]The Itinerary of Jacob ben Nathaniel ha-Cohen, ed. Grünhut, p. 7.

[114]Eisenstein, p. 58.

[115]M. Steinschneider, "Jüdische Schriften zur Geographie Palästinas," Jerusalem, ed. A.M. Luncz, III (Jerusalem, 1889), p. 48; Röhricht, Bibliotheca, p. 95.

[116]The Itinerary of Jacob ben Nathaniel ha-Cohen, ed. Grünhut, Introduction, p. 1.

[117]Ibid., pp. 4-5; Jewish Travellers, ed. E.N. Adler, pp. 98-99.

[118]The Itinerary of Jacob ben Nathaniel ha-Cohen, ed. Grünhut, Introduction, p. 1, n. 1.

[119]Ibid., p. 2.

[120]Ibid., p. 11; Jewish Travellers, ed. E.N. Adler, p. 98.

[121]Ya'ari, Travels to Palestine, p. 56.

[122]The Letters of Obadiah Jare Da Bertinoro, ed. E.N. Adler, Jewish Travellers, p. 233.

[123] Ya'ari, Travels to Palestine, p. 56.

[124] The Itinerary of Jacob ben Nathaniel ha-Cohen, ed. Grünhut, p. 9; Jewish Travellers, ed. E.N. Adler, p. 96.

[125] Jewish Travellers, ed. E.N. Adler, p. 92; Eisenstein, p. 58.

[126] Eisenstein, p. 58; Ya'ari, Travels to Palestine, p. 56.

[127] Eisenstein, p. 58.

[128] Jewish Travellers, ed. E.N. Adler, p. 92; The Itinerary of Jacob ben Nathaniel ha-Cohen, ed. Grünhut, p. 4.

[129] Ya'ari, Travels to Palestine, p. 56.

[130] Ibid.; The Itinerary of Jacob ben Nathaniel ha-Cohen, ed. Grünhut, Introduction, p. 3.

[131] Baron, A Social and Religious History of the Jews, VI, 225.

[132] Ibid., p. 226.

[133] Ibid.

[134] In 1926 A. Marmorstein published a medieval composition entitled Graves of Fathers (Kivre Avot), Zion-Measef, I (1926), 31-39. This contains a full list of holy graves in Palestine by an anonymous pilgrim. Except for Prawer ("The Jews in the Latin Kingfom of Jerusalem," Zion, XI [1945-46], 77) who ascribes it to the second part of the twelfth century (1146-1187), all scholars agree that we do not have here a twelfth century account. Thus it is not included in this study.

CHAPTER III

THE AIMS OF THE JEWISH TRAVELLERS

IN THE WEELFTH CENTURY

One of the fundamental questions is: What
were the aims of the travellers when they set upon
their journeys? Since the travellers' accounts do
not specifically state their aims, it is impossible to answer this question directly. We shall
have to try to attack the question in an indirect
way by analyzing the possible reasons which could
have motivated the travellers to embark on their
journeys. Furthermore, is it possible to find a
primary reason for the travellers' journeys?

Generally it is known that "the wandering Jew
is a very real character in the great drama of
History."[1] The Diaspora extended far beyond Palestine, even before the destruction of the First
Temple. After the Babylonian captivity, there
were always more Jews outside Palestine than within. Philo, Seneca and the author of the Acts of
the Apostles affirmed this fact.[2]

After the rise of Islam in the beginning of
the seventh century, the civilized world was parti-
tioned between Moslems and Christians.[3] There are
some similarities between the Jewish and Moslem
merchants and travellers. Sir T.W. Arnold, in his
discussion on "Arab Travellers and Merchants 1000-
1500"[4] notes:

> The journey of the Muslim travellers was
> facilitated by the brotherhood of Islam,
> which gave to the Mohammedan world its com-
> posite character. However many hundreds of
> miles the Muslim might travel from his na-
> tive town, he would confidently hope for a
> welcome and generous hospitality at the
> hands of his coreligionist, especially if
> he had any reputation for piety or religious
> knowledge.[5]

44

Similarly, the Jewish travelling merchant could
always be sure of a warm welcome at the hands of
his coreligionists. The assistance was not confined to mere hospitality. Information could be
obtained concerning conditions and possibilities
of trade, markets, prices, etc.[6] The linguistic
difficulties between East and West were not encountered by the Jews who had Hebrew as a common
language.[7] Furthermore, the uniformity of Jewish
law and commercial custom benefited the Jewish
traveller.[8]

W. Heyd gives full credit to the Jewish traders for keeping open the channels of international
trade.[9] Meyendorf states that "besides the travels of the pilgrims, the Vikings and the Arabs in
our period, there were two other types of travellers who added considerably to the knowledge of
the world among the Western peoples, namely, the
Jews, among whom Benjamin of Tudela may be considered the most prominent."[10] However, in contrast to Heyd, Meyendorf insists on the impossi-
bility of free movement of Jewish traders "under
the conditions of universal warfare prevailing between 800 and 1200...."[11] In contrast to Meyendorf, Baron sees in the very separation of the
world into Christianity and Islam an opportunity
for the Jews to acquire an important position in
international trade. Baron relies on contemporary
Jewish sources, which provide evidence to justify
his opinion.[12]

Benjamin of Tudela and Petachia, both of whom
passed between Christian and Mohammedan lands,
further substantiate the free mobility of Jews.
Nothing in their accounts suggests that they
thought they were exceptional in undertaking the
journey. Rabinowitz is correct in asserting that
there must have been many travellers and traders
who did not, however, leave an itinerary.[13] If
the journeys of Petachia and Benjamin had been exceptional, then we would have expected some reference in Petachia's accounts to the fact that two
European Jews visited Baghdad and other places in

the same decade. Petachia's statement "...when a Jew on his travels dies, the Sultan takes half of his property"[14] suggests that Jewish travellers frequently passed through the town of Baghdad. Our travellers visited Palestine which was under the crusaders' rule at that time, yet they passed safely. Thus, it can now be assumed that our travellers were not unique and that it was not unusual to find Jewish travellers on the road.[15]

History has always been a field in which people look for clarification and support for their actions and thoughts. The past could illuminate the present[16] and could encourage future deeds. This was especially so in the Middle Ages.[17] The author does not refer here to the continuous pilgrimages to the holy places,[18] or to the fact that there always was communication and travelling.[19] The concern here is with travellers whose itineraries covered Jewish communities over a wide area. This would provide new information concerning their coreligionists and become a foundation for the study of unique Jewish subjects, such as "a Jewish independent state," "the lost Ten Tribes," among others. Such stories, if they had been circulating in the twelfth century, could have been an inspiration for further inquiries.

Prior to our twelfth-century travellers we find one name which greatly influenced Jewish thinkers and was famous in both Jewish and non-Jewish circles. Eldad ha-Dani, a ninth-century traveller, told stories which caused a commotion, especially among the Jews.[20] Moreover, in the twelfth century we find his stories being quoted by Jewish leaders such as Rashi, Maimonides,[21] to mention just a few. Among non-Jewish circles we can also find his influence felt in the rumours about the Kingdom of Prester John.[22]

It is sufficient to list the names of Jewish travellers such as Alkharizi (1216),[23] Samuel ben Samson (1210),[24] Rabbi Jacob (1238-1244),[25] Estori ha-Parchi (1282-1357),[26] R. Meshullam of Volterra

(1481),[27] Obadiah of Bertinoro (1487)[28] and David
Reubeni (1522)[29] in order to establish the fact
that the twelfth-century travellers were but a link
in a long chain.

As previously noted, the crusading age bridged
the gap between East and West and witnessed a rapid
development in the realms of ideas and trade which
encouraged travelling.[30] Those who were educated,
sensitive, or possessed imagination felt it necessary to increase their knowledge and satisfy their
curiosity[31] regarding the "new" world. J.K. Wright
is correct when he states that "...curiosity...also
applied to the loftier and more impersonal impulse
that drives the astronomer to reach the depths of
the universe and the geographer to penetrate the
mysteries of terrae incognitae."[32] Man instinc-
tively craves to know and this is stimulated by the
atmosphere of the time. This instinct exhibited
itself in dangerous voyages for further geographical explorations in the fifteenth century. Can we
ignore this natural instinct in regard to our
travellers?

Certainly, for a twelfth-century Jew who was
living in West or Central Europe, there were more
powerful forces which encouraged such travelling.
These included concern about his brethren throughout the world, and his inquisitiveness about their
situation following the stormy period of the
crusades.

This curiosity can be clearly detected in the
itineraries of the travellers. It is especially
evident in that of Benjamin of Tudela. The rich-
ness of his itinerary with various subjects, cultural as well as non-cultural, makes it possible
for us to experience the atmosphere of the times
with him. His interest in architecture, for
example, and his descriptions of archaeological
remains in Rome,[33] places Benjamin unequivocally
among the educated people in his generation. His
itinerary reflects the growth of the economy and
commerce, exemplified by the commercial activity

47

in the international seaports. We can detect how
immensely impressed he was when he reports of the
commercial activity in Alexandria.[34] One should
not hesitate to picture Benjamin as a man gifted
with imagination and oriented to inquiry.[35]

The element of curiosity cannot be eliminated
with regard to the other two travellers. Petachia
of Regensburg not only intended to embark on a
pilgrimage to the Holy Land but to include a wide
circle of geographical areas, and his itinerary's
title Sivuv (World Tour) has an important significance in itself. Dubnov writes: "The yearning to
travel to the East, which was stimulated by the
crusades, carried away also a Jewish scholar of
Germany: Rabbi Petachia of Regensburg...."[36]

Even though Jacob ben Nathaniel ha-Cohen's
destination seems to have been the Holy Land, his
journey still included Egypt. The mention of
Aristotle in his short itinerary raises the question of his broader curiosity and interests. Our
traveller states: "In Alexandria of Egypt, I saw
the college of King Alexander.... There Alexander
used to learn of his teacher Aristotle,..."[37]
Aristotle's name has a unique significance in the
European Renaissance of the twelfth century.[38]

However, curiosity was apparently only one of
the elements which motivated our travellers to set
on their journeys. What, then, were the others?
If we examine their itineraries, we find one element which is common to all of them. Their voyages
primarily took them to the Jewish world, and we do
not see any attempt on their part to journey beyond
it. It is true that they reported rumours about
the non-Jewish world, but even these rumours referred mostly to Jewish subjects. For example, we
hear Benjamin of Tudela telling us about the lost
Jewish tribes in Persia and South Arabia,[39] although it is almost sure that he did not himself
visit there,[40] nor did he pretend to have done so.
His references to the Far East, then an area unknown to the West, are very short, and are done

partly as a result of curiosity. His world tour
remained strictly bound within the Jewish circle
of the twelfth century.

This is true, too, concerning R. Petachia,
who strongly emphasizes the main centre of Jewish
Diaspora, Babylonia, and his references to unknown
geographical areas are extremely vague. Once
again we have to remember that he never visited
Persia[41] or South Arabia and his references to
those areas are even poorer than those of Benjamin.

As far as R. Jacob ben Nathaniel ha-Cohen is
concerned, we surely can say[42] that only the Holy
Land and Egypt were included in his voyage; and
there is no mention of any other places. The fact
that the travellers limited themselves almost exclusively to the Jewish known world aids us in
narrowing our investigation about the travellers'
objects and aims. We conclude that our travellers' goals should be sought in the sphere of the
Jewish world, and if we were to find the ultimate
object, it probably would be within the realm of
Jewish issues derived from the Jewish situation in
the twelfth century.

Turning back to the itineraries, one can see
that the three travellers visited the Holy Land.
In light of the special significance the Holy Land
has had throughout Jewish history,[43] one can assume that one object of our voyagers was to pay a
pilgrimage. This possibility is further enhanced
if it is remembered that in the Middle Ages, Christians, Jews, and Moslems alike considered pilgrimages crucial to their spiritual life.[44] For example, it was incumbent upon a Moslem at least once
in his lifetime to journey to Mecca and Medina.[45]
The famous Ibn Jubayr is renowned for leaving a
brilliant account of his 1183-1185 pilgrimage to
the holy places of Islam. T.W. Arnold states:
"...another circumstance...served to stimulate
interest in geography and to induce many persons
to undetake lengthy journeys. This was the pilgrimage."[46] Moreover, it is impossible to under-

49

stand the crusades to the Holy Land without taking
into consideration the Holy Sepulchre in Jerusalem
and the entire concept of the Holy Land for Christianity.[47] In the Middle Ages, specificaly during
the period with which we are concerned, the Holy
Land had a very special meaning for Islam and
Christianity and was a bone of contention between
them during the twelfth century.[48]

For Jews it was impossible to think of redemption without connecting with it the destiny of the
Holy Land. There is ample literature to indicate
that the question of the destiny of the Patrimonium
Sancti came to light at the same time that a new
spirit concerning the Holy Land engulfed the Jews
in the Diaspora.[49] Is it not possible to consider
that our travellers had as their main object a pilgrimage to the Holy Land?

If we examine our accounts, we find a strong
support for this possibility in the itinerary of
Jacob ben Nathaniel ha-Cohen. His account opens
thus: "Account of the journeys to places in the
Holy Land and the tombs there of the righteous,
composed by R. Jacob ben R. Nathaniel ha-Cohen
when he entered the Holy Land."[50] In addition, we
find at the end of his account the following statement: "As I have been privileged to write about
the Holy Land, so may I be privileged to go there
and die there. Here end the words of me, Jacob ha-
Cohen, of all the sights I saw in the Holy Land."[51]
While Eisenstein states that Jacob did not reveal
to us the purpose of his journey,[52] these quota-
tions indicate, certainly, the clear purpose of the
journey—to visit the holy placed in the Holy Land.
Also, the entire account reveals a very strong emphasis on enumerating the holy places and the
graves in it. In fact, Jacob is the only one of
our travellers who indicates in a specific and concise fashion his purpose for the journey. Why did
he visit Egypt? Grünhut states that, like other
travellers before and after him, he entered the
Holy Land from Egypt through the Sinai Desert,[53]
and it is possible that he came to Egypt because

of its convenience and since it was cheaper to do
it that way. Thus, Egypt was secondary to his
main purpose in visiting the Holy Land.

Compared with Jacob ben Nathaniel's account
in which we have a clear indication of the purpose
of his voyage, we do not have a similar statement
in our other travellers' accounts.[54] Nevertheless, the Holy Land still occupies a prominent
place with elaborate descriptions. In Petachia's
World Tour, in addition to his singular detailed
description of Babylonia, it is only for the Holy
Land that he gives us such a detailed description.
While Grünhut is correct in his analysis of Petachia as being brief and failing to mention Hillah
and Hamath where Jews lived, the analysis should
be carried further to include his sudden wordy and
detailed descriptions of the Holy Land.[55] Petachia's account reveals a pious man who pays tribute to the holy places. He emphasizes tombs and
graves and tells extensively of miracles and spiritual powers connected with the graves of the righteous.[56] Interestingly, distances between graves
are what interested him rather than distances between cities. He goes into specific details when
he refers to the cave of Machpelah.[57]

It seems to be easy to say that his purpose
was similar to that of Rabbi Jacob ben Nathaniel
—visiting the Holy Land and paying a pilgrimage
to the graves of his forefathers. However, was it
really his main purpose? Although he was a pious
man who reminds us of Rabbi Jacob ben Nathaniel,
the route he chose and the extensive travels he
made, and the strong emphasis that he laid on giving detailed pictures of Jewish settlements in
Babylon, show that his objects could not be similar to that of Rabbi Jacob's pilgrimage to the
Holy Land. We cannot say for certain that when R.
Petachia came to the Orient, his visit to the Holy
Land followed conveniently or whether, had he not
been there, he would have travelled on a pilgrimage nevertheless.

A. Ya'ari believes that Petachia's main object was to make a pilgrimage to Palestine, and the letter of recommendation he got in Baghdad proves this point.[58] The author, however, maintains that being close to the holy places seemed to invite touring them and for that purpose a letter could be of help. The letter shows him to be on good and close terms with the Gaon.

If we analyze Benjamin of Tudela's itinerary, it seems to indicate that his main purpose was not to visit the Holy Land and the holy places.[59] Although it is true that he toured extensively through the Holy Land[60] and gave the best account of it, his very extensive journey that covered the entire known world seems to indicate that the Holy Land and its tombs were only secondary considerations.[61] His contemporaries, it seems did not consider his voyage a mere trip to the Holy Land. The author is not surprised that the Preface does not even mention the Holy Land, but rather that he "...passed through many remote countries,... In every place which he entered, he made a record of all that he saw, and was told of...matters not previously heard of in the land of Sepharad."[62]

Jacob ben Nathaniel who shows all the characteristics of a pious pilgrim remains limited to the Holy Land indicating it as his goal. The same is true concerning ibn Jubayr whose route led directly to the holy places of Islam.[63] On the other hand, returning to Petachia and especially to Benjamin, the very extensive area their journey covered took them far from the Holy Land, and this in itself excludes the possibility that the Holy Land was the main object. Furthermore, the long period of time they seemed to spend on their journeys weakens that possibility. As noted, if we were to examine the route those two travellers used, it would appear strange for travellers intending only to visit Palestine.

If the main object of Benjamin and Petachia was not to visit the Holy Land as a pilgrimage, could it have been that they had trade and merchantile operations in view? Could they have been agents of a commercial organization who were sent from their native city to enquire about the situation of trade as it was in that century as well as to investigate the possibilities of investments and commercial operations?

Many scholars consider Benjamin and Petachia as possible merchants. M.N. Adler states, when writing of Benjamin: "He certainly dwells on matters of commercial interest with considerable detail."[64] Graetz, too, suggests a possibility that Benjamin, although "the object of this journey is not quite known," could be an itinerant merchant.[65] Beazley states: "It is fairly certain that Benjamin was not only a Rabbi, but also a merchant, and that his object was as much to acquire and diffuse information about the commercial as about the religious state of his countrymen in distant lands."[66]

Looking into Benjamin's account, we can sense Benjamin's interest in commerce and trade. His observations of details concerning trade and merchandise reveal a man whose occupation probably was that of a merchant. It is no wonder at all that the history of commerce will always look upon him as one of the most valued sources on the subject. His descriptions of the international cities of the twelfth century and the observations he makes of their commercial value are excellent.[67] There is almost no city which Benjamin passed through that he did not fail to include observations of the city from its commercial aspect. The reference here is not only to international cities of which the descriptions are highly praised, but also to his inclusion of smaller cities.[68]

It seems to be generally accepted by scholars that Benjamin was a merchant. The nature of the information he gives us centring around the life style of Jews, makes it unacceptable to say that his main goal was trade and merchandise. This does not necessarily exclude the possibility that

53

he also may have had trade and mercantile operations in view.[69] Furthermore, the author agrees with E.N. Adler[70] that "His travels were too extensive to be those of a mere merchant...." If he were really an agent or a merchant whose main object were trade, we should find him limiting his visits to the more economically developed areas of the twelfth century. From his account, however, it becomes clear that the major theme is not trade, since non commercial centres are included. Moreover, if trade and mercantile operations motivated him to begin his journey, why should he hide it?

Returning to Petachia, whom E.N. Adler suspects to have been a merchant,[71] there is no indication in his account of being motivated by this purpose. Furthermore, his references to commerce and trade are very meagre compared with those of Benjamin. His route which took him through the East of Europe to Babylonia does not indicate that this was the purpose. Most of his account centres around the Jews in Babylonia without reference at all to commerce and trade. Descriptions of commercial centres like those we find in Benjamin's itinerary do not exist at all within Petachia's account. While we could say that Benjamin may have had trade and mercantile operations in mind, we cannot assume the same of Petachia. Thus, we can sum up this point by saying that none of our travellers was motivated by trade and commerce, although for Benjamin of Tudela, being a merchant, trade may have been a secondary factor.

If it be a correct assumption "that the Jew in the Middle Ages was much given to travel,"[72] then it might be said that the wandering Jew kept up communications between one area and another.[73] The Jewish Diaspora was scattered to the four corners of the earth. Benjamin's itinerary proves that in almost every city of importance Jews could be found. The common interests that unified the Jewish world always served as a motive for travel. Thus the traveller had the mission of enquiring about Jews and seeing the way they felt. We must keep in mind Chisdai's words in his letter to the

King of Khazar: "I always ask the ambassadors of
these monarchs about our brethren, the Israelites,
the remnant of the captivity, whether they have
heard anything concerning the deliverance of those
who have pined in bondage and had found no rest."[74]
This letter reflects that the wish to have information about their coreligionists was always an object of Jewish leaders, for which itinerant merchants were used.[75] Furthermore, if this be the
case in peaceful times, how much stronger must have
grown the desire for communication during the crusades. Benjamin's and Petachia's interests focus
around the Jewish sphere. Petachia almost completely ignores "world affairs" and centres his
information around the Jews. The careful reader
will find that in his accounts Benjamin of Tudela
reveals to us his efforts to indicate in each
place that he visited specific details of the life
of the Jews, especially their political situation,
and their security in the society in which they
were living. He concerned himself with the possibility of any existing hostility between the Jews
and the Gentiles around them. He also prides himself in supplying any fact, no matter how insignificant, that referred to independent Jews who were
not dominated politically by others.

What is the full meaning of this information
with which they supply us? Could they have been
messengers to provide communication between the
Jews and to preserve the unification of world
Jewry? Keeping in mind that the massacres at the
end of the eleventh century and of the twelfth
century created an atmosphere of confusion, there
must have been intense desire for such information.

Examining again the accounts by our travellers, we find serious obstacles to accepting the
above suggestion. It seems unlikely that Petachia
had been sent on his travels merely to inform his
brethren and to satisfy their curiosity.[76] Petachia spent a comparatively long portion of his
journey in Babylonia. It is true that Babylonia
contained a good portion of the world Jewry of the

twelfth century[77] but it is also true that Egypt was another important centre,[78] and Petachia did not pay a visit there. He completely ignored North Africa in which Jewish communities had existed for a long period.[79] He did not extend his travels into Persia and Arabia. If it is correct that following the first crusades new information was needed to update the picture of world Jewry, we do not find any emissaries or special messengers sent to Western Europe, including England.[80] The author maintains that Rabbi Petachia's mission was not to furnish information to satisfy his brethren's curiosity. Otherwise it is not clear why he gives a detailed picture of the Babylonian Jews. Furthermore, he completely neglects certain areas and cities in which, according to Benjamin, Jews were found.

Returning to Benjamin of Tudela, the suggestion which has been made again seems unacceptable. Although he gives us a detailed picture concerning the Jews whom he visited, his journey does not bring him to Western and Central Europe, where the established Jewish communities had been subject to persecution during the early crusades. If his mere intention were to update the picture by making a general observation, why, then, did he not go to North Africa and the rest of Europe from which news was especially needed as a result of persecutions?

Carefully examining the accounts, it is possible to detect within our travellers' minds aspirations for a better existence. We can sense their yearnings for a better society and life. Petachia was greatly impressed by the prosperous life of the Jews in Babylonia and he proudly identified with them. He is amazed at the tranquility in which the Jews were living. He gives a detailed picture of the Gaon and Exilarch. It appears that the new atmosphere he came across in Babylonia pushed him to describe life there in detail. Why should his enthusiasm surprise us—what more could we expect of a man coming from Germany in a generation that evidenced the massacres of Jews along the Rhine?

56

Furthermore, his longings for a better future can
be detected by his inquiries about the specific
time the Messiah was to arrive, and his stories of
Gentiles who convert to Judaism previous to Messianic times.[81] No one can deny Rabbi Petachia's
enthusiasm over his findings in Babylonia and one
feels that the entire voyage resulted from his
desire to focus on the Jews there.

Those aspirations for a better existence which
the author feels are evidenced by Petachia's account, can be even better shown by Benjamin of Tudela. His information concerning the Jews whom he
visited centred around typical questions which
bothered the European Jews of that century. In
coming to Byzantium, he clearly expresses the fact
on one hand that the Jews are in great despair
there, persecuted and hated by the Greeks, and on
the other hand he reminds us that no reason existed for that hatred since the Jews were "good and
very hospitable."[82] It is possible to share his
thoughts concerning the Jewish destiny in the
world and about the lot that befell the Jews in
history. In light of his meditations, we can expect him to aspire to a better life and future for
his people. He is proud when he has an opportunity
to speak about the Jews who are independent, the
masters of their own destiny. Reading his account
referring to the Jews of Kheibar[83] fills us even
today with a heroic awe that surely inspired Benjamin even more.[84] He does not omit any opportunity
to report of free Jews and warriors who have not
been persecuted. This report about the Lost Ten
Tribes—information he probably obtained in Baghdad—presents him as an astute inquirer, looking
to verify stories, legends and rumours circulating
for a long time among the Jews which, during the
twelfth century, reached a climax. He does not
omit the episode of the false Messiah, David Alroy,
of whom he furnishes us many details.[85] We wonder
if Benjamin was not looking for further informat-
tion to verify rumours of redemption soon to come,[86]
and if he himself was anxious to know of the expected day.[87] Graetz states: "The object of this

journey [Benjamin of Tudela] is not quite known. He was either an itinerant merchant, or a pious man of an inquiring turn of mind in search of traces of a Messianic redemption."[88] The very word "Messiah" hides within its rich content the yearning and hope for better existence.[89] Furthermore, his account is so fascinating that any reader would be entranced to look for verification of legends and rumours with the traveller. We should not forget that the rumours of the Lost Ten Tribes received further stimulus in the twelfth century through the famous letter which reported the legendary figure of Prester John.

From the above, it can be inferred that the accounts contain within them the psychological aspirations for a better era for the Jews. Furthermore, we can say that Benjamin took upon himself to investigate, to the best of his ability, the veracity of certain legends with which he was familiar. Nevertheless, to jump to the conclusion that our travellers set out on their journeys because they yearned for a better life and wished to verify stories would be wrong.

The situation of European Jews in the twelfth century indicated signs of decline. Liebeschütz emphasizes the development of the idea of a Christian society, which became an important factor from the eleventh century on.[90] This development is reflected well by the crusading movement, and resulted in Christian solidarity and a great awareness of any non-Christian group.[91] The Peasants' Crusade reflected an emotional atmosphere which was no longer controlled by the traditional conceptions. During the thirteenth century this combination of enthusiasm and emotionalism reached its full development.[92] Moreover, the sense of Christian solidarity was strongly felt in the towns which by now had reached an important place in society. The Jews were ultimately to remain outside this intensely developed religious and corporate life.[93] If Agus is correct that the historical evidences of the Pre-Crusade period indicates a

58

great social interaction between the Jews and their neighbours in Germany and France, and that every Jew depended chiefly on them for his daily living,[94] then, it is obvious that following the First and Second Crusades the social and economic life apparently changed little. Consequently, the First Crusade reflected a situation where the Jews needed protection not only as merchants but as non-Christians as well.[95] That is why, as a result of the persecutions of 1096, the Jews were included among those protected in the Mainz Imperial Land Peace of 1103 (the first of its kind).[96] This legal status of <u>homines minus potentes</u> found its important place in the Sachsenspiegel as well, and preserved its form for more than 120 years.[97] This legal protection applied to Jews "on all days and at all times."[98]

Jews began to consider emigration as a possible solution for their situation in Moslem Spain. Various ways had been suggested. One way reflected a revolutionary thought among the Spanish Jewry as exemplified by the emigration of ha-Levi to the Holy Land. He preached to his people that Jews could not consider themselves secure unless they would return to their own country. He himself set an example to be followed by others in the following generations.[99]

Another solution in Spain resulted in emigration of Jews from Moslem to Christian Spain in an attempt to reestablish Jewish life.[100] Abraham ibn Daud strongly approved of this movement.[101] In Germany the massacres forced Jews to consider emigrating further into Eastern Europe.[102] Individuals as well as entire communities moved from their native areas to quieter places. Maimonides is a famous example of those who emigrated to more secure area, as he himself left for Egypt. In support of this point, we have Maimonides' letter of consolation to his people in which he states that it is far better to emigrate to a land of greater security than to convert in a land of persecution.[103] We see then that emigration to a more peaceful area seemed to present itself as the best "temporary" solution.

Even in Tudela, Benjamin's native city, captured by Alfonso I in 1115,[104] the Jews decided in 1114 to emigrate fearing for their safety. They agreed to stay only at the special request of Alfonso I and his promise that they should be granted favourable municipal rights.[105] Furthermore, as the Jews continued to suffer from the hatred of the Christians, they made it clear that they would leave the city if the abuses were not stopped. Consequently, Sancho VII (1150-1194) in 1170 confirmed all the rights which Alfonso I granted them.[106] The defensive character of the Jewish quarter is very much emphasized in this privilege for Tudelian Jewry of 1170. Following the removal of the Jewish quarter in Tudela to the citadel, the king wrote that if anyone attacked the castle and anyone was hurt or killed, the Jews would not be held responsible, whether the incident happened in day time or at night.[107] Thus, the Jews were allowed to utilize the fortifications to defend themselves against possible mob violence. Furthermore, the king promised to keep the walls of the citadel in repair.[108] Not only that, for their greater security, the king assigned to them the fortress as a residence[109] and also freed them from the tax on merchandise.[110] He permitted them to freely sell their houses located in their former Juderia[111] and also showed tolerance in his regulation of their legal status.[112]

What is the meaning of all this? The most significant point is that the privileges listed above were granted in 1170, that is to say, while Benjamin was still on his journey. Secondly, we get the impression that the Jews in Tudela were being specially favoured. It should again be pointed out that the defensive character of the Jewish quarters is very strongly emphasized by Sancho VII. Therefore, it appears that the motivation behind this charter is the possible animosity of Christians towards the Jews forced the

60

latter to have a special stronghold where they
could find refuge in case of an attack. Moreover,
in 1170 it could have been a similar precarious
situation that forced granting favourable privileges to persuade the Jews to remain as King Alfonso
I had done in 1114. However, for our case, the
crucial point is that this was taking place around
the time Benjamin was on his travels.[113]

     At this point let us look again in the account
of Benjamin of Tudela. The account indicates that
Benjamin spent a considerable amount of time in the
following areas: Babylonia, Byzantium, Palestine
and Egypt.[114] All the other geographical areas
visited by him were, in the author's opinion, secondary to his voyage. Furthermore, the scholars
correctly indicate that it is doubtful whether our
traveller went beyond Babylonia into Persia. Surely he did not try to go farther east.[115] The same
is true of Arabia.[116] He reports of Jews in Arabia,
but only through hearsay. On this point, again,
the scholars are in agreement.[117]

     Therefore, is it possible that the role of
Benjamin of Tudela may have been as a special representative of Spanish Jewry sent to survey the
conditions of world Jewry, particularly in the a-
bove mentioned four areas in the hopes of finding
some asylum for his people in their crises?[118] The
most likely possibilities[119] were: Byzantium, into which Jews had emigrated previously;[120] Babylonia, which had been for a long time and still was
the Jewish centre in the twelfth century; and Egypt
which, during this time, absorbed many Jewish refugees from Palestine following the crusaders' conquest. Egypt itself was to become an important
Jewish centre. The Holy Land afforded another possibility as a place of refuge. The land of the
ancestors, to which ha-Levi had previously emigrated and had recommended as a refuge to his people,
was in the process of changing from Christian into
Moslem hands.[121] At this cross section of events,
the Holy Land, which had sent refugees to Egypt in
1096 was again in a position to be considered as a

refuge for persecuted Jews.[122] Furthermore, certain Messianic expectations foretold of the conquest of the Holy Land by Saladin who had, according to certain twelfth-century rumours, promised to surrender the Land to the Jewish Messiah.[123] Bearing all this in mind, can we assume that Benjamin had the intention of investigating various possibilities of asylum for his brethren? Can this be supported by the type of information he furnishes us with upon his return? He states the size of various Jewish communities, the economic opportunities available, plus the political situation of the jews there, and finally, a report of any present hostilities between Jews and the natives of these respective places.

The preface to his itinerary, which had been written by an unknown author, refers always to the authorities who tested and analyzed the information brought back by Benjamin.[124] Who are those authorities? Could they have been the people originally responsible for sending Benjamin of Tudela on his voyage with the specific purpose of seeking asylum for his people? Furthermore, the unknown author of the preface mentions a fact that we know from the itinerary itself: that is, that Rabbi Benjamin mentioned the leaders and scholars of the Jewish communities which he visited.[125] Were those the leaders with whom our traveller met in order to discuss the goal of his voyage, and was this the reason he mentioned these leaders and scholars by name? As to the question of why the authorities in Spain chose Rabbi Benjamin for this purpose, can we refer to what the unknown author of the preface has to say of him as a learned man, and a trustworthy person?[126] In addition to his personal attributes, Benjamin was further suited for such a difficult and responsible task because he was a merchant. As a long-time merchant, he had the necessary experience for extensive travelling.[127]

Coming back to Central Europe, not only had the First Crusade but the Second Crusade (1147) as well added Jewish martyrs. Jacob Tam himself

(From the end of the twelfth century the bishops
of Regensburg and the dukes of Bavaria competed to
obtain exclusive rule of the town.) It is important to keep in mind that the Jews migrated into
the King's cities in order to obtain effective royal
protection[148] because several princes could not secure peace in 1146 when Radulf spoke out emphati-
cally against the Jews.[149] The privilege extended
to the Jews by Frederick II in 1236 was directly
preceded by political events of an anti-Jewish
character,[150] just as had been the case with the
regulation in 1103. The anti-Jewish events that
led to the charter of 1236 reflected the insuffi-
ciency of even a country-wide peace.[151] Thus, it
is likely that the need for Regensburg Jewry to be
protected is connected with the charter of 1182,
as constant need for royal protection led eventually to the institution of the Chamber Serfdom
of the Jews.[152]

The 1182 charter also grants the right to
trade.[153] It is known that Frederick I opposed
the desire of guilds in Regensburg which may have
tried to restrict Jewish activities and to secure
the right to purchase raw material and food exclusively for themselves. The Emperor guaranteed the
Jews the rights of unlimited purchase.[154] The
charter then reveals to us the interesting process
by which the entire relationship between citizens
and Jews was about to deteriorate. While citizens
won their independence, Jews lost their liberty.
In Regensburg this development brought Jews into
the society where they could not be equal members.[155] Thus the charter of 1182 reflects a process by which the situation of the Jews in Regensburg was becoming less and less favourable, and
where even the protection of Frederick I could not
completely guarantee peace.[156] Above all, we
should keep in mind that Petachia set out on his
journey before the charter was granted.

Grünhut raises the possibility that Rabbi
Petachia might have met Rabbi Benjamin before the
former set out on his travels.[157] We have already

found that Rabbi Petachia started his journey soon
after Rabbi Benjamin returned home, and it is possible that Rabbi Petachia was motivated strongly by
the example of the Spanish traveller. Can one consider Rabbi Petachia as a special messenger of his
community to focus attention on Babylonia as a
place for possible emigration? We find that Rabbi
Petachia was concentrating in his account on Babylonia. Did he, as well as the leaders who had sent
him, consider Babylonia to be the most appropriate
place of refuge for his German brethren? Grünhut
correctly states that Rabbi Petachia, the pious and
devoted German Jew, instead of visiting the Holy
Land first, as any other pious Jew would have done,
came first to Babylonia.158 Furthermore, he did
not stay long in Palestine while he spent a considerable amount of time in Babylonia once he was
there. Again and again he returns to speak so
proudly of Babylonian Jews who lived peacefully in
prosperity. His admiration of Rabbi Samuel ben Ali
is so great that he refers to him as the most famous scholar in the world and believes that there
was none to be compared with him.159 In his account, Babylonia becomes deserving of the highest
praise. Do these indications to the nature of his
mission show it to be an investigation in Babylonia
as a possible refuge for his brethren in Europe?

     While visiting Babylonia, R. Petachia received
from Samuel ben Ali, the Gaon of Babylonia, a letter which gave him help and guidance.160 Again, is
it possible that discussion on the question of
Jewish emigration into Babylonia may have been responsible for this letter? Baron states: "Whatever the motives which induced this apparently
wealthy traveller to undertake such an arduous
'world tour,' he evidently learned less from, and
communicated less to his readers about his voyage
than his older Spanish contemporary."161 Baron is
right that Rabbi Petachia's account is poor compared with that of Rabbi Benjamin's. Is it because
Rabbi Petachia was anxious to fulfil a mission, and
being in Babylonia, his final object, he was not
interested much in anything else?

Is it, then, possible that while Rabbi Petachia was sent to investigate Babylonia, Rabbi Benjamin was delegated to investigate various possibilities for places of refuge? Is it possible that
our travellers did not specifically state in their
itineraries the object of finding asylum for Jews
because it could be quite dangerous to reveal the
intention of mass emigration?

The most serious objections to the assumption
that Petachia and Benjamin set upon their travels
to find an asylum for their brethren are not only
that there is not any clear and irrefutable proof
in their own accounts, but also because modern historical research shows that the Jewish situation
in Europe had not been seriously affected during
this period.[162] Though the crusading movement
started a series of persecutions and caused a deterioration in the Jewish situation, nevertheless,
the twelfth century as a whole still found the
Jews respected citizens, protected by the laws issued by the rulers of the state and by the heads
of the church. As noted above, the Jews were included in special acts of protection by rulers who
were defenders of the Jewish communities. In Germany, the central authority was still effective
and able emperors took active steps to guarantee
peace for the Jews. The grant of privileges to
Regensburg Jewry in 1182 reflects the determined
wish of the Emperor to protect the Jews. Only in
the thirteenth century is there a profound trans-
formation in the situation of European Jewry which
came about when the government and the church adop-
ted a clear, official policy to persecute the Jews
and to keep them in a subordinate position to the
rest of the society. Though there are signs of
deterioration in the Jewish situation following
the crusade of 1096, nevertheless, one has to wait
for over a century before one can see massive persecution of European Jewry.

The new Christian Spain, being on its way to
successful completion of the Reconquista, was also
in the process of rebuilding the country. The

Jews, because of their skills and experience in
various spheres of life, were needed and welcomed
here.[163]

Again, the Jews were inclined to establish
themselves in places where they were needed at the
time. Eastern Europe was at this period in the
process of westernization. Forests and swamps were
being cleared and new cities were springing up.[164]
The twelfth century was the heroic period for the
German people in moving east, north and southeast,
clearing forests and bringing new lands under cultivation. The colonisation movement pushed the
German frontier beyond Mecklenburg and Brandenburg
into Pomerania. In addition there was the less
striking German expansion in the southeast.[165]
Frontier lands, like the Magdeburg country and the
old Mark of Brandenburg, were in great need of immigrants.[166] A movement down the line of the Elbe
could be seen. The new German immigrants influenced the natives in the use of more modern methods
of cultivation. The economic capacity of the Cis-
tericians was highly prized,[167] and the Order attracted colonists, with easy terms.[168] The new
towns founded in colonial regions were still in
the course of development and needed new immigrants very badly. The Baltic area was soon to become a part of Western commerce.[169] That was one
aspect of the twelfth-century Renaissance. Everywhere there were signs of growing economy and new
prospects for life.[170] All this offered an easier
and better life here. The rulers of the new areas
in Central and Eastern Europe offered the Jews
privileges in order to attact them to build and
develop the new places.

Thus, the twelfth century witnessed mainly
the movement of Jews who, in the hopes of building
a new life for themselves, migrated from Central
to Eastern Europe. Baron must certainly have had
this in mind when he stated that:

> ...the European Jewish communities con-
> stantly increased in numerical, economic,

and cultural strength. By telescoping
the events of a whole century, modern
observers often received a totally erron-
eous impression...there was a tremendous
expansion of the Jewish population in
Christian Spain, and in the newer sections
of Central and Eastern Europe. Certainly,
by 1200 many more Jews lived under Christendom than had in 1095. Such tenacity in
the face of adversity and growing animo-
sities can be understood only against the
background of the vast economic and cultural changes throughout the western
world.[171]

Meanwhile, in spite of the glowing reports of Petachia, the Orient was declining.[172]

As to the question of what motivated Petachia
and Benjamin to set upon their travels, we are
forced to answer that due to the lack of documentation we are unable to isolate a specific goal.
However, given the difficulties of travel, it
stands to reason that the goals were multiple ones:
pilgrimage to the Land of the forefathers, curiosity, desire to travel, communication with the dispersed Jewish communities and bringing back information about them, or possible mercantile operations. Probably any one of the above reasons or
a combination of them motivated the travels of
Benjamin and Petachia.

We must also admit that there may be other
unknown reasons for their travels.

Footnotes

[1]Jewish Travellers, ed. E.N. Adler, Introduction, p. xi.

[2]Graetz, History of the Jews, II, 200-232;

69

Baron, A Social and Religious History of the Jews, I, 165-212.

[3]Baron, A Social and Religious History of the Jews, III, 75-119.

[4]Travels and Travellers of the Middle Ages, ed. A.P. Newton (New York, 1930), Chap. 5.

[5]Ibid., p. 89.

[6]Rabinowitz, Jewish Merchants' Adventures, p. 90.

[7]Baron, A Social and Religious History of the Jews, IV, 173.

[8]Ibid., 172-74.

[9]W. Heyd, Histoire du Commerce du Levant au Moyen Age, 2 vols., 2d ed.(Leipzig, 1936), I, 125-130.

[10]A. Meyendorf, "Trade and Communications in Eastern Europe from 800-1200," Travels and Travellers of the Middle Ages, p. 105.

[11]Ibid., p. 109.

[12]Baron, A Social and Religious History of the Jews, IV, 171-78, 322-26, ns. 26-34.

[13]Rabinowitz, Jewish Merchants' Adventures, p. 102.

[14]The Itinerary of Petachia. ed. Grünhut, p. 6; The Itinerary of Petachia, ed. E.N. Adler, Jewish Travellers, p. 68.

[15]Beazley, II, 218.

[16]P. Rousset, "La conception de l'histoire à l'époque féodale," Mélanges d'histoire du moyen âge, dédiés à la mémoire de Louis Halphen (Paris,

1951), p. 624.

[17]Ibid., pp. 623, 624, 629.

[18]Prawer, A History of the Latin Kingdom of Jerusalem, I, 42.

[19]Jewish Travellers, ed. E.N. Adler, Introduction, pp. xi-xii.

[20]On Eldad ha Dani see, Eldad Ha Dani, ed. A. Epstein (Pressburg, 1891), Introduction and the Itinerary; Rabinowitz, Jewish Merchants' Adventures, passim; I.A. Agus, Rabbi Meir of Rothenburg, 2 vols. (Philadelphia, 1947), I. 256; A. Neubauer, "Eldad the Danite," J.Q.R., III (1891), 541-544; J. Reifmann, "Comments on a Book: Eldad Hadani," Ha-Karmel, VIII (1870), 254, 262, 279-280, 286-87; L. Rabinowitz, "Eldad HaDani and China," J.Q.R., XXXVI (Jan. 1946), 231-38; Abraham ibn Ezra in his commentary on Ex. 2:22.

[21]Eldad Ha-Dani, ed. A. Epstein, Introduction, pp. xxii-xxiii.

[22]Ibid., pp. xxiii-xxiv.

[23]J. Alkharizi, Tahkemoni, ed. Y. Toporovski (Tel-Aviv, 1952); Baron, A Social and Religious History of the Jews, VII, 185.

[24]The Itinerary of Rabbi Samual Ben Samson, ed. E.N. Adler, Jewish Travellers, pp. 103-110; A.L. Sukenik, "Some Comments on Letters with Respect to Travels in Palestine from the Middle Ages," Zion-Measef, II (1927), 108.

[25]Eisenstein, pp. 65-71.

[26]Estori ha-Parchi, Caftor va-Pherach, ed. A.M. Luncz (Jerusalem, 1889-97).

[27]Eisenstein, pp. 86-106.

[28] Ibid., pp. 106-24. As to the influence of the stories concerning the Ten Tribes on the discoveries of the New World, see the article by H. Z. Hirshberg, "The Desire for Freedom in the Legends on the Ten Tribes," Mahnayim, LXXX (1963), 98.

[29] Eisenstein, pp. 139-166; Hirshberg, "The Desire for Freedom in the Legends on the Ten Tribes," 99.

[30] Newton, p. 2.

[31] Ibid., p. 43.

[32] J.K. Wright, Human Nature in Geography (Cambridge, Mass., 1966), pp. 72-73.

[33] The Itinerary of Benjamin of Tudela, ed. M.N. Adler, pp. 6-7; Haskins, The Renaissance of the 12th Century, pp. 119-121, 123-124; Mirabilia Urbis Romae, trans. F.M. Nichols (London, 1809), pp. 62, 117; F. Gregorovius, History of the City of Rome in the Middle Ages, trans. A. Hamilton, 8 vols. (London, 1894-1902), IV. 686.

[34] The Itinerary of Benjamin of Tudela, ed. M.N. Adler, p. 76.

[35] See Chapter II, Section 1 in the book.

[36] Dubnov, II, 724.

[37] Jewish Travellers, ed. E.N. Adler, p. 93; The Itinerary of Jacob ben Nathaniel ha-Cohen, ed. Grünhut, p. 12.

[38] J. Pieper, Scholasticism (New York, 1960), pp, 100-101.

[39] The Itinerary of Benjamin of Tudela, ed. M.N. Adler, pp. 47-51, 59.

[40] Beazley, II, 252.

[41] Ibid., p. 271.

[42] Baron, A Social and Religious History of the Jews, VI, 225.

[43] Prawer, A History of the Latin Kingdom of Jerusalem, I, 40.

[44] Ibid., pp. 42-43; Ish Shalom, Christian Travels in the Holy Land (Tel-Aviv, 1965), pp. 3-9; Deuteronomy, 16:16.

[45] Hitti states: "Pilgrimage is the fifth and last pillar of Islam. Once in a lifetime every Moslem of either sex who can afford it is supposed to undertake at a stated time of the year a holy visit to Makkah. 'Umrah is the lesser pilgrimage to Makkah and may be made individually and at any time." (P.K. Hitti, History of the Arabs [London, 1940], p. 133.)

[46] Newton, p. 91.

[47] Prawer, A History of the Latin Kingdom of Jerusalem, I, 38-48; Ish Shalom, Christian Travels in the Holy Land, pp. 4-9; Mähl, 11-26.

[48] S. Runciman, A History of the Crusades, 3 vols. (Oxford, 1951-52); Prawer, A History of the Latin Kingdom of Jerusalem, 2 vols.; K. Ritter, The Comparative Geography of Palestine and the Sinaitic Peninsula, W.L. Gage trans. of the Erdkunde von Asien, 4 vols. (New York, 1968), II. 39.

[49] See H. Schirmann, The Hebrew Poetry in Spain and Provence, 2 vols. (Jerusalem, 1960), I, 244-47, II, 381-85, 464-65, 485-92, 620-21.

[50] The Itinerary of Jacob ben Nathaniel ha-Cohen, ed. E.N. Adler, Jewish Travellers, p. 92.

[51] Ibid., p. 99.

[52] Eisenstein, p. 58.

[53] The Itinerary of Jacob ben Nathaniel ha-Cohen, ed. Grünhut, Introduction, p. 3.

[54] The researcher maintains that Beazley misunderstood Petachia's itinerary when he states: "He probably did not visit the river Sambation, which his narrative begins by fixing as the goal of his journey,..." (Beazley, II, 271). It is clear that Petachia did not visit that river; furthermore, there is no proof whatsoever in Petachia's itinerary that his goal was to visit it in order to find the Ten Lost Tribes. The Sivuv begins as follows: "These are the travels undertaken by Rabbi Petachia...who travelled all the lands till Sambation..." (The Itinerary of Petachia, ed. Grünhut, p. 1). To conclude from here that the goal of the journey was to reach Sambation would be, according to the author, an incorrect reading.

[55] The Itinerary of Petachia, ed. Grünhut, Part II, pp. xii-xiii.

[56] See Chapter V, Section 2 in the book.

[57] The Itinerary of Petachia, ed. Grünhut, pp. 33-34; Jewish Travellers, ed. E.N. Adler, pp. 89-90.

[58] Slutsky, "Pethahiah of Regensburg," E.J., XIII, 339.

[59] Ya'ari, Travels to Palestine, pp. 32-33.

[60] The Itinerary of Benjamin of Tudela, ed. M.N. Adler, pp. 18-29.

[61] M.N. Adler also does not consider that as his main purpose (ibid., Introduction, p. xiii).

[62] Ibid., Preface, p. 1.

[63] Hitti, History of the Arabs, p. 569.

⁶⁴*The Itinerary of Benjamin of Tudela*, ed. M. N. Adler, Introduction, p. xiii.

⁶⁵Graetz, *History of the Jews*, III, 388.

⁶⁶Beazley, II, 227. See also Benjamin of Tudela, *Sefer Masa'ot*, ed. Asher, II, x.

⁶⁷See Chapter VII in the book.

⁶⁸For example see *The Itinerary of Benjamin of Tudela*, ed. M.N. Adler, p. 3.

⁶⁹*Ibid.*, Introduction, p. xiii.

⁷⁰*Jewish Travellers*, ed. E.N. Adler, Introduction, p. xv.

⁷¹*Ibid.*, p. xvi.

⁷²*The Itinerary of Benjamin of Tudela*, ed. M.N. Adler, Introduction, p. xii.

⁷³Beazley, II, 218-19.

⁷⁴*The Epistle of R. Chisdai Ibn Shaprut to the King of the Khozars and the King's Reply*, ed. E. N. Adler, *Jewish Travellers*, p. 27.

⁷⁵*Ibid.*

⁷⁶Benisch believes that Petachia's object may be conjectured from the tenor of the book, that he was impelled thereto by a strong desire to visit his distant brethren, and to become acquainted with their fate (*The Travels of Rabbi Petachia of Ratisbon*, ed. and trans. A. Benisch [London, 1856], Introduction, p. vi).

⁷⁷Baron, *A Social and Religious History of the Jews*, III, 99.

⁷⁸S.D. Goitein, *A Mediterranean Society: The*

75

Jewish Communities of the Arab World as Portrayed in the Documents of the Cairo Geniza, Vol. 1 (Berkeley and Los Angeles, 1967); Vol. II (Berkeley, Los Angeles and London, 1971), I, Introduction; Baron, A Social and Religious History of the Jews, III, 99.

[79] Dubnov, II, 397-400.

[80] Baron, A Social and Religious History of the Jews, IV, 117-32.

[81] The Itinerary of Petachia, ed. Grünhut, pp. 7, 25.

[82] The Itinerary of Benjamin of Tudela, ed. M.N. Adler, p. 14.

[83] Ibid., pp. 46-50.

[84] See Chapter VI in the book.

[85] The Itinerary of Benjamin of Tudela, ed. M.N. Adler, pp. 54-56. Refer to this subject— Exile and Redemption in the twelfth century— in Chapter VI in the book.

[86] Benjamin of Tudela, Sefer Masa'ot, ed. Asher, I, 14-15.

[87] A. Sharf, Byzantine Jewry from Justinian to the Fourth Crusade (New York), p. 141.

[88] Graetz, History of the Jews, III, 388.

[89] R.J. Zwi Werbalowsky, "Messianiam in Jewish History," Journal of World History, XI (1968), 30-46.

[90] Liebeschütz, 98.

[91] Ibid., 101, 110; Dietrich, 97, 114.

[92] Liebeschütz, 109; Dasberg, pp. 156, 185.

[93]Liebeschütz, 109; Kisch, p. 338; Langmuir, 205; Dietrich, 94-95, 126-127; Dasberg, p. 193.

[94]I. Agus, The Heroic Age of Franco-German Jewry (New York, 1969), pp. 341-342.

[95]J. Parkes, The Jews in the Medieval Community (London, 1938), pp. 106, 79, 89.

[96]Kisch, p. 109.

[97]Ibid., pp. 131, 140-141.

[98]Ibid., p. 110.

[99]See Chapter VI in the book.

[100]Dubnov, II, 731.

[101]Abraham ibn Daud, Sefer Ha-Qabbalah, ed. S.D. Cohen, pp. 97-98.

[102]Dubnov, II, 790; Baron, A Social and Religious History of the Jews, IV, 118; Dietrich, 127.

[103]"Epistle on Apostasy-Iggeret ha-Shemad," A Maimonides Reader, ed. I. Twersky (New York, 1972), p. 10.

[104]Y. Baer, A History of the Jews in Christian Spain, 2 vols. (Philadelphia, 1961), I, 387, n. 23.

[105]F. Baer, Die Juden im christlichen Spanien, 2 vols. (Berlin, 1929), I, 920, No. 570.

[106]Ibid., pp. 933-935, No. 578.

[107]Ibid., p. 934, Nos. 4, 6; this provision was repeated in Sancho's privilege for the Jews of Funes (ibid., pp. 936-937, No. 579).

[108]Ibid., p. 934, No. 9.

[109]Ibid., p. 933, No. 578.

[110]Ibid., p. 934, No. 2.

[111]Ibid., p. 934, No. 1.

[112]Ibid., p. 934, Nos. 5, 7, 8.

[113]All this will probably explain the favourable policy of Sancho VII towards the Jews as documentdd in Baer, ibid., p. 933, No. 577; pp. 933-939, Nos. 578-581; M. Kayserling, Geschichte der Juden in Spanien und Portugal: I: Die Juden in Navarra (Berlin, 1861), pp. 21-22. In fact, Sancho VII was admonished by Gregory IX for his favourable policy towards the Jews (Grayzel, p. 272, No. 72).

[114]Beazley, II, 227-28.

[115]Ibid., p. 255.

[116]Ibid., p. 253.

[117]Baron believes, however, that the scholars have gone too far in denying that he reached the countries east of the Persian Gulf. (Baron, A Social and Religious History of the Jews, VI, 224.)

[118]Jewish Travellers, ed. E.N. Adler, Introduction, pp. xii-xiii; Asher, II, Introduction, ix-x; F. Uspensky, "Benjamin of Tudela's Notes on His Journey," Annaly, III (1923), 19-20.

[119]Prawer, A History of the Latin Kingdom of Jerusalem, I, 313-14; Z. Ankori, Karaites in Byzantium (New York, 1959), pp. 87-100.

[120]Ankori, Karaites in Byzantium, pp. 87-106.

[121]Prawer, A History of the Latin Kingdom of Jerusalem, I, 292, 296, 299; see Chapter VI in the book.

[122]Dinur, Israel in Diaspora (2)I, 180; Prawer, A History of the Latin Kingdom of Jerusalem, II, 388; M. Nahmanides, Sefer Hasagot Haramban Zal

Sehsig 'Al Rabenu Mose bar Maimon Zal Beminyan
Hamitsvot (Constantinople, 1510), Commandement 4;
see Chapters V and VI in the book.

[123]Dinur, Israel in Diaspora (2)II, 284-86; see
Chapter VI in the book.

[124]The Itinerary of Benjamin of Tudela, ed. M.
N. Adler, pp. 1-2.

[125]Ibid., p. 1.

[126]Ibid., pp. 1-2.

[127]See Chapter II, Section 1 upon this point.

[128]Neubauer and Stern, II, 60; Haberman, p. 121;
Dietrich, 122.

[129]Neubauer and Stern, II, 67-68; Haberman, pp.
124-25; Dietrich, 123; R. Chazan, "The Blois Incident of 1171," P.A.A.J.R., XXXVI (1968), 13-31.

[130]Neubauer and Stern, II, 68; Graetz, History
of the Jews, III, 355; Baron, A Social and Religious History of the Jews, IV, 118-19.

[131]C.J. Hefele, Histoire des Conciles d'après
les documents originaux, trans. and ed. H. Leclerq,
9 vols. (Paris, 1907-21), Tome V, deuxième partie,
pp. 1086-87.

[132]Mansi, XXII, 259.

[133]Could the success be ascribed to the influence of Rabbi Yechiel, the treasurer of Pope Alexander III, mentioned by Benjamin of Tudela at Rome?
(The Itinerary of Benjamin of Tudela, ed. M.N.
Adler, pp. 5-6.)

[134]Dinur, Israel in Diaspora (2)I, 288, n. 7.

[135]Ibn Verga, Shevet Yehudah, ed. A. Sohat
(Jerusalem, 1947), p. 146.

[136]As early as 1179 one could detect the harsh policy of the Church against the Jews, as expressed later in the Fourth Lateran Council. (Pfaff, pp. 181-184, 185-190.) The growing animosity of the Church legislation against the Jews explains the fear the Jews had on the eve of the Third Lateran Council of which we read in Shevet Yehudah, see n. 135 above.

[137]Mansi, XXII, 231.

[138]Ibid.

[139]Dinur, Israel in Diaspora (2)I, 157.

[140]see Chapter I in the book.

[141]The Itinerary of Petachia, ed. Grunhut, Part II, p. viii.

[142]See footnote 102 above.

[143]Aronius, Regesten, No. 135.

[144]Neubauer and Stern, II, 2, 37 and especially 48.

[145]B. Altmann, "Studies in Medieval German History," P.A.A.J.R., X (1940), 49.

[146]Aronius, Regesten, pp. 123, No. 280; p. 139, No. 314a; also Pfaff, pp. 196-197.

[147]Altmann, "Studies in Medieval German History," p. 70.

[148]Aronius, Regesten, No. 233.

[149]Neubauer and Stern, II, 58-59; Dietrich, p. 122.

[150]Aronius, Regesten, Nos. 460, 474, 497.

[151]Burchard Von Ursberg (1177-1231) asserts that

the peace laws were not properly obeyed (Kisch, p. 143; Dasberg, pp. 151, 154, 156, 158-163, 169).

[152]Altmann, "Studies in Medieval German History," pp. 56, 73-75; Dietrich, p. 119.

[153]Aronius, Regesten, No. 250.

[154]Altmann, "Studies in Medieval German History," p. 53.

[155]Kisch, pp. 118-119; Altmann, "Studies in Medieval German History," 6, 48, 51, 56-57, 77.

[156]Pfaff, p. 200.

[157]The Itinerary of Petachia, ed. Grünhut, Part II, p. viii.

[158]Ibid., p. ix.

[159]Ibid., p. x.

[160]Ibid., p. 12; Jewish Travellers, ed. E.N. Adler, p. 73.

[161]Baron, A Social and Religious History of the Jews, VI, 225.

[162]Chazan, Medieval Jewry in Northern France, pp. 26-29, 36, 38, 62; Chazan, "Jewish Settlement in Northern France 1096-1306," p. 43; Chazan, "The Bray Incident of 1192," pp. 5-6, 14; Baron, A Social and Religious History of the Jews, IV, 283, n. 1; 308, n. 62; 311, n. 71; Roth, "European Jewry in the Dark Ages: A Revised Picture," HUCA, XXIII (1950-51), 151-169; Kish, pp. 4, 21-22; Parkes, The Jew in the Medieval Community, pp. 59-89; Altmann, "Studies in Medieval German History," p. 77 and n. 220.

[163]Y. Baer, A History of the Jews in Christian Spain, I, 47, 78; II, 78-110; A.A. Newmann, The Jews in Spain, 2 vols. (Philadelphia, 1942), I, 4-5.

[164] J.H. Clapham and E. Power (eds.), _Cambridge Economic History of Europe_ (Cambridge, 1941), I, 80.

[165] M. Clagett, G. Post and R. Reynolds, _Twelfth Century Europe and the Foundations of Modern Society_ (Madison, 1961), p. 160.

[166] C.E.H., I, 81.

[167] _Ibid._, p. 85.

[168] _Ibid._, p. 86.

[169] _Ibid._, II, 179.

[170] Haskins, _The Renaissance of the 12th Century_, pp. vi, 15.

[171] Baron, _A Social and Religious History of the Jews_, IV, 148-149; Dietrich, p. 127. There is a widely held opinion that the European population was increasing throughout the twelfth and thirteenth centuries. Studies by Génicot show the tendency towards the creation of new towns during this period (L. Génicot, _On the Evidence of Growth in the West from the Eleventh to the Thirteenth Century, Change in Medieval Society_, ed. Sylvia Thrupp [New York, 1964], pp. 14-29), a view that would support our suggestion of expanding Jewish population in Europe despite the persecutions.

[172] See Chapter IV, Section 1, 3, 4.

WORLD JEWRY AND ITS POLITICAL, ECONOMICAL

AND CULTURAL SITUATION ACCORDING

TO THE TRAVELLERS

This chapter is an attempt to depict world Jewry as it is reflected by our travellers. Since it is convenient to follow the regional guide in this survey, we shall start with Europe, followed by the Byzantine Empire with its adjacent European territories. Then we shall proceed to Egypt and Syria, followed by the Abbasid Caliphate. The discussion of the Holy Land has been assigned its own chapter due to its unique significance.

Europe

The history of Spanish Jewry provides an important element in the story of the struggle for the reconquest of Spain. During the early stages of the reconquest, both the Jews and Moslems suffered from the violence of the newly-founded Christian state.[1] Gradually, however, Christians began to consider Jews to be a useful part of the population, and inter-group relations changed. This period saw the emergence in northwest Spain of organized communities, influential in trade and industry. It is important to note that from the beginning of the eleventh century to the middle of the twelfth, during the invasion of the fanatic Almohades, many Jews from the Moslem region made their way to the Christian kingdom, attracted by the advantages offered to new settlers. As a matter of fact, the older Jewish settlements were destroyed and a new centre of Jewish life began to form in Christian Spain.[2]

Benjamin of Tudela started his journey from

his native city, and came first to Saragossa, "and
thence by way of the River Ebro to Tortosa."[3] Then
he travelled to Tarragona, and made a two-day journey from that city to the city of Barcelona, after
which he travelled for a day and a half to reach
Gerona. From there he crossed to the south of
France. Thus we see that our traveller visited few
places in Spain, all of which had already come under Christian rule. Jews had been residing in
Saragossa for a long time. It seems strange that
Benjamin of Tudela contented himself with mentioning only the name of the city, giving us little
else in the way of detail. For instance, he fails
to report the number of Jews, their occupations, or
their famous leaders, subjects which he generally
discusses in relation to the other cities he visits.
Benjamin is silent concerning Tortosa and Tarragona
as well.[4] In Tortosa, which is located in Catalonia, Jews had lived and owned property since the
time of Rome, while Taragona is called by Edrisi
the "city of the Jews," and contained a Jewish community of a very early date.[5] Benjamin is highly
impressed with Taragona for "Its Cyclopean and
Greek buildings" and for the fact that "it is situated by the sea,"[6] but he is completely silent in
regard to the Jews there.

Benjamin gives more information when he comes
to Barcelona, "where there is a holy congregation,
including sages, wise and illustrious men, such as
R. Shesheth, R. Shealtiel, R. Solomon, and R.
Abraham, son of Chisdai. This is a small city and
beautiful, lying upon the sea coast."[7] Shealtiel,
the name mentioned by Benjamin, is the name of one
of the most respected families of Catalonia. They
were descendants of the celebrated R. Jehuda B.
Barzillai who lived about 1130.[8] Alkharizi also
finds at Barcelona R. Shealtiel, the Nasi[9] and
praises him and his sons, probably descendants of
the man mentioned by Benjamin of Tudela.

Barcelona, a port in Aragon, was the seat of
the oldest Jewish communities in the country. In
the twelfth century, we learn about Abraham b.

Hiyya using his mathematical knowledge in the service of the King of Aragon. The Jews were mainly
occupied as artisans and merchants.[10] Benjamin
refers to this community as "holy," revealing its
religious role in Spain, and it is possible that
he was impressed with the religious atmosphere in
Barcelona where, in the following century, we find
Nahmanides leading a study group of learned men
whose purpose was the study of mysticism. Sheshet
ben Isaac ben Joseph Benveniste, who is mentioned
by our traveller, was a physician and writer,[11]
and was titled "Nasi." He received his education
in Narbonne, and it is known that he owed his high
position to his knowledge of Arabic. It is no
wonder that Benjamin notes his name, since in Barcelona and Saragossa the families of Sheshet and
Benveniste were important.[12]

Gerona, the last city in Spain to be mentioned by our traveller, had, he states, "a small
congregation of Jews."[13] Here the Jews owned
houses and lands which they could hold without restrictions.[14]

The political position and the cultural level
of the Jews in the north was different from that
of the south of Spain. The borders were never
closed.[15] In the northeast of Spain through which
Benjamin journeyed, the centres of Judaeo-Arabic
culture-Saragossa, Tudela, Tortosa—lay close to
the Jewish settlements under Christian rule, and
"a more lively traffic in cultural values must
have been carried on across the frontiers than the
existing sources reveal."[16] The fact that Benjamin of Tudela was able to enter the south of France
from Gerona illustrates this cultural exchange.
When writing of Narbonne, he says: "a city pre-
eminent for learning; thence the Torah (Law) goes
forth to all countries."[17] This statement gives
further evidence of the flow of ideas to which Baer
refers.

Before moving with our traveller into France,
it is necessary to admit that Benjamin is a poor
source from which to learn the history of the Jews

in this part of Spain in the middle of the twelfth
century. With the exception of Barcelona, we cannot rely on Banjamin to describe the Jewish settlements of the time in any detail. Benjamin does not
mention the Jewish migration from south to north
that took place in Spain at this time. Furthermore, the occupations and the intellectual positions of the cities are not revealed to us by him
(except, of course, those of Barcelona). This portion of the account is one of the few sections that
fail to satisfy the curiosity of scholars interested in Jewish history of the period. The author
feels that our traveller, starting his journey in
Tudela, and moving through towns close to it, felt
it unnecessary to repeat facts that would be familiar to his readers. No wonder, then, that in
Taragona he deems it important to mention archaeological remains that were unknown to others at
that time. It is also possible that the editors
of the itinerary omitted the details which they
felt the readers already might know.

Moving into southern France,[18] Benjamin makes
a round of the most important cities. After leaving Spain, Benjamin arrives at Narbonne, of which
he reports:

> ...a city pre-eminent for learning: thence
> the Torah (Law) goes forth to all countries.
> Sages and great illustrious men abide there.
> At their head is R. Kalonymos, the son of
> the great and illustrious R. Todros of the
> seed of David, whose pedigree is established.
> He possesses hereditaments and lands given
> him by the ruler of the city, of which no
> man can forcibly dispossess him. Prominent
> in the community is R. Abraham, head of the
> Academy; also R. Machir and R. Judah, and
> many other distinguished scholars. At the
> present day 300 Jews are there.[19]

From 1134 the city was administered by Alfonse,
Count of Toulouse. During the ten-year reign of
this alien feudal lord, the population was oppressed with heavy taxes, and the Jewish community

suffered the most.[20] Todros ha-Nasi, the head of
the community, tried to ease the situation,[21] but
many Jews had to leave Narbonne. As a result, the
community of Narbonne was reduced from 2,000 families to a mere three hundred persons, at the time
of Benjamin's visit. We can almost hear in the
words "At the present day..." that our traveller
is familiar with the above facts.

Benjamin found in this city an established
Jewish community, headed by R. Kalonymos,[22] the
son of the "great and illustrious" Nasi, mentioned
above. Kalonymos himself was a renowned teacher
of the Law.[23] According to R. Benjamin, the head
of the community "possesses hereditaments and
lands given him by the ruler of the city." Moreover, Benjamin seems to stress the fact that "no
man can forcibly dispossess him." This information reflects the political status of the Jews in
this part of France at this time. The permission
to become a landed proprietor was granted as a
favour.[24]

R. Benjamin is impressed with Kalonymos, and
continues to inform us of his father, "R. Todros
of the seed of David, whose pedigree is established." We know that Davidides, or descendants
of the house of David, were found among the Jews
in different periods from the Roman period through
the Persian era.[25] As a result of dispersion, the
genealogical records were lost. Petachia of
Regensburg was shown a pedigree by R. Nehorai in
Galilee which extended up to Jehuda the Patriarch.[26]
The princes of the exile were acknowledged as
Davidides, and there existed pedigrees of the latest of these princes which reached back to David.[27]
Thus we are aware of transferring the Davidic no-
bility to the famous families of the Nesiim in
Narbonne.[28]

In his account, Benjamin informs us of an
academy in Narbonne, headed by the famous R. Abraham (d. 1178). It is no wonder that Benjamin does
not miss this man, who was the author of the

Rabbinic code Ha-Eshkol,[29] and was one of the intermediaries between the Talmudists of France and
the scholars of Spain.[30] From among "many other
distinguished scholars" residing at Narbonne,[31]
our traveller mentions only two others by name.

Reaching Montpellier, Benjamin reports that
the town had a flourishing commerce due to its location.[32] This probably contributed to the flourishing Jewish community there. When speaking of
the Jews, he says they are "rich and charitable,
who lend a helping hand to all that come to
them."[33] He does not specify who those people are
who seek a helping hand. Could they be refugees
driven from Spain? It is important to note that
at Lunel, too, Benjamin states that there are "men
of great benevolence, who lend a helping hand to
all their brethren both far and near."[34]

Thus we find the Jewish communities in southern France undisturbed by the crusading movement.
Benjamin concludes by saying: "May the Lord preserve them,"[35] thus expressing a secret wish that
the violence of the crusades be prevented from
disturbing this quiet area. From this point of
view, we can see how this section of the itinerary
reflects the history of the time.

Let us note again the following information
which Rabbi Benjamin gives concerning Montpellier,
which he calls Har Gaash:[36]

In the city there are scholars of great
eminence....they have among them houses
of learning devoted to the Talmud.[37]

This statement takes on a special importance when
we consider that we are dealing here with the centre of the French Talmidists, and a centre of
learning known in the European Jewish world of the
twelfth century. Combined with the cities in the
northeast of Spain, Montpellier helped to make
this area an intellectual region for both Jewish
and Christian European culture and scholarship.[38]

The three-hundred-member community of Lunel
was also noted for its scholars and for its Talmudical academy. The complete and excellent description provided by Benjamin shows a community which
includes "a congregation of Israelites, who study
the Law day and night."[39] The academy of Lunel
attracted students from all over the world. As
Rabbi Benjamin states, the foreign students are
"taught, boarded, lodged and clothed by the congregation, so long as they attend the house of
study."[40] This helped to establish the reputation
of the Academy of Lunel.[41] It also shows that the
time of importance of the great Babylonian academies was drawing to a close, and that we are dealing with a time in which the Jewish academies in
the West were well established.

Among those scholars of Lunel whom Benjamin
names, we find "R. Judah the Physician, the son of
Tibbon, the Sephardi."[42] He is the celebrated
translator, born in Granada, who lived in Lunel
prior to 1161.[43] It is to be noticed that our
traveller calls him "the Sephardi" to indicate his
Spanish origin. He was on friendly terms with the
family of R. Meshullam, and was the most famous
Jew of Lunel at that time.[44] It is no wonder,
then, that our traveller included him in the list
of eminent scholars at Lunel.[45]

Benjamin finds a similar academy in Posquières.[46] Like the congregation at Lunel, the
wealthy Jews here were able to take care of the
many students "so long as they attended the house
of study."[47] Rabbi Benjamin is again greatly impressed by the eminent scholars he finds here. He
mentions by name Rabbenu Meshullam[48] "the great
rabbi...and his five sons, who are wise, great,
and wealthy."[49] One of the sons, R. Asher, is referred to by Benjamin as "the recluse, who dwells
apart from the world, he pores over his books days
and night, fasts periodically and abstains from
all meat. He is a great scholar of the Talmud."[50]
This R. Asher was one of a group of pious Rabbis
known as Perushim, whom I. Twersky calls "quasi-

monkish scholars." Twersky adds that at this time "Perishut was becoming fashionable and Provence was one of its best agents."[51]

In Posquières, "which is a large place containing about forty Jews,"[52] our traveller mentions, among other famous Rabbis, the eminent Talmudist "the great Rabbi, R. Abraham, son of David," known as "The Rabad,"[53] the son-in-law of the R. Abraham of Narbonne,[54] to whom our traveller has previously referred. Besides heading the local Academy, R. Abraham, son of David, was himself "an energetic and wise man, great as a Talmudical authority. People came to him from a distance to learn the Law at his lips, and they find rest in his house...of those who are without means he also pays the expenses, for he is very rich."[55] From this we may conclude that Posquières is also a Talmudical centre, with a famous teacher and many students.[56]

The last French city to be mentioned by our traveller is Marseilles, which contained at the time approximately three hundred Jewish families. The community was divided geographically into two parts: one resided in the upper part of the city, near the fortress; the other was situated on the seashore below.[57] The Jewish community supported "a great academy of leaned men."[58] Once again Benjamin lists its Rabbis and leaders.[59] As Benjamin correctly states, Marseilles is "a very busy city upon the sea coast."[60] The city carried on a very lively trade with Italy, and though Italian merchants had almost managed to oust the Jews from maritime trade, those Jews in Marseilles and some other cities continued to influence the trade until after the period under discussion.[61]

In summary, we may say that the first century of the crusades did not significantly impair relations between the Jews and Christians in southern France. The local counts and bishops at this time showed a certain liberalism which was, perhaps, a result of certain free, radical trends in spiritual life and thought which came from Arab Spain,

and which eventually led to the formation of the
Albigensian movement. Another reason for the improved attitude toward the Jews in southern France
was the fact that the Jews wielded considerable
economic and cultural influence.[62] Jews here gradually acquired administrative rights in their tax
districts. This led to the appointment of Jews to
administrative posts in local government, such as
the post of bailiff, as Rabbi Benjamin has stated.
It is also true, however, that not all the seig-
neurs were so liberal.[63] From Spain the Renaissance spread into the southern part of France.
This, along with the political ties that existed
between France and Castile and Navarre, tended to
bind together the Jews of those countries. At
this time also the Jewish cultural leadership
passed from Moslem Spain to Christian Spain and
to neighbouring southern France. Among other communities in southern France, Marseilles, Arles,
Montpellier and Narbonne were cultural leaders of
European Jewry.[64] As we have seen, our traveller's
account of this part of France reflects well the
actual state of affairs.

On his journey homeward Benjamin mentions the
rest of France briefly, saying: "Scholars are
there, unequalled in the whole world, who study
the Law day and night. They are charitable and
hospitable to all travellers, and are as brothers
and friends unto all their brethren the Jews."[65]
In the face of these generalities we can be almost certain that Benjamin did not visit that part
of France. But he well knows that there are great
Talmudists there, who are "unequalled in the whole
world," and who care about their Jewish brethren.
The author maintains that by stating the prayer:
"May God, the Blessed One have mercy upon us and
upon them," Benjamin is referring to the suffering
experienced by the nearby German Jewry as a result
of the crusades.[66]

Because of the general nature of Benjamin's
remarks,[67] we may also conclude that he did not
visit Germany either. Even though Benjamin is
able to give us the names of the cities in which

91

there were Jews at that time, the description
shows a very general picture, and Aronius[68] is correct when he doubts as to whether Benjamin actually
visited Germany.

From Marseilles, Rabbi Benjamin boarded a
ship, and in four days reached Genoa. During the
High Middle Ages, many small Jewish groups, consisting mainly of traders, were to be found throughout
northern Italy, especially in the commercial centres. The most important of these centres were
Pavia and Lucca.[69] The expulsion of the Jews from
Verona was typical with the advance of the Middle
Ages.[70] Some of the settlements which existed
during the tenth century disappeared afterwards.
The majority of the Italian Jewry lived south of
Rome, where the former Byzantine communities had
not yet lost their importance.[71] In Italy the interest to participate in the crusades was mainly
of an economic nature, though a reference to a persecution in Lombardy at this time is available.[72]

Benjamin of Tudela gives us the first detailed
account of Italian Jewry of this period. He visited
the country on two occasions—between 1165 and 1167
—while on his way to the Orient,[73] and on his way
home.[74] As Baron correctly states,[75] the Jewish
community of Genoa, which had flourished in the
sixth century, had dwindled so greatly in six hundred years, that Benjamin was able to find only two
Jews there: "...both of them good men."[76] C. Roth
expresses the opinion that the population decrease
may have been due to the previous issuing of an
edict of expulsion.[77] The area to the north of
Genoa was economically backward, which perhaps explains the fact that Benjamin probably did not
visit there.

From Genoa, Benjamin came to Pisa, then powerful as a trading centre. Pisa's policy towards the
Jews was relatively tolerant, and Benjamin found
there twenty Jewish families,[78] who probably took
part in the city's trade.[79]

From Pisa Benjamin continued on to Lucca, a
commercial city which commanded the trade route to
France. Here Benjamin found about "forty Jews."[80]
The Jewish settlement here was important even before 1000. Abraham Ibn Ezra was living and writing
here in 1140, a fact that shows that the place still
deserved its old reputation for being a centre of
learning.[81] The forty families which Benjamin
found here composed a large population for those
times.[82]

Rome was the major attraction in Italy for
travellers.[83] Benjamin had eyes for the beauties
and monuments of the city and attached a Jewish
association to many of them.[84] Here Benjamin found
not less than 200 Jewish families which constituted,
according to C. Roth, about twenty per cent of the
total population.[85] Benjamin states that:

> [The Jews] occupy an honourable position and
> pay no tributes, and amongst them are offi-
> cials of the Pope Alexander.... Great scho-
> lars reside here, at the head of them being
> R. Daniel, the chief Rabbi, and J. Jechiel,
> an official of the Pope. He is a handsome
> young man of intelligence and wisdom, and
> he has the entry of the Pope's palace; for
> he is the steward of his house and of all
> that he has. He is a grandson of R. Nathan,
> who composed the Aruch and its commentaries.
> Other scholars are R. Joab,... R. Menachem,
> head of the Academy, R. Jechiel...and R.
> Benjamin.[86]

Here the Jews paid no special taxes and were generally honoured.[87] Moreover, they were eminent in
their learning. A certain R. Daniel was the best
known scholar, and R. Menachem headed the Academy.[88] Jechiel was the administrator of the fi-
nances of Pope Alexander III.[89]

From Rome, Benjamin went by a roundabout route
to Otranto, ignoring Gaeta, where there was a Jewish group of dyers.[90] First he came to Capua,
where he found "About 300 Jews...among them great

93

scholars and esteemed persons."[91] In general, as
far as the north of Italy is concerned, it seems
clear that the population figures we receive from
Benjamin are too small, while his estimate of the
total population in the south seems to be exaggerated.[92]

At Naples, our traveller found approximately
500 Jews.[93] In the eleventh century, the Jewish
community paid about five per cent of the town's
taxes, thus forming approximately 1,500 residents
out of the total 30,000.[94]

Salerno, a day's journey to the south, had a
Jewish population of 600, and a medical school.[95]
The majority of the Jewish community lived in the
Jewish quarter (Judaica) with its wooden houses.
This section is mentioned repeatedly from 1004 on,
and remains the oldest reference in medieval history to a section of a town in which Jews resided.[96] In Salerno, Rabbi Benjamin also mentions
prominent scholars in the community. He mentions
Melchizedek, "the great Rabbi."[97] This "great
Rabbi," whose commentaries upon several sections
of the Mishna have survived, was quot ed by authors from 1160 to 1200.[98] It is no wonder that
Rabbi Benjamin mentions Melchizedek even though he
was already dead.

Rabbi Benjamin then travelled to Amalfi, a
city which was now experiencing a period of decline.[99] This is reflected in the fact that the
Jewish community dwindled to no more than twenty.[100] On the other hand, in the city of Bene-
vento, under Papal rule, there were two hundred
Jews.[101] They obviously lived happily since three
parish churches adjoined the Jewish quarter by the
end of the century.[102]

The next stop was made at Melfi, "In the country of Apulia,...where about 200 Jews reside...."[103]
Melfi was the administrative capital of Apulia.
Benjamin found a certain Ahimaaz as the leader of
the Jews. C. Roth expressed the idea that Ahimaaz
could have been the last survivor[104] of a famous

94

family which had been prominent two centuries before.[105] At Ascoli, there were 40 Jews.[106] Their
role in commerce was significant, for the taxes
they paid at this time were considered an important source of income.

The "south of Italy" had some ports important
in Levantine trade, especially with Palestine. At
Trani, "where all the pilgrims gather to go to
Jerusalem...a community of about 200 Israelites"
lived.[107] The members of this community[108] consisted of refugees fleeing from the Almoravide persecutions of 1144 in Spain.[109] Taranto, lying on
the border of Calabria, had a community of 300
where Greek was still the dominant language.[110]
Several individuals were "men of learning."[111] A
document of 1133 refers to them as Affidati, protected non-citizens.[112] However, Brindisi, a day's
journey away, had only ten Jews who were primarily
dyers.[113] At Otranto, on the other hand, there
were about 500 Jews.[114] The large community here
was obviously attracted by the trade with the
Levant, and from here Rabbi Benjamin set sail.[115]

During his return trip in 1170 Benjamin passed
through Sicily. This island had been reconquered
by Robert and Roger Guiscard, in a series of campaigns between 1060 and 1090.[116] Influences from
the Moslem period continued to be felt. The Jewish community was known by the same Arabic name—
Aljama—as it had been in Spain.[117] Many of the
Jews had Arabic names, and maintained Moslem customs, some of which were observed until the fifteenth century. R. Obadiah Da Bertinoro reported
these customs in great detail.[118] The Arabic influence was still evident when Benjamin visited
Messina. There he was amazed to find a community
of 200 living in luxury.[119] They enjoyed equal
rights with their neighbours under a charter of
1129.[120]

At Palermo, he estimated the Jewish population to be no less than 1,500.[121] This is the
largest figure mentioned by our traveller concerning the population of an Italian community. There

is evidence that the number of Jews had increased
earlier when Roger II had brought a group of Jews
to the city as prisoners from his campaign of 1147
against Byzantium. In the following century, there
was further immigration from Morocco. The new-
comers were permitted to establish their own synagogue.

These are the only places on the island for
which we have data for the twelfth century.[122] C.
Roth states the following: "There is every reason
to believe that the kingdom of Sicily at this time
contained the most numerous, most populous, and
most industrious Jewish communities of all
Italy."[123]

The Jews of the southern part of Italy had
been interested in overseas trade. The southern
rulers encouraged Jewish traders.[124] This is opposite to the policy carried out by leaders in the
northern republics. Thus, Benjamin found the largest Jewish communities in harbour towns. The market dues paid by these Jewish traders were considered to be an important source of revenue. Jews
were often employed in financial administrative
positions. This was the case in Salerno and
Capua.[125] Jews also were engaged in the field of
medicine.[126] Benjamin mentions one individual who
was the head of the community of Amalfi.[127]

Circumstances also encouraged Jews to live in
the countryside, and they were found, especially
in the south, as landowners and peasants.[128] They
often were found in occupations which required
special handicraft skill. They were particularly
associated with dyeing and weaving.[129] According
to our traveller, the communities in Greece and
Byzantium gained their main source of income from
these industries.[130] The Jewish community at
Brindisi was entirely dependent upon this trade.[131]
The association of the Jews with weaving and dyeing was so significant that Frederick II entrusted
the administration of th is monopoly exclusively
to Jews.[132] C. Roth states: "more than ever, the
term 'Jew' was quasi-synonymous with 'dyer' and

'weaver.'"[133]

During the Byzantine period, important centres
of Rabbinical studies had been founded in Bari and
Otranto. However, the most important schools could
be found in Rome. From this city, in the middle of
the eleventh century, came one of the great Medieval Jewish scholars—Nathan ben Jehiel.[134] Nathan
and his contemporaries (Rashi and al-Fasi) were
regarded as key figures through whom Talmudic lore
passed to later generations. Nathan's Talmudic
dictionary, called the Aruch, is still used by
scholars. No wonder that Benjamin mentions both
the book and its author.[135]

Palermo was also a famous centre of Jewish
learning.[136] It was the Talmud and related legal
subjects which chiefly interested Italian Jewry.
Abraham ibn Izra, who passed through the country
between 1140 and 1146, remarked that some of the
scholars had difficulty in explicating simple biblical passages.[137]

Yet, the most significant aspect of Jewish intellectual life in southern Italy had a different
emphasis. Here, where the Latin, Italian, Byzantine, Moslem and Jewish elements mixed, there was
a period of remarkable intellectual activity. No
place was better suited for the transmission of
Islamic culture to Europe.[138] The cosmopolitan
court of Roger II produced a circle of scholars.
Successive rulers were also alive to the new intellectual developments.[139] In Benjamin's description of the palace of the King,[140] one can almost
breathe the atmosphere of the cosmopolitan court.
The intellectual flowering reached its highest
peak under Frederick II—stupor mundi—King of
Sicily and Apulia. It was intellectual activity
of this sort which formed the earliest stages of
the Latin Renaissance, in which Jewish participation was significant.[141]

In summary, one fundamental fact must be kept
in mind. In Benjamin's day, all the communities
of major importance were located south of Rome.

97

However, the situation changed as a result of the
expulsions of 1492 and 1542. From then on, all
communities of importance existed from Rome north-
wards.

Finally, we should note here that Benjamin's
account of European Jewry reflects one more important development in Jewish medieval life. We have
already seen that he has listed Jewish academic
centres in Spain, Northern and Southern France,
and Italy. Furthermore, he has stated the names
of many eminent rabbis to whom students had come
from many parts of the world. This reflects the
vital nature of Jewish scholarship in the West.
The hegemony of the Babylonian academies was already broken in this period by the rise of the
schools in the West. During the twelfth century,
the Orient was in a process of decline both economically and spiritually,[142] and Islamic culture
was yielding place to the dynamic vigour of the
West, as Grunebaum's paper at least partly
reveals.[143] From the Jewish point of view, both
the scholarly learning and cultural life were
shifting their source of activity from East to
West.[144]

In the twelfth century, we meet in Egypt several scholars from Christian countries, such as
Isaac b. Benveniste of Narbonne,[145] Joseph b. Ger-
shon, Anatoli b. Joseph—Dayyanim in Alexandria in
Maimonides' time,[146] Phineas ben Meshullan from
Provence,[147] and others.[148] Egyptian Jewry was at
that time dependent on Europe for its spiritual
leaders, whereas before the twelfth century, these
leaders would have come from the Babylonian and
Palestinian academies.[149]

The time is over when the Orient sent its
scholars to act as spiritual leaders in the West.
However, the most fascinating proof of this comes
from Maimonides' epistle, directed to the congregation of Lunel. The author finds this letter to
be of utmost importance:

...To you my honored friends, may you remain
confident and strong, I have now to tell the
truth; you, members of the congregation of
Lunel, and of the neighboring towns, stand
alone in raising the banner of Moses. You
apply yourselves to the study of the Talmud,
and also cherish wisdom. The study of the
Torah in our communities has ceased: most
of the bigger congregations are dead to
spiritual aims: the remaining communities
are facing the end. In the whole of Palestine there are three or four places only,
and even these are weak, and in the whole of
Syria none but a few in Aleppo occupy themselves with the Torah according to the
truth, but even they have it so much at
heart. In the Babylonian Diaspora there
are only two or three groups in Yemen, and
in the rest of Arabia they know little of
the Talmud and are merely acquainted with
aggadic exposition.... The Jews of India
know nothing of the Torah and of the Laws,
save the Sabbath and circumcision. In the
towns of Berbery which belong to the realms
of Islam, the Jews read the Torah and observe it according to its literal meaning.
What was inflicted upon the Jews of Maghreb
as punishment for their sins you know. Thus
it remains for you alone to be a strong support to our religion. Therefore be firm and
courageous for the sake of our people and
our God: make up your minds to remain here
brave men. Everything depends on you: the
decision is in your hands. Do not rely upon
my support, because I am an old man with
gray hair. And know that for this not my
age but my weak body is responsible....[150]

Thus, this important letter, which was written by the most intellectual Jewish authority of
the twelfth century, does not paint an encouraring
picture of the intellectual life of the Jews in
the Orient.[151] The letter is uniquely significant
concerning the decline of the Jewish learning in
Orient in the second half of the twelfth century.

99

Concerning the intellectual life of Europe,
Maimonides clearly states that the hope of Jewish
learning in the future is to be in the West. Benjamin mentions that students from many parts of
the world came to the West to study. Maimonides
believes that the hegemony of Jewish culture and
vitality was moving swiftly from the Orient to the
West. This fact was also evident from the descriptions made by Benjamin of Tudela, although the tendency was not as clear to him and Petachia as it
was to Maimonides.

The Byzantine Empire

In 1168, Benjamin of Tudela visited the Byzantine Empire.[152] He is the only traveller who states
specifically how many Jews lived there. He is also
the principal authority on the types of work in
which the urban Jews were chiefly employed. The details that Benjamin provides are valuable not only
by themselves, but also in relation to Byzantine
history: for Byzantine society, as a whole, was
undergoing an important change in the twelfth century.[153]

Byzantium could not fight the whole crusading
West, and consequently, its foreign policy concentrated on searching for western allies.[154] To finance this policy, Alexius I had to expand his economic concessions to Italian trading cities. This
turn to the West influenced the internal life of
the empire. The Byzantines copied Western customs
and received Western advisers, especially during
the reign of Manuel I (1143-1180). Except for the
reaction against foreign influence which led to the
massacre of Western residents in Constantinople in
1182,[155] the Western ideas prevailed. These influenced the Byzantine from of feudalism which eventually gave way under Western pressures to resemble
a feudal system of the West. This in itself dam-
aged imperial authority.[156]

While the Byzantine Empire was weakened during

the period of the crusades and eventually fell in
the Fourth Campaign (1204), the Jews found more
freedom. The old despotism of the empire gave
way.[157] More importantly, as we shall see, Benjamin of Tudels reflects the rise of the Jewish communities in Byzantium. However, before analyzing
the detailed picture presented by Benjamin, it is
important to depict briefly the Jewish background
of the Byzantine Empire prior to the twelfth
century.

The second half of the tenth century saw continual Byzantine military victories which had no
equal since Justinian the Great.[158] The Byzantine
victories led to the incorporation of Moslem territories into the Byzantine Empire. This annexation
opened new routes for immigration further inland.
Both the non-Jewish and Jewish merchants were attracted to the trade centres which eventually led
to permanent settlements of eastern trade groups
within Byzantium. Constantinople alone absorbed a
hundred thousand easterners during the early eleventh century,[159] despite the restrictions on
"alien" movement within Constantinople's walls.
These migrations repeated themselves during the
late tenth century and the first half of the eleventh.[160] Also, in the early eleventh century, refugees came from Egypt.[161] The document, "A Letter
of Historical Importance from Seleuceia, Cilicia,
Dated 21 July 1137,"[162] confirms the above thesis
presented by Ankori. It is evident that the Seleu-
ceian Jews were an immigrant community, and that
they felt safe in their new location. The immigrants, as it appears, were soon integrated into
the Byzantine Empire; however, they were still connected, both culturally and emotionally, to their
native Egypt. Concerning this document, Goitein
states: "Our letter constitutes thus an interesting testimony of an important demographic fact in
the history of the Jewish people: the immigration
from the Islamic countries into Byzantium."[163]

We find Benjamin arriving in Otranto situated
"on the coast of the Greek Sea,"[164] the last part
of sourthern Italy which was still under the domin-

101

ion of Byzantium. Here, Benjamin found that there
was a well-organized Jewish community of 500 members under the leadership of a collegium of rabbis.
From Otranto, Benjamin travelled for two days to
reach Corfu[165] where he found one Jew.[166] Next,
Benjamin found about a hundred Jews in the city of
Arta.[167] Moving to the Gulf of Corinth, Benjamin
found no Jews at Aetolicum,[168] but when he crossed
the Gulf to Patras, he found 50 Jews there.[169]
Journeying to the Parnassos Mountain, Benjamin
found a group of 200 Jews who lived by themselves
in the village, Crissa.[170] Here Benjamin discovered that the Jews sowed and reaped on their
own land.[171] Then, Benjamin returned to the Gulf
and visited Corinth, in which he found a Jewish
community of 300 members.[172]

Benjamin then journeyed northward to Thebes,
the most imposing community in Greece.[173] This
city, in Benjamin's time, contained about 2000 Jews,
the greatest number of Jews in Greece.[174] The The-
ban Jews were skilled manufacturers of silk and
purple cloth, in fact, the most skilled throughout
Greece.[175] Concerning this textile art, Gibbon
states that the artists enjoyed exemption from personal taxes; he continues:

> These arts which were exercised at Corinth,
> Thebes, and Argos, afforded food and occu-
> pation to a numerous people; the men, women,
> and children were distributed according to
> their age and strength: and if many of
> these were domestic slaves, their masters,
> who directed the work and enjoyed the pro-
> fits, were of a free and honorable condi-
> tion.[176]

Benjamin continues to report that the Jews in Thebes "have scholars learned in the Mishnah and the
Talmud, and other prominent men...and there are
none like them in the land of the Greeks, except
in the city of Constantinople."[177] The Jewish community of Thebes was prosperous. It enjoyed a
large membership, economic success, and extensive
scholarship. Certainly, the city impressed

Benjamin very much.

Benjamin also noted smaller communities in
Eubea and on the border of Valachia.[178] At Sinon
Potamo (the modern city Lamia in Thessaly)[179]
Benjamin found a community of 50 Jews and a group
of Wallachians who plundered the Greek cities and
killed the Christian inhabitants. Concerning the
Wallachian's questionable identity, Benjamin states:

> They do not hold fast to the faith of the
> Nazarenes, but give themselves Jewish
> names. Some people say that they are Jews,
> and, in fact, they call the Jews their
> brethren, and when they meet with them,
> though they rob them, they refrain from
> killing them as they kill the Greeks.[180]

To this, Rapaport adds that the similarity of names
should have given the Wallachians the idea of a
Jewish origin.[181] Moreover, Benjamin reports that
the Wallachians of Lamia had acquired Jewish inclinations.[182] Significantly, these war-like Wallachians, some twenty years after Benjamin's visit,
revolted, and won their independence from the Byzantine Empire.[183]

Continuing, Benjamin travelled to the maritime
city Armiros, a port for traders from Venice, Pisa,
Genoa, and other cities. Here, Benjamin found a
Jewish community of 400 members under the leadership of a collegium of three men: the rabbi, the
"parnas" or warden, and the "rosh" or leader.[184]
Such a collegium consisting of three men, a rabbi
and two elders, was the administration which Benjamin generally encountered in the Byzantine communities.

From Armiros, Benjamin went next to Salonica
where he found a community of about 500 Jews.
Salonica's Jews were under a provost-like leader,
a certain R. Samuel, appointed by the king.[185] Besides R. Samuel, Benjamin also found a governing
body of three additional elders.[186] Thus, expecting Thebes, Salonica contained in Benjamin's time

more Jewish inhabitants than any other Grecian
city. The location of Salonica made the city a
prosperous commercial centre and consequently a
reason for its large Jewish population. Benjamin
found the Jews in Salonica employed in silk weaving.[187] However, Benjamin also noticed oppression;
he simply but directly states: "The Jews are oppressed."[188] This oppression readily accounts for
the Messianic movement that had great success in
Salonica.[189]

        Benjamin's account gives no information con-
cerning the Jews who lived in the relatively unknown Jewish settlements in the cities such as
Tarsus, Trebizond, Smyrna, Amaseia, Laodiceia, Apa-
meia, Magnesia, Caesareia, to name a few. However,
we have the account of the Jewish gathering in Aby-
dos in 1096 in the expectation of Messianic miracles.[190] According to Ankori, there is no reason
to suppose that the economic factors that had jus-
tified Jewish settlement there previously had suddenly disappeared.[191] Also, Ankori assumes the
existence of Jewish communities in many ports and
commercial cities of Asia Minor at different
periods of Byzantine history.[192] But generally,
we know little about Jewish history in Asia Minor
between the first and fourth crusades.[193] Nevertheless, for Asia Minor, the main goal of all roads
was Constantinople, the "city which reigns supreme
over all others."[194] Here, in Constantinople, was
the centre of world trade; its treasures were
talked about in the West.

        In spite of restrictions,[195] there was a con-
tinuous growth of foreign merchants in Constantinople. Undoubtedly, Jews were included among these
foreign merchants.[196] Concerning the Jews of the
city, Benjamin states:

        No Jews live in the city, for they have
        been placed behind an inlet of the sea.
        An arm of the sea of Marmora shuts them
        in on the one side, and they are unable
        to go out except by way of the sea, when
        they want to do business with the inhabit-

104

ants. In the Jewish quarter are about 2000
Rabbenite Jews and about 500 Karaites, and
a fence divides them. Amongst the scholars
are several wise men, at their head being
the chief rabbi R. Abtalion, R. Obadiah, R.
Aaron Bechor Shoro, R. Joseph Shir-Guru, and
R. Eliakim, the warden. And amongst them
there are artificers in silk and many rich
merchants. No Jew there is allowed to ride
on horseback. The one exception is R. Solomon Hamistri, who is the King's physician,
and through whom the Jews enjoy considerable
alleviation of their oppression. For their
condition is very low, and there is much
hatred against them, which is fostered by
the tanners, who threw out their dirty water
in the streets before the doors of the Jewish
houses and defile the Jew's quarter (the
Ghetto), for the Greeks hate the Jews, good
and bad alike, and subject them to great oppression, and beat them in the streets, and
in every way treat them with rigor. Yet the
Jews are rich and good, kindly and charitable, and they bear their lot with cheerfulness. The district inhabited by the Jews
is called Pera.[197]

Since about the tenth or eleventh century, the
Jewish quarter of Constantinople, the suburb Pera,
was located across the Golden Horn.[198] Benjamin
calls this Pera the Jews' "migrash."[199] Towards
the end of the eleventh century, Pera became the
main Jewish residential area.[200] This was offi-
cially confirmed by Alexus I's allocation of residential areas for different communities.[201] Benjamin saw Pera after it had existed for nearly a hundred years, when this situation had become permanent.[202]

The status of the Jewish quarter in Constantinople, deserves a re-examination. This view was
first presented by Baron:

The continued development of the guild system in the Byzantine Empire...inevitably

stimulated the Jews to organize along occu-
pational lines...such (Jewish corporations)
are, indeed, clearly implied in Benjamin of
Tudela's description of the Jewish craftsmen in Constantinople and elsewhere in the
Balkans.[203]

Analyzing the status of the Jewish quarter, Ankori
states that the district of Constantinople in which
the quarters (including Pera) were located had a
"colorful cosmopolitan character." Moreover, an
increasing shift of the city's economic enterprise
to this district argues against a ghetto concept.[204]
According to Ankori, the report of Benjamin on
Christian animosity caused by the Jewish tanner's
"dirty water" is greatly overemphasized. One feels,
Ankori continues, that Benjamin received his information in Constantinople only from the skilled
craftsmen who manufactured silk garments. Apparently, Benjamin shared their bias against the tanning profession.[205]

Ankori also presents evidence that there were
scattered Jewish groups who lived in various sections of Constantinople.[206] He concludes that the
area which impressed Benjamin as the Jewish quarter
because of its large Jewish population was merely
a "migrash" (the common ground) of the silk manufacturers' guild and the tanners' guild. The Jewish dominance of these guilds turned the quarter
into a Jewish one.[207] Thus, while to Benjamin,
Pera seemed segregated, a forced concentration of
Jews in Pera alone does not seem to be the case.[208]

On the other hand, Sharf attaches a special
significance to Benjamin's report of animosity towards the Jews as indicative of the change which
the Byzantine Empire was undergoing in the twelfth
century and which was expressed chiefly in Constantinople.[209] Sharf contrasts the mere mention of
Jewish oppression in Thessalonica[210] to the Jewish
oppression in Constantinople which Benjamin describes as "great oppression": "their condition is
very low," "much hatred against them," "the Greeks
hate the Jews, good and bad...and beat them in the

streets."[211] The mention of the beatings may have
been an exaggerated generalization, but, for Sharf,
Benjamin would not make a generalization that was
unfounded, because he had an obvious admiration for
Constantinople.[212]

R. Petachia of Regensburg, who visited the
area about ten years later, supports Benjamin's report. Petachia reports: "In Greece the Jews are
subject to great oppression: and even compelled to
perform menial work in their own persons."[213] It
is doubtful whether he was anywhere besides Constantinople, for Petachia's only other comment, in
the same passage, was: "There were so many congregations in Greece, that the land of Israel could
not contain them were they settled therein."[214]
Evidently, Petachia limited his comments to the Jews
in Constantinople due to its population size. Thus,
Petachia's reference to the "great oppression" of
the Jews confirms Benjamin's observation: the
worst treatment of Jews was in Constantinople.

What were the causes of this hostility? Benjamin said one was the disgust at the Jewish tanners.[215] Even if the tanning occupation was new in
Constantinople, Sharf argues, it was an example of
servile work, and this employment would be the result of oppression, not the cause.[216] Thus, the
hatred of the Jews must be found elsewhere, a hatred that was applied to all classes, both "good
and bad."

These feelings did much more than just express
themselves in words or blows, they influenced Byzantine legislation. For example, in 1148, Manuel
passed two new ordinances. First, he abolished the
custom in which certain cases involving Jews were
settled by an official responsible for the peace of
the Jewish quarter, and instead decreed that all
were to be judged by the ordinary courts.[217] Second, in 1148, after a Jew of Attaleia converted to
Christianity and turned his house into a monastery,
the Jewish community took possession of the furni-
ture and, consequently, a suit was brought before
Manuel for its return.[218] It was then that the

107

Jewish party was ordered to follow a humilating procedure: an insulting variation of the oath more judaico appeared.[219]

To agree with Sharf,[200] this hatred of the Jews does remind one of the West. Benjamin suggests the real nature of these anti-Semitic feelings when he speaks of the privileged position of R. Solomon, the king's physician. Solomon's position was the "classic western situation" where a favoured Jew was the only defence of a Jewish community.[221] Thus, the influx of western ideas influenced the treatment of the Jews in Constantinople: Solomon symbolized something quite new.[222]

Returning to Benjamin's itinerary, we find that he leaves Constantinople and the remainder of his journey within the Empire is by ship. He first sailed through the Sea of Marmora, stopping at Raedestus (Rososto),[223] where he found a community of 400 Jews,[224] and at Gallipoli,[225] where he found a Jewish community of 200.[226] Benjamin concludes his journey by visiting the islands in the Aegean and the Mediterranean. At Mytilene, Benjamin found "Jewish congregations in ten localities on the island," although he fails to note their numbers.[227] On Chios, Benjamin found 400 Jewish families, on Samos, 300 families, and on Rhodes 400.[228] On Cyprus, although again he failed to note the number, Benjamin found Rabbanites, Karaites, and a group he called "Epikorsi,"[229] heretics. In addition, Benjamin reports that other unnamed "islands have many congregations of Jews."[230]

From Benjamin's report, we conclude that there were flourishing Jewish communities in provincial Greece and on the islands. According to Sharf, Benjamin's figures show that the Jews in Constantinople constituted less than 30 per cent of his total.[231] The size of some communities was great: e.g., the Jewish population of Thebes was comparable to that of Constantinople. The figure of 500 for Thessalonica—which Benjamin called "a very large city"[232] —was comparable to those figures given for Corinth, Halmyros, Rodesto, Chios, Samos, and Rhodes. Also,

the communities which Benjamin saw were well established and had recognized leaders. On the other
hand, Abraham ibn Daud, a contemporary of R. Benjamin, has only a brief mention of Byzantine Jewry
in his book Sefer ha-Qabbalah[233] where he includes
a survey of contemporary Jewry. In Byzantium these
Jewish communities were prosperous, especially in
the important silk trade in cities such as Thebes
and Thessalonica.[234] Benjamin's report reflects
that those communities recovered from the second
crusade and the Norman invasion which destroyed
many areas.

Benjamin's report, Sharf states, also indicates a basic demographic development. There was
a tendency for the Jews to settle in smaller population areas: with the exception of Thebes,
Corinth, and Thessalonica, Benjamin's list consisted of placed which were never before mentioned
in a Jewish connection and they were smaller than
the above three.[235] The same conditions are true
regarding the islands: Mytilene and Samos are
fairly large islands, but the islands with the
"many communities" are insignificant spots in the
Aegean or Mediterranean, and all these islands had
no previous mention. On the other hand, Jewish
communities existed before on the larger islands:
Chios, Rhodes and Cyprus.[236]

In Benjamin's report on the provinces there
was no mention of hatred of Jews, with the exception of Thessalonica,[237] and there, since there are
no details as in Constantinople, Sharf concludes
that the oppression could not have been serious.[238]
Furthermore, Eustathius, the archbishop of Tessa-
lonica (1175-1194), confirms the existence of favourable conditions for the Jews.[239]

Regarding the intellectual life of the Byzantine Jews, we turn to literature. There are echoes
of the crusades in the sermons of Toviah ben Eliezer, the author of the Midrash Lekah Tov.[240] Abraham ibn Ezra refers to Byzantine Jewish scholars in
the second part of the twelfth century.[241] In
poetry, Alkharizi, who visited Greece at the begin-

109

ing of the thirteenth century, found poets who
wrote in Hebrew but lacked talent.[242] At this time,
the talented Karaite Hadassi lived in Constantinople
and wrote his book Eshkol Ha-Kofer.[243]

Importantly, Benjamin does not refer to Jewish
academies in Byzantium as he does in France, where,
while visiting few places in Provence, he noted the
existence of academies under notable scholars with
students from many places, and in Italy where he
was able to find in Rome the famous author of the
Aruch and its commentaries. Benjamin does not mention one academy throughout his travels through the
Byzantine Empire, even though the Byzantine communities were relatively larger than the places he
visited in Provence.[244] In Constantinople with
2000 Rabbanite Jews and 500 Karaites, all Benjamin
states is that "amongst the scholars are several
wise men."[245] In Salonica, which Benjamin called
"a very large city" with about 500 Jews, he merely
mentions the chief rabbi and his sons, referring
to them as scholars.[246] Only in Thebes which had
2000 Jewish families, does Benjamin give more details: "They have scholars learned in the Mishnah
and the Talmud, and other prominent men"[247]—but
still, we do not hear of an academy.

It is clear that the Jewish intellectual centres in the twelfth century were to be found in the
West. The East was in decline. Traditional Jewish
studies had moved from its old centres in the East
to new centres north of the Alps and in Spain.

Why did the large, prosperous, well-estab-
blished communities of Constantinople, Thessanlon-
ica, and other communities in Greece and Asia Minor
contribute so little to Jewish learning? Even
Sharf admits that the answer can only be conjectured in the light of the sources.[248] However,
according to him, part of the answer may be the decline of orthodoxy due to the Karaite influence
which weakened the way of life necessary for the
development of Jewish learning.[249] Another reason
may be the relative absence of barriers between
Jews and Christians due to their ability to work

together in guilds in Greece and Asia Minor. The isolation of Jews living in Byzantine Italy, concludes Sharf, encouraged the intellectual development,[250] while the limited assimilation of Jews in Byzantine society discouraged learning.[251]

Fatimite Egypt and Moslem Syria

Concerning the history of the Jews in Egypt and Syria, the Genizah documents[252] serve to illuminate political, economic and intellectual life during the eleventh and twelfth centuries. This is especially true concerning Fustat and the neighbouring cities.[253]

The Jews were forced out of the kingdom of Jerusalem by the crusaders, an event which resulted in the strengthening of Jewish centres in Syria, Mesopotamia, and Egypt. At this time, as Benjamin of Tudela was returning home by way of Egypt, the Fatimites experienced a great crisis. For several years Egypt was a battlefield between the Syrians and the Franks,[254] and on November 12, 1168, Fustat was burned.[255] Putting an end to Fatimite dominion, Saladin caused the name of "Abbasid Caliph" to be proclaimed in the mosques on Friday, September 10, 1171.[256]

In 1174 Saladin seized Damascus and became ruler of Syria and Egypt.[257] Benjamin of Tudela entered Egypt in which Saladin was still ruling under Nur-ed-din. He ran the country efficiently and in a few months it had regained its prosperity.[258]

Benjamin gives us a detailed description of the most important communities of Egypt.[259] He recognized Kutz as "the commencement of the land of Egypt," and in the new section of Kutz found there 300 Jewish families.[260] The old town, which was second in size to Fustat and a chief centre of Arabian trade, had by now entirely vanished.[261] In Fayum, "which is Pithom,"[262] he recorded 200 Jewish families.[263] This ancient city is described by

111

Edrisi as large and located in a fertile country.[264]

The next stop for Benjamin was Fustat. Here is Benjamin's report of the Jewish community there:

> This Mizraim is the great city situated on the banks of the Nile, which is Pison or Al-Nil. The number of Jewish inhabitants is about 7,000. Two large synagogues are there, one belonging to the men of the land of Israel and one belonging to the men of the land of Babylon. The synagogue of the men of the land of Israel is called Kenisat-al-Schamiyyim, and the synagogue of the men of Babylon is called Kenisat-al-Irakiyyim. Their usage with regard to the portions and sections of the Law are not alike; for the men of Babylon are accustomed to read a portion every week, as is done in Spain, and is our custom, and to finish the Law each year; whilst the men of Palestine do not do so, but divide each portion into three sections and finish the Law at the end of three years. The two communities, however, have an established custom to unite and pray together on the day of the rejoicing of the Law, and on the day of the giving of the Law. Among the Jews is Nethanel the Prince of Princes and the head of the academy, who is the head of all the congregations in Egypt. He appoints Rabbis and officials, and is attached to the court of the great king, who lives in his palace of Zoan-el-Medina, which is the royal city for the Arabs,... The Jews that dwell there are very rich.[265]

Thus, the Jewish community which Benjamin comes across here is a large and well established one. The Jewish concentration was found in the old section of the city (Fustat) and was divided into two groups: the Babylonians (al-Irakiyyim) and the Palestinians or Syrians (al-Schamiyyim in Arabic). Each group had separate customs and prayers held in their own synagogue. The official representa-

tive, or Nagid, of Egyptian Jewry resided in Cairo.
He also headed the academy and served the King.
Although Cairo became the government seat, for the
Jews it occupied a secondary place to Fustat. Abul-
feda adds that living in Fustat was cheaper.[266]

The centre of Judaism and the Jewish people
was the local community which was organized around
one or two synagogues. It was called The Holy Congregation, a biblical term to signify "a Kingdom
of Priests and a holy nation" (Ex. XIX:6). During
the whole period of the Genizah documents, this
title was in use.[267] The community functionaries
regarded themselves as having been selected by the
congregation and by God.[268]

In most large towns in the twelfth century,
two synagogues existed:[269] one Palestinian and
the other Babylonian. While the congregations had
been formed originally by arrivals from the countries of the former Byzantine Empire and the lands
of the Abbasid Caliphate,[270] to follow one or the
other of the two rites became a question of taste.
Thus the two synagogues competed with each other
for new members. The Genizah documents illuminate
this situation.[271] Obviously the competition led,
at times, to friction. "We, the two congreations"
(the text states: synagogues) "here came together
and united and made peace between ourselves," indicating that peace had not existed before.[272] The
competition between the community leaders, especially during the first half of the eleventh century, has been described by Jacob Mann in detail.[273]
Benjamin, on the other hand, who reports differences and rivalries between the two rites, at the
same time says that "the two communities, however,
have an established custom to unite and pray together on the day of Rejoicing of the Law and on
the day of the Giving of the Law.[274] This also indicates that there was an effort to soften the
differences between the two.

It is interesting that in the Genizah documents the two congregations appear throughout as belonging to the local community. This is expressed

by the fact that the community chest was common.[275]
Consequently it is not surprising to read in a Genizah letter in which a woman in trouble simply writes
to the Qahal (Congregation) of old Cairo.[276]

As a result of the invasions of the Bedouins
into Tunisia and the Seljuks into Syria and Palestine, and later of the massacre by the crusaders in
the Holy Land, refugees came from these countries
to Egypt, causing both congregations to cooperate
more. The recently created office of the Nagid also advanced their unity. It is obvious, then, that
when Benjamin visited Egypt the replacement of the
congregations by a local community was a return to
a situation as existed before the schism between
"Easterners" and "Westerners" represented by their
synagogues took place.[277] Rabbi Benjamin mentions
that the main difference in his time between the
two synagogues was the differing customs with regard to the portions and sections of the Law.[278]
The Palestinian Jews completed the readings in a
period of three years, while the Babylonian, and
later the European Jews who followed them, completed the reading of the Law in a period of only
one year. "This difference must be old,"[279] and
indeed is mentioned in the Talmud.[280]

In spite of the fact that the majority of Jews
followed the Babylonian custom, Benjamin still
found congregations in Egypt which were Palestinian
in this respect. In 1180, Maimonides writes that
the custom of extending the reading of the Law over
a period of three years was widely accepted,[281] and
this indicates that many synagogues probably followed this observance.[282] Some time later, his son,
Abraham, confirms this fact. At the same time he
gives an account of differences with other religious
customs which took place.[283] According to Graetz,
those who followed the Palestinian custom of reading
the Law came from Palestine to Cairo as a result of
the persecution during the first crusade,[284] but
according to Büchler, this cannot be verified.[285]

Benjamin found in Fustat, "Nethanel, the Prince
of Princes and the head of the Academy, who is the

114

head of all congregations in Egypt, he appoints Rabbis and officials...."[286] Thus we have here a reference to the head of the Egyptian Jews, actually to the office of Nagid. Jacob Mann states: "From the Fatimite regime (868)...Egyptian Jewry was strongly organized under the Nagid,...recognized by the government of Ra-is al-Yahud."[287] During the Fatimite period, the Egyptian and the Syrian Jews enjoyed not only religious freedom and equal privileges, but also had a recognized representative.[288] Besides three others, Samuel b. Hananya is the only Nagid known in Fatimite Egypt,[289] (1140-1159). But Zuta, an ambitious man, caused Samuel to be removed. In the scroll of Zuta[290] we read that Zuta paid a certain sum of money to obtain the post.[291] However, after a period of 66 days Samuel b. Hananya was restored.[292] Following his death (1159)[293] the post was neglected for some time,[294] though ultimately according to Graetz, Nethanel, mentioned above by Benjamin, succeeded Samuel b. Hananya as Nagid.[295] Nevertheless, in a marriage contract issued in Fustat in 1160, Nethanel is mentioned and we read, "To His Excellency, the most honorable, glorious, dear, and holy master, teacher and lord, the Gaon Nethanel Halevi, the Head of the academy of the Diaspora...."[296] It is obvious that Benjamin omits the word "Halevi" and that the two documents, both the one quoted, and that of Benjamin of Tudela, do not mention the word "Nagid." Neubauer implies that the title was temporarily not in use.[297] Is it possible that Nethanel did not accept the title "Nagid" after Maimonides, to whom the title had been offered, refused it?[298] In any event the title of "Nagid" is not attached to him,[299] and he was, as Benjamin titles him, "head of the academy" being thus one of the very last Gaons of Fustat college.[300]

Our traveller tells of some of the duties of Nethanel. Besides heading the academy, he was responsible for appointing Rabbis and officials.[301] R. Obadiah da Bertinoro, who visited Egypt at the end of the fifteenth century, still was able to report that the Nagid appointed the Dayyanim in every community.[302] Generally speaking, his duty was to

unite the Jews, to be the legal authority and judge
according to the laws and customs.[303] Among other
duties, he was responsible for order in the community and also for carrying out the restrictions imposed by the state on non-Moslem subjects.[304]

In 1071, when Jerusalem was conquered by the
Seljuks, the Palestinian Yeshiva moved to Damascus.
The academy in Fustat benefited from this move,
since some of the Palestinian members joined it.[305]
The hatred which existed between the Abbasides and
the Fatimites led eventually to the election of a
head of the Egyptian Jews.[306] This last fact contributed also to the position of the Fustat Academy, at the head of which, in Benjamin's time,
stood Nethanel. When Benjamin visited Egypt, the
Fustat Academy had already attained significance.
Most of the deeds of the Jewish law courts, which
were issued in the twelfth century, speak of the
Gaonim as the highest authority of Egyptian
Jewry.[307] Under Zuta, the office of Nagid declined
and the head of the Fustat Yeshiva became the highest authority among the Egyptian Jewry.[308]

It also seems clear that the Yeshiva of Fustat
was a branch of the ancient Palestinian academy,
similar to the Damascene Yeshiva which existed in
that time. Both the heads of the Fustat and the
Damascus Yeshivas had the title of "Rosh Yeshibat
Gaon Ya'akob" or "Rosh Yeshibat Eres hashbi": that
is, they pretended to be the successors of the
Palestinian Gaonim. Since both the Gaon of Damascus and that of Fustat claimed to be the inheritors
of the Palestinian Yeshiva, there was a rivalry between them. The Yeshiva in Damascus was under the
influence of Samuel b. 'Ali in Baghdad while Nethanel b. Moses Halevi communicated with Ali's competi-
tor—the exhilarch Daniel ben Hisdai.[309] While the
Gaon of Damascus claimed to have juridical authority
over the Jews of Egypt, the head of the Fustat Yeshiva, Nethanel b. Moses Halevi, was appointed by
the Babylonian Exilarch as the spiritual head of
the Jews in Egypt.[310] In a letter to Nethanel in
1161, the Exilarch says that the Palestinian or the
Damascus Academy and its Gaon have no authority over

Egypt.[311] Strauss is sure that Nethanel publicized
this letter.[312]

Benjamin's time saw the establishment of close
relations between the Jews of Egypt and the Babylonian Exilarch, and this was something new in the
history of the Egyptian Jews. According to Strauss,
this new orientation cannot be explained only by
the competition between the Yeshiva of Fustat and
that of Damascus.[313] Rather, this was a result of
the weakness of the Fatimite dynasty, and with
Saladin ascending to power the tendency became ever
stronger. Saladin swore allegiance to the Abbasid
caliph and it was natural for the Egyptian Jews to
follow this new orientation. This resulted in re-
cognizing once more the Exilarch as the supreme
head.[314]

Benjamin of Tudela left Fustat for old Mizraim
which is the ancient Memphis,[315] and found it be be
in ruins.[316] Outside the city, in Dimuh, he reports of an ancient synagogue "of Moses our Master
...and the overseer and clerk of this place of worship is a venerable old man: he is a man of learning."[317] This was a place of pilgrimage for the
Egyptian Jews, who believed that Moses had built
this synagogue. Near this synagogue there was a
tree with evergreen leaves which, according to the
belief of the Egyptian Jews, had sprung up from the
rod of Moses.[318] Macrizi, the Egyptian historian
of the fourteenth century, relates that during his
time numerous Jewish pilgrims still came to this
Moses Synagogue on the festival of Shavout in order
to honour the memory of the creator of the Torah.
"They do this," Macrizi states, "instead of making
the Hajj to Jerusalem."[319]

In Alexandria, "a commercial market for all
nations," Benjamin found a huge Jewish community
of 3,000 Jews.[320] This trade centre flourished,
especially during the epoch of the crusaders, when
an economic relationship between Europe, Asia, and
Africa was established. Interestingly, R. Obadiah
Da Bertinoro found at the end of the fifteenth century only 25 Jewish families and two old synagogues

in Alexandria.[321]   Obviously in Bertinoro's time,
Alexandria on the whole lost its Jewish significance.

In Damietta, a harbour which gained in reputation during the crusading era, Benjamin found about
200 Jews.[322]   Our traveller lists other cities located in the Delta where he found existing Jewish
communities.[323]   It seems obvious that Benjamin had
as his object the enumeration of only the locations
in Egypt which contained Jews, and this is reflected by his route in Egypt.   It is also obvious that
most of the Jewish populations in Egypt concentrated in the Delta area.   Only Fayum and Kutz were
located in upper Egypt.   Organized and active Jewry
was then to be found in the trade centres of the
Egyptian Delta.   Those communities had a strong connection with Cairo, and were like a unified and
highly organized community.[324]   Maimonides and
others address those cities like a single unit.[325]
The twelfth century was a period of prosperity for
the entire Delta region, and was characterized by
large populations, as testified to by the Arab geographers.[326]   Benjamin of Tudela confirms this when
he describes the Delta and the branches of the Nile:
"Along both banks of these four river heads are
cities, towns, and villages, and people visit these
places either by ship or by land.   There is no such
thickly populated land as this anywhere.   It is extensive too, and abundant in all good things."[327]
During the thirteenth century a great change took
place in the Jewish settlements of this area.   Most
of the cities of the Delta disappeared,[328] and the
travellers from the end of the fifteenth century
tell of only a few settlements.[329]   Possibly the
cause was the decline of the economy in the area,
but this question still remains uncertain.[330]

Thus, Benjamin's account reflects the times.
In the epoch of the last Fatimite, the status of
the Jews in Egypt was especially good.   Large communities were established in Cairo, Fustat and
Alexandria; the communities in other cities expanded and did their self-administration.   Though
Baghdad again had an Exilarch, Egypt had its own

Nagid. It can be concluded that Benjamin visited
Egypt in a time of transition. The Ayyubid government, established by Saladin, developed a new attitude toward the non-Moslem groups. The Fatimites
had relied greatly on the support of Christians and
Jews.[331] They had participated in financially supporting the religious institutions of Christians
and Jews and took part in their ceremonies. The
number of Jews who held government positions was
large. No wonder the Fatimite period is considered
to be the golden age in the history of the Jews in
Egypt. This is reflected in the anger and jealousy
shown by the Moslems themselves.[332] All this
changed when Saladin came to power.[333] The new
ruler tried to create a feeling of superiority a-
mong the Moslems over the non-Moslems.[334] He rejected the tolerance of the Fatimites in the religious sphere. However, the Ayyubids were educated
and the people were not yet fanatics as were the
Mameluks later on.[335] Therefore, the social relations between Moslems and Jews continued.[336] Saladin did not touch the communal autonomy of the Jews.
However, the change in the political situation affected that autonomy as well as other spheres of
social life. This began about 15 years before the
downfall of the Fatimite caliphs, when they became
weak, and reached its peak in the first years of
Saladin's reign.[337]

It has been stated that Moslem Syria offered
asylum to the academies and other Jewish institutions that had been transferred from the crusader's
Palestine. While Benjamin found a sad picture of
Jewish life in the Holy Land he gives a totally
different account when he moves from the Holy Land
to Moslem Syria. Here the Jewish centres are stimulated once more by refugees from Palestine. If
in Antiochia, which was under the crusaders, Benjamin found only ten Jewish families,[338] in Damascus, which was under the Moslems, the Jewish community expanded to 3000 families! Here is what
Benjamin reports of the Jewish community in Damascus:

Three thousand Jews abide in this city,

and amongst them are learned and rich men.
The head of the Academy of the land of
Israel resides here. His name is R. Aza-
riah, and with him are his brother Sar
Shalom, the head of the Beth Din; R. Joseph
the fifth of the academy, R. Mazliach, the
lecturer, the head of the order; R. Meir,
the crown of the scholars; R. Joseph ben Al
Pilath, the pillar of the academy, R. Heman,
the warden; and R. Zedekiah, the physician.[339]

Petachia of Regensburg visited Damascus also, and
he reports:

This is a large city, the King of Egypt
rules over it. There are about 10,000 Jews
there, who have a prince. The head of their
academy is Rabbi Ezra, who is full of the
knowledge of the Law, for Rabbi Samuel, head
of the academy of Babylon, ordained him.[340]

We see then that Petachia estimated the number of
Jews to be 10,000, a fact supporting the opinion
that Benjamin refers only to the heads of families
in his figures.[341] In this large trade centre
from which the Kingdom of Nur-ed-din began,[342]
Palestinian scholars and public personalities settled. At the head of the community of Damascus
were Ezra, the rector of the academy; Shar Shalom,
the chairman of the court of arbitration; some individuals carrying the title of Rosh-Seder (elders
of the academy), also a "darshan," lecturer or
preacher; parnas—an elder—and one physician.
Here we have the entire apparatus of the academy
which had formerly been in Palestine.[343] Benjamin
clearly states that "the head of the academy of the
land of Israel resides here,"[344] and it seems that
Benjamin is aware of the fact that the academy had
moved recently from the Holy Land to Damascus.[345]
W. Bacher correctly observes that at the time of
the crusades, the traditions of the Palestinian
Gaonate seems to have survived at Damascus.[346] As
we said above, the Egyptian Jews under Saladin came
to recognize the authority of the Exilarchate at
Baghdad, and the Yeshiva at Fustat lost some of its

120

independence. Damascus, on the other hand, seems
to have preserved its authority independently.
Petachia, however, states that R. Samuel, head of
the academy of Babylon, ordained Rabbi Ezra, the
head of the academy of Damascus. This seems to indicate that the Damascus academy also came under
the supervision of Baghdad at this time.

As regards a licence to act as judge, apart
from ordination (Semikhah), the rights of the Exilarch of Baghdad are more extensive than those of
the Palestinian Gaon in our travellers' time. This
fact is stated explicitly by Maimonides about 1167,
in his commentary.[347] This agrees with Petachia's
account which reads:

> In all the land of Assyria and Damascus, in
> the cities of Persia and Media, as well as
> in the land of Babel, they have no juddge
> that has not been appointed [by] Rabbi Sam-
> uel, the head of the academy [Babylonian].
> It is he that gives license in every city
> to judge and to teach. His authority is
> acknowledged in all countries and also in
> the land of Israel.[348]

From the twelfth-century accounts it becomes obvious that there are three elements which charac-
terize the Jewish community of Damascus: first,
a large Jewish community, though the figures given
by Petachia are exaggerated; the Damascus academy
that moved from Palestine; and a famous prince pre-
siding at the head of the community there. However,
the attempt to continue the Palestinian academy in
Syria was not lasting success, and its influence
was felt only on a small scale. The same can be
said of the Fustat academy and its Gaons.[349]

En route across the Syrian desert, between
Damascus and Mesopotamia, Benjamin came across Pal-
myra, where he reports a Jewish community of some
2000 families, characterized by military power, who
supported the Arab neighbours in the struggle
against the crusaders, and against the Bedouins of
Arabia.[350] The community was headed by a council

121

of three individuals.[351]

The second largest community, after Damascus, was located in Aleppo, where the Sultan Nureddin resided. Aleppo, together with Damascus, had Jewish communities a long time before they had been visited by our travellers. One of the seven gates of Aleppo was called Bab-el-Yahud,[352] and the Persian traveller Nasir-i-Khusrau, who visited the city in 1047 mentions four gates, one of which is the Jewish gate.[353] Rabbi Petachia does not mention the existence of the Jewish community here, while Banjamin states not only its size, 5,000 Jews, but also that it was headed by a council of three figures.[354] Rabbi Judah Alkharizi, who visited the city at the beginning of the thirteenth century calls it the "blessed city." He mentions by name some of the leaders of the community because of their learning and riches. His account reflects a well established community.[355]

The largest community was the Mesopotamian city of Mosul, not far from the ruins of Nineveh, the ancient capital of Assyria.[356] Our account refers to it as Assur or "New Nineveh."[357] Benjamin reports, "...Mosul, which is Assur the great, and here dwell about 7,000 Jews, at their head being R. Zakkai the Nasi, the seed of David, and R. Joseph, surnamed Burhan-al-mulk the astronomer to the King Sin-ed-din the brother of Nur-ed-din King of Damascus."[358] We hear then that the city was ruled by the brother of Nureddin, who employed a Jewish astronomer. He was one of the leaders of the Jewish community. It was Zakkai the Nasi, "of the seed of David," who was regarded as the official spokesman of the community of Mosul. Close to Baghdad, Mosul came under the impact of the Exilarchate and Gaonate of Baghdad. Rabbi Petachia reports of the Jewish community at Mosul:

> At New Nineveh is a large congregation numbering more than six thousand souls. It has two princes. The name of one is Rabbi David and the other Rabbi Samuel. They are sons of two brothers and the seed of King

David. Everyone pays there annually a
gold Florin: of that coming from the Jews
half belongs to the King or Sultan...who
is subject to the King of Babel...the other
half belongs to the princes: they have
fields and vineyards.

In those countries there are no precen-
tors nor have they any in the lands of
Persia, Media, and Damascus. But among
the households of the princes there are
many scholars. Sometimes they call upon
this man, and sometimes upon that, to recite the prayers. The prince has also a
prison wherein he locks up the wicked. If
a Gentile and a Jew have a dispute, he imprisons the guilty party whether Jew or
Mohammedan.... At Nineveh there was an
astrologer whose name was R. Solomon. There
is among all the sages in Nineveh, and the
land of Assur, none as expert in the planets
as he....[359]

Thus, Rabbi Petachia confirms Benjamin's report in
respect to the large Jewish community that existed
at Mosul. He also found at Mosul two cousins who
claimed to belong to the royal House of David, and
who probably belonged to the house of R. Zakkai,
mentioned before by R. Benjamin. One of these,
David, has been praised by Alkharizi[360] who generally had no high opinion of the intellectual life
of the Mosul community. Also, R. Petachia found
an astrologer in Mosul, where there was none like
him as "expert in the planets."

In addition to this R. Petachia tells us that
half of the Jewish taxes belong to the princes who
"have fields and vineyards." Moreover, the prince,
the supreme leader of the Jewish community, has the
authority to imprison those who should be punished,
and the most interesting point is that the prince
"imprisons the guilty party whether Jew or Mohammedan." Rabbi Petachia was astounded at the high
level of education he found in the East.[361] At
Mosul, "there are many scholars." He found no permanent cantors in those countries, but a different

123

man is asked to recite the prayers, a fact which
indicates an educated community.

Though the literary production of the Jews in
the Orient is poor at this time,[362] that does not
indicate that the level of the general education
was low. The Genizah documents contain lists of
private libraries which show that even physicians
and merchants were concerned in the advancement of
education, religious, as well as secular.[363] Alkharizi, being in Aleppo, records that R. Joseph, a
renowned scholar from the west, arrived in the city.
There he encouraged many to study.[364] We get the
impression that the intellectual life here was stimulated by scholars coming from the west. The
general picture described by Alkharizi is not one
of ignorance.[365] Although a certain educated man
who arrived in Egypt possibly from Byzantium wrote
a letter to the Egyptian Nagid complaining of the
ignorance of the Egyptian Jews.[366] His letter indicates that the man was angry at not being supported financially as he had hoped.[367]

To sum up, Moslem Syria was inhabited by many
Jewish congregations, which were economically and
intellectually well established. R. Petachia correctly states: "From Nineveh, and further on,
there are congregations in every city and village."[368] The early period of the crusaders forced
Jews to leave the Holy Land and settle in Moslem
Syria, a fact reflected by our travellers' accounts.[369]

Ibn Jubayr, who visited Syria in the second
half of the twelfth century, was surprised to find
that the crusaders did not rob the Arab farmers under their rule and he condemns the Moslem despots
who took advantage of the farmers.[370] Based on
this, some historians concluded that the situation
of the non-Christians under the crusaders was better than that under the Moslems.[371] The history
of Syria in the twelfth century, however, indicates
that the crusaders did not succeed in gaining the
trust of their subjects, oriental Christians or
Moslems. In the war between the crusaders and

Zengi, Nur-ed-din, and Saladin the natives sided
with the Moslems.[372]

The Moslems tried to unify the oriental population behind them and stir up hatred against the
crusaders. Therefore, they favoured the Jews, as
indicated by the fact that when Zengi conquered
Edessa in 1144, 300 Jewish families, on whose loy-
alty he could depend, were transferred into the
city.[373] The most significant argument for this
can be brought from Benjamin's account, listing
only three Jewish communities of medium size in the
crusaders' cities. In Latikiya he found 100
Jews,[374] in Gebal 150,[375] and in Tyre 500,[376] not
to mention the Holy Land in which we hear of a number of medium-sized Jewish communities.[377] In contrast he reports of 3,000 Jewish families in Damascus and 5,000 in Aleppo, and two other communities
on the Syrian border that contained 2,000 Jewish
families. We are forced to ask then if the situation of the Jews under the crusaders was better
than under the Moslems, as Lammens agrues,[378] why
did the Jews not come to settle in the crusaders'
cities? As the crusaders' cities were then important trade centres, would this not motivate the
Jews to emigrate to them? Why were 5,000 Jews found
in Aleppo, while in Antioch, a flourishing city,
there were only ten Jewish families?[379] It is also
important to remember that Maimonides, fleeing from
North Africa, came to Acre where he concealed his
religion. Interestingly enough, he did not stay in
the area of the crusaders but preferred to move to
a Moslem country— Egypt. Thus Strauss disagrees
with Lammens who believes that the situation of the
Jews under the crusaders was better than that under
the Moslems; however, Strauss does not present enough
proof to show that the situation under the crusaders
became worse while it improved under the Moslems.
He argues that if the situation of the Jews under
the crusaders was better, then Jewish communities
from Syria would have left to come to the crusaders'
country. The same can be asked concerning the Moslem countries. If the situation were better there,
why did the Jews not leave the crusaders' countries
entirely and go to Moslem Syria? As for the Jewish

community in Antioch, the last source to refer to it
is from the sixth century, and it is difficult to
conclude from a single twelfth-century source the
exact reasons that led to the decrease of the number of Jews there.[380]

Finally, we can try to figure out the total
Jewish population in those countries in relation to
the general population. We have stated already
that Benjamin furnishes information, quite uncommon
in other contemporary sources dealing with Jewish
history, regarding the size of the Jewish Communities he visited.[381] Based on the figures found
within Benjamin's accounts and on isolated information in other contemporary sources,[382] Strauss
reaches a conclusion that in Egypt there were almost 40,000 Jews,[383] and in Syria about 40,200[384]
at this time.

Generally speaking, the total population in
Egypt at the second half of the thirteenth century
is considered to be about 4,000,000.[385] Consequently, Jews formed at that time only one percent
of the total population. Syria contained at that
time no more than 3,000,000,[386] and therefore Jews
were numerically a more important element here than
in Egypt and formed around two percent of the total
Syrian population. Furthermore, in Syria the size
of the Jewish population was much more imporant if
we remember that the Syrian population was broken
into many religious groups with no clearly dominant
majority. In Egypt, on the other hand, almost all
the Moslems were orthodox and most of the Christians were Copts and only a minority were Greeks.

However, one must remember that Benjamin's figures can be used only for general evaluation in regard to the sizes of the communities, but have no
value for serious statistics.[387] It is the proper
place to remember W.B. Stevenson's statement that:
"the numbers (given by the chroniclers in the time
of the crusades) ...are a mere fashion of speech
intended to express proportions and relations, and
may be called illustrative or pictorial numbers."[388]

126

The Abbaside Calphate and the Surrounding Areas

The religious efforts of the Moslems were
aroused by the crusades, which reunited them against
a common enemy. As Lebrecht puts it "...the deeds
of this period remind the observer of the virgin
time of the Islam, of its golden age under the two
legitimate Caliphs."[389] A highly significant event
of this period is the emancipation of the Abbaside
Caliphs.[390] In the first half of the twelfth century, they established a small kingdom around Baghdad which depended in name only on the "great Sultans" of Persia. The highest degree of independence
was secured by the Calph Al-Moktafi (1136-1160)
whose aspiration was to renew the ancient glory of
the Abbasides.[391] This Caliph also restored to the
Jews of Babylon the internal autonomy that they had
enjoyed in the golden age of the Caliphate. Once
again Babylonian Jewry held the highest organs of
temporal and spiritual authority: The Exilarchate
and the Gaonate were strong factors in the life of
Oriental Jewry.[392]

Benjamin, during his visit to Baghdad (1168),
noted the importance of the Jewish community there
when he saw the considerable number of synagogues
attended by 40,000 Jews.[393] The account describes
the Jewish political conditions favourably. Benjamin was so impressed by the King and his life that
he wrote a lengthy description of him.[394] This
long, favourable account is proof of Benjamin's
sympathetic attitude toward the Caliph who is "kind
unto Israel, and many belonging to the people of
Israel are his attendants."[395] Benjamin also reported that the Caliph possessed a knowledge of the
Hebrew language and of Jewish law.[396] Although this
knowledge of Hebrew cannot be verified, the Caliph's
attitude towards the Jews was well known in Baghdad
and its provinces during the time of Benjamin's
visit. Petachia states that the Caliph "was a
friend of Rabbi Solomon because the monarch was of
the seed of Mahomet, and the head of the captivity
descended from King David."[397] Petachia later
claims that the same Caliph intended to accept

127

Judaism with his own people, however, "had not time to become a convert and convert his people before he died."[398] No matter how this particular report is interpreted, his conclusion that "the Jews in the land of Babel live in peace"[399] is correct. This is consistent with Benjamin's statements.

Benjamin's report of the Exilarch Daniel Ben Hisdai is very significant. The Jews called Daniel b. Hisdai the head of the captivity (Resh Galuta) of all Israel. Benjamin relates:

> And at the head of them all is Daniel the son of Hisdai, who is styled 'our Lord and Head of the Captivity of all Israel.' He possesses a book of pedigrees going back as far as David, King of Israel. The Jews call him 'our Lord, Head of the Captivity,' and the Mohammedans call him 'Saidna ben Daoud,' and he has been invested with authority over all the congregations of Israel at the hands of the Emir al-Muminin, the Lord of Islam. For thus Mohammed commended concerning him and his descendants: and he granted him a seal of office over all the congregations that dwell under his rule, and ordered that every one, whether Mohammedan or Jew, or belonging to any other nation in his dominion, should rise up before him (the Exilarch) and salute him, and that any one who should refuse to rise up should receive one hundred stripes.
> And every fifth day when he goes to pay a visit to the great Caliph, horsemen, Gentiles as well as Jews, escort him, and heralds proclaim in advance, 'Make way, before our Lord, the son of David, as is due unto him....' He is mounted on a horse, and is attired in robe of silk and embroidery with a large turban on his head, and from the turban is suspended a long white cloth adorned with a chain upon which the cipher of Mohammed is engraved. Then he appears before the Caliph and kisses his hand, and the Caliph rises and places him

on a throne which Mohammed had ordered to
be made for him and all the Mohammedan
princes who attend the court of the Caliph
rise up before him. And the Head of the
Captivity is seated on his throne opposite
to the Caliph.... The authority of the
Head of the Captivity extends over all the
communities of Shinar, Persia, Khurasan and
Sheba which is El-Yemen, and Diyar Kalach
and the land of Aram Naharaim (Mesopotamia),
and over the dwellers in the mountains of
Ararat and the land of the Alans.... His
authority extends also over the land of
Siberia, and the communities in the land of
the Togarmim unto the mountains of Asveh
and the land of Gurgan.... Further it extends to the gates of Samarkand, the land
of Tibet, and the land of India. In respect
of all these countries the Head of the Captivity gives the communities power to ap-
point Rabbis and Ministers who come unto him
to be consecrated and to receive his authority. They bring him offerings and gifts
from the ends of the earth. He owns hospices, gardens and plantations...and much
land inherited from his fathers, and no one
can take his possessions from him by force.
He has a fixed weekly revenue arising from
the hospices of the Jews, the markets and
the merchants, apart from that which is
brought to him from far off lands. The man
is very rich, and wise in the Scriptures as
well as in the Talmud, and many Israelites
dine at his table everyday.[400]

The extent of the power of the Exilarch is,
no doubt, exaggerated. It is possible that, at that
time, the authority of the Head of Captivity was
recognized in certain places, such as Persia, Arme-
nia, and the Caucasus, areas in which Jewish communities were permitted to renew their relations with
Baghdad.[401] Can some of these exaggerations be explained by the fact that Benjamin was under the influence of the old description of the Exilarchate

in the work of Nathan-ha-Babli?[402]

Benjamin continues to give us further information of the Head of the Captivity:

> At his installation, the head of the Captiv-
> ity gives much money to the Caliph, to the
> Princes and the Ministers. On the day that
> the Caliph performs the ceremony of invest-
> ing him with authority, he rides in the sec-
> ond of the royal equipages, and is escorted
> from the palace of the Caliph to his own
> house with timbrels and fifes.[403]

Thus the appointment of the Exilarch had to be confirmed by the Caliph, the Princes and the Ministers.
It is quite interesting to compare this account with
that of the installation of the Egyptian Nagid,[404]
Samuel ben Paltiel, as given by the Nagid himself.[405]
In both cases, the office (Exilarch in Babylonia
and Nagid in Egypt) was hereditary: the support of
the community was needed, especially if the dignitary did not have children. An amount of money on
that occasion was paid to the Caliph, who performed
the ceremony. Benjamin reports that a sum of money
was given to the Princes and the Ministers, a fact
different from the case of the Nagid in Egypt. The
dignitary rides in the street, in Benjamin's report
"from the Palace of the Caliph to his own house with
timbrels and fifes." In the case of the Egyptian
Nagid, a copy of the mandate which has been written
in the name of the Caliph was read to announce the
Nagid in his office, accompanied by a procession
and rejoicing. In both instances it seems that the
man in the office needed both—the support of the
leaders of the community and an official appointment by the Caliph. In spite of the similarities
we have noted, it is clear that the Exilarch in
Baghdad, backed by a long tadition, held a more established and exalted position than did the Nagid
in Egypt, whose office was relatively recent.[406]

The office of the Exilarchate also greatly impressed Petachia.[407] He writes that a year before

his arrival at Baghdad, the Exilarch Daniel died. When the deceased Exilarch left no heir, the community could not agree on a successor. One party favoured R. David, and the other favoured R. Samuel.[408] Both were of Mosul and traced their origins to the Exilarchs of Baghdad. Finally, according to R. Petachia, David, a cousin to Daniel b. Hisdai,[409] became Exilarch jointly with R. Samuel b. 'Ali, the head of the great Academy.[410]

We have to remember that the office of Exilarch was a transitional stage when Benjamin and Petachia visited Baghdad. Soon, as indicated by Petachia, the privileges of the Exilarch would be transferred to the Gaon. Moreover, the appointment of the Gaonim would be made by the government rather than by the Exilarch. Thereafter, the historical function of the Exilarchs ceased, and the Gaonim enjoyed all the religious and political privileges. The exact process of this important change of power remains obscure because of the lack of accurate documentation. A possible cause can be related to the death of Daniel b. Hisdai, who left no heir. The subsequent division of the community as to succession weakened the office considerably. When the new Exilarch was finally nominated, the office already had lost its independence, and its privileges had to be shared with the famous Gaon of the twelfth century, Samuel b. Ali.

As for the Gaonim and the Yeshivot, the twelfth century may be viewed as a revival of the Talmudic Academies as they had once existed in Sura and Pumbedita. Benjamin reports that each of the ten Academies had its own rector. One of them, Samuel ben 'Ali Halevi, had the title Gaon, and together with the other rectors formed a spiritual collegium. This collegium had jurisdiction over the internal religious and legal affairs of the communities. Communal affairs referred to them by periphery courts were handled by a group of rabbis who formed the Judicial Collegium. Once a week, when the Gaon Samuel participated in their sessions, more important questions were considered. Benjamin reports:

In this city there are ten Acedemies. At
the head of the great Academy is the chief
rabbi R. Samuel the son of Eli. He is the
head of the Academy Gaon Jacob. He is a
Levite, and traces his pedigree back to
Moses our teacher. The head of the second
Academy is R. Hananya his brother.... R.
Daniel is the head of the third Academy;
R. Elazar the scholar is the head of the
fourth Academy; and R. Elazar,...., is the
head of the order, and his pedigree reaches
to Samuel the Prophet.... He and his brethren know how to chant the melodies as did
the singers at the time when the Temple was
standing. He is head of the fifth Academy.
R. Hisdai, the glory of the scholars, is
head of the sixth Academy. R. Haggai is
head of the seventh Academy. R. Ezra is the
head of the eighty Academy. R. Zakkai, the
son of Bostanai the Nasi, is the head of the
Sium. These are the ten Batlanim,[411] and
they do not engage in any other work than
communal administration: and all the days
of the week they judge the Jews their countrymen, except on the second day of the
week, when they all appear before the chief
rabbi Samuel, the head of the Yeshiba Gaon
[Jacob], who in conjunction with the other
Batlanim judges all those that appear before
him.[412]

Mann believes that Benjamin, as an outsider,
misunderstood the functions assigned to the ten
leading members of the school (including the Gaon)
to be identical with activities of separate academies. Samuel ben 'Ali always speaks of "the school"
in the singular. He also frequently associates himself in correspondence with his brother, Hananyah,
who is the vice president of the Academy (סגן הישיבה).
According to Benjamin, Hananyah was to have been the
head of the second Academy.[413] We also know that a
scholar served under the Gaon in the position of Ab
Bet Din. Hence we have ten leading members of one
school under the Gaon. This number is similar to
that given by Natan the Babylonian (10th century),

132

according to whom there were seven Allufim, the
heads of the rows, and three "Haberim" who established the Bet Din of the school.[414] The only difference in accounts between Natan and Benjamin is
in the titles of the scholars,[415] except for the
Gaon, who retained his title. The title "Alluf"
(Resh Kallah) was given to people outside the school
and did not fit the resident members. The formerly
leading Alluf, head of the first row, appears now
to have been called vice president (סגן הישיבה).
Other titles mentioned by Benjamin are The Third in
rank (יסוד הישיבה), Haber (a reminiscence of the
same title of Natan's day), "head of the Order"
(ראש הסדר), "the glory of the scholars" (פאר החב-
רים), "the counsel of the Academy" (סוד הישיבה) and
"head of the Sium" (בעל הסיום).[416] In Samuel ben
'Ali's time, they had certain duties of teaching.
Benjamin, being unfamiliar with the internal organization of the Academy, thought that there were ten
academies, where there was actually only one, called
by Benjamin himself "the Great Acedemy."[417] This
Academy was presided over by Samuel ben 'Ali, who
alone held the title "the head of the Academy" and
Gaon.

The most important fact is that Petachia was
impressed by the learned community and reports that
"There is no one so ignorant in the whole of Babylon,
Assyria, Media, and Persia, but knows the twenty four
books, punctuation, grammar, the superfluous and
omitted letter for the Precentor does not recite the
scripture lesson, but he that is called up to the
scroll of the law recites it himself."[418] No matter
how exaggerated this fact is, it has been confirmed
that the intellectual level of the community was at
a high enough level to impress Petachia who came
from Germany. Jewish learning in Babylonia was interrupted by a long decline after Hai Gaon (1038),[419]
but resumed in this period with an encouraging up-
lift. The Academy of Baghdad now replaced Sura and
Pumbedita as the major centre of Jewish learning.[420]
Petachia reports that the students came from many
places, and "they are all well informed."[421] Furthermore, before they are allowed to enter the Academy, they study in the city under other teachers.

Only when they are ready are they brought before
the head of the Academy.[422]   Thus the Academy maintained high standards.   As to the Academy's relations with the previously existing Academies, it is
apparent from our travellers' accounts and Genizah
letters[423] that many customs and traditions were
preserved.

The Gaon Samuel ben 'Ali (1164-1194) was known
before the discovery of the Genizah.[424]   He became
famous not only through the description our travellers left and the preserved correspondence which he
carried on with scholars, but mainly through a dispute with Maimonides.   Petachia leaves a record of
a few details about the character of this Gaon who
became better known in the light of the Genizah letters.   The Gaon wrote Petachia a letter of recommendation[425] known as "iggereth Arahith" or "iggereth-
Dikar."[426]   Petachia reports of the Gaon:

> Rabbi Samuel has a book of genealogy going
> back as far as Samuel of Ramah, son of El-
> kanah.   He has no sons, but only one daugh-
> ter.   She is expert in Scripture and Talmud.
> She gives instruction in Scripture to young
> men through a window.   She, herself, is with-
> in the building, whilst the disciples are
> below outside and do not see her.[427]   In all
> the land of Assyria and Damascus, in the
> cities of Persia and Media, as well as in
> the land of Babel, they have no judge that
> has not been appointed by Rabbi Samuel, the
> head of the Academy.   It is he that gives
> licence in every city to judge and to teach.
> His authority is acknowledged in all coun-
> tries, and also in the land of Isreal.   They
> all respect him.   He has about sixty beadles
> who held the people in submission by means
> of rods.   After the departure of the dis-
> ciples, the elders derive instruction from
> Rabbi Samuel in the science of planets and
> other branches of knowledge.[428]

Petachia here speaks highly of the Gaon.   He may
have exaggerated when he relates that the Gaon

occupied a large residence which was covered with
tapestry and he himself was clothed in garments
adorned with gold.[429] Considering new information
derived from the Genizah documents, the Gaon could
not have been that wealthy, for such a rich man
would not have written such pitiful letters beg-
ging for money.[430]

The Gaon's authority was, as Petachia reported,
quite extensive, reaching even Europe. R. Moses of
Kiev turned to the Gaon for answers to Halachic
questions, and the Gaon's response has been preserved.[431] In Petachia's time, Samuel b. 'Ali became joint Exilarch with R. David. Furthermore,
Petachia carried his letter of recommendation with
him "and the people did all that he required."
Petachia adds that the people feared Samuel.[432]
This shows the respect that this Gaon enjoyed and
the authority he had in the Jewish communities.[433]

The Gaon was involved in several controversies
with Maimonides. It is clear that these two leaders
did not agree on many important theological and
ritual problems. For example, Maimonides' view of
physical resurrection after death brought attacks
and caused unrest among the Jews of Yeman.[434] One
of these Jews wrote to the Gaon of Baghdad, in 1190,
on this affair.[435] His reply has not been preserved, but Maimonides refers to it in the following way:

> This year, in the year 4951 (1191), some cor-
> respondence written by our colleagues and
> friends of Baghdad reached us. They mention
> that a Yemenite enquirer asked about these
> problems of the Gaon...and he compiled...a
> dissertation on the resurrection of the dead.
> And he put my opinions concerning this prob-
> lem partly in a mistaken way, and partly in
> a form which can be justified.... The Gaon's
> dissertation in its original form was sent to
> me. I saw in it all the homilies and Agga-
> doth which he compiled.... And more wonder-
> ful still are some strange ideas mentioned
> by him pretending that they are philosophi-

135

cal views on psychology.[436]

We may learn from this that Samuel was not only a
well-known talmudist but was also knowledgeable in
philosophy. Petachia also testified to this for
the phrase "wisdom of Egypt" in the following refers to philosophy: "He is the superior, full of
wisdom both in the written and oral law and in all
the wisdom of Egypt. Nothing is hidden from him.
He knows the Holy names, and is profoundly versed
in the Talmud."[437] The Gaon's treatise had an impact on Baghdad. One person, probably Daniel by
name,[438] found it necessary to compose a refutation
of the Gaon's attack on Maimonides.[439]

This was not the only controversy occurring
between the two. Another resident of Baghdad,
Joseph ibn Gabir, turned to Maimonides with a question about Hilkhoth Niddah,[440] and we can gather
from one of these letters that Maimonides participated in a local quarrel between the Gaon and the
Exilarch. A preserved Genizah letter reveals that
Maimonides sides[441] with a candidate for the Exilarchate who was not favoured by the Gaon.[442] Maimonides was criticized for taking part in the
strife and for writing to a man whom he did not
know and from whom scholars kept their distance.[443]
This controversy reflects the account we have of
what occurred after the Exilarch Daniel b. Hisdai
died in 1174, leaving no heirs. As reported by
Petachia, the community could not decide which of
Daniel's two brothers should succeed him. The Gaon
supported one brother while Maimonides supported
the other.

The Gaon and Maimonides were involved in other
controversies as well, but they were of lesser importance.[444] Ultimately, the quarrel about the
election of the Exilarch was the chief cause of all
disagreement. In relation to the office of Exilarch, after the death of the Exilarch in 1190 the
Gaon tried to abolish the office altogether. According to the Gaon, there was no need for the office since not worldly, but spiritual leadership
was needed.[445]

Historians are able to gather much information about the Jewish life in the Orient from this Gaon's Responsa. These letters were sent by special messengers[446] to all communities of Syria, Mesopotamia and Persia, whose collected funds supported the Gaonate and the Academy. The Jews of these countries were governed by a well-organized adminstration set up by Samuel b. 'Ali Gaon.[447]

In summary, in the second half of the twelfth century, the Gaon Samuel b. 'Ali assumed the added temporal power of the Exilarchate. Samuel b. 'Ali was the actual Exilarch, while David and Samuel, the brothers of Daniel, were satisfied with bearing the title. The Caliph, it should be noted, recognized the merging of temporal and spiritual functions into one office. Since the time of the downfall of the Gaonate, Samuel b. 'Ali was the first and last Gaon whose authority was recognized in the Orient and the West. Just as the Gaon of the preceding era did, he answered questions from many places about religious matters. Again, at the time our travellers visited Baghdad, the office of the Gaonate was in its final glory.

Up to this point, our travellers found in Baghdad a secure Jewish community, which had a harmonious relationship with the revived Abbaside Caliphate. As Benjamin puts it, the Jews there "dwell in security, prosperity and honour under the great Caliph, and amongst them are great sages,..."[448]

There is no greater contrast than between the reports of Benjamin and Petachia and that of the poet Judah Alkharizi. While the twelfth century travellers were impressed by the intellectual activity and high education in Baghdad, Alkharizi, who visited Baghdad at the beginning of the thirteenth century, presented a different picture. What he described was actually a picture of decline. In the twelfth century, Baghdad was a place of wealth and learning and the Jewish community reflected religious vitality.[449] Benjamin found twenty-eight synagogues in Baghdad.[450] Petachia reports that in

137

Babel there are thirty synagogues "besides that of Daniel."[451] The Jewish community was painted in bright colours. According to Alkharizi's report, however, the population was depicted as being pleasure-seekers and sinners. Synagogues as well as houses of study were now in ruins or being used for some profane purpose. Alkharizi wrote: "At one time the glory of all the countries, where there were Gaonim and men of wisdom, from time im-memorial...the flour disappeared, and only the chaff was left; the devout are gone, and only troublemakers are left."[452]

Indeed, the whole of Jewish life in the Abba-side Caliphate was in a period of transition when our travellers came upon it. With the death of the Gaon Exilarch Samuel b. 'Ali,[453] the extinction of the autonomous centre of Baghdad gradually began. The entire Jewish political and spiritual institu-tion was in decline.[454] The sphere of influence was narrowing as the large communities of Syria (Mosul-Aleppo-Damascus) chose their own leaders. Alkharizi found here greater vitality both socially and literally. Politically, they were under the jurisdiction of the local Sultans, who were not dependent upon the Caliph. Palestine, on its way to freedom from the crusaders, was becoming the sphere of influence of Egypt. Thus the Caliphate of Baghdad was nearing an end. The Mongol invasion (1258) put an end even to this remnant.[455] From the Jewish point of view, with the downfall of the Abbaside dynasty a glorious epoch of Jewish history also ended. It is clear then that the significance of the facts recorded by our travellers lies in their description of Jewish life within the Abba-side Caliphate during its temporary twelfth-century revival.[456]

Benjamin lists cities in the areas surrounding Baghdad in which there were large Jewish communi-ties. In fact, the accounts include nearly all the stations on the modern caravan routes. It is still evident, states Layard, that a considerable Jewish population lived in the cities of Babylonia. Layard continues to state that, in his journey to Mesopo-

tamia, it is evident that the Jewish population
has greatly diminished and in some places had disappeared entirely.[457]

Benjamin found a large Jewish community numbering 10,000 in Okbara,[458] a city on the Tigris
near Baghdad, which was famous during the Caliphate.[459] In the maritime city of Basra, Benjamin
found 10,000 Jews "and among them are scholars and
many rich men."[460] This was a place of great importance in the time of Edrisi, Abulfeda and Ibn
Batuta since it attracted all the foreign commerce
of Persia and the Euphrates.[461] Benjamin cites
other large Jewish communities in Mesopotamia.[462]
It is important to note that Benjamin travelled a
zigzag route to reach Baghdad, a fact reflecting
his thorough search of the area.

Some doubt exists as to whether Benjamin had
personally satisfied himself in regards to the Jewish population for all of the places in Babylonia
and Persia. Scholars agree that up to this point
Benjamin always seems to underestimate the Jewish
population, while from now on he gives exaggerated
numbers. This strengthens Beazley's opinion that
Benjamin did not proceed beyond Isfahan, but found
his way directly to Egypt. It is no longer a record of personal travel, it is rather an attempt
to supplement the first part of things seen, by a
second part of things heard. Thus the statements
concerning the intervening places must be interpreted as hearsay.[463] It is interesting to quote
here Petachia's statement in regard to Mesopotamia
and Persia:

> But in the Land of Cush and Babel there are
> more than sixty myriads of Jews: and there
> are as many in the land of Persia. But in
> Persia the Jews are subject to hard bondage
> and sufferings. Therefore, Rabbi Petachia
> visited only one city in Persia.[464]

It is obvious that Petachia only estimated the numbers of Jews in Babylonia, Persia and their neibh-
bouring areas. Clearly it was in Baghdad that our

travellers collected their information in respect
to the neighbouring areas.[465]

The Jewish communities of those distant countries (Persia and Arabia) formerly constituted an
integral part of the Abbaside Caliphate. They were
a world unto themselves, with their own religious
and national peculiarities, although they were
linked to the spiritual authorities of Baghdad.
For example, Benjamin reported a number of Jewish
communities under the leadership of a special Nasi
in the cities of Northern Arabia.[466] He noted that
the Jewish population included scholars, wealthy
men, and warriors, as well as nomads. Among them,
Benjamin says, were found groups of ascetics who
lamented Zion.[467] Benjamin speaks of Aden:

> The country is mountainous. There are many
> Israelites here, and they are not under the
> yoke of the Gentiles, but possess cities and
> castles on the summits of the mountains,
> from which they make descents into the plain
> country called Lybia, which is a Christian
> Empire. These are the Lybians of the Land
> of Lybia, with whom the Jews are at war. The
> Jews take spoil and booty and retreat to the
> mountains, and no man can prevail against
> them. Many of these Jews of the Land of Aden
> come to persia and Egypt.[468]

This part of Arabia, including Abyssinia on the
other side of the Red Sea, was considered part of
middle India, while Benjamin refers to it as the
"land of Aden."[469] Benjamin speaks of independent
Jews who possess cities and castles, and who engage
in wars against Lybia ("which is a Christian Empire"), and retreat to the mountains. Does Benjamin
intend to say that the independent Jews who lived
in the mountainous country in the rear of Aden
crossed the straits of Bab-el-Mandeb and made war
against the inhabitants of the Plains of Abyssinia?
In the twelfth century Nubia slowly was becoming
Islamised, but this process was completed later. The
"Christian Empire" which Benjamin mentions might refer to the kingdom of Prester John in Abyssinia.[470]

140

The Jews of Aden fought against the Christian ruler
of Abyssinia, and found safety in the mountainous
area there. These Jews, who settled in Abyssinia,
later came to be known as Falasha Jews. Interestingly, Obadiah Da Bertinoro, being in Egypt at the
end of the fifteenth century, reports: "I saw two
of them in Cairo; they were black [Falashas?] but
not so black as the negroes...."[471]

Benjamin concludes his report on the Jews of
Aden[472] with the statement: "Many of these Jews
of the land of Aden come to Persia and Egypt." It
seems probable that, being in Baghdad and Egypt,
Benjamin met some Jews who had come into contact
with those Jews of south Arabia and they served as
a source of information.

The history of the Jews in Yemen in the Middle
Ages is still shrouded in mystery. Neubauer has
stated that we are ignorant concerning the history
of the Yemenite Jews in the period between the sixth
century and 1171, the year Maimonides sent them his
famous letter.[473] However, we do have a letter dated 1153[474] which reflects the role Aden occupied in
Indian trade,[475] and in addition furnishes some details in regard to the Jews of Yemen in this period.
At the head of this letter we read: "The permanent
court in Aden and from the mouth of our prince head
of our exile and from the mouth of our Nagid, his
soul be in Paradise, and from the mouth of our Nagid
Halfon...."[476] It is known that Heads of Captivi-
ties were in Baghdad, Mosul, Fustat, Palestine, Damascus and Aleppo,[477] but we do not know of such dig-
nitaries in Yemen. Mann can present no other documents other than Benjamin's report in regard to the
Jews in Arabia: "At this place lives Salmon the
Nasi, the brother of Hanan the Nasi, and the land
belongs to the two brothers, who are the seed of
David, for they have their pedigree in writing."[478]
Scholars once doubted Benjamin's account of Arabia,
but these two sources agree that a head of captivity was residing also in Arabia at the time, thus
corroborating each other. Halfon the Nagid was the
owner of a ship which suffered disaster,[479] and in
his presence the writer of the letter clarifies the

141

entire case in the synagogue.[480] His title "Nagid" is unusual, as Nagidim existed in Egypt and Palestine,[481] Kairuan and Spain, but we have no information of a Nagidate in Yemen and Aden. Was there such a hereditary office there? This problem cannot be solved due to the lack of documentation.

In addition, the writer of the letter emphasizes, on behalf of the people of Aden, that everything should be done according to the Talmudic law and the Gaon's edicts.[482] For a long time it had been believed that the Jews of Yemen did not have a knowledge of and did not follow Talmudic law,[483] but, slowly, this belief has been rejected.[484] The letter also shows that the Jewish community of Aden was under the influence of Egyptian Jews.[485] Even before the Epistle of Yemen (1171), Jewish merchants resided in Aden; the above letter verifies that contacts existed between the Jews of Yemen, Aden, and their brothers in the Orient, during the period under discussion.

In the Persian Provinces of the former Baghdad Caliphate, Benjamin found large Jewish communities in various cities. The spread of the Jewish Diaspora into Persia, Caucasus, India, China, etc., is an obscure chapter in Jewish history. As Fischel puts it, "The whole continent of Asia is still to a large degree terra incognita for the Jewish historians."[486] Few Jewish communities in Asia (Baghdad, Isfahan) can be traced through all the stages of their histories.[487] For example, a history of the city of Meshhed in Khorasan has only recently been established.[488]

In Khuzisten "which is Elam,"[489] Benjamin is occupied with the tomb of Daniel at Shushan, the capital. He reports of "about 7,000 Jews and fourteen synagogues,"[490] while Petachia found only two Jews there, dyers by profession. The significant fact in Petachia's account is that the traveller showed those two Jewish dyers "the seal of the head of the academy" and they then showed him the coffin of Daniel.[491] It is well documented that the Jews

142

here were under the influence of the Babylonian
Jewish centre.

From Shushan,[492] Benjamin continues his enumeration of localities, but not in any real itinerary
of his own, to the river Halwan and the district of
Mulehet. He reported about 20,000 Israelites in
Rudbar,[493] "and among them are learned and rich men.
But the Jews live under great oppression."[494] Here
we should remember Petachia's statement that the
"Jews in Persia are subject to hard bondage and sufferings."[495] However, neither of our travellers
explain what is meant by this oppression. At the
same time, it is important to note that while Petachia in this instance refers to Persian Jews in
general, Benjamin speaks of oppression only in reference to Rudbar. In respect to Mulehet, near the
south coast of the Caspian Sea, Benjamin reported
on the "Old Man of the Mountain"[496] and four communities of independent Jews who participated with the
Assassins in time of war. In addition, according
to Benjamin, more than 100 Jewish communities inhabited those mountains, and Benjamin refers to them
as belonging to the Lost Ten Tribes.[497] We also
hear that "the Jews are under the authority of the
Head of the Captivity of Babylon,"[498] again indicating the contact between the Persian Jews and the
Babylonian Jewish centre at Baghdad. Asher interprets this statement to mean that it was in Baghdad,
a place to which Jews of all parts of Asia came,
that Benjamin collected his information.[499]

At Amadia, a city situated in the Mountains of
Kurdistan, northeast of Mosul, Benjamin reported a
Jewish community that numbered 25,000.[500] This community had a leading position among the Jewish communities of Kurdistan,[501] and letters and documents
from the sixteenth century also confirm this.[502]
The Jews here are under the authority of the King
of Persia "and he raises a tribute from them," but
Benjamin adds that this was a tax to be paid by all
males in the land of Islam who are over the age of
fifteen.[503] Amadia gave rise to a false Messiah of
whom Benjamin reports;[504] however, we shall deal
with this messianic episode in Chapter VI.

Azerbaijan, the northwestern province of the Persian empire, is an interesting historical area. Its leading cities in Islamic times, such as Tabriz and Urmia played a significant role in the history of Asia.[505] Marco Polo passed through its territory on his way to China. Benjamin, however, makes no mention of Jews there. Is it possible that he meant to include them when he listed the countries which stood under the authority of the Exilarch in Baghdad?[506] The important correspondence of Samuel ben 'Ali with Oriental Jewish communities contains the names of Jewish settlements in Persia, many of which may refer to communities in Azerbaijan.[507] In a way the obscurity surrounding the Jews in this region in the twelfth century was illuminated by Samuel el-Maghribi (d. 1174), who moved from Baghdad to Azerbaijan and settled in its capital, Maragha. He reported that, concerning the support of the Pseudo-Messiah David Alroy, "Jews in Khoy, Salmas, Tabriz, Maragha and Urmia...used to swear in the name of David Alroy, praised him at all their meetings and continued to believe in him as the expected Messiah...."[508] Thus, although Benjamin did not mention any Jews in this area, it is clear that there were Jewish communities there. Azerbaijan entered Jewish history in the thirteenth century.[509]

Samarkand in Transoxiana, to the northeast of Khorasan,[510] is mentioned by Benjamin who states that the city was "on the confines of Persia," inhabited by a large number of Jews (about 50,000). The chief of the Jews of Samarkand was Rabbi Obadiah ha-Nasi, and Benjamin notes: "Among them are wise and very rich men."[511] Bukhara, the important centre of Islamic culture, was, strangely enough, not mentioned by Benjamin, and remained obscure until modern times.[512]

Benjamin mentions Hamadan, a city in west Persia, in which he reports a Jewish community that numbered "30,000 Israelites" and he noticed here the tombs of Mordecai and Esther.[513] The existence of a Jewish community in Hamadan is confirmed by an epistle of Samuel ben 'Ali, which mentions that an academy existed there under the supervision of the

144

Jewish authorities in Baghdad.[514] Actually Hamadan
was one of the main stations on Khorasan road from
Baghdad.[515]

Isfahan served as the capital of Persia, and
Benjamin reports: "...and about 15,000 Israelites
reside there. The chief Rabbi is Sar Shalom, who
has been appointed by the Head of the Captivity to
have jurisdiction over all the Rabbis that are in
the Kingdom of Persia."[516] In fact, this Jewish
community attracted the attention of many Arab and
Persian geographers as many legends and traditions
from various sources are connected with this city.
The Arabic[517] and the Talmudic references[518] both
refer to the same territory and same motive: the
search of the exiled for a new place, similar to
Jerusalem, in which to settle. Different explanations in regard to the origin of Yahudiya (Isfahan)
point to the fact that Jews inhabited Isfahan at an
early date.[519] The community of Isfahan was not
only significant numerically, but also economically.
From the ninth and tenth centuries, the Jews were
active in international trade, when Isfahan became
an important commercial and intellectual centre.[520]
The community had early come under the influence of
the Baghdadian authorities. We learn this, however,
only from Benjamin's report, for, strangely enough,
the epistle of Samuel b. 'Ali makes no mention of
Isfahan.[521] Benjamin's account also shows how important the community was, for the chief Rabbi of
all Persia resided there.[522]

The area of the Persian Gulf has remained neglected by Jewish scholars,[523] though it has been
associated with Jewish events from Islamic times.
Benjamin, speaking generally of the area of the
Persian Gulf, does not mention Bahrain. Similarly,
Siraf on the Persian shore of the Persian Gulf had
a Jewish settlement towards the end of the tenth
century. It was an important trade station[524] which
also served as the centre of commercial activities
for Jews dwelling in the interior of Persia.[525]
Siraf though, was declining in the eleventh century,
which perhaps explains why Benjamin did not mention
it. The island of Kish in the Persian Gulf, however,

145

became the great centre of the overseas trade to India.[526] It is important to realize that Benjamin's account reflects the fact that the Jews moved along with the translocation of the commercial centres in the Persian Gulf, for Benjamin states that Kish is an important market.[527] He reports the existence of a Jewish community there of about 500 Jews.[528] Katifa, located on the east coast of Arabia of the Persian Gulf, also had a considerable Jewish settlement in Medieval Islam,[529] and was a significant city in Benjamin's time.[530] Benjamin notices that the place was famous for its pearl fishery and the existence there of a Jewish community of about 5,000.[531] A reference to "Jews on the islands of the Persian Sea" by R. Hai Gaon (990-1038) might indicate that R. Hai Gaon knew of the existence of Jewish communities in this area.[532] If these "islands" include also the island of Kish, then it could be taken as evidence that Jews resided there over a hundred years previous to Benjamin's journey.

After Benjamin's report on the Persian Gulf, no further mention of Jews there is made in the existing sources.[533]

Footnotes

[1] Baer, A History of the Jews in Christian Spain, I, 46-47.

[2] Ibid., p. 39; Sefer Haqabbala, ed. G.D. Cohen, pp. 96-99.

[3] The Itinerary of Benjamin of Tudela, ed. M. N. Adler, p. 2.

[4] Ibid.

[5] Baron, A Social and Religious History of the Jews, III, 109; IV, 34; Benjamin of Tudela, Sefer Masa'ot, ed. Asher, II, 2, n. 5.

[6] The Itinerary of Benjamin of Tudela, ed. M. N. Adler, p. 2.

[7] Ibid.

[8] Benjamin of Tudela, Sefer Masa'ot, ed. Asher, II, 5, n. 7.

[9] Alkharizi, Tahkemoni, p. 346.

[10] Baer, A History of the Jews in Christian Spain, I. 46.

[11] The name "Sheshet" is used frequently, between the eleventh and fourteenth centuries, by the Jews of Catalonia, Aragon and Provence, but almost nowhere else (Benjamin of Tudela, Sefer Masa'ot, ed. Asher, II, 3-5, n. 6).

[12] One of the most famous of the Spanish Jews in the second half of the twelfth century was Sheshet ben Isaac Benveniste, who was alfaqim (physician) and bailiff to Alphonso II and Pedro II of Aragon. He owned urban and rural properties throughout Aragon and Catalonia. The brothers were famous as scholars, poets, and patrons of learning (Baer, A History of the Jews in Christian Spain, I, 91, 55).

[13] The Itinerary of Benjamin of Tudela, ed. M. N. Adler, p. 2.

[14] Baer, A History of the Jews in Christian Spain, I, 42.

[15] Ibid., I. 45.

[16] Ibid., p. 46.

[17] The Itinerary of Benjamin of Tudela, ed. M. N. Adler, p. 2.

[18] Languedoc and Provence (H. Gross, Gallia Judaica [Paris, 1897], p. 489. A resource of the Jews of Languedoc, see G. Saige, Les Juifs du Languedoc

antérieurement au xive siècle (Paris, 1881). For
rabbinic cultural achievements of Southern French
Jewry, see B.Z. Benedict, "On the History of the
Torah-center in Provence," Tarbiz, XXII (1951), 85-
109.

[19] The Itinerary of Benjamin of Tudela, ed. M.
N. Adler, pp. 2-3.

[20] Dubnov, II, 688; Gross, Gallia Judaica, pp.
404-05.

[21] Neubauer (ed.), Sefer Haqabbala, in Medieval
Jewish Chronicles, I, 82-83; Mann, Texts and Studies
in Jewish History and Literature, I, 17, 31; J.
Régné, Étude sur la Condition des Juifs de Narbonne
du ve aud xive Siècle (Narbonne, 1912), p. 64.

[22] His ancestor, R. Machir, came to Europe in
the time of Charlemange (Régné, pp. 150, 181, 227-
228; Saige, pp. 137-38, No. VIII; pp. 65, 70-71;
A. Zukerman, A Jewish Princedom in Feudal France
768-900 [New York and London, 1972] , pp. 59-60).

[23] Gross, Gallia Judaica, p. 406.

[24] Golb, "New light on the persecution of French
Jews at the time of the First Crusade," p. 16.

[25] Benjamin reports of similar pedigrees as produced by the princes of the independent Jews of
Arabia (The Itinerary of Benjamin of Tudela, ed. M.
N. Adler, p. 48), and again he reports that in Mosul, the head of the Jews was called, "the Nasi of
the seed of David" (ibid., p. 33). When he was in
Baghdad, again he did not fail to remind us that
Daniel, the head of the Jews in captivity, "possesses a book of pedigrees going back as far as David,
King of Israel" (ibid., p. 39). Petachia does the
same while in Baghdad (The Itinerary of Petachia,
ed. Grünhut, p. 9). Alkharizi refers to such pedigrees in Damascus (Alkharizi, pp. 24-25). The desire for nobility reduced to nothing and unreal
descents from biblical persons are mentioned by the
Talmud (Gittin, 57b). Petachia testifies to this

(The Itinerary of Petachia, ed. Grünhut, p. 9).
The author believes that the fact that Benjamin and
Petachia do not forget to mention this fact shows
that they are concerned greatly about pedigrees
which reach back to David, since David in Medieval
Jewish life was associated with the Messianic redemption with which our travellers are much concerned. See the recent work by Zukerman where the
author advances the thesis relating to the establishment of a Principate of the Jews by the Carolingian rulers, and describes the powers and functions of these royal institutions during more than
a century (pp. 35; 59-60; 63; 74-101; 167-168).

[26]The Itinerary of Petachia, ed. Grünhut, p.
29; Jewish Travellers, ed. E.N. Adler, p. 86.

[27]J. Mann, "The Office of the Exilarchate in
Babylonia and Its Branches at the End of the Period
of the Gaonate," A Memorial Book to A. Poznanski
(Jerusalem, 1969), p. 32; Graetz, Geschichte der
Juden, II, 509.

[28]The Itinerary of Benjamin of Tudela, ed. M.
N. Adler, p. 2; Alkharizi, p. 347.

[29]S. Schwarzfuchs, "Supplément bibliographique:
Additions et corrections à l'ouvrage de H. Gross,"
Gallia Judaica (Amsterdam, 1969), p. 29.

[30]Gross, Gallia Judaica, pp. 414-15.

[31]The Itinerary of Benjamin of Tudela, ed. M.
N. Adler, p. 3.

[32]Ibid.

[33]Ibid.

[34]Ibid., pp. 3-4.

[35]Ibid., p. 4. See also I. Twersky, Rabad of
Posquières: A Twelfth Century Talmudist (Cambridge,
Mass., 1962), pp. 21-22; 36-37.

[36] For the name Har Gaash, see Gross, Gallia Judaica, p. 323.

[37] The Itinerary of Benjamin of Tudela, ed. M. N. Adler, p. 3.

[38] Gross, Gallia Judaica, pp. 324-25; Haskins, The Renaissance of the 12th Century, p. 285; Graetz, History of the Jews, III, 370-1; see also the study by A. Azemard, Etude sur les Israélites de Montpellier au moyen âge (Nîmes, 1924), et passim.

[39] The Itinerary of Benjamin of Tudela, ed. M. N. Adler, p. 3.

[40] Ibid.

[41] Gross, Gallia Judaica, p. 279.

[42] The Itinerary of Benjamin of Tudela, ed. M. N. Adler, p. 3.

[43] He is one of those who introduced Spanish culture into France describing the condition of Jewish learning in Provence as he found it in the middle of the twelfth century. He states, "Also in the lands of the Christians there was a remanant of our people. From the earliest days there were among them scholars proficient in the knowledge of Torah and Talmud, but they did not occupy themselves with other sciences because their Torah-study was their [sole] profession and because books about other sciences were not available in their regions" (Judah ibn Tibbon, Introduction to Hobbot ha-Lebabot, ed. A. Zifroni [Jerusalem, 1928], p. 2. This is quoted from I. Twersky's article "Aspects of the Social and Cultural History of Provencal Jewry," Journal of World History, XI [1968], 195).

[44] Benjamin of Tudela, Sefer Masa'ot, ed. Asher, II, 12, n. 21; Twersky, "Aspects of the Social and cultural History of Provencal Jewry," 196-97; Gross, Gallia Judaica, pp. 279, 282.

[45]Concerning other famous sages at Lunel, see Gross, Gallia Judaica, pp. 282-90; Schwarzfuchs, "Supplément bibliographique: Additions et corrections à l'ouvrage de H. Gross," pp. 23-24. Concerning R. Abba Mari, mentioned by Benjamin, see H. Gross, "Notice sur Abba Mari de Lunel," R.E.J., IV (1882), 192-207.

[46]The Itinerary of Benjamin of Tudela, ed. M. N. Adler, p. 4.

[47]Ibid., p. 3.

[48]Concerning this celebrated man, see Twersky, Rabad of Posquières, pp. 12-13.

[49]The Itinerary of Benjamin of Tudela, ed. M. N. Adler, p. 3.

[50]Ibid.

[51]Twersky, Rabad of Posquières, pp. 26-29. R. Asher (for details on him see Gross, Gallia Judaica, pp. 279-81) reminds us of the "mourners of Sion and Jerusalem" mentioned by Benjamin later as dwelling in Arabia (see Chapter VI in the book). Is R. Asher a Karaite? (Concerning this Jewish sect see Dinur [2] I, pp. 247-56.) We can assume safely in the negative since R. Benjamin states clearly, "He is a great scholar of the Talmud." This same R. Asher wrote a book by name The Customs (ed. S. Assaf, Safran Shell Rishonim [Jerusalem, 1935], pp. 129-82) on liturgy and prayers. Extracts of this book are found in an Italian rites manuscript and in one of them is to be found the following passage: "This was explained by my elder brother, R. Jacob Nazir" (Assaf, Safran Shell Rishonim, p. 105). The word Nazir indicates that he led a life similar to that of his brother R. Asher, whom Benjamin titles "the recluse." We can sum up that in the period under discussion, there were, in various places in Europe and the Orient, certain Jews who led an ascetic life, either individually or in isolated groups who had some characteristics similar to the Karaite

Abele Sion (concerning the group see Dinur [2] I, p, 215), and yet, were not Karaites. The common point is that all those pietists were supplicating God for restoration of Zion, and redemption. See also G. Scholem, "Jüdische Mystik in Westeuropa im 12. und 13. Jahrhundert," p. 43.

[52] The Itinerary of Benjamin of Tudela, ed. M. N. Adler, p. 4.

[53] On this eminent man see Twersky, Rabad of Posquières, et passim.

[54] Ibid., pp. 7-10.

[55] The Itinerary of Benjamin of Tudela, ed. M.N. Adler, p. 4.

[56] Gross, Gallia Judaica, p. 447.

[57] The Itinerary of Benjamin of Tudela, ed. M.N. Adler, pp. 4-5.

[58] Ibid., p. 5.

[59] Of the famous sages in this community see Gross, Gallia Judaica, pp. 370-73.

[60] The Itinerary of Benjamin of Tudela, ed. M.N. Adler, p. 5.

[61] Gross, Gallia Judaica, p. 367. For Marseilles, see A. Crémieux, "Les Juifs de Marseilles au moyen âge," R.E.J., XLVI (1903), 1-47, 246-268; XLVII (1903), 62-86, 243-261.

[62] Pfaff, p. 201.

[63] Twersky, Rabad of Posquières, pp. 20-21; 36-37.

[64] Ibid., p. 35; Twersky, "Aspects of the Social and Cultural History of Provencal Jewry," p. 189. H. Malter states: "As center for this widespread learning of the age, Provence stood second only to

Spain. Its geographical situation made it the meeting point for the scientific culture developed under
Arabic influence in Spain and Talmudic learning of
the French Jews.... There also appeared many famous
scholars, who united a comprehensive knowledge of
the Talmud with broad general learning, and who ex-
erted a lasting influence upon later ages" (H. Malter, "Shem Tob Ben Joseph Palquera," J.Q.R., I
[1910], 153). Thus the significance of Provence
has always been recognized. See also Scholem,
"Jüdische Mystik in Westeuropa im 12. und 13. Jahrhundert," pp. 39, 40, 45, 53.

[65]The Itinerary of Benjamin of Tudela, ed. M.
N. Adler, p. 81.

[66]As to the situation of the Jews in northern
France, see Chazan's article "Jewish settlement in
Northern France, 1096-1306," pp. 41-65; Chazan, Med-
ieval Jewry in Northern France, et passim; also
Golb, "New light on the persecution of French Jews
at the time of the First Crusade," especially 18-45.

[67]The Itinerary of Benjamin of Tudela, ed. M.
N. Adler, pp. 79-80.

[68]Aronius, Regesten, p. 131, n. 306.

[69]C. Roth, The History of the Jews of Italy,
(Philadelphia, 1946), p. 71.

[70]Dinur, Israel in Diaspora (1)II, p. 141.

[71]Baron, A Social and Religious History of the
Jews, IV, 20, 25.

[72]Roth, The History of the Jews of Italy, p.
73.

[73]The Itinerary of Benjamin of Tudela, ed. M.N.
Adler, pp. 5-10.

[74]Ibid., pp. 78-79.

[75]Baron, A Social and Religious History of the
Jews, IV, 26.

[76]The Itinerary of Benjamin of Tudela, ed. M.
N. Adler, p. 5.

[77]Roth, The History of the Jews of Italy, P.
75; Dubnov, II, 779.

[78]The Itinerary of Benjamin of Tudela, ed. M.
N. Adler, p. 5.

[79]Baron, A Social and Religious History of the
Jews, IV, 26.

[80]The Itinerary of Benjamin of Tudela, ed. M.
N. Adler, p. 5.

[81]Baron, A Social and Religious History of the
Jews, IV, 26.

[82]The Places which we have previously mentioned
are the only ones visited by R. Benjamin in northern
Italy. It is clear that Benjamin's account in northern Italy is rather incomplete, and there were other
communities which he did not mention. At the same
time, it is certain that any centre of real economic, numerical, or intellectual importance could not
have escaped Benjamin's notice. Thus Roth concludes
that the north, which was later to become the centre
of Italian Jewry, contained as yet only a sparse
Jewish population (Roth, The History of the Jews of
Italy, p. 77).

[83]See Chapter III, n. 33 in the book.

[84]The Itinerary of Benjamin of Tudela, ed. M.
N. Adler, pp. 6-7. For details see Benjamin of
Tudela, Sefer Masa'ot, ed. Asher, II, 25-26, n. 39,
40: Josippon, pp. 314, 371, 392, 394; A. Ibn Zacut,
p. 119B; R. Jehiel, Part I, p. 157; Gittin, 56B; R.
Gershom ben R. Asher from Scarmelo, pp. 23, 62, 104;
Meloh Hofnayim, documents collected and ed. A. Geiger
(Berlin, 1840), p. 31 (Hebrew part).

[85]Roth, The History of the Jews of Italy, p.
78.

[86] The Itinerary of Benjamin of Tudela, ed. M. N. Adler, pp. 5-6.

[87] Heavy taxes were to be levied later on in the fifteenth and sixteenth centuries (Roth, The History of the Jews in Italy, p. 367).

[88] Benjamin of Tudela, Sefer Masa'ot, ed. Asher, II, 20, n. 35.

[89] Ibid., p. 16, n. 32, p. 17, n. 33; Roth, The History of the Jews of Italy, p. 77.

[90] Roth, The History of the Jews of Italy, p. 78.

[91] The Itinerary of Benjamin of Tudela, ed. M. N. Adler, p. 7.

[92] Roth, The History of the Jews of Italy, p. 78.

[93] The Itinerary of Benjamin of Tudela, ed. M. N. Adler, p. 8.

[94] Roth, The History of the Jews of Italy, p. 79; Baron, A Social and Religious History of the Jews, IV, 24.

[95] The Itinerary of Benjamin of Tudela, ed. M. N. Adler, p. 8.

[96] Roth, The History of the Jews of Italy, p. 79.

[97] The Itinerary of Benjamin of Tudela, ed. M. N. Adler, p. 8.

[98] Benjamin of Tudela, Sefer Masa'ot, ed. Asher, II, 28, n. 46.

[99] Baron, A Social and Religious History of the Jews, IV, 24.

100 The Itinerary of Benjamin of Tudela, ed. M. N. Adler, p. 9.

101 Ibid.

102 Roth, The History of the Jews of Italy, p. 79.

103 The Itinerary of Benjamin of Tudela, ed. M. N. Adler, p. 9.

104 Roth, The History of the Jews of Italy, p. 79.

105 Aḥima'as ben Paltiel, The Chronicle of Aḥima'as, ed. B. Klar (Jerusalem, 1944) et passim.

106 The Itinerary of Benjamin of Tudela, ed. M. N. Adler, p. 9.

107 Ibid.

108 Concerning "R. Nathan the expounder," see Benjamin of Tudela, Sefer Masa'ot, ed. Asher, II, 33, n. 51.

109 Baron, A Social and Religious History of the Jews, IV, 21; Roth, The History of the Jews of Italy, p. 80.

110 E.N. Adler, "The Jews in Southern Italy," J.Q.R., XIV (1902), 111-15.

111 The Itinerary of Benjamin of Tudela, ed. M. N. Adler, p. 9.

112 Roth, The History of the Jews of Italy, p. 80.

113 The Itinerary of Benjamin of Tudela, ed. M. N. Adler, p. 9.

114 Ibid., pp. 9-10.

[115]There were other places in the southern part of Italy where Jews lived, although these communities were outside of Benjamin's route (Roth, The History of the Jews of Italy, pp. 80-81).

[116]Hitti, History of the Arabs, p. 606. On the history of a late phase of southern Italian Jewry, see R. Strauss, Die Juden im Königreich sizilien unter Normannen und Staufern (Heidelberg, 1910), et passim.

[117]Roth, The History of the Jews of Italy, p. 81.

[118]Jewish Travellers, ed. E.N. Adler, pp. 210-14.

[119]The Itinerary of Benjamin of Tudela, ed. M. N. Adler, p. 78.

[120]Baron, A Social and Religious History of the Jews, IV, 23.

[121]The Itinerary of Benjamin of Tudela, ed. M. N. Adler, p. 78.

[122]Jews could also be found at Naso, a city between Palermo and Messina, and at Catania, although R. Benjamin did not visit these towns (Roth, The History of the Jews of Italy, p. 82).

[123]Ibid., p. 83.

[124]Ibid., p. 85.

[125]Ibid.

[126]Dinur, Israel in Diaspora (2) II, p. 144.

[127]The Itinerary of Benjamin of Tudela, ed. M. N. Adler, p. 9.

[128]Roth, The History of the Jews of Italy, p. 86.

[129] Ibid.

[130] See the following section.

[131] The Itinerary of Benjamin of Tudela, ed. M. N. Adler, p. 9.

[132] C.M.H., VI, 148-51.

[133] Roth, The History of the Jews of Italy, p. 87.

[134] Baron, A Social and Religious History of the Jews, IV, 308, n. 61 and VI, 28.

[135] The Itinerary of Benjamin of Tudela, ed. M. N. Adler, p. 6.

[136] Roth, The History of the Jews of Italy, p. 92.

[137] Ibid.

[138] Hitti, History of the Arabs, pp. 602-14.

[139] Ibid.

[140] The Itinerary of Benjamin of Tudela, ed. M. N. Adler, pp. 78-79.

[141] Roth, The History of the Jews of Italy, p. 96; Twersky, "Aspects of the Social and Cultural History of Provencal Jewry," p. 191; Haskins, The Renaissance of the 12th Century, pp. 290-93.
It is interesting to note that the Jews were contributing to Italian literature in this period. Spitzer shows us this by an analysis of an anomymous Judeo-Italian elegy (L. Spitzer, "The Influence of Hebrew and Vernacular Poetry on the Judaean Italian Elegy," in Clagett-Post-Reynolds, pp. 118-30). The poem (ibid., pp. 115-117) is written in the tradition of the Hebrew elegies to commemorate the destruction of Jerusalem and the Temple. The text of the poem confirms the belief that the Jews

of the period participated in the Gentiles' cultural life. However, it also shows linguistic
traits of the Jewish community (ibid., p. 119).
According to Spitzer, the structure of the poem
has "Dantean overtones which are made possible by
the use of the Romance vernacular." Spitzer concludes by saying that the "elegy is indeed an Italian poem about Jewish subject matter: Sion Lamen-
tata," (ibid, p. 130).

[142]Rabad testifies to this in his Sefer Haqabbalah, ed. Neubauer, Medieval Jewish Chronicles,
I, 84.

[143]Clagett-Post-Reynolds, pp. 189-207.

[144]At the beginning of the thirteenth century,
Alkharizi visited the Orient. He speaks of the
Jewish community at Aleppo as being intellectually
dead, and mentions a famous scholar, R. Joseph,
Maimonides' student (Dinur, Israel in Diaspora [I]
II, p. 187, n. 14), whom he titles "The Westerner,"
and who came to settle in Aleppo, thus bringing
about an intellectual resurgence there (Alkharizi,
p. 359).

[145]Mann, The Jews in Egypt and Palestine under
the Fatimid Caliphs, I, 218.

[146]Ibid., pp. 175, 247.

[147]Graetz, History of the Jews, III, 444.

[148]Mann, The Jews in Egypt and Palestine under
the Fatimid Caliphs, I, 232.

[149]Ibid.; Dinur, Israel in Diaspora (3) II, pp.
5-6, 115.

[150]"A Letter to the Rabbis of Lunel," ed. and
trans. Twersky, A Maimonides Reader, pp. 481-82.
Hebrew text in Ginze Yerushalayim, ed. S.A. Wurtheimer (Jerusalem, 1896), Part I, pp. 36-37.

[151]Note sections 3 and 4 in this chapter.

152Sharf, p. 132.

153Ibid.

154Ibid., p. 133.

155William of Tyre gives a vivid picture of this uprising, II, 461-67.

156Sharf, p. 134.

157Dubnov, II, 783.

158Ankori, Karaites in Byzantium, pp. 87, 92, 95-97; Prawer, A History of the Latin Kingdom of Jerusalem, I, 16-21.

159Ankori, Karaites in Byzantium, p. 103.

160Ibid., pp. 102, 104.

161Dinur, Israel in Diaspora (2) II, p. 151; Goitein, A Mediterranean Society, I, 39.

162S.D. Goitein, "A Letter of Historical Importance from Seleuceia, Cilicia, Dated 21 July 1137," Tarbiz, XXVII (1958), 521-35.

163Ibid., p. 524. Also other documents published by Mann reflect relations between Egypt and Byzantium and indicate that Egyptian Jews settled in Byzantium (Mann, Texts and Studies in Jewish History and Literature, I, 48-59).

164The Itinerary of Benjamin of Tudela, ed. M. N. Adler, p. 9.

165Corfu was taken by Manuel in 1149. Benjamin's statement, "here ends the Kingdom of Sicily" (ibid., p. 10)—as interpreted by Asher—signifies that Corfu was Benjamin's first stop after leaving the Kingdom of Sicily (Benjamin of Tudela, Sefer Masa'ot, ed. Asher, II, 34, n. 55).

[166] *The Itinerary of Benjamin of Tudela*, ed. M. N. Adler, p. 10.

[167] *Ibid*. Here, too, one of the leaders bore a characteristic Greek name. On the question of the identification of the place, see J. Starr, *The Jews in the Byzantine Empire 641-1204* (Athens, 1939), p. 233; M.A. Denidas, "Leucas or Arta?" *Ipeirotica Khronica*, VI (1931), 23-28.

[168] *The Itinerary of Benjamin of Tudela*, ed. M. N. Adler, p. 10.

[169] *Ibid*. The author questions why Dubnov (II, 785) states that Benjamin found 500 Jews here. Even Asher does not read that number and is in agreement with Adler (Benjamin of Tudela, *Sefer Masa'ot*, ed. Asher, I, 46).

[170] No authority to identify it with the modern village Khrissa (Sharf, p. 137).

[171] *The Itinerary of Benjamin of Tudela*, ed. M. N. Adler, p. 10. Significantly, Benjamin records the rare event of Jewish agriculture, their own land, and their independence in Byzantine land— as had been the original status of the fifteen families on Chios (Sharf, p. 147). It seems that here the Jewish community lived an undisturbed life.

[172] *The Itinerary of Benjamin of Tudela*, ed. M. N. Adler, p. 10.

[173] Benjamin of Tudela, *Sefer Masa'ot*, ed. Asher, II, 36, n. 66.

[174] *The Itinerary of Benjamin of Tudela*, ed. M. N. Adler, p. 10.

[175] *Ibid*.

[176] E. Gibbon, *The Decline and Fall of the Roman Empire*, ed. O. Smeaton, 3 vols. (New York, 1932), III, 270.

[177]The Itinerary of Benjamin of Tudela, ed. M. N. Adler, p. 10.

[178]Ibid., n. 5, and pp. 10-11; Benjamin of Tudela, Sefer Masa'ot, ed. Asher, II, 37, ns. 69, 70, 71; Sharf, p. 137.

[179]Sharf, p. 137.

[180]The Itinerary of Benjamin of Tudela, ed. M. N. Adler, p. 11.

[181]Benjamin of Tudela, Sefer Masa'ot, ed. Asher, II, 38, n. 73; Sharf, p. 149.

[182]Concerning this problem, Sharf maintains that the Wallachians could have acquired Jewish inclinations due to their nomadic nature. In Benjamin's day, the nomadic tribes spread into Greece and Thessaly. To the north, the Wallachians became the allies of the Bulgarians fighting for independence against the Byzantines. These tribes became Christianized (G. Ostrogorsky, History of the Byzantine State, trans. J.M. Hussey [Oxford, 1956], pp. 358-59, n. 4). However, in Thessaly, the Byzantines held contempt for the Wallachians; consequently, the Wallachians became an alien people (Sharf, p. 149). Rejected by local Christians, they could have been attracted to Judaism, although they did not necessarily change their means of support (Sharf, p. 150).

[183]Ostrogorsky, pp. 403-406; 404, n. 1.

[184]The Itinerary of Benjamin of Tudela, ed. M. N. Adler, p. 11.

[185]Ibid.

[186]Ibid.

[187]Ibid.

[188]Ibid.

[189]See Chapter VI of the book.

[190]The text in Mann, "The Messianic Movement in the Time of the Early Crusades," Hattekufah, XXIII (1925), 253; also Starr, The Jews in the Byzantine Empire 641-1204, p. 203, No. 153.

[191]Ankori, Karaites in Byzantium, p. 114; Dinur, Israel in Diaspora (2) II, pp. 151, 157; p. 192, ns. 192-93.

[192]Ankori, Karaites in Byzantium, p. 171.

[193]Sharf, pp. 151-53.

[194]Joinville & Villehardouin, Chronicles of the Crusades, trans. M.R.B. Shaw (London, 1973), p. 59.

[195]S. Runciman, Byzantine Civilization (New York, 1955), p. 172.

[196]Ankori, Karaites in Byzantium, p. 138. Reporting on the city's riots in 1044, Bar Hebraeus states: "And at that time when there were many aliens, Armenians and Arabs and Jews, in the royal city, a great tumult broke out against Constantine the King.... And the king, having inquiried into the cause of the tumult, was told that the aliens had made the tumult, so that they may loot the city. Then the king commanded that there should not remain anyone who had entered it during the last thirty years, and that the men who stayed should have their eyes gouged out. Then there went out about one hundred thousand souls," (Abul Faraj [Bar Hebraeus], Chronography, 2 vols [Oxford, 1932], Vol. I, ed. and trans. E.W. Budge, I, 203).

[197]The Itinerary of Benjamin of Tudela, ed. M. N. Adler, p. 14; Sharf notes correctly that M.N. Adler reads "זרוע יד רומי" (arm of the Roman hand) which is meaningless, and translates "Sea of Marmora" which geographically is incorrect, since the Sea of Marmora does not divide the old city from Pera. The manuscript variant "וזרוע ים רוסיה" is

at least explicable as the Golden Horn (Sharf, p. 158, n. 5).

[198]Sharf, p. 16; Starr, The Jews in the Byzantine Empire, p. 43.

[199]The Itinerary of Benjamin of Tudela, ed. M. N. Adler (Hebrew), p. 16.

[200]Sharf, p. 117.

[201]Ibn Verga states that a predecessor of Manuel Comnenus issued an edict prohibiting the Jews from residing anywhere else except Pera, and restricted their occupations to tanning and shipbuilding. However, this was an older administration (Shevet Jehudah, p. 70).

[202]Sharf, p. 154.

[203]S.W. Baron, The Jewish Community, 3 vols. (Philadelphia, 1948), I, 365; Baron, A Social and Religious History of the Jews, IV, 171. The reevaluation of Pera can be detected also in Starr's work (The Jews in the Byzantine Empire, p. 43).

[204]Ankori, Karaites in Byzantium, p. 141.

[205]Ibid., n. 205.

[206]Ibid., p. 142, ns. 210-211.

[207]Ibid., p. 143.

[208]Ibid.

[209]Sharf, p. 154.

[210]The Itinerary of Benjamin of Tudela, ed. M. N. Adler, p. 11.

[211]Ibid., p. 14.

[212]Sharf, p. 154.

[213] Grünhut, ed., *Sivuv*, p. 36; *Jewish Travellers*, ed. E.N. Adler, p. 91.

[214] *The Itinerary of Petachia*, ed. Grünhut, p. 36; *The Itinerary of Petachia*, ed. E.N. Adler, *Jewish Travellers*, p. 91.

[215] *The Itinerary of Benjamin of Tudela*, ed. M. N. Adler, p. 14.

[216] Sharf, p. 155.

[217] Dinur, *Israel in Diaspora* (2) II, p. 154.

[218] *Ibid.*, p. 156; Starr, *The Jews in the Byzantine Empire*, p. 219, n. 167; p. 221, n. 171.

[219] Sharf, p. 156.

[220] *Ibid.*, p. 157.

[221] *The Itinerary of Benjamin of Tudela*, ed. M. N. Adler, p. 14.

[222] The influence of western ideas centred strongly in Constantinople where a pro-western emperor ruled and a pro-western nobility lived. However, the change also weakened the imperial power outside the capital. This is the reason, Sharf maintains, that the Jews were attracted to provincial settlements (Sharf, p. 157).

[223] Benjamin of Tudela, *Sefer Masa'ot*, ed. Asher, II, 54, n. 112; *The Itinerary of Benjamin of Tudela*, ed. M.N. Adler, p. 14, n. 2.

[224] *The Itinerary of Benjamin of Tudela*, ed. M. N. Adler, p. 14.

[225] Benjamin of Tudela, *Sefer Masa'ot*, ed. Asher, II, 55, ns. 114-15.

[226] *The Itinerary of Benjamin of Tudela*, ed. M. N. Adler, p. 14.

[227] Ibid.

[228] Ibid.

[229] Ibid., pp. 14-15.

[230] Ibid., p. 14.

[231] Sharf, p. 142.

[232] The Itinerary of Benjamin of Tudela, ed. M. N. Adler, p. 11.

[233] Abraham ibn Daud, Sefer HaQabbalah, ed. S.D. Cohen, p. 93.

[234] It is evident, according to Starr, that there was also Jewish silk manufacturing in Corinth (Starr, The Jews in the Byzantine Empire, p. 148, n. 85).

[235] Sharf, p. 145.

[236] Ibid., pp. 145-46.

[237] The Itinerary of Benjamin of Tudela, ed. M. N. Adler, p. 11.

[238] Sharf, p. 147.

[239] Ibid., and p. 160, n. 52.

[240] Toviah Berabi Eliezer, Midrash Lekah Tov (Wilna, 1884), Introduction, p. 1.

[241] R. Abraham ibn Ezra, Commentary on Book of Jonah 1:2.

[242] Alkharizi, p. 191.

[243] See Bibliography.

[244] Note previous section of this book.

[245] The Itinerary of Benjamin of Tudela, ed. M. N. Adler, p. 14.

[246] Ibid., p. 11.

[247] Ibid., p. 10.

[248] Sharf, p. 175.

[249] Ibid., p. 177

[250] Ibid.

[251] Ibid., pp. 178-79, 182-84.

[252] Genizah-documents written in Hebrew characters but mostly in Arabic language, originating from a synagogue in old Cairo and dispersed at present in many libraries all over the world.

[253] Goitein, A Mediterranean Society, I, Preface, vii; E. Strauss, History of the Jews in Egypt and Syria under the Rule of the Mameluks, 2 vols. (Jerusalem, 1944-70), I, 26; S.D. Goitein, "Jewish Society and Institutions under Islam," Journal of World History, XI (1968), 172.

[254] Prawer, A History of the Latin Kingdom of Jerusalem, I, 328-58; Goitein, A Mediterranean Society, I, 36.

[255] William of Tyre, II, 353.

[256] Behâ-Ed-Dîn, "The Life of Saladin," 61-62; S. Lane-Poole, A History of Egypt in the Middle Ages (London, 1968), p. 193.

[257] Prawer, A History of the Latin Kingdom of Jerusalem, I, 439.

[258] Lane-Poole, pp. 194-96.

[259] It seems doubtful whether Benjamin really travelled in upper Egypt. This portion of his account is characterized as legendary and the topography is not precise. The entire picture becomes different once the traveller reports of the Delta.

Here the journey is organized and logical and we
see that the traveller is familiar with the topography of lower Egypt. The distances given are
acceptable.

[260]The Itinerary of Benjamin of Tudela, ed. M.
N. Adler, p. 69.

[261]Ibid., n. 2. Kutz, says Abulfeda, was, after
Fustat, the largest city of Egypt and a centre for
merchants who came from Aden. Makrizi reports:
"C'est le premier endroit où s'arrêtent les caravans
qui viennet des mers de l'Inde, de l'Abyssinie, du
Yêmen et du Hedjaz, en traversant le désert d'Aidab.
Kous renferme un grand nombre de fondouks, de mai-
sons particuliers, de bains, de collèges, de jar-
dins, de vergers et de potagers. Sa population se
compose d'artisans de toute espèce, de marchande,
de savans et de riches propriétaires" (Benjamin of
Tudela, Sefer Masa'ot, ed. Asher, II, 196, n. 338).

[262]Ibid., II, 196, n. 339; The Itinerary of
Benjamin of Tudela, ed. M.N. Adler, p. 69, n. 3.
In the Middle Ages, Fayum was wrongly called Pithom.

[263]The Itinerary of Benjamin of Tudela, ed. M.
N. Adler, p. 69.

[264]A. Edrisi, Géographie d'Edrisi, ed. and
trans. P.A. Jaubert, 2 vols. (Paris, 1836-1840),
I, 308-09.

[265]The Itinerary of Benjamin of Tudela, ed. M.
N. Adler, pp. 70-71.

[266]E.J. Worman, "Notes on the Jews in Fustat
from Cambridge Genizah Documents," J.Q.R., XVIII
(1905), 2.

[267]S.D. Goitein, "The Local Jewish Commnunity
in the Light of the Cairo Geniza Records," J.J.S.,
XII (1961), 133.

[268]Examples in Goitein, A Mediterranean Society,
II, 68-91.

[269] Worman, p. 11.

[270] Goitein, "The Local Jewish Community in the Light of the Cairo Geniza Records," p. 137.

[271] Ibid., p. 138.

[272] Mann, Texts and Studies in Jewish History and Literature, I, 455, n. 17.

[273] Mann, The Jews in Egypt and Palestine under the Fatimid Caliphs, I, 118, 124.

[274] The Itinerary of Benjamin of Tudela, ed. M. N. Adler, p. 70. C. Roth expresses the opinion that it is very likely that this was based on personal observation, and that Benjamin attended the synagogue services in Cairo on the Rejoicing of the Law in September, 1171 and thereafter started his way back home (C. Roth, "Benjamin of Tudela: The Last Stage," Annuario di Studi Ebraici, ed. Elio Toaff [1968-69] p. 48).

[275] Goitein, "The Local Jewish Community in the Light of the Cairo Geniza Records," pp. 138-139; Goitein, A Mediterranean Society, II, 112-21.

[276] J. Mann, "A Second Supplement to 'The Jews in Egypt and in Palestine under the Fatimid Caliphs,'" HUCA, III (1926), 291-92.

[277] Goitein, "The Local Jewish Community in the Light of the Cairo Geniza Records," p. 141.

[278] The Itinerary of Benjamin of Tudela, ed. M. N. Adler, p. 70.

[279] A. Buchler, "The Reading of the Law and Prophets in a Triennial Cycle," J.Q.R., V (1893), 420.

[280] B. Megilla, 29b; Dinur, Israel in Diaspora (4) I, 322.

[281] Hilchot T'Fillah, XIII, 1.

[282]Mann, The Jews in Egypt and Palestine under the Fatimid Caliphs, I, 222, no. 2; Mann, Texts and Studies in Jewish History and Literature, I, 416, n. 3.

[283]Büchler, 421-22; Mann, Texts and Studies in Jewish History and Literature, I, 416-17. The Egyptian, Joseph Sambary in 1672 speaks of them (Neubauer, [ed.], Medieval Jewish Chronicles, I, 118). I. Abrahams observes that Sambary must have had Benjamin's itinerary before him and thus he repeats only Benjamin's account (I. Abrahams, "Sambary and Benjamin of Tudela," J.Q.R., II [1890], 107).

[284]Graetz, Geschichte der Juden, VI, 285.

[285]Büchler, 423. What were the Haphtarahs according to the Palestinian practice? Büchler tries to illuminate this question, looking into a manuscript which lists the Haphtarahs of the first seventy portions according to the Triennial cycle (ibid., 39-42). He traces the Haphtarahs from their origin to the last stage of their Palestinian development (ibid., 1-73). According to him there is no doubt that the present form of the Haphtarahs was also a slow growth from small beginnings. E.N. Adler discovered a genizah fragment which seems to have been a collection of Haphtarahs of the Triennial Cycle. He ascribes it to the eleventh or twelfth century (E.N. Adler, "MS. of Haftaras of the Triennial Cycle," J.Q.R., VIII [1895-96], 528). The fragment adds five late Haphtarahs to the seventy referred to above.

[286]The Itinerary of Benjamin of Tudela, ed. M. N. Adler, pp. 70-71.

[287]Mann, Texts and Studies in Jewish History and Literature, I, 394.

[288]Strauss, History of the Jews in Egypt and Syria under the Rule of the Mameluks, I, 39.

[289]Goitein, A Mediterranean Society, II, 25-26.

[290] Published by Neubauer, "Egyptian Fragments," J.Q.R., VIII (1896), 544-51.

[291] Scroll of Zūtā, ibid., p. 545.

[292] Ibid.

[293] Mann, The Jews in Egypt and Palestine under the Fatimid Caliphs, I, 233.

[294] Strauss, "Saladin and the Jews," 313.

[295] Neubauer, "Egyptian Fragments," p. 553.

[296] Ibid., p. 554.

[297] Ibid.

[298] S.D. Goitein, "The Life of Maimonides in the Light of New Finds from the Cairo Geniza," Peraqim, IV (1966), 31.

[299] Mann, Texts and Studies in Jewish History and Literature, I, 235-36.

[300] Ibid., I, 258-59; Mann, "A Second Supplement to 'The Jews in Egypt and in Palestine under the Fatimid Caliphs,'" p. 296.

[301] The Itinerary of Benjamin of Tudela, ed. M. N. Adler, p. 71.

[302] Jewish Travellers, ed. E.N. Adler, p. 229.

[303] Strauss, "Saladin and the Jews," p. 313.

[304] Goitein, A Mediterranean Society, II, 27.

[305] Mann, "A Second Supplement to 'The Jews in Egypt and in Palestine under the Fatimid Caliphs,'" p. 293.

[306] Benjamin of Tudela, Sefer Masa'ot, ed. Asher, II, 197, n. 340. D. Neustadt rejects the idea that the office of Nagid was created to compete with the

office of Exilarch (D. Neustadt, "Some Problems Concerning the 'Negidut' in Egypt during the Middle Ages," _Zion_, IV [1938], 148.

[307] Strauss, "Saladin and the Jews," p. 314.

[308] Mann, _Texts and Studies in Jewish History and Literature_, I, 395.

[309] Strauss, _History of the Jews in Egypt and Syria_, I, 46; Mann, _Texts and Studies in Jewish History and Literature_, I, 230.

[310] Strauss, "Saladin and the Jews," pp. 315-16; S. Assaf, (ed), "Collection of R. Samuel b. 'Ali Letters and of His Contemporaries," _Tarbiz_, I (1929-30), Book I, 115.

[311] Mann, _Texts and Studies in Jewish History and Literature_, I, 229; Assaf, (ed), "Collection of R. Samuel b. 'Ali Letters and of His Contemporaries," Book 3, pp. 66-77; specifically pp. 68-69. One of the chief points of contention was the problem of Semikhah (ordination). On "ordination" see the discussion by I. Bornstein, "The Custom of Ordination and Its History," _Hattekufah_, IV (1919), 393-426.

[312] Strauss, "Saladin and the Jews," p. 316.

[313] _Ibid._

[314] _Ibid._; Mann, _Texts and Studies in Jewish History and Literature_, I, 236.

[315] _The Itinerary of Benjamin of Tudela_, ed. M. N. Adler, p. 73, n. 3.

[316] _Ibid._, p. 73.

[317] _Ibid._, p. 74.

[318] Graetz, _History of the Jews_, III, 445.

[319] Richard J.H. Gottheil, "A Cairo Synagogue Eleventh Century Document," _J.Q.R._, XIX (1907), 502;

S. Assaf, "An Ancient Synagogue in Damoha (Egypt),"
Texts and Studies in Jewish History (Jerusalem,
1946), p. 155.

[320]The Itinerary of Benjamin of Tudela, ed. M.
N. Adler, pp. 76-77.

[321]Jewish Travellers, ed. E.N. Adler, p. 222.

[322]The Itinerary of Benjamin of Tudela, ed. M.
N. Adler, p. 77.

[323]For other cities in which Benjamin found existing Jewish communities, ibid., pp. 74, 77, 78.
See also Worman, p. 10; L. Goldziher, "Bücherbesprechungen," Zeitschrift des Deutschen Palästina-
Vereins, XXVIII (Leipzig, 1905), 153.

[324]Mann, The Jews in Egypt and Palestine under
the Fatimid Caliphs, I, 202; II, 239-40.

[325]Ibid., II, 259, 317.

[326]D. Neustadt, "Contributions to the Economic
History of the Jews in Egypt in the Middle Ages,"
Zion, II (1937), 246, n. 6.

[327]The Itinerary of Benjamin of Tudela, ed. M.
N. Adler, p. 73.

[328]Neustadt, "Contributions to the Economic History of the Jews In Egypt in the Middle Ages," p.
247.

[329]Jewish Travellers, ed. E.N. Adler, pp. 161,
171, 222, 225, 230, 231.

[330]Neustadt, "Contributions to the Economic History of the Jews in Egypt in the Middle Ages," p.
247.

[331]Strauss, History of the Jews in Egypt and
Syria under the Rule of the Mameluks, I, 28, 30.

[332]Ibid., p. 30. The following lines, composed

by one of the educated Moslems living then, reflects feelings of anger accumulated within the Moslem population: "The Jews of this time attained their goals and became the rulers. Theirs is the power and the glory; among them is to be found the confidential adviser and even the king: Sons of Egypt, this is my advice to you—be Jews since even the heavens have been Judaized" (ibid.).

[333]Strauss, "Saladin and the Jews," p. 306.

[334]Ibid.

[335]Of this fanatic atmosphere during the Mameluks period we have the evidence of Bertinoro who visited Egypt at the end of the fifteenth century. He states that, "the Mameluks were at this time in the habit of beating and plundering Jews as well as Arabs" (Jewish Travellers, ed. E.N. Adler, p. 231).

[336]Strauss, "Saladin and the Jews," p. 309.

[337]Ibid., pp. 313-14.

[338]The Itinerary of Benjamin of Tudela, ed. M. N. Adler, p. 16.

[339]Ibid., p. 30.

[340]The Itinerary of Petachia, ed. E.N. Adler, Jewish Travellers, p. 85; The Itinerary of Petachia, ed. Grünhut, p. 28.

[341]The Itinerary of Benjamin of Tudela, ed. M. N. Adler, p. 30, n. 3; p. 16, n. 2; Mann, The Jews in Egypt and Palestine under the Fatimid Caliphs, I, 25-26.

[342]The Itinerary of Benjamin of Tudela, ed. M. N. Adler, p. 29.

[343]Mann, Texts and Studies in Jewish History and Literature, I, 251-52.

[344]The Itinerary of Benjamin of Tudela, ed. M.

N. Adler, p. 30.

[345]Mann, Texts and Studies in Jewish History and Literature, I, 251.

[346]W. Bacher, "Das Gaonat in Palästina und das Exilarchat in Aegypten," J.Q.R., XV (1908), 95.

[347]Maimonides' commentary to Bekhoroth, 4, 4.

[348]The Itinerary of Petachia, ed. E.N. Adler, Jewish Travellers, p. 71; The Itinerary of Petachia, ed. Grünhut, p. 10.

[349]Mann, Texts and Studies in Jewish History and Literature, I, 254; 258-59.

[350]The Itinerary of Benjamin of Tudela, ed. M. N. Adler, p. 31.

[351]Ibid.

[352]G. Le Strange, Palestine under the Moslems (Beirut, 1965), p. 361.

[353]Ibid., p. 362.

[354]The Itinerary of Benjamin of Tudela, ed. M. N. Adler, p. 32.

[355]Alkharizi, pp. 358-63.

[356]The Itinerary of Benjamin of Tudela, ed. M. N. Adler, p. 33.

[357]The Itinerary of Petachia, ed. Grünhut, p. 5. On the term "Assur" see Mann, "Texts and Studies in Jewish History and Literature, I, 477.

[358]The Itinerary of Benjamin of Tudela, ed. M. N. Adler, p. 33.

[359]The Itinerary of Petachia, ed. E.N. Adler, Jewish Travellers, pp. 67-68; The Itinerary of Petachia, ed. Grunhut, pp. 5-7.

[360] Alkharisi, p. 365.

[361] See next section of this chapter.

[362] Graetz, History of the Jews, III, 444.

[363] Strauss, History of the Jews in Egypt and Syria under the Rule of the Mameluks, I, 46-47.

[364] Alkharizi, pp. 358-63. See note 144 above.

[365] Mann, Texts and Studies in Jewish History and Literature, I, 266, and poem cited there on pp. 269-305 to reflect the literary ability of the Orient.

[366] Mann, The Jews in Egypt and Palestine under the Fatimid Caliphs, I, 230; II, 288-89.

[367] Ibid., II, 289.

[368] The Itinerary of Petachia, ed. E.N. Adler, Jewish Travellers, p. 69; The Itinerary of Petachia, ed. Grünhut, p. 7.

[369] Benjamin and Petachia list other cities in Syria where they found existing Jewish communities (The Itinerary of Benjamin of Tudela, ed. M.N. Adler, pp. 30, 31, 32, 33; The Itinerary of Petachia, ed. Grünhut, pp. 4-5, 28; The Itinerary of Petachia, ed. E.N. Adler, Jewish Travellers, pp. 67, 85.

[370] Ibn Jubayr, The Travels of Ibn Jubayr, trans. and ed. R.J.C. Broadhurst (London, 1952), pp. 316-17.

[371] Strauss, History of the Jews in Egypt and Syria under the Rule of the Mameluks, I, 36.

[372] Ibid., p. 37.

[373] A.S. Tritton and H.A.R. Gibb, "The First and Second Crusades from an Anonymous Syriac Chronicle," J.R.A.S. (April 1933), p. 291.

176

[374] The Itinerary of Benjamin of Tudela, ed. M. N. Adler, p. 16.

[375] Ibid., p. 17.

[376] Ibid., p. 18.

[377] See Chapter IV, section 1.

[378] H. Lammens, "Sha'm," Encyclopaedia of Islam, IV (1934), 296.

[379] The Itinerary of Benjamin of Tudela, ed. M. N. Adler, p. 18.

[380] Prawer, "The Jews in the Latin Kingdom of Jerusalem," p. 70, n. 37.

[381] Neustadt, "Contributions to the Economic History of the Jews in Egypt in the Middle Ages," p. 222. See references cited in footnote 387 below.

[382] Dinur, Israel in Diaspora (2)II, p. 24; Mann, The Jews in Egypt and Palestine under the Fatimid Caliphs, II, 259, 286; Mann, Texts and Studies in Jewish History and Literature, I, 80, 231, 249; Assaf (ed.), "Collection of R. Samuel b. 'Ali Letters and of His Contemporaries," Book II, 62-63.

[383] Strauss, History of the Jews in Egypt and Syria under the Rule of the Mameluks, I, 33. See also references cited in footnote 387 below.

[384] Strauss, History of the Jews in Egypt and Syria under the Rule of the Mameluks, I, 34; Dinur reaches the same number (Israel in Diaspora [2] II, p. 168, n. 15).

[385] Strauss, History of the Jews in Egypt and Syria under the Rule of the Mameluks, I, 34.

[386] Ibid.; H. Lammens, La Syrie, Précis Historique, 2 vols. (Beyrouth, 1921), I, 120; Lammens, "Sha'm," Encyclopaedia of Islam, IV, 298-99.

[387]Prawer, "The Jews in the Latin Kingdom of Jerusalem," p. 79. See also Goitein, "Jewish Society and Institutions under Islam," p. 173; E. Strauss, "Prolegomena to the Medieval History of Oriental Jewry," J.Q.R., L. (1959), 55-68, 147-66; N. Golb, "The Topography of the Jews of Medieval Egypt," J.N.E.S., XXIV (1965), 251-70.

[388]W.B. Stevenson, "The First Crusade," C.M.H., V, 278.

[389]F. Lebrecht, "Essay on the Caliphate of Baghdad During the Latter Half of the Twelfth Century," Benjamin of Tudela, Sefer Masa'ot, ed. Asher, II, 353.

[390]Ibid., p. 354.

[391]Ibid., pp. 378-387; A. Ben Jacob, A History of the Jews in Iraq from the End of the Gaonic Period to the Present Time (Jerusalem, 1965), p. 16.

[392]Ben Jacob, p. 16; Mann, Texts and Studies in Jewish History and Literature, I, 208.

[393]Asher gives the Jewish population at 1,000 (Benjamin of Tudela, Sefer Masa'ot, ed. Asher, I, 100). Petachia makes the same estimate (The Itinerary of Petachia, ed. Grünhut, p. 8), a fact which is inconsistent, however, with his other statement that "The Head of the Academy has about two thousand disciples at once, and more than five hundred sit around him" (ibid.) M.N. Adler used the British Museum and Casanatense manuscripts which have the reading "forty thousand." According to him, these manuscripts have the preferable reading (The Itinerary of Benjamin of Tudela, ed. M.N. Adler, p. 39 and n. 1).

[394]The Itinerary of Benjamin of Tudela, ed. M. N. Adler, pp. 35-38. See Ibn Jubayr's description of Baghdad, The Travels of Ibn Jubayr, pp. 226-39.

[395]The Itinerary of Benjamin of Tudela, ed. M.

N. Adler, p. 35.

[396] Ibid.

[397] The Itinerary of Petachia, ed. E.N. Adler, Jewish Travellers, pp. 71-72; The Itinerary of Petachia, ed. Grunhut, pp. 10-11.

[398] The Itinerary of Petachia, ed. E.N. Adler, Jewish Travellers, p. 84; The Itinerary of Petachia, ed. Grünhut, p. 27.

[399] The Itinerary of Petachia, ed. E.N. Adler, Jewish Travellers, p. 71; The Itinerary of Petachia, ed. Grünuut, p. 10.

[400] The Itinerary of Benjamin of Tudela, ed. M. N. Adler, pp. 39-41.

[401] Assaf (ed.), "Collection of R. Samuel b. 'Ali Letters and of His Contemporaries," Book I, p. 118.

[402] Nathan the Babylonian's report in Medieval Jewish Chronicles, ed. Neubauer, II, 85-87.

[403] The Itinerary of Benjamin of Tudela, ed. M. N. Adler, p. 41.

[404] See the former section.

[405] E.N. Adler, "The Installation of the Egyptian Nagid," J.Q.R., IX (1897), 717-20.

[406] As a matter of fact, no full text of a Caliph's charter of appointment of an Exilarch has been preserved. According to Baron it probably was similar to the decrees issued in regard to the Nestorian Catholicoi (Baron, A Social and Religious History of the Jews, V, 6). Such a decree, issued by Al Muktafi II in 1138, was addressed to the Catholicoi. See the text in D.D. Mingana, ed. and trans. of "A Charter of Protection Granted to the Nestorian Church in A.D. 1138 by Muktafi II, Caliph of Baghdad," Bulletin of the John Rylands Library, X (1926), 132.

[407] The Itinerary of Petachia, ed. E.N. Adler, Jewish Travellers, pp. 70-71; The Itinerary of Petachia, ed. Grünhut, p. 9.

[408] Ibid.

[409] Mann, Texts and Studies in Jewish History and Literature, I, 228.

[410] On Samuel ben 'Ali, see further on in the present section.

[411] "Batlanim" is a talmudic term which refers to scholars who uninterruptedly devoted themselves to cummunal affairs (Megilla 5a:21b; Sanhedrin 17b).

[412] The Itinerary of Benjamin of Tudela, ed. M. N. Adler, p. 39.

[413] Ibid.; Mann, Texts and Studies in Jewish History and Literature, I, 215.

[414] Medieval Jewish Chronicles, ed. Neubauer, II, 87.

[415] Mann, Texts and Studies in Jewish History and Literature, I, 216.

[416] About several of these titles see Mann, The Jews in Egypt and Palestine under the Fatimid Caliphs, I, 277-79.

[417] The Itinerary of Benjamin of Tudela, ed. M. N. Adler, p. 39.

[418] The Itinerary of Petachia, ed. E.N. Adler, Jewish Travellers, pp. 69-70; The Itinerary of Petachia, ed. Grünhut, p. 8.

[419] Dinur, Israel in Diaspora, (3)I, p. 7.

[420] Mann, Texts and Studies in Jewish History and Literature, I, 217, 227; Assaf (ed.), "Collection of R. Samuel b. 'Ali Letters and of His Contemporaries," Book I, pp. 110-11.

[421]The Itinerary of Petachia, ed. E.N. Adler, Jewish Travellers, p. 70; The Itinerary of Petachia, ed. Grünhut, p. 8.

[422]Ibid.

[423]Assaf (ed.), "Collection of R. Samuel b. 'Ali Letters and of His Contemporaries," Book I, p. 111.

[424]His activities have been described in detail by S. Poznansky, Babylonische Geonim im nachgaonäischen Zeitalter (Berlin, 1914), pp. 15-36, 54-61; Assaf (ed.), "Collection of R. Samuel b. 'Ali Letters and of His Contemporaries," Book I, pp. 102-103.

[425]The Itinerary of Petachia, ed. E.N. Adler, Jewish Travellers, p. 73; The Itinerary of Petachia, ed. Grünhut, p. 12.

[426]For such letters of recommendation, see S.D. Sasson, "Iggeroth Paras We-Teman," Hazofeh, IX (1925), 210, 214.

[427]Does this throw light on the intellectual standard of Baghdad women in this century? It is quite interesting to quote here R. Petachia to illuminate the status of the woman in Baghdad at that time, which contrasted with his native country's custom: "Nobody there looks upon any woman, nor does anybody go into the house of his friend lest he should see the wife of that neighbour, who would immediately say unto him: Insolent man, wherefor art thou come? But he knocks with a tin (knocken), when the other comes forth and speaks to him," (The Itinerary of Petachia, ed. E.N. Adler, Jewish Travellers, p. 69). No doubt we can detect here the Moslem influence upon the Jews, according to which the woman should not be seen by others. Ibn Jubayr states: "Muslim women,...wrap their cloaks about them, and are veiled," (p. 350); see also Meshullam ben R. Menahem's report (1481), Jewish Travellers, ed. E.N. Adler, p. 158. This same custom still exists today in those areas.

[428] The Itinerary of Petachia, ed. E.N. Adler, Jewish Travellers, p. 71; The Itinerary of Petachia, ed. Grünhut, pp. 9-10.

[429] The Itinerary of Petachia, ed. E.N. Adler, Jewish Travellers, p. 70; The Itinerary of Petachia, ed. Grünhut, p. 9.

[430] Assaf (ed.), "Collection of R. Samuel b. 'Ali Letters and of His Contemporaries," Book II, pp. 58-62; Book III, p. 33.

[431] Meir ben Baruch of Rothenburg, Sha'are Teshuboth; Responsa of R. Meir ben Baruch of Rothenburg, ed. M.A. Blach (Berlin, 1891-1892), P. 64; Poznanski, Babylonische Geonim im nachgaonäischen Zeitalter, p. 54; Ben Jacob, p. 26.

[432] The Itinerary of Petachia, ed. E.N. Adler, Jewish Travellers, p. 73; The Itinerary of Petachia, ed. Grünhut, p. 12.

[433] J. Mann, "An Answer from R. Samuel b. 'Ali, Gaon of Baghdad," Hazofeh LeHochmat Yisrael, VI (1922), 106; Mann, Texts and Studies in Jewish History and Literature, I, 214.

[434] "Maimonides' Treatise on Resurrection; The Original Arabic and Ibn Tibbon's Hebrew Translation and Glossary," ed. J. Finkel, P.A.A.J.R., IX (1939), 65, 67.

[435] A. Harkavy, "Fragment einer Apologie des Maimonidischen," Zeitschrift für hebräische Bibliographie, trans. H. Brody (Berlin, 1897), II, 125; "An Answer from R. Samuel b. 'Ali, Gaon of Baghdad," p. 106.

[436] Moses Maimonides, Kobez Teshubot ha-Rambam, ed. A. Lichtenberg, 2 vols. (Leipzig, 1859), II, 8-9.

[437] The Itinerary of Petachia, ed. E.N. Adler, Jewish Travellers, p. 69; The Itinerary of Petachia, ed. Grünhut, p. 10.

[438] Harkavy, "Fragment einer Apologie des Maimonidischen," 125.

[439] A fragment of it was discovered and published by Harkavy, ibid., II, 125-58, 181-88.

[440] Moses Maimonides, Maimonidean Responsa, ed.
A.H. Freimann (Jerusalem, 1934), No. 98.

[441] Ibid., No. 99.

[442] Assaf (ed.), "Collection of R. Samuel b.
'Ali Letters and of His Contemporaries," Book I,
pp. 126-27; Book II, pp. 62-63.

[443] Poznanski, Babylonische Geonim im nachgaonäischen Zeitalter, p. 32.

[444] Maimonides, Kobez Teshubot ha-Rambam, II,
31; Maimonides, Maimonidean Responsa, Nos. 67, 68,
69.

[445] Mann, Texts and Studies in Jewish History
and Literature, I, 237-38; Assaf (ed.), "Collection
of R. Samuel b. 'Ali Letters and of His Contemporaries," Book I, p. 126; Book II, pp. 62-70; Ben
Jacob, p. 22.

[446] For example, Zechariah b. Berakhel (Assaf
(ed.), "Collection of R. Samuel b. 'Ali Letters and
of His Contemporaries," Book I, p. 107; Book II, p.
62).

[447] This energy is reflected in the letters generally and especially in the one published by Assaf
(ed.), "Collection of R. Samuel b. 'Ali Letters and
of His Contemporaries," Book II, pp. 62-70.

[448] The Itinerary of Benjamin of Tudela, ed. M.
N. Adler, p. 39.

[449] Ben Jacob, pp. 35-36; Baron, A Social and
Religious History of the Jews, III, 158; V, 85; VII,
155; VIII, 63, 141, 249.

[450] The Itinerary of Benjamin of Tudela, ed. M. N. Adler, p. 42.

[451] The Itinerary of Petachia, ed. Grünhut, p. 16.

[452] Alkharizi, p. 365.

[453] Between 1193 and 1194 (Mann, Texts and Studies in Jewish History and Literature, I, 219).

[454] Ibn Jubayr being in Baghdad in June 1184 wrote: "Today we may apply to her the saying of the lover: 'You are not you, and the houses are not those I knew'" (p. 239).

[455] Prawer, A History of the Latin Kingdom of Jerusalem, II, 413; Mann, Texts and Studies in Jewish History and Literature, I, 229.

[456] In fact, by the twelfth century the centre of gravity already had begun shifting to Western Europe. Observers, like Maimonides in his letter to the sages of Lunel (see section I in the present chapter), could already foresee that western Jewry would soon become the chief bearers of Judaism. However, this pessimistic description of the neglect of Jewish learning in the Orient must have sounded exaggerated to Maimonides' contemporaries before the end of the twelfth century.

[457] A.H. Layard, Discoveries among the Ruins of Nineveh and Babylon (New York, 1875), p. 446.

[458] The Itinerary of Benjamin of Tudela, ed. M. N. Adler, p. 35.

[459] Benjamin of Tudela, Sefer Masa'ot, ed. Asher, II, 135, n. 258.

[460] The Itinerary of Benjamin of Tudela, ed. M. N. Adler, p. 51.

[461] Benjamin of Tudela, Sefer Masa'ot, ed. Asher, II, 149, n. 286.

[462] The Itinerary of Benjamin of Tudela, ed. M. N. Adler, pp. 34-35.

[463] The correspondence of Samuel b. 'Ali Gaon contains a long list of places inhabited by Jews: some of these cities are not mentioned by our twelfth-century travellers. Such are Dakuka, Wasit, Kirkuk, Mardin, Seruj, El-Kal'ah (Assaf [ed.]), "Collection of R. Samuel b. 'Ali Letters and of His Contemporaries," Book III, p. 58, 28, 38, 19-20, 54, 59; Dinur, Israel in Diaspora (2)II, pp. 33-34 and p. 33, ns. 10-12, p. 34, ns. 13-15).

[464] The Itinerary of Petachia, ed. E.N. Adler, Jewish Travellers, p. 71; The Itinerary of Petachia, ed. Grünhut, p. 10.

[465] Being now on the Persian borders, Benjamin lists other places located around Baghdad in which Jewish communities could be found (The Itinerary of Benjamin of Tudela, ed. M.N. Adler, pp. 42, 43, 45).

[466] Ibid., p. 48.

[467] Ibid. See footnote 51 in this chapter.

[468] Ibid., p. 67.

[469] Ibid. Marco Polo divided India into the greater, lesser and middle, and called middle India "Abascia" (Abyssinia); and he included the coast of Arabia, as far as the Persian Gulf, as part of that middle division. Then Marco Polo goes on to describe Abyssinia as an extensive country governed by three Christian and three Mohammedan kings and notes that the Jews are numerous in the country (Marco Polo, The Book of Ser Marco Polo, the Venetian, Concerning the Kingdoms and Marvels of the East, trans. and ed. Henry Yule, 2 vols. [New York, 1926)], II, 427-31; see also H. Yule's notes on pp. 432-37).

[470] Beazley, II, 260.

185

[471] Jewish Travellers, ed. E.N. Adler, pp. 238-239. See end of note 533 below.

[472] A Jewish community had existed in Aden from time immemorial. A modern Jewish traveller, Jacob Saphir, devotes Vol. II, Chapters I-X of his Eben Saphir to give a full account of the Jews of Aden (J.E. Saphir, Travels of Rabbi Jacob Saphir, 2 vols. [Mainz, 1847]. He reports the area of Aden to be desolate and extremely hot, with mountains covered with black stones and without good drinking water (ibid., II, 3-4). He goes on to say that the Jews he visited in Aden were poor and oppressed, although it is traditionally reported that they have occupied that territory from time immemorial (ibid., 9, 14). Many Jews from Yemen joined them as a result of persecution. Their religious customs are similar to those of the Yemenite Jews (ibid., 8; S.B. Miles, The Countries and Tribes of the Persian Gulf, 2 vols. [London, 1919-20], II, 375).

[473] Mann, "A Second Supplement to 'The Jews in Egypt and in Palestine under Fatimid Caliphs,'" p. 301.

[474] Ed. E. Strauss, "A Journey to India," Zion, IV (1938), 217-31.

[475] Note Chapter VII in the book.

[476] Strauss, "A Journey to India," p. 227.

[477] Poznanski, Babylonische Geonim im nachgaonäischen Zeitalter, 111.

[478] The Itinerary of Benjamin of Tudela, ed. M. N. Adler, p. 48.

[479] Strauss, "A Journey to India," p. 223.

[480] Ibid., p. 225.

[481] Mann, The Jews in Egypt and Palestine under the Fatimid Caliphs, I, 257.

186

[482] Strauss, "A Journey to India," p. 225.

[483] Eldad ha-Dani, ed. Epstein, pp. xii, xiii, xvii.

[484] Neubauer, "Eldad the Danite," J.Q.R., III (1891), 542.

[485] Strauss, "A Journey to India," p. 226.

[486] W.J. Fischel, "Azarbaijan in Jewish History," P.A.A.J.R., XXII (1953), 1; W.J. Fischel, "The Jews of Central Asia (Khorasan) in Medieval Hebrew and Islamic Literature," Historia Judaica, VII (1945), 29.

[487] Fischel, "Azarbaijan in Jewish History," p. 1.

[488] W.J. Fischel, "Isfahan," The Joshua Starr Memorial Volume (New York, 1953), p. 111.

[489] In the Gaonic literature it is called also by its ancient name of "Elam" (Le Strange, The Lands of Eastern Caliphate, p. 245). There are references to the Jewish communities of Elam and their customs (Mann, "The Responsa of the Babylonian Gaonim as a Source of Jewish History," VII, 471.

[490] The Itinerary of Benjamin of Tudela, ed. M. N. Adler, p. 51. Benjamin's report on the coffin of Daniel, pp. 52-53.

[491] The Itinerary of Petachia, ed. Grünhut, p. 20. On the legends of Daniel's tomb, see R. Jehiel, Part I, pp. 130-31; Benjamin of Tudela, Sefer Masa'ot, ed. Asher, II, 152, n. a; The Itinerary of Petachia, ed. Benisch, p. 98, n. 69; Uri Ben Simeon, pp. 80-82; Le Strange, The Lands of Eastern Caliphate, p. 240; A.H. Layard, Early Adventures in Persia, Susiana, and Babylonia, 2 vols. (New York, 1887), II, 295; E. N. Adler, Jews in Many Lands, p. 224.

[492] On the site of Shushan, see Layard, Early Adventures in Persia, Susiana, and Babylonia, II, 295.

[493]On this locality see Benjamin of Tudela, Sefer Masa'ot, ed. Asher, II, 155, n. 293.

[494]The Itinerary of Benjamin of Tudela, ed. M. N. Adler, p. 53.

[495]The Itinerary of Petachia, ed., E.N. Adler, Jewish Travellers, p. 71; The Itinerary of Petachia, ed. Grünhut, p. 10.

[496]The Itinerary of Benjamin of Tudela, ed. M. N. Adler, pp. 16-17, 53-54. The mountains are evidently grouped by him with the range of Chafton or Zagros (Beazley, II, 255).

[497]See Chapter VI in the book.

[498]The Itinerary of Benjamin of Tudela, ed. M. N. Adler, p. 54.

[499]Benjamin of Tudela, Sefer Masa'ot, ed. Asher, II, 158, n. 296.

[500]The Itinerary of Benjamin of Tudela, ed. M. N. Adler, p. 54.

[501]Layard, Discoveries among the Ruins of Nineveh and Babylon, pp. 330-31, a note on p. 331.

[502]Mann, Texts and Studies in Jewish History and Literature, I, 480. See also W.J. Fischel, "Kurdistan," J.S.S., VI (1944), 195-226.

[503]The Itinerary of Benjamin of Tudela, ed. M. N. Adler, p. 54.

[504]Ibid., pp. 54-56.

[505]Fischel, "Azarbaijan in Jewish History," p. 2.

[506]The Itinerary of Benjamin of Tudela, ed. M. N. Adler, p. 40.

[507]Fischel, "Azarbaijan in Jewish History," p. 3; Assaf (ed.), "Collection of R. Samuel b. 'Ali

Letters and of His Contemporaries," Book I, p. 120;
Book III, pp. 22-24.

[508]Fischel, "Azarbaijan in Jewish History," p.
3; Joseph ha-Cohen, pp. 35-36.

[509]Fischel, "Azarbaijan in Jewish History," p.
4.

[510]Khorasan is mentioned by Benjamin as one of
the areas over which the authority of the Exilarch
extended. He even gives details in regard to some
of its cities.

[511]The Itinerary of Benjamin of Tudela, ed. M.
N. Adler, p. 59. For more on the city see Benjamin
of Tudela, Sefer Masa'ot, ed. Asher, II, 170, n. 309.

[512]Fischel, "The Jews of Central Asia (Khorasan)
in Medieval Hebrew and Islamic Literature," p. 43.

[513]The Itinerary of Benjamin of Tudela, ed. M.
N. Adler, p. 57. On the tombs see Yihus Ha-Avot,
p. 80; R. Gershom ben R. Asher from Scarmelo, pp.
37-38; R. Jehiel, Part I, p. 132; E. Herzfeld,
Archaeological History of Iran (London, 1935), p.
105; W.J. Fischel, "The History of Persian Jews
during the Sefevid Dynasty," Zion, II (1937), 291;
Ish Shalom, "Tradition of Graves in Palestine," pp.
234-35.

[514]Assaf (ed.), "Collection of R. Samuel b. 'Ali
Letters and of His Contemporaries," Book I, p. 122;
Book III, p. 26.

[515]Rabinowitz, Jewish Merchants' Adventures, p.
49.

[516]The Itinerary of Benjamin of Tudela, ed. M.
N. Adler, p. 58.

[517]Le Strange, The Lands of Eastern Caliphate,
p. 203.

[518]Sanhedrin 94a.

189

[519] Fischel, "Isfahan," pp. 113-14; Rabinowitz, Jewish Merchants' Adventures, p. 48.

[520] Mann, Texts and Studies in Jewish History and Literature, II, 68, 104.

[521] Assaf (ed.), "Collection of R. Samuel b. 'Ali Letters and of His Contemporaries," Book I, pp. 120-25.

[522] For a description of the geography of the area see H.B. Hynch, "Across Luristan to Ispahan," Royal Geographical Society, Proceedings, New Series (Sept. 1890), pp. 538, 542, 544, 546.

[523] W.J. Fischel, "The Region of the Persian Gulf and Its Jewish Settlements in Islamic Times," Alexander Marx Jubilee Volume (New York, 1950), p. 203.

[524] Ibid., p. 207.

[525] W.J. Fischel, Jews in the Economic and Political Life of Medieval Islam (New York, 1969), p. 32.

[526] The Itinerary of Benjamin of Tudela, ed. M. N. Adler, pp. 62-63; Benjamin of Tudela, Sefer Masa 'ot, ed. Asher, II, 175, n. 315.

[527] P.M. Sykes, Ten Thousand Miles in Persia, or Eight Years in Iran (London, 1902), p. 58. On its commercial significance, see Chapter VII in the book.

[528] The Itinerary of Benjamin of Tudela, ed. M. N. Adler, p. 63.

[529] Fischel, "The Region of the Persian Gulf and its Jewish Settlements in Islamic Times," p. 208.

[530] Benjamin of Tudela, Sefer Masa'ot, ed. Asher, II, 178, n. 317; S.B. Miles, The Countries and Tribes of the Persian Gulf, 2 vols. (London, 1919-1920), II, 415.

[531] The Itinerary of Benjamin of Tudela, ed. M.

N. Adler, p. 63.

[532]Mann, "The Responsa of the Babylonian Gaonim as a Source of Jewish History," VII, 471.

[533]Fischel, "The Region of the Persian Gulf and Its Jewish Settlements in Islamic Times," p. 208. The settlements of Jews in India and China before the end of the twelfth century are meagre. As Godbey asserts, the Chinese Jews are "the last link in a chain of Jewish communities," (Godbey, p. 368; Glover A. Kingsley, "The Jews of the Extreme Eastern Diaspora," American Monthly Menora, V [1888], 11). Concurrently large numbers of Jews from the Caliphate were absorbed by India, a natural result for Jews who once were in Khorasan. See J. Saadiah, The Book of Beliefs and Opinions, trans. S. Rosenblatt, ed. S. Landauer (New Haven, 1948), p. 21; J. Braslavsky, "Jewish trade between the Mediterranean and India in the Twelfth Century," Zion, VII (1941), 135-39; W.C. White, Chinese Jews, 2d ed. (New York, 1966), Part I, pp. 9-10. Benjamin and Petachia, as noted earlier, provide good evidence that such a chain existed in Persia and Khorasan. In Khulam (Quilon) and in the surrounding towns, Benjamin places the several thousand black Jews, called Bene Israel (The Itinerary of Benjamin of Tudela, ed. M. N. Adler, p. 65). For details and claims of origin see Saphir, II, 44-49, 56-69; David D'Beth Hillel, The Travels of R. David D'Beth Hillel, ed. W.J. Fischel (New York, 1973), pp. 113-121; David G. Mandelbaum, "The Jewish Way of Life in Cochin," J.S.S., I (1949), 423-60; Rabinowitz, Jewish Merchants' Adventures, p. 61. According to Benjamin, the journey from Quilon to Ibrig, where he locates about 3,000 Jews, lasts twenty-three days (The Itinerary of Benjamin of Tudela, ed. M.N. Adler, p. 65). Ibrig cannot be identified. Asher reads "the island of Kandy" which he believes to refer to Ceylon (Benjamin of Tudela, Sefer Masa'ot, ed. Asher, I, 141; II, 185, n. 325). Renaudot states that in the tenth century Jews on the island enjoyed religious liberty (Pinkerton, VII, 217). Edrisi testifies to the fact that Jews had great influence (Edrisi, I, 72).

From Ibrig, according to Benjamin, it takes
forty days to reach "Zin (China)...in the uttermost
East," (The Itinerary of Benjamin of Tudela, ed. M.
N. Adler, p. 66). It is difficult to specify the
time the first Jewish settlement in China took
place. In a ninth century account (851) it is
stated that "the Jews have been settled in that Empire (China) from time immemorial," (Pinkerton,
VII, 42; see also H. Yule, Cathay and the Way Thither, 4 vols. [London, 1915], I, 251). According to
Ibn Battuta (1346) the Chinese city Al-Khansa had
a "Jews' Gate" (Dinur, Israel in Diaspora (2)II, p.
166). The most important proof of the existence of
Jews at that time and earlier in China is furnished
by the information known concerning the Chinese community of K'ai-feng-fu (White, especially Part I,
pp. 31-37; 165-69; 188-89; also D.D. Leslie, The
Survival of the Chinese Jews: The Jewish Community
of Kaifeng [Leiden, 1972], pp. 3-24). Marco Polo
was able to refer (1274) to the powerful commercial
influence of the Jews in China in his time (Marco
Polo, I, 60, 75, 182, 187, 217, 219). Benjamin,
interestingly, does not mention the Jews of China
themselves. Does this indicate ignorance in respect of Jews existing there in his time?
        Benjamin had little more information about
African Jewry south of Egypt. All he had to say
about Jews in Abyssinia (Falashas) was that they
included successful warriors and that they had communications with Aden (The Itinerary of Benjamin of
Tudela, ed. M.N. Adler, pp. 67, 69). Abyssinia disappeared from Jewish history after the sixth century. See W. Leslau, Falasha Anthology: The Black
Jews of Ethiopia (New York, 1969), pp. 19-20, et
passim; also an article on the Falashas, Eldad ha-
Dani, ed. Epstein, pp. 141-89.

CHAPTER V

THE HOLY LAND IN THE BOOKS OF THE TRAVELLERS

The Jews in the Holy Land in the Period

under Discussion

As befits three Jewish travellers conscious of the heightened religiosity of the times, their accounts centre upon a description of the Holy Land, and generally are considered to be among the finest to emerge from the Medieval period. After careful scrutiny of Benjamin's statements, Conder, for example, finds them to be more accurate in detail than other travelogues compiled in the time of the crusades. In regard to this he says: "The medieval Jewish pilgrims appear as a rule to have had a much more accurate knowledge both of the country and of the Bible. Their assertions are borne out by existing remains, and are of the greatest value."[1] The three European Jews saw the Holy Land in the hands of the victorious crusaders, prior to Saladin's reconquest.[2] It is evident that their observations engender the Jewish view of the ancestral homeland in the final half of the twelfth century.[3]

Even though the Seljuk invasion had not caused severe disturbance among the Jewish population, this period prior to the crusaders' triumph had seen a substantial diminution of the Jewish populace and a deterioration of the Jewish settlements.[4] The cities—functioning during times of invasion as primary strategic points of both attacker and defender[5]—underwent massive upheaval in comparison to the rural communities. The country settlements, offering only negligible resistance to the invaders, experienced comparatively mild disturbance to their way of life. Consequently, the Jewish city population as part of the urban mass suffered in the extreme, whereas their rural counterparts remained relatively unaffected.[6]

193

Due to the effects of the Seljuk conquest in 1070, the Jews who remained of the reduced population were in a perilous position. The instability of the situation is reflected in the transfer of the Yeshiva of Gaon Jacob from its location in Jerusalem to Tyre and later to Damascus.[7] What the Seljuks left intact, the crusaders destroyed. This is not to imply that the crusaders did not leave any settlement in existence.[8] Benjamin of Tudela notes the survival of the Jewish populace in twenty different areas. Barring the highly unlikely possibility that these Jewish islands of settlement were colonized during the crusading era proper, it is evident that destruction by the crusaders, of the Jews, was not complete.

Whereas the dearth of Moslem sources yields little of worth concerning the Moslem population in the conquered areas, the Genizah documents capture the feelings of the Jews. The extreme state of anxiety is indicated in a letter written by a Syrian Jew representing the local officials whose community was imperilled by the invading crusaders. The letter closes with a request for the Damascus community to offer prayers for their safety and to save them.[9] As a consequence of the fear of these advancing Christian warriors, the largest community of Jews in the Holy Land, located in the fortified city of Ramleh—a provincial capital on the road to Jerusalem—was completely depopulated, its population escaping to the coastal cities. A similar fate befell the Jewish community in Jaffa. Of greater symbolic importance was the fall of Jerusalem to the crusaders on July 15, 1099 with the inevitable ensuing result: the death of a considerable number of Jewish inhabitants.[10] In recalling the massacre, William of Tyre could not suppress his involuntary revulsion:

> It was impossible to look upon the vast numbers of the slain without horror...everywhere lay fragments of human bodies...it was not alone a spectacle of headless bodies and mutilated limbs strewn in all directions that roused horror in all that looked upon them.

> Still more dreadful was it to gaze upon the
> victors themselves, dripping with blood.[11]

The Moslem historian, Ibn al-Qalānisī, records that
the crusaders, upon discovering the Jews assembled
in a synagogue, burnt it to the ground.[12] Baron,
after judiciously weighing the evidence, confirms
the fact.[13]

Testimony to the chaos spreading through the
country is given in a genizah letter composed by
a Jewish pilgrim who witnessed the situation in the
Holy Land. Writing in 1100, this sojourner had
waited a number of years in Egypt, vainly expecting
the cessation of hostilities in the Holy Land before
travelling to Jerusalem.[14] As additional proof,
Abraham bar Hiyya asserted that "not a single Jew
is found in Jerusalem at the time."[15] A genizah
letter describes the efforts of Jewish fund-raisers
in Egypt to ransom the remaining captives in Ascalon. According to this letter these twenty survi-
vors were only a few of those who had reach Ascalon.[16] Some Jewish refugees found shelter in Gaza
and Ascalon where Egypt remained in control. The
crusaders did not occupy that area until 1153.[17]

Statesmanship gradually replaced religious fanaticism. The crusaders eventually realized that
their future depended upon the continued existence
of the local native population. The outnumbered
crusaders had to repopulate the land, and, of course,
could not do this alone. Therefore, neither the Jews
of Tiberias nor those of Tripolis, after its conquest by the crusaders in 1109, suffered seriously.[18]
Similarly, the large Jewish population of Tyre was
not destroyed in 1124 when the city surrendered.[19]
This policy continued during all of the later con-
quests.[20]

Economic pressures also favoured the slow rejuvenation of Jewish life. Thus, our three travellers'
accounts of their visits to the Holy Land towards
the end of the century reflect the disruptions
caused by the previous crusader and Seljuk invasions
on the one hand, but also the results of the new

crusader policy towards the non-Frankish populations on the other.

The rural areas, as has been stated, generally suffered less than the urban centres. This largely explains the considerable Jewish settlement in the upper and central Galilee in the twelfth century.[21] It is improbable that these Jewish settlements had been created during the turbulent period of the creation of the crusader states. That the rural populations were not exterminated is, of course, not surprising, if we remember that Tancred, conqueror of the Galilee, was fondly remembered by the natives. William of Tyre wrote that "even to this day his memory is held in benediction by the people of that land."[22]

Tiberias, the capital of the Galilee from 1100-1247, and Safed, its important fortification, had Jewish settlements in the second half of the twelfth century. Strangely, none of our travellers visited Safed[23] even though they passed through Meron which was close to that important city. Indeed, Safed was a second Jewish centre, after Tiberias.[24] Our knowledge of it comes from the early thirteenth-century traveller Alkharizi.[25] Samuel ben Samson, a Jewish traveller to Palestine in 1210, gives us further evidence of Safed being a Jewish centre in the Galilee.[26]

Maimonides visited Tiberias in the twelfth century and was buried there in 1206.[27] All three of our travellers visited this city.[28] When Benjamin visited Tiberias it was a fief of the Kingdom of Jerusalem. R. Benjamin found there "about fifty Jews,"[29] headed by three rabbis, one of whom was an astronomer.[30] Petachia, having been in Tiberias, reports:

> ...at which place there is a congregation...
> of the posterity of Rabbi Judah as descen-
> dent exists, whose name is Rabbi Nehorai.
> He has a son whose name is Judah, after...
> Judah, the Prince. He possesses a book of
> genealogy going back to Rabbi Judah. Rabbi

Nehorai is a physician and sells spices in
the market. His children are with him in
the shop. They are kept secluded that they
may not look about.[31] He is a disciple of the
wise and righteous.

Oddly, R. Benjamin never mentions him.

R. Jacob b. Nathaniel ha-Cohen does not mention Jews being in Tiberias, except at the hot
springs which "consist of some four baths on the
shore of the Lake."[32] Mann states[33] that many Jews
visited these springs and the poor among them required financial support. The Genizah contains several appeals from them.[34] These two Jewish centres,
Tiberias and Safed, were surrounded by smaller Jewish settlements in Biriya, Gush Haleb, Dalton, Kefar
Nebratha, Kefar Amukah, Kefar Bara'm, Ein Zethem,
Al-Alviya,[35] Meron and Almah. Our three travellers
visited the last two of these places. Benjamin does
not mention any Jews in Meron,[36] but at Almah he
found about fifty Jews[37]—similar to the size of the
Tiberias Jewish community! In Sepphoris Benjamin
found only a huge cemetery.[38]

Jerusalem, too, was visited by all our travellers.[39] R. Jacob b. Nathaniel ha-Cohen, as usual,
does not report how many Jews were in the city at
that time. Nevertheless, from his statement: "Then
said I, Jacob, to the Rabbis..."[40] it can be inferred that he did find Jews in Jerusalem. Petachia,
however, states: "The only Jew there is Rabbi Abraham, the dyer, and he pays a heavy tax to the King
to be permitted to remain there."[41] Several years
before, Benjamin reported a different situation:

Jerusalem...contains a dyeing house, for
which the Jews pay a small rent annually
to the King, on condition that besides the
Jews no other dyers be allowed in Jerusalem.
There are about 200 Jews who dwell under
the Tower of David in one corner of the
city.[42]

Benjamin's report provides information regarding

the political and economic situation of the Jews in
the crusaders' capital. Economic needs favoured
the slow renewal of Jewish life in Jerusalem. With
the feudalization of the country under the crusaders and the development of an overseas trade,
the crusaders established royal monopolies. As in
Sicily where the Norman rulers entrusted the manage-
ment of some of these industries to Jews,[43] so here,
as Benjamin and Petachia observed, Jews cared for
the dyeing shop in Jerusalem.

The other two travellers affirm Benjamin's reports of Jews coming to pray before the Wailing Wall
and of dyers settled in the city. William of Tyre,
however, relates that all non-Christians were expelled following the conquest of Jerusalem.[44] Jewish sources which refer to Jerusalem and the fate
of the Jews there during the siege and immediately
following the crusader conquest, also affirm the
fact that no Jews remained there.[45] Thus, our travellers attest to the fact that the crusaders eventually allowed Jews to come to the city. This policy began, according to Prawer, in the first quarter
of the twelfth century for the purpose of stimulat-
ing the trading life of the city and expanding its
population.[46]

We note, however, a further difficulty in the
reports of our travellers. While Petachia found
only one Jewish family in the city, Benjamin reports
200 Jews there several years earlier. That it was
dangerous for Jews to even visit the city during the
Christian reign is testified to by Maimonides[47] and
by Alkharizi.[48] Jews definitely were not allowed
to settle in Jerusalem. However, it is unclear
whether Adler and Asher correctly read that Benjamin
reports of an actual 200 Jews living in Jerusalem.
The Roman manuscript reads "four"[49] which conforms
to Petachia's report of only one Jew there during
his visit some years later. According to Adler[50]
the Hebrew letter " ד ", meaning four, could easily
be misread for " ר ", meaning 200. If we accept
Adler's reading that Benjamin found 200 Jewish families in the city, we should be surprised that Petachia reported only one. Is it possible that the Jews

of whom Benjamin speaks all fled Jerusalem in the
light of Saladin's approaching conquest? Baron,
too, believes that, because of the continued prohibition of Jews residing in Jerusalem, the reading
of "dalet" (four) instead of "resh" (200) families
in Benjamin's travelogue appears to be more correct.[51] Even after Saladin's conquest of Jerusalem
in 1187, only a few Jews returned there, despite
the removal of the crusaders' prohibition. Indeed,
according to Alkharizi, the new administration even
issued a call to Jews to resettle in the Holy
City.[52]

The first members of the renewed community came
from Ascalon[53] which had been destroyed.[54] Soon after, Jews from North Africa came as a result of persecutions there in 1198.[55] In 1211 three hundred
French and English Jews came to Jerusalem.[56] Some
of these are even known by name: R. Jonathan son
of David ha-Cohen from Lunel who travelled with R.
Samuel son of Samson and others.[57]

Of Ramleh,[58] Benjamin wrote: "about three hundred Jews dwell there. It was formerly a very great
city: at a distance of two miles there is a large
Jewish cemetery."[59]

In the eleventh century Ramleh had the largest
Jewish population of any city in the Holy Land, a
population which included Samaritans.[60] However,
many fled because of the approaching crusaders.[61]
But the city's population was comparatively unmo-
lested, explaining the large number of Jews living
there in Benjamin's time. However, Asher reads:
"about three Jews dwell there."[62] Adler considers
this a wrong reading. He thinks that the copyist
took the Hebrew letter "   " to be an abbreviation
for "   " meaning "three."[63] Actually, according
to Adler, the "   " stands for its numerical value
of 300. Moreover, the large Jewish cemetery, mentioned by Benjamin, probably indicates that the city
was inhabited by a great number of Jews.[64] Today
scholars are of the opinion that Asher's reading is
preferable and that Benjamin found only three Jewish
dyers there, living in the midst of extensive

cemeteries.[65] Prawer further states that Ramleh
lost its greatness of the preceding period and it
is therefore hard to assume the existence of a
large Jewish settlement there in Benjamin's time.[66]

While Benjamin found few Jews living in the interior of the country,[67] except in the upper and
central Gailee, his picture of the maritime cities
differs radically. Significantly, Benjamin found
that the largest Jewish communities were in Tyre
and Ascalon, which were the last to be captured by
the crusaders.[68] This is certainly due to a crusader policy change regarding conquered cities. Often these cities surrendered according to an agreement promising security to the local population.[69]
These agreements made it possible for the Jewish
communities to continue their existence, thus explaining the large Jewish populations our travellers found there. In Tyre, Benjamin wrote:

> Tyre is a beautiful city. It contains about
> 500 Jews, some of them scholars of the Tal-
> mud,... The Jews own sea-going vessels, and
> there are glassmakers amongst them who make
> that fine Tyrian glass-ware which is prized
> in all countries.[70]

In the preceding century Tyre attained the Jewish
cultural leadership of Jerusalem and Tiberias. Here
Benjamin found a large community of 500, including
several skilled glass-blowers. That glass was manufactured in Tyre during the Middle Ages is well
known.[71] Benjamin provides a further important detail when he reports that "The Jews own sea-going
vessels." It seems that he mentions this fact as
something exceptional, since it was unusual to meet
Jewish shipowners.[72] The Genizah records show that
the Tyrian Jews' income came from the manufacturing
of glass and the exporting of glass products. They
also traded in spices and flax with Egypt and with
the Maghreb merchants who came there on business.

Benjamin's account proves that there was a
flourishing Jewish community in Tyre then. Ephraim
the Egyptian and Meir from southern France headed

the community. Obviously, this reflects that there
were Jews from both Egypt and France in Tyre. It
might be the case that two separate Jewish communities existed there. At this time Maimonides was
communicating with the heads of this community.
From his Responsa and from Benjamin's account it
seems that this large Jewish community was not only
well established economically, but was also highly
organized. Indeed, Tyre was the only known Jewish
centre of learning during this period.[73]

After the crusaders' conquest, the Jews lived
in the Venetian quarter of the city, which was under the direct rule of the Venetian republic.[74] An
account of the Venetian commune and of its property
from the middle of the thirteenth century exists.
This report indicates the number of Jews as nine
families (meaning about 50 members).[75] Benjamin
speaks of about 500 Jews, ten times as many. Can
it be assumed that in Benjamin's time not all of
the Jews there living in the Venetian quarter, and
some must have lived in other parts of the city?

Unlike other Jewish communities in Palestine,
Tyre was unaffected by Saladin's wars; he did not
capture the city and thus Jewish life there continued undisturbed during the thirteenth century.[76]

Ascalon, because of its geographical position,[77] was, throughout its long history, one of
the most flourishing maritime cities of the country.
Under the Fatimids, Jews are mentioned in a genizah
letter as "Qehal Ascalon" ("the Ascalon congregation") and "Qehal Kadosh" ("holy congregation").[78]
From Benjamin's account we know that the Jews, Samaritans and Karaites numbered some 540.[79] Thus after
the crusaders' conquest in 1153, part of the Jewish
population remained,[80] and in fact Ascalon contained
the largest Jewish community in the country, consisting of three congregations. As noted above, during the first period of the crusaders' rule, Ascalon
sheltered a large number of refugees from various
localities.[81] Thus the Ascalon Jewish population
grew. The Jewish community had its own court and,
as late as 1145, was still able to issue official

documents.[82] During this period members of the
Jewish community there were in touch with Jewish
centres abroad.[83] Benjamin does not provide any
details regarding the economic pursuits of the Ascalon Jews. Did they participate in the city's
overseas trade?[84]

Benjamin found much smaller Jewish communities
in the other martime cities. Acre is an exception.
Of this last city Benjamin reports: "It is the
commencement of the land of Israel. It possesses
a large harbour for all the pilgrims who come to
Jerusalem by ship.... About 200 Jews live there,
..."[85] Petachia merely writes, "There are Jews at
Acre."[86] The Christian traveller, William of Olden-
burg, also relates in 1211 that every man in Acre
keeps his own religion and that there are Jews
there.[87] Letters in the Cairo Genizah refer to
"Kehal Akko" and "Rasheha" ("its leaders").[88] Maimonides visited Acre in 1165 and thenceforth cor-
responded with the local dayyan, Japeth b. Elijah.[89]
The Jewish community was boosted by the arrival of
300 rabbis from France and England in 1211.[90] Some
of these settled in Jerusalem, and others in Acre.

Acre was of the utmost strategic importance to
the crusaders in the period between the second and
third crusades, when Benjamin visited there. By
that time they realized that entry into the Holy
Land by sea was preferable to the land routes. They
took the city in 1104.[91] From then on Acre enjoyed
a glorious period lasting 200 years.[92] Benjamin's
statement that Acre "is the commencement of the land
of Israel" shows that he recognized its belonging to
the ancient Jewish state.[93] Alkharizi, who mentions
the city more than once, acclaims its geographical
setting—the beauty of its surroundings and its
closeness to the Shekina (the presence of God).[94]
On the other hand he condemns its population.[95]
From these travellers' accounts and also from a
question sent to Maimonides,[96] it seems the Acre
Jewish community was well organized.[97]

Haifa was another interesting place from the
Jewish point of view. Benjamin does not mention

any Jews actually living there—only "many Jewish graves."[98] Thus, it is unclear why Benvenisti states that Jews lived in Haifa.[99] On the eve of the crusaders' conquest, the Persian traveller Nasir Khusrau passed through Haifa and noted: in Haifa there are "shipbuilders, who build very large craft: the seagoing ships of this place are known under the name of Judi."[100] Prior to the crusaders' conquest there was a Jewish community in Haifa. It received special privileges from the Fatimids for which the Jews paid taxes.[101] It is surprising to find Jews living there since the economic opportunities of the small city were limited.[102] Could it be that there was a connection between these Jews and the shipbuilders mentioned above? Or, is it possible that the Jews settled here because of the cemetery near the city which was within the boundaries of the Holy Land?[103] The Jews participated heroically in the defence of the city against the crusaders.[104] Haifa was taken (in 1100) and like Jerusalem, the population was slaughtered.[105]

Jaffa was conquered by the crusaders in the summer of 1099. It became the main gateway to Jerusalem for the first four crusades.[106] Benjamin reported "one Jewish dyer lives here."[107] The Jewish community, along with the Moslems, fled the city making it possible for the crusaders to take it without a battle.[108] Further south, at Ashdod "now in ruins: no Jews dwell there."[109]

We can now identify different periods in the history of the Jews in the Holy Land under the crusaders' rule. During the period 1099-1124, Jews were destroyed along with the Moslems. Thus the Jewish communities in Acre, Haifa and Jerusalem were totally destroyed. Other Jewish communities, e.g., Ramleh and Jaffa, escaped this physical destruction by fleeing before the crusaders came. On the other hand the rural settlements were not destroyed; they fell to the crusaders without resistance. This explains the existence of Jewish communities in the Galilee, the northern part of the Holy Land. By the end of the first quarter of the

twelfth century the crusaders' religious enthusiasm
declined and cities were taken under specific terms
of surrender. Tyre and Ascalon fell under this
policy and their Jewish communities continued to
exist. At the same time, some transplanted Jewish
communities returned to the cities they had fled
and renewed themselves. Indeed, only the Jerusalem
community seemed unable to renew itself, because of
a law prohibiting Jews to reside there. Though
even here the crusaders could not ignore economic
realities. Eventually they had to allow Jews engaged in the dyeing profession to settle in the Holy
City.

In the middle of the twelfth century Jewish
settlements in the Holy Land were encouraged by the
Kingdom of Jerusalem, now at its zenith. Benjamin's
and Petachia's accounts are from this period; they
therefore reflect this rejuvenation of Jewish life.
In this light the significance of Petachia's general
statement that "...there are also congregations in
the land of Israel, numbering, however, only one
hundred, two hundred, or three hundred families"[110]
can be understood. He made this statement while
reporting that there was a congregation at Tiberias[111] without giving a specific number. Petachia's
statement does reflect the true overall picture.
What he is saying is that there are different Jewish
communities of varying sizes dispersed throughout
the Holy Land and that Tiberias was not the only Jewish centre. Petachia knows that some are large, numbering three hundred families, others number only
two hundred and still others have only one hundred
families. Indeed, Petachia is classifying the Jewish communities according to numerical strength. A
look into Benjamin's accounts also reveals various
Jewish communities in the Holy Land, the largest
with 500 families, and the smallest with twenty families, as well as a few isolated Jewish families
living in various localities. It is clear that
Petachia's statement is a generalization while Benjamin's reports reflect the true situation in detail.

In fact Petachia's estimate is significant not

204

because it gives the exact numerical size of the
Jewish population in the Holy Land, but because it
confirms two facts: (1) there were Jewish communities in the Holy Land under the crusaders, and (2)
on the eve of Saladin's conquest the Jews had already overcome the partial destruction by the crusaders, although they remained numerically small.
Actually the number of Jews was three times greater
than the highest number given by Petachia. According to Benjamin there were more than one thousand
Jewish families from Acre southwards.

Jewish life then was centred primarily in the
maritime cities. There were also important Jewish
centres at Ramleh (if we accept Adler's reading)
in the south and in Tiberias in the north. In the
Judean mountains there were isolated Jews. Benjamin reported isolated Jewish dyers living at Beit
Nuba,[112] and at Beit Jibrin close to the crusader
fortification.[113] Other isolated Jewish families
were reported in Bethlehem,[114] Ludd,[115] and Hebron.[116] Petachia speaks of only one Jew at Elone
Mamre, near Hebron—an old man and his son.[117] If
there had been more Jews in Hebron both Petachia
and Benjamin would have mentioned this fact. In
1211, R. Samuel b. Samson visited the Holy Land and
found in Hebron one Jewish dyer,[118] probably the
same Jew mentioned previously by Petachia.[119]

Strangely, the crusaders who caused the Jews
suffering in Europe treated them equally with the
other religious groups in the Holy Land. The Jews
were not granted, as in Europe, special privileges,
but neither were they subject to restrictions.
There was no parallel in Palestine to the legislation of Innocent III which opened a dark page of
Jewish history in Europe.[120]

Under these circumstances we find limited Jewish participation in the flourishing trade which
developed in the coastal cities.[121] Most Jews were
craftsmen, especially dyers. It is interesting to
remember here that the Moslem traveller Mukaddasi
writes of Jerusalem at the end of the tenth century
that most of the dyers, coin assayers, money

205

changers and tanners were Jews, while most physicians and scribes were Christians.[122]   In general the Jewish professions were connected with the handicrafts. Benjamin reinforces this impression when he writes of the Druses, saying" "There are no resident Jews among them, but a certain number of Jewish handicraftsmen and dyers come among them, for the sake of trade, and then return,..."[123] Interestingly, the dyeing profession was held in contempt in southern Europe.[124]

The Jewish physicians were famous. Indeed, William of Tyre chastised the Christian rulers for preferring Jewish physicians.[125] The historical sources also mention Jewish spice sellers and pedlers wandering between villages.[126] In the Funda of Tiberias, Petachia found Nehorai selling spices, a trade related to medicine.

It seems, then, that this short period of prosperity in the crusaders' Holy Land encouraged prosperity in the Jewish communities. The fact that Maimonides and our travellers were able to tour the land certainly testifies to a certain degree of safety.[127] The renewed Jewish settlements in the Holy Land were a result of renewed emigration. Although the individual motivations were always the same—to fulfil the religious duty of settling in Zion—it should be remembered that the crusade and the crusaders' policy encouraged the renewal of Jewish life in the country.

The ascendancy of Saladin opened a new era in the history of Jewish life in the Holy Land. The Jews saw the divine hand at work in the failure of the crusaders to maintain their position in the Holy Land.[128] This period, similar to that of the first crusade, was a source of messianic hopes heightening the Jewish spirit. An emigration movement to the Holy Land began. It had its roots among the European Jews at the end of the twelfth century and continued during the next century: the emigration of R. Yehiel of Paris who desired to sacrifice in Jerusalem;[129] the emigrations of R. Abraham Abulafia who had messianic expectations;[130]

Nahmanides' emigration;[131] Maharm of Rotenburg's attempt to emigrate to the Holy Land[132]—all outline this movement whose roots can be detected among European Jews in the second half of the twelfth century and which continued in the following century. Jews took the command to settle the Holy Land seriously; it became considered as a mitsvah (commandment).[133] In the thirteenth century the Holy Land was no longer merely an object of prayer, but became a reality in the religious life of the Jews.[134] Jews were constantly coming to the Holy Land, some for permanent settlement, some as pilgrims.[135] Our travellers' accounts reflect the impact of this movement upon the rejuvenation of Jewish life in the Holy Land during this period. Pilgrims were attracted here at a rate unparalleled in the past. Egyptian Jews were immigrating now.[136] French Jews also came. Benjamin wrote that the second head of the community in Tyre was from southern France.[137] In Jerusalem, Benjamin tells us, there was a Jew from Byzantium, R. Abraham al-Constantine.[138] Our travellers themselves were from Spain and Germany, not to mention ha-Levi, Alkharizi, Ibn Ezra and others. A special literature, unknown before in Jewish history, emerged—a literature dealing with Palestine.[139] The religious sentiments which motivated the first crusade eventually resulted in Jewish emigration to the land of their fathers. This became easier now because of the renewed communications between East and West created by the crusades.

In the past the Palestinian Jewish community had also been strengthened through immigration. But the immigrants came primarily from the neighbouring countries: Egypt, Syria, Babylonia, Persia and Byzantium. Of course a few Jews came from Europe too, but they were a minority. The crusades changed this pattern through the creation of commercial contacts with Europe. The impression is that the Jewish communities renewed during the second half of the twelfth century were strengthened primarily by European immigrants.[140] Benjamin provides partial evidence for this. He mentions names of people which are clearly European. For example,

207

he speaks of "R. Meir from Carcassone"[141] as one of
the leaders of the Jewish community in Tyre. Moreover, Benjamin's descriptions of the Holy Land contain many crusader or Western expressions and references to Christian traditions.[142] Prawer states
that Benjamin's guides were probably European Jews,
since if they had had deep roots in the Moslem traditions this would have been reflected in the account itself.[143] In this connection, the influence
of the famous poet ha-Levi cannot be neglected. He
motivated Spanish Jews of his day to emigrate and
resettle Zion. He himself set an example by settling there. Benjamin relates that ha-Levi's grave
is in Tiberias.[144]

These small and mostly unrecorded rumblings of
an emigration movement in the twelfth century seem
to have been larger than previously suspected. They
turned into a stream flowing into the Holy Land in
the thirteenth century. Moreover, the second Kingdom of the crusaders might not have feared this
flow; indeed, it might have welcomed it. R. Samuel
b. Samson made a pilgrimage to Palestine in 1210.
At the end of his narrative he wrote: "Journeying
from Jerusalem and from the Galilee in the year 970
(1210). I have a firman with the seal of the King
of Jerusalem attesting the truth of the Present
Writing."[145] He was carrying a letter from the
King of Jerusalem, i.e., John de Brienne. Scholars
have suggested that this letter recommended Jewish
emigration to Palestine and resulted in the famous
pilgrimage of three hundred French and English
rabbis the following year (1211).[146] The crusaders,
interested in repopulating the remainder of the
kingdom after 1187, may indeed actually have planned
and encouraged immigration from Europe. Although
European Christians showed little enthusiasm for
doing so, this effort stimulated the interest of
many Jews who eventually did leave Europe to return
to the land of their fathers.

The Jewish settlements of the Holy Land maintained their contacts with their brethren in Egypt
and Syria on one hand, and with Europe on the other.
The custom of burying the dead in the Holy Land was

popular in this period among the Egyptian Jews as
testified by Benjamin's account.[147] Furthermore,
Jacob b. Nathaniel ha-Cohen, at the end of his account, expresses a clear wish to be privileged to
die in the Holy Land.[148]

The Holy Places and the Holy Graves

The subject of holy tombs, and places determined to be holy by Jewish tradition is one of the
most interesting to be found in our travellers'
accounts. All three visited the celebrated holy
places because the medieval mind could not ignore
saints, or other persons with prominent roles in
the religious past. Through miracles ascribed to
them, such saints continued to play a role, even
after their physical deaths. The awakening of religious fervour must have also affected Jews living
in that period.[149]

For many, travelling had one object—that of
visiting holy spots and praying there.[150] Jacob b.
Nathaniel ha-Cohen seems to be one whose only motive for travel is visiting the Holy Land and seeing
the holy localities. Benjamin and Petachia also do
not ignore the subject. Most of the sites venerated
by Jews were concentrated in the Holy Land. If
Palestine were holy as a country, then the holy
graves were the holiest areas. This factor kept
the memory and meaning of the Land alive within the
Jewish mind.

It seems that venerating the graves of the forefathers had become an established religious custom
although Judaism did not actually encourage it.[151]
The Talmud supplies us with information about people
marking graves in the first month of Adar,[152] and a
legend speaks of Caleb, one of the twelve spies sent
out by Moses (Numbers 13:6) who briefly made a pilgrimage to the patriarchs' sepulchres.[153] This custom in Palestine is known also from the New Testament,[154] and the Karaite Sahl Ibn Masliah from the

tenth century complains that the people in his own time were venerating the graves, lighting candles, making vows and pleading with the dead to intercede for them.[155] In one book from the Fatimid period, there are prayers to be said in cemeteries,[156] which were probably written for those intending to visit the holy graves. Ha-Levi wrote many poems to venerate the Land and its stones.[157] Alkharizi, telling of his intention to visit the grave of Ezra in the Orient, wrote beautiful poems to commemorate those sepulchres of the prophets.[158] Furthermore, Rabbi Jacob the messenger of Rabbi Jechiel of Paris (1238-44) opens his account to the Holy Land with the following lines:

> These are the journeyings of the Children of Israel who wish to go to contemplate and pray at the graves of the Patriarchs, the right-eous and the saints of the Holy Land, and to our holy and glorious temple wherein our fathers prayed in Jerusalem, may it be re-built and established soon in our days.[159]

Such accounting would not have been necessary if no journeys were being made.

Since Judaism generally discouraged the custom, it is no wonder that few traditions concerning graves and tombs are left to us from the early per-iod in Jewish history. However, with the increasing movement to visit the Holy Land and the holy places in it, old graves were rediscovered and new tradi-tions and legends were created regarding them. These legends may have been developed by people living in Palestine to augment the value and sanctity of the Holy Land in the eyes of the people living abroad. Or, these legends may have been spread by Pilgrims themselves to enhance their prestige among their un-travelled peers. Yet, the research of these tradi-tions is important. In some cases, the remnant of a grave might indicate the remnant of an old settle-ment.[160]

Unquestionably, the contesting Crusaders and Moslems awakened the Jewish longing for the Land of

210

their Fathers. This spirit made every spot pre-
cious to Jews who strongly associated the Land with
the future Messiah. Jewish travellers wanted to
simply touch the sacred ground or pray at the holy
places. A special literature to guide pilgrims was
under development at this time. The holy places
needed proper identification if they were to be
visited. Moreover, Benjamin and Petachia leave the
impression that they were attempting to guide the
visitor in the Land. They indicate in their accounts the places, distances, and landmarks of such
holy sites. This is especially true of the accounts of Petachia and Jacob b. Nathaniel, as well
as of that of R. Jacob the messenger from Paris.
This is the only information they seek to record in
their itineraries.

While the medieval Jew was living and working
in the real world, the memory of the holy sites accompanied him in his daily thoughts. R. Jacob ben
Nathaniel ha-Cohen ends his account with a wish to
be buried in the Holy Land. This would, he believed, permit him to continue feeling the presence
of the Holy Spirit of the Land (and the saints
buried there) even after his death. R. Jacob, the
messenger, likewise expresses the same wish, and
takes it a step further. He hopes to witness soon
the Messianic Age which would bring with it the resurrection of the righteous people whose tombs he
had visited.[161]

Medieval Jews held mystically to the idea that
Jewish piety would hasten the Messianic Age. The
generations which suffered persecution in Europe
during the crusading movement became humble. These
Jews concentrated upon studying their religion and
their God, believing that such devotion was a powerful deterrent to the evil forces which plagued Jews.
The Hassidic movement and Jewish mysticism developed.[162] Persecution was seen as Divine punishment
for past and present sins. The safety and preservation of the Jewish nation was partially dependent
upon the lives of past martyrs and righteous Jews.
Thus, pilgrims who visited and prayed at the holy
tombs felt they were helping in the preservation
process.[163]

211

It is relatively easy to establish a relationship between such ideas and our travellers, if we first establish their belief that past righteous sages preserved a world which deserved destruction. Holy sages pleaded with the Deity to withhold destruction, just as Abraham pleaded to save the cities of Sodom and Gomorrah. Those cities could not count ten righteous men among the populace and were destroyed (Genesis 18:17-33). Thus, we cannot be surprised to read the following lines in the opening account of Rabbi Samuel ben Samson (1210): "These words deserve to be written in order that we might know the places of the graves of our forefathers, by whose merit the world exists."[164] An astonishing premise—that the entire world exists by the merits of the forefathers! Therefore, enumerating the tombs and graves, and relating the stories associated with those places, became significant for the travellers. They wanted such a record for their generation and future generations.

The twelfth-century travellers' accounts reflect the impact of the new times on the Jew and represent the new spirit of the age. They reflect that pious feeling of the medieval Jew concerning the Holy Land and holy sites; they also reflect the various traditions concerning these sites. Most of the sites which they mention were known previously, and were considered universally holy among the Jews. They are mentioned by almost every traveller before and after the twelfth century. Some others were in the process of becoming important; still others were being recorded for the first time.

Because of conflicting biblical accounts, confusing landmarks and traditions, and disagreements among legends and stories related to the holy sites, problems with identification of these sites arise. This is why it is interesting to survey the holy sites and holy graves visited by these twelfth-century travellers and compare their accounts. This study includes holy cities, holy items in the cities, synagogues, as well as holy graves.

Hebron, the city of the Fathers,[165] has a

212

special meaning for the religious Jew. In the Cave
of the "Machpelah" (double Cave) are buried the
three Patriarchs and their wives.[166] Naturally the
field of the Machpelah became a symbol for Jews of
the past and future redemption.[167] In 1166, Maimonides visited the place and prayed there. The
day he visited the tomb he later established as a
personal feast day.[168]

Benjamin's account of Machpelah[169] is the most
detailed of the three travellers. He visited the
Cave and speaks of it as a large place of worship
called St. Abram. This title was commonly applied
to the Haram by the twelfth-century Christian
writers.[170] Ossuaries similar to those mentioned
by Benjamin have been described in the Talmud.
Many others have been discovered in tombs near Jerusalem, also bearing Hebrew inscriptions, and are
generally referred to as osteophagi.[171] The fact
that Benjamin mentions such a detail makes it probable that he actually entered the Cave's interior.
Some years later, Petachia visited the Cave and
reported:

> He saw over the cave a large palace, which
> Abraham our father built. There are in it
> large stones of twenty-seven or twenty-
> eight cubits...he gave to the keeper of the
> key of the cave a gold piece to take him to
> the graves of the fathers; and the keeper
> opened the door, and behold there was over
> the entrance an image, and inside three
> cells. The Jews of Acre had told him pre-
> viously: beware, for they have placed three
> corpses at the entrance of the cave and say
> that these were the Patriarchs.... The
> Rabbi therefore gave him another gold piece
> to take him inside the cave. The keeper
> then opened the (inner) door, saying 'I
> never permitted a Gentile before to enter
> thiy doorway.' The keeper then brought
> lights and they went inside and had to des-
> cend steps.... They then came to a very
> spacious cave. In the midst of the cave
> there is an entrance in the ground. The

ground consists all of rocks, and all the
graves are in the hollow of the rock: and
over that entrance, in the middle, are
placed very thick iron bars, the likes no
man can make by earthly means but with
heavenly help only. And a storm wind blows
from between the holes between bar and bar.
He could not enter there with lights. Then
he understood that the Fathers were there
and he prayed there. Whenever he bent towards the mouth of the cave, a storm wind
went forth and cast him backwards.[172]

It is obvious, then, that the crusaders allowed
Jews to visit the holy place. It seems that only
Jacob b. Nathaniel casts some doubts on this, because he states in his report that he entered the
Cave "in the guise of a Gentile,"[173] which might
suggest that he had experienced difficulties trying
to enter the Cave as a Jew.[174] By comparing the accounts, we realize that the crusaders did not freely
allow visitors to see the actual tombs.[175] Jacob
b. Nathaniel even noticed a new construction built
to separate the actual graves from the false
ones.[176] All three travellers speak of the three
graves of the Patriarchs facing those of the Mat-
riarchs, a fact mentioned also by Edrisi in 1154.[177]

To reach those graves, one had to descent
steps, although the number of steps descended differs between Petachia and Jacob b. Nathaniel. Light
was also necessary to find the way. Jacob[178] and
Petachia report strong winds blowing within the
Cave. These winds indicated to Petachia the actual
burial place where he was to offer his prayer. Both
Petachia and Benjamin report finding many other
graves and casks filled with bones within the same
site.

The Jewish custom of bringing the bones of
deceased parents and friends to Palestine arose
from Talmudic interpretation of a biblical verse:
"The land will reconcile the sins of his people"
(Deuteronomy 32:43). This verse has been interpreted to mean that burial in Palestine was

sufficient to erase the sins of a lifetime.[179]
Pious Jews living in exile from their Land, arranged
to be buried there after death.[180] Where could one
find a more sacred ground than the area around Hebron surrounding the Cave of Machpelah? Benjamin
clearly states: "One finds there many casks filled
with the bones of Israelites, as the members of the
House of Israel were wont to bring the bones of
their fathers thither and deposit them there to
this day."[181]

Jacob b. Nathaniel reports: "There is the
place out of which Adam, the first man, was created.
They take earth from it and build houses with it,
but it never grows less, and is always full."[182]
According to Talmudic tradition, the earth of the
first man, Adam, was gathered from the area around
Hebron (Sanhedrin 38a). There is also a Jewish
tradition that Adam was buried in Hebron.[183] Traditions linking the ground from which Adam was created
and Hebron are also known among Christians.[184]
Among the crusaders, John of Würzburg (1100),[185]
Theodorich (1172),[186] and Jacques of Vitry (1120)[187]
still speak of the Tomb of Adam in Hebron. In 1173,
the Arab writer Ali added the sepulchres of Noah,
and Noah's son, Shem, to those already known to be
buried in Hebron. Ali also confirms the fact that
visitors could enter the Cave only after proper payment. Mention is also made of the strong wind within the Cave.[188]

Another report by Benjamin places the Well of
Abraham near the Cave. Bertinoro states that the
Arabs call it the Well of Isaac.[189] Benjamin fur-
ther states: "out of reverence for the Patriarch
Abraham, no one is allowed to build in the neighbor-
hood."[190]

Logically, the Cave of Machpelah became a centre for other stories. R. Jacob b. Nathaniel speaks
of a building which had been erected by "Joseph the
Righteous."[191] Antonius Placentius also located
Joseph's burial in the Cave of Machpelah.[192] Jacob
b. Nathaniel notes this tradition and carefully mentions: "And others say that King Solomon buried him

215

[Joseph] there."[193] This is a reversal of the direction of influence which flowed from the crusaders
to the Jews. Jacob b. Nathaniel is the first European Jew to enlighten the Europeans about the Christian tradition concerning Joseph's burial place in
relation to the Machpelah Cave. This Christian tradition was then passed along to the Arabs. Moslems,
even today, speak of Joseph's tomb being located
there.[194]

Petachia tells of a curious incident which
occurred at Mamre, close to Hebron. There an old
man instructed his son to show Petachia the tree
under which the angels rested (Genesis 18:4, 8).
Petachia was led to a fine olive tree: "They have
a tradition that when the angels sat down the tree
was cleft into three parts, each resting under one
part whilst sitting on the stone. The fruits of
the tree are very sweet...they also showed him a
stone...upon which Abraham was circumcised."[195]
Such holy trees and stones associated with biblical
stories are to be found in various localities in
Palestine.[196] All these indicators add proof to
the theory that the Machpelah Cave became the centre of holy items connected with Abraham, or the
Patriarchs in general.[197]

The second famous holy sepulchre which the
three travellers mention is the Tomb of Rachel.
Petachia reports:

> ...The Rabbi then came to Rachel's grave,
> at Ephrath, half a day's journey from
> Jerusalem. Upon her grave are eleven
> stones, according to the number of the
> eleven tribes: and because Benjamin was
> only born at her death, there is no stone
> erected for him. They are of marble.
> The stone of Jacob, however, consisting
> of one piece of marble, above all of them,
> is very large, a load for many persons.[198]

Then he continued to relate that priests took away
the large stone from the grave and used it for a
church, but in the morning it was seen on the grave

as before. This was repeated several times until
at last they "abstained from carrying it away."[199]

Based upon the accounts of the twelfth-century
travellers,[200] the tombstone consisted of eleven
stones, reportedly laid by the eleven sons of Jacob.
The large stone was supposedly placed at the top by
hands of Jacob. Edrisi confirms this in a writing
dated 1154.[201] Petachia and Jacob b. Nathaniel mention the tradition that Benjamin, being the youngest
son, did not have the strength to bring his own
stone, so his father (Jacob) helped him. Another
tradition is brought by Rabbi Jacob the Messenger,
the mid-thirteenth century traveller, who added:
"Joseph did not give a stone because he was only
about eight years old, or because of his grief at
having lost his mother."[202] The tomb was roofed
over with a dome supported by four pillars, which
R. Jacob b. Nathaniel chose to call "four doors."

The sepulchre has already been mentioned by
Eusebius at the beginning of the fourth century.[203]
Felix Fabri refers to it at the end of the fifteenth century.[204] Estori ha-Parchi mentions, too,
the tomb and describes it.[205] The place was greatly
venerated by Christians, Jews, and Moslems.[206]
Rachel has been an inspiration to literature and
art. Historically, she serves as a gentle "mother"
who pleads with God to have mercy upon the people
of Israel, and to return them to their Land.[207]
Many Jewish travellers visited the tomb to carve
their names upon the stones, as has been reported
by Benjamin.[208]

Jerusalem, city of peace, has always held a
unique place in the minds and hearts of Jews. Our
twelfth-century travellers visited Jerusalem as a
matter of course, to view the city and the holy
sites within it.[209]

According to an old tradition, that part of
the Valley of Kidron that separates the Mount of
Olives from the Temple Mount is called by the name
Jehoshaphat. This tradition which Eusebius mentions in the early fourth century[210] is reported by

the twelfth-century travellers.[211] The tradition
holds the valley to be the scene of the judgment of
the nations of which Joel and Ezekiel prophesy (Joel
4:2-13; Ezek. 20:35). Benjamin reports: "The gate
of Jehoshaphat leads to the Valley of Jehoshaphat,
which is the gathering place of nations."[212] Historically, Jews considered it a privilege to be
buried in that valley.[213] Here were found four
ancient tombs—two of which are mentioned by Benjamin: Absalom's and King Uzziah's.[214] Those two
structures are visible. The other two are underground tombs. All these four monuments in the
valley date back to the period of the Second Temple.[215] The Monument of Absalom is mentioned by
Jacob b. Nathaniel[216] while Petachia does not speak
of it.

The first information regarding the graves in
this valley is by the fourth-century Christian
travellers. A traveller from Bordeaux (333) mentions those monuments for the first time.[217] The
Tower of Jehoshaphat that Arculf mentions in his
itinerary (695),[218] is Absalom's monument, and hundreds of years later we still hear of the tradition
which refers to this monument as the grave of King
Jehoshaphat, probably influenced by the very name
of the valley.[219]

Benjamin and Jacob b. Nathaniel are the first
Jewish travellers in the twelfth century who men-
tion the monuments in this valley. According to N.
Avigad,[220] the sepulchre of King Uzziah, which Benjamin mentions,[221] is probably the grave of sons of
Hazir. King Uzziah was buried on Mount Zion, close
to other kings of Judah (II Kings 15:7). The name,
"Hand of Absalom" originated in the story of II
Samuel (18:18).[222] The identification of this place
was influenced by Josephus Flavius who describes the
"Hand of Absalom" of II Samuel as a monument located near Jerusalem (7.10.3 Antiq.). In later periods the "Hand of Absalom" changed to the "Pillar
of Absalom."[223] Benjamin merely states: "Here is
the pillar called Absalom's Hand."[224]

218

According to Prawer[225] Jacob b. Nathaniel describes a Christian funeral when he says: "I also
saw the Valley of Jehoshaphat into which they throw
stones, and every day, at least one hundred die and
their bodies are brought from Benjamin's Gate down
between the monument and the waters of Siloam, a
great descent, until they come to Mount Olivet."[226]
As to the throwing of stones, to which Jacob refers,
this could reflect the Jewish custom of pelting
Absalom's monument with stones.[227] Even present day
Jews customarily pelt this monument with stones in
memory of Absalom's disobedience to his father, King
David. It could also be that Jacob b. Nathaniel
refers to a Christian custom of laying stones to
reserve a spot in the Valley of Jehoshaphat, the
place where the tradition suggests the Day of Judgment will take place.[228]

The monuments in the Valley of Kidron (Jehoshaphat) are well preserved. This fact makes it possible to trace ancient burial traditions in the
Orient.[229]

The Mount of Olives is mentioned by our travellers. While Petachia[230] and Jacob b. Nathaniel[231]
mention it only by name and location, Benjamin,
after identifying the mountain, states:

From the Valley of Jehoshaphat one ascends
the Mount of Olives: it is the valley only
which separates Jerusalem from the Mount of
Olives.... Facing Jerusalem for a distance
of three miles are the cemeteries belonging
to the Israelites, who in the days of old
buried the dead in caves, and upon each
sepulchre is a dated inscription, but the
Christians destroy the sepulchres, employ-
ing the stones thereof in building their
houses. These sepulchres reach as far as
Zelzah in the territory of Benjamin.[232]

Benjamin notices the surrounding cemeteries, dating
from preceding periods. This mountain enjoys a
doubly holy location. It faces Jerusalem, the holy
city, and borders on the Valley of Jehoshaphat.

219

The special role it is to play in the Messianic
Era (Ezekiel 11:23) makes it attractive as a burial
place. An additional sanctification of the Mount
of Olives, according to Midrashic tradition, occurred when the "Divine Presence" (Shechinah) rested
on the mountain.[233]

The mountain, a fitting place for pilgrims to
worship,[234] especially after the eighth century
when Jews were forbidden the Temple Mount as a place
for viewing the Temple Mount. Thus did the mountain acquire additional significance for Jews. Rabbi Jacob, the Messenger from Paris, relates that he
and his companions walked along the Valley of Jehoshaphat, until they reached the Mount of Olives,
"...we go uphill to the platform which faces the
Temple Gate. Thence we see the Temple Mount and all
buildings upon it, and we pray in the direction of
the Temple."[236]

The tombs of the Prophets Haggai, Habakkuk and
Hulda have not been mentioned by our twelfth-century
travellers. Except that of Hulda[237] they were noted
by Obadiah da Bertinoro on the Mount of Olives. In
addition to this, Obadiah confirms Benjamin's account when he refers to the Mount of Olives: "Everywhere, outside and inside, both in fields and houses,
the caves are innumerable...."[238]

Saewulf, who visited the country under the rule
of the crusaders, also mentions the mountain, in
order to state that from there are visible "...the
extreme western walls of the city...and how much it
is since increased."[239] Like Bishop Arculf (7th
century)[240] he also continues to associate the mountain with a Christian tradition.[241]

Mount Zion with its Royal Sepulchres occupies
one of the most memorable localities in ancient Jewish history.[242] Benjamin is the first to notice
that on Mount Zion there are no buildings, except
for a Christian "place of worship."[243] He is obviously referring to the Church of the Apostles
identified then with the Coenaculum.[244] Furthermore, Benjamin tells us that on Mount Zion are to

be found the sepulchres of the House of David and
those of the kings who reigned after him, but "...
the exact place cannot be identified."[245] It is
interesting to note that Petachia and Jacob b.
Nathaniel, who were deeply interested in visiting
the holy places, failed to report the tradition
locating the sepulchres of the House of David on
Mount Zion.[246] Jacob b. Nathaniel, however, after
enumerating the holy sites in Jerusalem, adds:
"these things are known and none knows more."[247]
In spite of this, Benjamin relates a story which
had been told to him[248] concerning an incident which
took place fifteen years prior to his visit. One
wall of the Church of Mount Zion fell. The Patriarch commanded that workers restore the Church. Two
workmen raised a certain stone and discovered the
entrance to a cave.

> They entered the cave, and reached a large
> chamber resting upon pillars of marble
> overlaid with silver and gold. In front
> was a table of gold and a sceptre and crown.
> This was the sepulchre of King David. On
> the left...was the sepulchre of King Solo-
> mon: then followed the sepulchres of all the
> kings of Judah that were buried there....
> The two men essayed to enter the chamber,
> when a fierce wind came forth...and smote
> them, and they fell...like dead men....
> And there came forth a wind like a man's
> voice, crying out: 'Arise and go forth
> from this place!' So the men rushed forth
> in terror,...

Being questioned, Rabbi Abraham el Constantini told
the Patriarch:

> 'These are the sepulchres of the House of
> David: they belong to the Kings of Judah,
> and on the morrow let us enter, I and you
> and these men....' And on the morrow they
> sent for the two men and found each of them
> lying on his bed in terror, and the men said,
> 'We will not enter there, for the Lord doth
> not desire to show it to any man.' Then the

221

Patriarch gave orders that the place should
be closed up and hidden from the sight of
man unto this day.[249]

Benjamin's account has verisimilitude. It
leaves the impression that something actually happened. Perhaps, as the Jews of Jerusalem believe,
the Hand of God protects the holy places. The
event which had supernatural overtones, according
to Prawer, was a bolt of lightning which hit the
Church on Mount Zion.[250] William of Tyre relates
that lightning hit the Church in 1146 and also hit
the Holy Sepulchre.[251] This probably encouraged
the Jews in the city who believed that it was God
taking revenge upon the Crusaders by thunder and
lightning. However, with the Church on Mount Zion,
many thoughts were associated. It was known that
David was buried in the "City of David" (I Kings 2:
10), which is Zion (I Kings 8:1).[252] Zion was actually Mount Zion, the assumed burial place of David
and all the royal kings who succeeded him.[253] Benjamin's reference to the incident fifteen years
prior to his visit, confirms the time given by William of Tyre. This, like many traditions, could
have been transmuted in the re-telling.

Rabbi Jacob, the Messenger, seems to have a
clear knowledge of the royal sepulchres located on
Mount Zion.[254] Thus, we realize that the tradition
locating the royal tombs on Mount Zion was known a
few years after Benjamin. Interestingly, Isaac
Chello who visited the Holy Land in 1334, states:
"But the sepulchres of the House of David which were
on Mount Zion are no longer known today either to
Jews or Mussulmans."[255] Isaac Chello was familiar
with the tradition locating the royal tombs on Mount
Zion, however, it is unclear when they were lost.

The royal sepulchres are recorded in Moslem
literature dating only from the tenth century.[256]
The Arab traveller, Ali, who visited Jerusalem a
few years after Benjamin says nothing about discovering the royal tombs.[257] Early Christian tradition
(fourth to eighth century) believed the sepulchre of

222

David to be in or around the city of Bethlehem,[258] and Yakut, the Arab traveller, testifies to this.[259] At the beginning of the crusades, Raymond de Aguilers specifies the tradition of David's tomb on Mount Zion.[260] However, Saewulf,[261] who gives details of Mount Zion, and associates it strongly with Christian tradition, does not mention the royal sepulchres.

Strangely, the story recorded by Benjamin concerning treasure buried within the royal sepulchres is not recorded elsewhere. Perhaps it was decided to obscure the location of the tombs to discourage grave-robbers. Not until the fourteenth and fifteenth centuries do the Christian pilgrims, Marinus Sanuto (1310)[262] and Felix Fabri (1484),[263] again mention the location of David's tomb on Mount Zion. When it became common knowledge that David's tomb was there, Jews (1427) attempted to purchase it from the Franciscans.[264]

The Temple area is the most holy area in the city of Jerusalem.[265] This area was naturally visited by the twelfth-century travellers. Benjamin of Tudela reports:

> ...the gate of Gushpat...facing our ancient
> Temple, now called Templum Domini. Upon
> the site of the sanctuary Omar...erected an
> edifice with a very large and magnificent
> cupola, into which the Gentiles do not bring
> any image or effigy, but they merely come
> there to pray. In front of this place is
> the Western Wall, which is one of the walls
> of the Holy of Holies. This is called the
> Gate of Mercy, and thither come all the Jews
> to pray before the wall.... In Jerusalem,
> attached to the palace which belonged to
> Solomon, are the stables built by him, form-
> ing a very substantial structure,...and the
> like of it is not to be seen anywhere in
> the world. There is also visible up to this
> day the pool used by the priests before of-
> fering their sacrifice, and the Jews coming
> thither write their name upon the wall.[266]

Benjamin apparently is familiar with the legend[267] associated with the building of the mosque (also reported by Petachia) "with a very large and magnificent cupola" upon the site of the sanctuary. Petachia says the Moslem king urged an old Jewish man to point out the locality of the temple.

> Then the king grew urgent with that old man until he pointed it out. the king was a friend of the Jews, and said: 'I will build here a temple, and none but Jews shall pray therein.' He built the temple of marble stone, a beautiful structure consisting of red, green, and variegated marble.[268]

Benjamin states that the Gentiles do not bring in images, but merely come there to pray. While Petachia states: "Then came Gentiles and put images in it, but they fell down. They then fixed the images in the thickness of the wall, but in the Holy of Holies they could not place any."[269]

The entire area of the Temple Mount is considered sacred. Specific spots, holy in themselves, build to a crescendo of holiness that peaks at the Temple Mount—the sanctuary, the holy of holies. The deep religious meaning of the area is reflected in the halachic interpretations which allegorically related the city of Jerusalem to the "camp of Israel"; the Temple Mount to the "camp of Levites"; and the Temple Courts to the camp of the "Divine Presence."[270] Virtually every Jew who made his pilgrimage there emotionally felt the impact of this spot. Following the twelfth-century travellers, Rabbi Jacob the Messenger from Paris reports that he looked at the Temple Mount from a nearby hill, and he lists the sites of the Altar, the Temple, and the sanctuary. He also notices the Mosque of Omar erected on the site of the holy of holies around the Eben Shethiah (considered to be the foundation stone of the Temple).[271] Furthermore, he adds that the Moslems gather there in crowds on their festival days to dance.[272] It is important to keep in mind that this mid-thirteenth century traveller came to the city shortly after it had been reconquered by

Saladin. Thus, his report indicates the long-standing struggle for possession of the Holy Land. Mere possession of the city heightened its holy value to the Moslems. On the other hand, our twelfth-century travellers were reflecting the period of Christian ownership of the Land. Benjamin's account indicates that every spot had been Christianized. Saewulf (1102) associates everything in the Temple area with the Christian tradition. It is obvious that the crusaders' influence strengthened the Christianization of the Land.[273] The crusaders opened the Temple area to public visitation. The monks attempted to identify scriptural events with their actual locations, exemplifying the caution which must be used in the interests of historical accuracy.

Petachia does not specifically name the Western Wall (Murum de Lamentatione), but he probably has reference to it when he refers to the entire area; however, Benjamin and Jacob allude to the Western Wall by name. Benjamin states that it is one of the walls of the holy of holies, and all Jews come there to pray. Jacob notices that: "its upper stones are new,"[274] which indicates slight restoration of the wall for unknown reasons.

The Western Wall was sanctified because of its proximity to the Temple Mount, from which, the Jews believe, the Divine Presence never departed.[275] It simultaneously symbolized a mourning for past Jewish glory and hopes of future salvation.[276] However, the Western Wall gains in significance only from the beginning of the sixteenth century in Jewish sources.[277]

Shiloh, the capital of Israel during the period of the Judges, was the centre of Israelite worship (I Samuel 1:2; Jeremiah 7:12, 14; 26:6, 9; Psalms 78:60). Theodorus Lector records that the Byzantine Emperor Arcadius (383-408) removed the bones of Samuel to Constantinople in 406.[278] However, pilgrims searched for the grave site of Samuel at Ramah, using biblical evidence for this conclusion (I Samuel 25:1; 28:3). They unearthed evidence proving that Ramah was in fact Ramleh as it is testified by

Benjamin.[279]   Therefore, the tomb of Samuel was
sited at Ramleh.[280]   Benjamin states:

> Three parasangs further (from Beit Jibrin)
> one reached St. Samuel of Shiloh. This is
> the Shiloh which is two parasangs from
> Jerusalem. When the Christians captured
> Ramleh, the Ramah of old...they found there
> the grave of Samuel the Ramathite close to
> a Jewish synagogue. The Christians took
> the remains, conveyed them into Shiloh, and
> erected over them a large church, and called
> it St. Samuel of Shiloh unto this day.[281]

Benjamin records that the crusaders removed
Samuel's remains from Ramleh to the highest mountain
overlooking Jerusalem, El Nabi-Samwil,[282] which is
Shiloh.[283]   According to Benjamin the crusaders
found at Ramleh (Ramah of Old) a synagogue, in addition to the grave of Samuel. It is known that the
Karaites had a synagogue at Ramleh in 1013.[284]   Benjamin also relates that the crusaders erected a
church over Samuel's tomb. It is known that Baldwin
the Second (1118-1131) gave the area to the Premon-
stratensian Order, which built a church on the site
in 1157.[285]   Following Saladin's conquest, Moslems
and Jews turned the ruins of that Church into prayer
houses.[286]   Jewish pilgrims also identified the
site with the graves of Hannah, Elkanah, and his
two sons.[287]   On the twenty-eighth of Iyyar, the
traditional date of Samuel's death, thousands of
Jews gathered there in Medieval times to offer prayers and kindle lights. Meshullam ben Menahem (1481)
clearly testifies to this.[288]   Further reading of
this account makes it apparent that Benjamin's account reflects the period of the crusades, and Meshullam's the later Moslem period.

Benjamin and Jacob b. Nathaniel mention the
Tomb of Joseph in Shechem.[289]   Jacob b. Nathaniel
states:

> Joseph the righteous is buried in a cave
> where there are two coffins, and candles
> are lighted every evening. Once a knight

226

came in...and said, who is this. And they
said, it is Joseph.... And he had an axe
in his hand and struck the grave, and be-
hold a miracle. He died instantaneously.[290]

While one of the coffins holds the remains of Joseph,
it is unclear who is buried in the other one. It
seems that Jacob actually entered the cave, while we
cannot determine actual entry by Benjamin. Since
the latter states that no Jews lives in Shechem,[291]
it can be implied that Jacob might have relied upon
stories told by Samaritans who honoured the place
as well.

Isaac Chelo (1334) refers to pilgrims who come
to visit Joseph's tomb, and mentions a well allegedly dug by the Patriarch.[292] This tradition is not
supported by twelfth-century travellers' accounts.
However, Jacob b. Nathaniel speaks of Miriam's well,
close to the hot springs of Tiberias.[293] A similar
well is mentioned by Benjamin in Ascalon, located
centrally in the city "...which they called Bir
Abraham: this the patriarch dug in the days of the
Philistines."[294] Jacob b. Nathaniel also mentions
this well.[295] It is interesting to state that Ali
of Herat, Benjamin's contemporary, writes: "Askelon
is a fine city. There is near here the well of
Abraham, which they say he dug with his own hand."296
Ibn Battuta in 1355 found Ascalon in ruins. However,
he still mentions the well.[297]

Jacob's well is famous, and considerable material can be found in the Palestine Exploration Fund
relating to its history and associations.[298] Tid-
bits of information concerning wells (i.e., near
Shechem and Ascalon) and other items are given relating to many places. Thus, Petachia mentions that
he saw the stone over the well near Haran, which
Jacob moved for Rachel.[299] Furthermore, in Mamre,
close to Hebron, he noticed the well of Sarah with
its waters "clear and sweet" and not far from it he
saw Abraham's well and found its waters to be "very
agreeable."[300] Rabbi Petachia continues that an old
Jewish man living at Mamre affirmed with an oath,
that on the fast Day of Atonement, he had seen a

fiery angel offering up his devotions and a fiery
horse by the well of Sarah.[301]

In the neighbourhood of Shechem, Jacob b.
Nathaniel speaks of a cave "in which Baasha, King
of Israel, is buried, and on a high hill in the
forest is the grave of Zipporah, and a lion guards
her and man may not enter or cut wood from the
forest...."[302] Jacob continues that many other unknown graves are around, including a great cave
"which some say is the grave of Jonah, the son of
Amittai."[303] However, at the beginning of his account, he says that he saw the grave of Jonah "in
Kiriath Arba, which is Hebron."[304] At the same
time, Benjamin and Petachia locate the prophet's
grave in different places. Benjamin records that
Jonah is buried in Sepphoris,[305] once a chief city
in Galilee,[306] while in Mosul he found the "synagogue of Obadiah, built by Jonah."[307] It is true,
however, that Benjamin is careful and speaks of the
place as a synagogue. Nevertheless, local Moslems
believe that Jonah is buried there. After examining the place Layard concluded that the tradition
which locates Jonah's tomb here is nothing but a
legend.[308] Petachia, on the other hand, general-
izes, locating the tomb between upper Galilee and
Rachel's grave. We read:

> From thence he went to the grave of Jonah,
> son of Amittai. There is a beautiful pal-
> ace built over it. Near it is a pleasure
> garden, wherein all kinds of fruit are
> found. The keeper of the pleasure garden
> is a Gentile. Nevertheless, when Gentiles
> come there he gives them no fruit, but
> when Jews come he gives them a friendly
> reception, saying Jonah...was a Jew, there-
> fore, it is due to you to partake of what
> is his....[309]

The place where recent authors locate the sepulchre
of Jonah is "K'far Kana, or Kina"[310] located between Sepphoris and Tiberias.[311] They also mention
his magnificent monument, which might be the same
described by Petachia. Clearly many legends and

traditions surrounding Jonah's tomb make its exact location subject to inquiry, as indicated by the conflicting reports of our travellers.

In Caesarea, Jacob b. Nathaniel speaks of the grave of the ten Mishnaic martyrs, among whom Rabbi Akiva is the most famous.312 Jacob states that the site of their martyrdom is located by the ruins of a great marble stone. He further relates that a Gentile was buried close to the cave, and

> In a dream he came to the rulers...and cried ... 'Take me away...for they smite me with iron rods heated in the fire,' and he said to them that in this cave there are twelve dead men clothed in prayer cloaks...that Gentile was a fisherman and all the fishermen died.... Furthermore, they say that the great marble stone was the throne of Caesar and never does any grass grow in the place where the righteous were martyred.313

Generally speaking, the Galilee area is filled with holy memories of localities ascribed to biblical prophets and to Tannaim, Amoraim, and Gaonim. Jews continuously visited those holy places, following the true spirit of tradition. Many circulating traditions concerning holy places in Babylonia314 and the Holy Land can be found by anyone who reads Ish Shalom's article315 and the twelfth-century accounts. When the Jewish population in the Holy Land decreased, many spots were forgotten. With the return of Jewry after the Spanish expulsion (1492), these localities were renewed to the Jewish experience. Naturally pilgrims identified Jerusalem, Hebron, Safed, and Tiberias as being most sacred, but other small localities in the Galilee (K'far Alma, K'far Kana, Peqiin, K'far Yasif, and S'efaram, etc.) gained prominence as holy spots and attracted many pilgrims.316

Thus our travellers reflect twelfth-century traditions regarding holy spots in the Galilee. Benjamin states that in Sepphoris there "are the graves of Rabbenu Hakkadosh,...and of Rabbi Chiya,...they

are all buried in the mountain. Many other Jewish
graves are here."[317] Petachia adds, "a pleasing
odor ascends from his grave [Rabbi Jehudah's].
This odor is smelled at a distance of a mile from
his grave."[318] Rabbenu Hakkadosh is Rabbi Judah
the Patriarch, founder of the Mishnah, and Rabbi
Chiya is the author of the Tosefta (Supplementary
Mishnah). Later, the graves of the sons and scholars of Rabbi Judah were located at Sepphoris,
while those of Rabbi Chiya and his two sons were
re-located at Tiberias.[319]

Most of the later travellers also report Rabbi
Judah the Prince's grave at Sepphoris, reflecting
a talmudic tradition.[320] Only Estori ha-Parchi is
uncertain about this.[321] Both Benjamin and Petachia indicate that many other graves are to be
found around Sepphoris, without specifying ownership. It is obvious that the tradition credited the
graves to famous Jewish personalities of ancient
times. However, the individual identification of
the graves has been obscured by history.

At Tiberias itself, Petachia mentions a synagogue traditionally built by Joshua, son of Nun.[322]
While Benjamin states that "nearby [Tiberias] is
the synagogue of Caleb, Ben Jephunneh."[323] The sepulchres of both were shown in the same proximity on
Mount Gaash,[324] where Jacob b. Nathaniel also reported two graves existing: "One of our Lord
Joshua, the son of Nun, and one of Caleb, Ben Jephunneh."[325] Interestingly, we read in Petachia's
account:

> Mt. Gaash is very high:[326] ...the mountain
> is ascended by means of steps, formed in
> it. In the midst of the mountain Joshua,
> son of Nun, is buried, and by his side Caleb,
> son of Jephunneh. Close by a spring of good
> water gushes from the mountains: there are
> beautiful palaces erected near the graves.
> ...Near one of the palaces a foot-print is
> perceptible, like that of a human being
> treading on snow. This is that which the
> angel imprinted after the death of Joshua,

230

...when the land of Israel was shaken.[327]

Obviously, Petachia explains the sweetness of the
water due to its location close to the holy graves.
He identifies footprints and associates them with
the biblical story of an earthquate.[328] He also
notices two structures over the grave. It is apparent that Jacob and Petachia are in agreement in
the identification of those two graves.[329]

In the lower Galilee, without specifying the
exact locality, Petachia

> [found]...a cave...spacious and high....
> On one side of the cave are buried Shammai
> and his disciples: and on the other Hillel
> and his disciples. In the middle...there
> is a large stone, hollow like a cup....
> When worthy men enter, the stone sppears
> full of sweet water: these may then wash
> hands and feet, and pray, imploring God
> for what they desire.... The water appears
> in honour of a man who is worthy...though
> men were to draw from the stone a thousand
> jugs of water its quantity could not be
> diminished....[330]

Jacob b. Nathaniel also does not specify the place
in which he saw[331] the graves of those two famous
sages from the Second Temple Period.[332] Benjamin,
being more accurate, states that the Cave, in which
those famous Rabbis' graves are to be found, is
located in the neighbourhood of Meron.[333] Rabbi
Samuel ben Samson speaks of the sepulchre at Meron,
"and thirty-six other tombs as well."[334] Recently,
the tradition transported the graves of Shammai and
his pupils to a cave close to the Meron River,[335]
removing them from their previously accepted spot
in conjunction with Hillel's.

Benjamin and Petachia do not mention the famous tomb of Rabbi Simeon ben Yohai at Meron, while
Jacob b. Nathaniel does. He states: "At Meron,
Rabbi Simeon ben Yohai and his son are buried, and
there are two monuments thereon, and his college is

231

still standing. From there it is three parasangs
to Kefar Hanan, and his synagogue is there in the
hill with only one wall built."[336] Implied then
is the famous sepulchre of the well-known tanna
from the mid-second century[337] along with his son,
Eleazar. Those two graves are quite prominent and
were known according to a Talmudic legend.[338] The
legend speaks of the father appearing in a dream
to the Jews of Meron with the request that his
son's grave be re-located near his own at Meron.
Jacob notices the college, which is substantiated
in 1210 by Samuel ben Samson, with further details.[339] Both travellers mention other unknown
graves in the vicinity.[340]

Benjamin places the grave of the famous sage
of the Second Temple period, Rabbi Johanan ben
Zakkai, close to the hot springs of Tiberias.[341]
Later catalogues also mention his sepulchre in
Tiberias.[342] Jacob b. Nathaniel mentions the famous scholar,[343] buried along with some of his pupils. He adds: "The people of all nations kindle
lights there, and sick and barren come there and
are healed."[344] Thanks to Jacob b. Nathaniel comes
information about this sepulchre as a pilgrimage
site for various faiths. On the other hand, it is
difficult to decide whether Jews used to bury their
dead near those famous graves since many bone-
filled coffins are mentioned in Jacob's account.[345]

Benjamin speaks of the tomb of Barak ben Abi-
noam at Kedesh Naphtali.[346] The identification
seems to be correct.[347] Josephus places it on the
frontier of Galilee, and Eusebius and St. Jerome
place it near Banias,[348] a one-day journey from
Kedesh Naphtali according to Benjamin.[349] Barak
is known from the Book of Judges (Chapter 4). The
Books of Yihus Hazzadikkim and haAvot add there
the sepulchres of Deborah and Yael.[350]

Here it is interesting to discover the birth
of traditions. Many pilgrims located the burial
place of Barak at Kedesh Naphtali. As mentioned
above, some added the tomb of Deborah there. Ish
Shalom notices[351] that the origins of this tradi-

tion is in the biblical verse (Judges 4:9) and
fledgling traditions which matured by association
with biblical stories. Some of these traditions
escape exact verification because of divergent elements of composition. Often the tradition ignored
the biblical source. Thus, from the Scripture it
is known that Miriam, sister of Moses, is buried
in Kadesh in the desert (South Palestine) (Numbers
20:1-2). However, the tradition ignored the facts
and refers to Miriam's burial site at Tiberias, as
mentioned above by Rabbi Jacob b. Nathaniel ha-
Cohen. Where did this tradition originate? Another known tradition, as mentioned previously by
our traveller Jacob, refers to Miriam's well near
Tiberias. Apparently, pilgrims created their own
explanations relating her burial site nearby, as
verified by Jacob ben Nathaniel.[352]

The most primitive type of tradition regarding graves, is that which is based upon the very
name of the place where the personality lives and
acted. Usually tradition locates burial places
within the locality. Many examples substantiate
this, such as the previously mentioned account of
Petachia which places the grave of Nitai the Arbe-
lite in Arbel.[353] Furthermore, all the travellers
mention the burial places of Hillel and Shammai in
Meron, where nearby is a place called Shamma. It
was natural to assume that the sepulchre of Shammai would be near a place called Shamma, and equally logical to assume that of Hillel is nearby.
Furthermore, in the book Caphtor Va Perach by
Estori ha-Parchi[354] we read: "You will find that
most of the tribes are in the villages spread out
in Palestine, and that village is called according
to the tribe buried there." The truth lies in
diametric opposition to the tradition as proved by
the following: 1) Estori ha-Parchi tries to find
Dan's tomb in the village of Danna, in the Jezreel
Valley;[355] 2) the twelfth-century travellers locate
Rabbi Akiva's grave in the neighbourhoos of Tiberias, where the village by the name 'Akaba is close
by.[356]

To summarize, the graves in the Galilee were

sanctified by their association with famous pious
personages of Jewish history. These personages
originated during the biblical period, and continued through the pre- and post-talmudic periods.
The mysterious traditions arose later when pilgrims
attempted to restore them to their former glory.
Clearly, unknown personalities were buried around
the famous graves, as testified by the twelfth-
century travellers. The exact locations of the famous graves are difficult to determine because of
conflicting accounts.[357] Even a man with tenden-
cies towards belief in the supernatural, such as
Jacob b. Nathaniel, sometimes admits cautiously
that the tradition may not be accurate historically.
Renan states:

> We shall not insist on the apocryphal char-
> acter of the tombs of the doctors whom the
> Jewish pilgrims in the middle ages place in
> every one of the cities of Galilee. In or-
> der to understand how little foundation in
> fact this tradition possesses, it suffices
> to remark that many of the men supposed to
> be buried in Galilee never even went there.
> ... As the traditions of Galilee were Tal-
> mudic, this country was filled with Talmu-
> dic legends.[358]

The fact that R. Jacob b. Nathaniel admits frequently that identification is unknown is clear
evidence to the circulation of various traditions
concerning those holy graves in the various spots
in the Holy Land.[359] Wilson states: "Ancient
tombs are thickly scattered over the whole of Palestine, especially near those places where there are
traces of the site of a town or a village,"[360] and
especially in the Galilee. The isolation of the
Galilee, geographically speaking, is a sufficient
explanation for the existence of the most numerous
and contradictory traditions in regard to the location and identification of the holy graves there.
The account of Benjamin is too cautious to include
the circulating traditions; however, the other two
travellers give us insight into those traditions
by simply including them in their accounts.

234

The smallest item in most localities within
the Holy Land becomes significant by association
with the Jewish historical past. From this point
of view, the Jewish travellers (especially Jacob
and Petachia) may be likened to Christian pilgrims
of the early Middle Ages (and even the twelfth-
century ones) who associated many areas of the Holy
Land with Christian tradition. Stones, trees,
bodies of water, wells, walls— all acquired a special sanctity by association with the past. Surrounding items were reputed to have special healing
powers gained by their proximity in relation to the
holy person. Imaginative imprints (i.e., the
angel's footprints recorded by Petachia) reflect
the growing core of stories and legends circulating
around the holy grave.

The accounts of the holy tombs and sites indicate additionally the familiarity of these travellers with their historical past (at least with the
names they mentioned). This implication might be
further extended to reflect the travellers' broad
general knowledge of the geography of the Holy
Land.[361] In this light, the travellers' special
attachment to the Holy Land is hardly surprising.
Palestine, therefore, occupies a special part of
their accounts. In fact, it is the only one in
Jacob's itinerary. "Terra Sancta" had a deeply-
rooted connection with the Jewish past and held
the seeds for future Jewish redemption. This last
point leads to the next chapter, which furnishes a
more detailed analysis of the subject.

Footnotes

[1]Quoted from The Itinerary of Benjamin of
Tudela, ed. M.N. Adler, p. 21, n. 4. See also Beaz-
ley, II, 241; Ritter, The Comparative Geography of
Palestine and the Sinaitic Peninsula, II, 55.

[2]See Chapter II in the book.

235

[3]The crusaders' chronicles omit mention of
the Jewish settlements to any degree. Prawer thinks
that this underlines the fact that the crusaders
were not generally concerned with the native population (Prawer, "The Jews in the Latin Kingdom of Jerusalem," p. 39; B.Z. Dinur, "A Study of the History
of the Jews in Palestine during the First Crusade,"
Zion-Measef, II [1927], 38, n. 2).

[4]M. Ish Shalom, Christian Travels in the Holy
Land (Tel-Aviv, 1965), p. 88; Prawer, A History of
the Latin Kingdom of Jerusalem, I, 420; Dinur,
Israel in Diaspora (1)I, 198.

[5]Mann, The Jews in Egypt and Palestine under
the Fatimid Caliphs, II, 199-200; Mann, Texts and
Studies in Jewish History and Literature, II, 42.

[6]M. Benvenisti, The Crusaders in the Holy Land
(Jerusalem, 1970), p. 18.

[7]Yishuv, The Book of Yishuv, ed. S. Klein
(Jerusalem, 1938-39), II, Introduction.

[8]Prawer, "The Jews in the Latin Kingdom of
Jerusalem," pp. 38-39; Dinur, "A Study of the History of the Jews in Palestine during the First Crusade," pp. 51, 55, 64.

[9]Dinur, Israel in Diaspora (1)II, 405; Mann,
"The Messianic Movements in the Time of the Early
Crusades," p. 260.

[10]Prawer, A History of the Latin Kingdom of
Jerusalem, I, 141.

[11]William of Tyre, I, 372.

[12]Ibn al-Qalānisī, History of Damascus, ed. H.
F. Amedroz (Leyden, 1908), Arabic text, p. 137; S.
Munk, Palestine (Paris, 1845), p. 260.

[13]Baron, A Social and Religious History of the
Jews, IV, 110.

[14] S.D. Goitein, "New Sources on the Fate of the Jews in the Time Jerusalem was Conquered by the Crusaders," Zion, XVII (1952), 144.

[15] Abraham Bar Hiyya, Sefer Megillat ha-Megalleh, ed. A. Poznanski (Berlin, 1924), p. 99.

[16] Ibid.; Goitein, "New Sources on the Fate of the Jews in the Time of Jerusalem Was Conquered by the Crusaders," 136.

[17] Prawer, A History of the Latin Kingdom of Jerusalem, I, 313-14.

[18] Ibid., pp. 191, 166.

[19] Ibid., p. 216.

[20] Ibid., p. 427.

[21] Dinur, Israel in Diaspora (1)II, 400.

[22] William of Tyre, I, 399.

[23] Of this city, history, archaeology, see Ritter, The Comparative Geography of Palestine and the Sinaitic Peninsula, II, 256-62.

[24] Ya'ari, Travels to Palestine, p. 69.

[25] Alkharizi, p. 350.

[26] Itinerary of R. Samuel ben Samson, ed. E.N. Adler, Jewish Travellers, p. 107.

[27] A fact already noticed by the Jewish traveller Rabbi Jacob, the Messenger of Rabbi Jechiel of Paris, 1238-44 (Jewish Travellers, ed. E.N. Adler, p. 124). See also Uri Ben Simeon, Yihus Ha-Avot, Genealogia Patriarcharum, Prophetarum, Fustorum, Tannaorum, Amoraorum, Super Quibus Pax, in Terra Israëlis, Extraeam, ed. Joh. Henricus Hottingerus, Cippi Hebraici (Heidelberg, 1659), p. 57.

237

[28]Edrisi describes this famous place in more than usual length (Edrisi, I, 347).

[29]The Itinerary of Benjamin of Tudela, ed. M. N. Adler, p. 28.

[30]It is well known that, during the Middle Ages, Jews were often employed as astrologers by Arab rulers. Petachia and Benjamin testify to this (The Itinerary of Benjamin of Tudela, ed. M.N. Adler, pp. 33, 80; The Itinerary of Petachia, ed. Grunhut, p. 7).

[31]The Itinerary of Petachia, ed. E.N. Adler, Jewish Travellers, p. 86; The Itinerary of Petachia, ed. Grünhut, p. 29.

[32]The Itinerary of Petachia, ed. E.N. Adler, Jewish Travellers, p. 96; The Itinerary of Petachia, ed. Grünhut, pp. 13-14.

[33]Mann, The Jews in Egypt and Palestine under the Fatimid Caliphs, I, 166.

[34]Mann published such a letter (ibid., II, 193). Edrisi names four springs which were used as baths. In addition, he says there were other ones further south which were much resorted to by the sick (Edrisi, I, 347). Mukaddasi also refers to these hot springs to which sick people with certain diseases would come to bathe (Le Strange, Palestine under the Moslems, pp. 335-36; Al. Mukaddasi, Description of Syria Including Palestine, Palestine Pilgrims Text Society, III [London, 1886], 83). For more details see Ritter, The Comparative Geography of Palestine and the Sinaitic Peninsula, II, 246-48.

[35]Prawer, A History of the Latin Kingdom of Jerusalem, I, 428.

[36]The Itinerary of Benjamin of Tudela, ed. M. N. Adler, p. 29.

[37] Ibid.

[38] Ibid., p. 28.

[39] Of the history of Jerusalem, meaning and archaeology, see Ritter, The Comparative Geography of Palestine and the Sinaitic Peninsula, IV, 1-212.

[40] The Itinerary of Jacob b. Nathaniel ha-Cohen, ed. E.N. Adler, Jewish Travellers, p. 99.

[41] The Itinerary of Petachia, ed. E.N. Adler, Jewish Travellers, p. 88; The Itinerary of Petachia, ed. Grünhut, p. 32.

[42] The Itinerary of Benjamin of Tudela, ed. M.N. Adler, p. 22. For details on the population of the city, see Ritter, The Comparative Geography of Palestine and the Sinaitic Peninsula, IV, 189-212.

[43] See Chapter IV, section 1.

[44] William of Tyre, I, 378.

[45] "Megillat Obadiah the Proselyte," ed. S.A. Wurtheimer, Ginze Yerushalayim (Jerusalem, 1896), Part II, pp. 16-17; Abraham bar Hiyya, Sefer Megillat ha-Megalleh, p. 99; Alkharizi, p. 247.

[46] Prawer, "The Jews in the Latin Kingdom of Jerusalem," p. 46.

[47] Benjamin of Tudela, Sefer Masa'ot, ed. Asher, II, 89, n. 171.

[48] Alkharizi, p. 248.

[49] The Itinerary of Benjamin of Tudela, ed. M. N. Adler, p. 22, n. 2.

[50] Ibid.

[51] Baron, A Social and Religious History of the Jews, IV, 297, n. 32; Dinur, "A Study of the History of the Jews in Palestine during the First

239

Crusade," p. 54.

[52]Alkharizi, p. 248; Goitein, "Letter from Eretz Israel Dating to the Crusader Period," Yerushalayim, Review for Eretz Israel Research, II/V (1955), 56.

[53]Alkharizi, p. 350.

[54]Ish Shalom, Christian Travels in the Holy Land, p. 95.

[55]D. Corcos-Abulafia, "The Attitude of the Almohadic Rulers towards the Jews," Zion, XXXII (1967), 158.

[56]Ibn Verga, Shevet Jehudah, p. 147; Chazan, Medieval Jewry in Northern France, pp. 80, 87. On the supposed philosophic and religious motivations see S. Krauss, "L'émigration de 300 rabbins en Palestine en l'an 1211," R.E.J., LXXXII (1926), 333-343.

[57]Itinerary of R. Samuel ben Samson, ed. E.N. Adler, Jewish Travellers, p. 103.

[58]Ritter, The Comparative Geography of Palestine and the Sinaitic Peninsula, IV, 260-65; Mann, The Jews in Egypt and Palestine under the Fatimid Caliphs, I, 41-42, 155; II, 176-178. See also the account of Nasir-i-Khusrau, who visited Ramleh in 1047 (Le Strange, Palestine under the Moslems, pp. 306-7).

[59]The Itinerary of Benjamin of Tudela, ed. M.N. Adler, p. 27.

[60]Edrisi states that Ramleh was a great centre of trade (Edrisi, I, 339).

[61]The last known document regarding Jews in Ramleh prior to the crusaders' conquest dates from 1094 (Yishuv, II, 63, No. 42). See also Mann, The Jews in Egypt and Palestine under the Fatimid Caliphs, II, 200-1.

[62] Benjamin of Tudela, Sefer Masa'ot, ed. Asher, I, 79.

[63] The Itinerary of Benjamin of Tudela, ed. M. N. Adler, p. 27, n. 4; Dinur, "A Study of the History of the Jews in Palestine during the First Crusade," p. 42, n. 9.

[64] Those who accept Adler's reading assume that it was the Jews of Marseilles who re-established the Jewish community there (Dinur, ibid., pp. 43, 44). Prawer rejects this opinion because of various difficulties (Prawer, "The Jews in the Latin Kingdom of Jerusalem," p. 40). Dinur believes that the Jews who fled before the approaching crusaders returned to re-establish their community, but not before the middle of the twelfth century (Dinur, "A Study of the History of the Jews in Palestine during the First Crusade," pp. 43, 49 and 42, n. 9).

[65] Prawer, A History of the Latin Kingdom of Jerusalem, I, 426.

[66] Ibid., p. 431, n. 114.

[67] See further on in this chapter. On the divisions of Palestine into Judaea, Samaria, and Galilee, and the physical basis of this partition, see Ritter, The Comparative Geography of Palestine and the Sinaitic Peninsula, III, 191-200.

[68] Tyre fell in 1124, and Ascalon in 1153 (Prawer, A History of the Latin Kingdom of Jerusalem, I, 311-12, 216-17).

[69] Ibid., p. 428.

[70] The Itinerary of Benjamin of Tudela, ed. M.N. Adler, p. 18.

[71] Edrisi, I, 349.

[72] See Chapter VII in the book.

[73] Yishuv, II, Introduction; Mann, The Jews in

Egypt and Palestine under the Fatimid Caliphs, I,
178-93; Mann, Texts and Studies in Jewish History
and Literature, I, 249 and 249, n. 3.

[74]Prawer, A History of the Latin Kingdom of
Jerusalem, II, 400-401.

[75]R. Röhricht, Regesta Regni Hierosolymitani
(Innsbrück, 1893-1904), No. 1114, p. 290.

[76]Prawer, A History of the Latin Kingdom of
Jerusalem, II, 400.

[77]On the history of the city and its ruins, see
Ritter, The Comparative Geography of Palestine and
the Sinaitic Peninsula, III, 214-20.

[78]Mann, The Jews in Egypt and Palestine under
the Fatimid Caliphs, II, 198.

[79]The Itinerary of Benjamin of Tudela, ed. M.N.
Adler, p. 28.

[80]J. Prawer, "The City and Duchy of Ascalon in
the Crusader Period," Eretz Israel, V (1958), 233-
34; S.D. Goitein, "A Letter from Ascalon during its
Occupation by the Crusaders," Tarbiz, XXXI (1962),
287, 290.

[81]Yishuv, II, Introduction, p. 21.

[82]Prawer, A History of the Latin Kingdom of
Jerusalem, I, 314.

[83]Mann, The Jews in Egypt and Palestine under
the Fatimid Caliphs, I, 170; II, 201.

[84]Benjamin attempts to locate the ruins of Ascalon as well, though the location he gives is unreli-
able. See Survey of Western Palestine. Memoirs,
ed. E.H. Palmer and W. Besant (London, 1881-83), III,
244-45.

[85]The Itinerary of Benjamin of Tudela, ed. M.N.
Adler, p. 19.

[86] The Itinerary of Petachia, ed. E.N. Adler, Jewish Travellers, p. 86.

[87] Dinur, Israel in Diaspora (1) II, 495.

[88] Mann, The Jews in Egypt and Palestine under the Fatimid Caliphs, II, 371, n. 2.

[89] Prawer, "The Jews in the Latin Kingdom of Jerusalem," p. 57.

[90] Mann, The Jews in Egypt and Palestine under the Fatimid Caliphs, II, 370, 383. See note 56 above.

[91] Benvenisti, pp. 78, 80-82. Edrisi states correctly that the city comprised a harbour within itself (Edrisi, I, 348). Edrisi wrote at a time when the city was in its prime, having a crowded population. See also Ibn Jubayr, p. 318.

[92] Prawer, A History of the Latin Kingdom of Jerusalem, I, 181.

[93] Some of the talmudic rabbis, however, considered Acre as a frontier town, and not as part of Palestine. See Mann, The Jews in Egypt and Palestine under the Fatimid Caliphs, I, 191; II, 225; The Travels of Petachia, ed. Benisch, p. 103, n. 97.

[94] Alkharizi, pp. 369-70.

[95] For the reason for his condemnation of the Jewish community, see Prawer's hypothesis developed in "The Jews in the Latin Kingdom of Jerusalem," p. 59.

[96] Maimonides, Maimonidean Responsa, No. 159.

[97] On Acre and its ruins see Ritter, The Comparative Geography of Palestine and the Sinaitic Peninsula, IV, 361-68.

[98] The Itinerary of Benjamin of Tudela, ed. M.N. Adler, p. 19.

[99]Benvenisti, p. 18.

[100]Palestine Pilgrims Text Society, III, 20; Le Strange, Palestine under the Moslems, p. 446.

[101]Mann, The Jews in Egypt and Palestine under the Fatimid Caliphs, I, 42, 188.

[102]At the time of Edrisi, Haifa must have been a large and flourishing place (Edrisi, I, 348).

[103]Mann, The Jews in Egypt and Palestine under the Fatimid Caliphs, I, 191; II, 225; Prawer, A History of the Latin Kingdom of Jerusalem, I, 170.

[104]Albertus Aquensis, RHC, HOcc., III, 521.

[105]Prawer, A History of the Latin Kingdom of Jerusalem, I, 170, 425-26. Benjamin found existing Jewish communities in other coastal cities (The Itinerary of Benjamin of Tudela, ed. M.N. Adler, pp. 17, 18, 20).

[106]Survey of Western Palestine, II, 276-77. For Jaffa and its past, see Ritter, The Comparative Geography of Palestine and the Sinaitic Peninsula. IV, 253-59.

[107]The Itinerary of Benjamin of Tudela, ed. M.N. Adler, p. 27.

[108]Prawer, A History of the Latin Kingdom of Jerusalem, I, 426; Yishuv, II, 15, n. 3.

[109]The Itinerary of Benjamin of Tudela, ed. M.N. Adler, p. 27. For details on the ruins, see Ritter, The Comparative Geography of Palestine and the Sinaitic Peninsula, III, 224-25, 221.

[110]The Itinerary of Petachia, ed. E.N. Adler, Jewish Travellers, p. 86.

[111]Ibid.

[112]The Itinerary of Benjamin of Tudela, ed. M.N.

Adler, p. 27.

[113]Ibid., p. 26. See A. Socin, Palestine and Syria, Handbook for Travellers, ed. R.K. Baedeker (London, 1876), p. 309.

[114]The Itinerary of Benjamin of Tudela, ed. M.N. Adler, p. 25. Bethlehem was, as it still is today, predominantly Christian (Benvenisti, p. 157).

[115]The Itinerary of Benjamin of Tudela, ed. M.N. Adler, p. 28.

[116]Ibid., pp. 25-26.

[117]The Itinerary of Petachia, ed. Grunhut, p. 35.

[118]Itinerary of R. Samuel ben Samson, ed. E.N. Adler, Jewish Travellers, p. 105.

[119]There are, however, some evidences indicating a Jewish settlement there during our period. See Mann, The Jews in Egypt and Palestine under the Fatimid Caliphs, II, 329-30; also Dinur, Israel in Diaspora (1)II, 547, n. 64.

[120]Prawer, A History of the Latin Kingdom of Jerusalem, I, 361-420; Prawer, "The Jews in the Latin Kingdom of Jerusalem," pp. 66-67.

[121]E.H. Byrne, "Genoese Trade with Syria in the Twelfth Century," A.H.R., XXV (1919-20), 191-219. A detailed description of commerce will be given in Chapter VII in the book. Two late documents dated 1274 and 1280 indicate Jewish involvement in banking in the Holy Land, but of course it cannot be taken as a proof for an earlier period. (Röh-richt, Regesta Regni Hierosolymitani, Nos. 1399, 1435).

[122]Yishuv, II, 135; Palestine Pilgrims Text Society, III, 77.

[123]The Itinerary of Benjamin of Tudela, ed. M.N. Adler, p. 18.

[124] Yishuv, I, 36. Goitein states: "Character-
izing dyeing as despised or low is an unjustified
generalization" (Goitein, "Jewish Society and Institutions under Islam," p. 177).

[125] William of Tyre, II, 292.

[126] Maimonides, Maimonidean Responsa, No. 159.

[127] Indeed, it is questionable whether Benjamin
actually visited all of the places in the Holy Land
mentioned in his itinerary. His visit occurred
close to the time of the second crusade when Palestine was suffering with internal conflicts and the
attack by Nur-ed-din of Damascus (Prawer, A History
of the Latin Kingdom of Jerusalem, I, 346-58).
However, it is interesting to quote here Ibn Jubayr
who states: "One of the astonishing things that is
talked of is that though the fires of discord burn
between the two parties, Muslim and Christian, two
armies of them may meet and dispose themselves in
battle array, and yet Muslim and Christian travellers will come and go between them without interfer-
ence" (Ibn Jubayr, p. 300).

[128] See Chapter VI in the book.

[129] Estori ha-Parchi, pp. 81-82.

[130] A. Berger, "The Messianic self-consciousness
of Abraham-Abulafia," Essays on Jewish Life and
Thought, eds. L. Blau et al. (New York, 1959), pp.
55-61.

[131] B. Chavel, Ramban (New York, 1960), p. 62.

[132] Irving A. Agus, Rabbi Meir of Rothenburg, 2
vols. (Philadelphia, 1947), I, 125-127.

[133] See Nahmanides' Commandment Four, quoted in
footnote 37 of Chapter VI in the book.

[134] See Chapter VI in the book. Also see Prawer,
"The Jews in the Latin Kingdom of Jerusalem," p.

74; Prawer, "Jewish Resettlement in Crusader Jerusalem," _Ariel_, XIX (1967), 62.

[135]S.H. Kuk, "R. Jechiel from Paris and Palestine," _Zion-Measef_, V (1933), 97.

[136]Maimonides, _Maimonidean Responsa_, No. 180.

[137]_The Itinerary of Benjamin of Tudela_, ed. M.N.
Adler, p. 18.

[138]_Ibid._, p. 24.

[139]Prawer, "The Jews in the Latin Kingdom of
Jerusalem," p. 66.

[140]Prawer, _A History of the Latin Kingdom of
Jerusalem_, I, 430 and 430, n. 113. See also Prawer,
"Jewish Resettlement in Crusader Jerusalem," 64.

[141]_The Itinerary of Benjamin of Tudela_, ed. M.N.
Adler, p. 18.

[142]_Ibid._, pp. 17-19, 21-26, 28.

[143]Prawer, _A History of the Latin Kingdom of
Jerusalem_, I, 430.

[144]_The Itinerary of Benjamin of Tudela_, ed. M.N.
Adler, p. 29. See Chapter VI in the book; also Uri
Ben Simeon, p. 73.

[145]_Itinerary of R. Samuel ben Samson_, ed. E.N.
Adler, _Jewish Travellers_, p. 110.

[146]_Ibid._, p. 103. It seems that the impact of
the Albigensian Crusade on the Jews of Southern
France should be considered here. See P. Bourdrel,
Histoire des Juifs de France (Paris, 1974), pp. 38-
46. R. Samuel b. Samson exemplified it. For different views on the reasons for the emigration of
300 French and English Rabbis in 1211, see references cited in note 56 above.

[147]_The Itinerary of Benjamin of Tudela_, ed. M.N.

Adler, p. 26. See also the next section of the present chapter.

[148]The Itinerary of Jacob b. Nathaniel ha-Cohen, ed. Grünhut, p. 14.

[149]It is the same spirit of the age which gave rise to the Acta Sanctorum, the fifty-three volumes of which are devoted to the lives of saints and personages reputed holy. Interestingly, Ibn Jubayr on his visit to Damascus states: "The venerated shrines in this city are more than can be recorded, and we have but outlined those that are celebrated and known.... Prayers said in this blessed place are answered, as has been experienced by many..." (Ibn Jubayr, pp. 290, 293).

[150]J.D. Eisenstein (ed.), A Collection of Itineraries by Jewish Travellers to Palestine, Syria, Egypt and Other Countries (Tel-Aviv, 1969), p. 329.

[151]Thus we read: "And why did Moses' grave remain hidden? To prevent Israel from...worshipping and sacrificing there" (M. Ish Shalom, "Tradition of Graves in Palestine," Sinai, VII (1940-41), 82,

[152]Mishnah Sekalim, 1.1.

[153]Sotah, 34b.

[154]Matt. 23:29, Luke 11:47-48.

[155]S. Pinsker, Likkute Kadmoniyot, 2 vols. (Jerusalem, 1968), Appendix, pp. 31-32.

[156]Mann, The Jews in Egypt and Palestine under the Fatimid Caliphs, II, 357.

[157]H. Schirmann, The Hebrew Poetry in Spain and Provence, 2 vols. (Jerusalem, 1960), II, 485-90.

[158]Alkharizi, pp. 287-94.

[159]R. Jacob, the Messenger of R. Jechiel of Paris, ed. E.N. Adler, Jewish Travellers, p. 115.

For a similar example, see the opening of the book
Yihus ha-Avot, p. 27.

[160]See Ritter, The Comparative Geography of
Palestine and the Sinaitic Peninsula, II, 217.

[161]R. Jacob, the Messenger of R. Jechiel of
Paris, ed. E.N. Adler, Jewish Travellers, p. 129.

[162]G. Scholem, "Jüdische Mystik in Westeuropa
im 12. and 13. Jahrhundert," 41, 43, 45. See Chapters I and VI in the book.

[163]The author of Yihus ha-Avot opens his book
with the statement that he is planning on enumerating the holy tombs and wishes that "Deus justitiam
eorum in bonum nostrum cedere jubeat, Amen" (Uri
Ben Simeon, p. 26). Prayer at these tombs will
hasten the redemtpion (ibid., p. 29).

[164]Itinerary of R. Samuel ben Samson, ed. E.N.
Adler, Jewish Travellers, p. 103.

[165]As to the city, its history and archaeology,
see Ritter, The Comparative Geography of Palestine
and the Sinaitic Peninsula, III, 290-323.

[166]For full details on the Cave, see Ritter,
ibid., pp. 306-16; also J. Joachim, Heiligengräber
in Jesu Umwelt (Göttingen, 1958), pp. 90-94.

[167]R. Gershom ben R. Asher from Scarmelo, Sefer
Yichus Hazzaddikim, ed. A.M. Luncz (Jerusalem,
1896), p. 153. For Arab tradition about the Cave
see Le Strange, Palestine under the Moslems, pp.
316, 319, 253, 512.

[168]Maimonides introduction to commentary on Mishnah "Rosh Hashanah."

[169]The Itinerary of Benjamin of Tudela, ed. M.N.
Adler, p. 25.

[170]R.M. ha-Cohen, The Cave of Machpelah (Israel,
1970), p. 76; Survey of Western Palestine, III, 344;

Yishuv, II, 6-7.

[171] Survey of Western Palestine, III, 344.

[172] The Itinerary of Petachia, ed. E.N. Adler, Jewish Travellers, pp. 88-90; The Itinerary of Petachia, ed. Grünhut, pp. 33-34.

[173] The Itinerary of R. Jacob b. Nathaniel ha-Cohen, ed. E.N. Adler, Jewish Travellers, p. 98.

[174] The next Jew who made a pilgrimage to Hebron, Samuel ben Samson in 1210, in company with the distinguished scholar, R. Jonathan ha-Cohen de Lunel, had more difficulty in gaining access to the Cave. They were permitted to pay a secret visit at midnight (Itinerary of R. Samuel ben Samson, ed. E.N. Adler, Jewish Travellers, p. 105).

[175] See the reports of Bertinoro, The Letters of Obadiah Da Bertinoro, ed. E.N. Adler, Jewish Travellers, p. 233) and Meshullam ben R. Menahem (ibid., p. 185). The same is reported by Uri Ben Simeon, p. 31.

[176] The Itinerary of Jacob ben Nathaniel ha-Cohen, ed. E.N. Adler, Jewish Travellers, p. 98. At this time the monks had already begum to form legends and to enrich themselves at the expense of credulous pilgrims who came there (Ritter, The Comparative Geography of Palestine and the Sinaitic Peninsula, III, 313).

[177] Ha-Cohen, The Cave of Machpelah, p. 76.

[178] The Itinerary of Jacob ben Nathaniel ha-Cohen, ed. E.N. Adler, Jewish Travellers, p. 98.

[179] Benjamin of Tudela, Sefer Masa'ot, ed. Asher, II, 93, n. 175.

[180] Baron, A Social and Religious History of the Jews, II, 289-290; Braslavsky, Studies in Our Country: Its Past and Remains, pp. 95-96.

[182] The Itinerary of Jacob ben Nathaniel ha-Cohen, ed. E.N. Adler, Jewish Travellers, p. 98.

[183] See Rashi on Genesis 23:2.

[184] Joachim, pp. 96-97; Ritter, The Comparative Geography of Palestine and the Sinaitic Peninsula, III, 293; Ha-Cohen, The Cave of Machpelah, p. 74. See also S. Mähl, "Jerusalem in mittelalterlicher Sicht," Die Welt als Geschichte, XXII (1962), p. 17.

[185] Palestine Pilgrims Text Society, V. 58.

[186] Ibid., p. 53.

[187] Survey of Western Palestine, III, 343.

[188] Le Strange, Palestine Under the Moslems, p. 316. Ibn Jubayr speaks of Adam's tomb near Mecca (Ibn Jubayr, pp. 104, 286). The tradition concerning the sepulchres of Noah and Noah's son, Shem in Hebron, is originated in the Talmud (Sota, 13a; Baba Batra, 58a). For more details see R. Gershom ben R. Asher, p. 152; Ha-Cohen, The Cave of Machpelah, pp. 145-46.

[189] The Letters of Obadiah Da Bertinoro, ed. E.N. Adler, Jewish Travellers, p. 233.

[190] The Itinerary of Benjamin of Tudela, ed. M.N. Adler, p. 26.

[191] The Itinerary of Jacob ben Nathaniel ha-Cohen, ed. E.N. Adler, Jewish Travellers, p. 98. See also Ritter, The Comparative Geography of Palestine and the Sinaitic Peninsula, III, 296, 300. Another tradition locates there the burial place of Nathan the prophet (ibid., 302).

[192] P. Thomsen, Loca Sancta (Halle an der Saale, 1907), p. 116.

[193] The Itinerary of Jacob ben Nathaniel ha-Cohen, ed. E.N. Adler, Jewish Travellers, p. 98.

251

[194] P.E.F., Quarterly Statement (London, 1882), p. 197. Some believe that the origin of this tradition emerged as a result of a confusing Talmudic legend (Ish Shalom, "Tradition of Graves in Palestine," p. 91). This legend (Sota 13a; Uri Ben Simeon, p. 31) speaks of Esau's head being cut in the Cave of Machpelah. From the name "Esau" a near name "Joseph" was corrupted, and included into the non-Jewish tradition.

[195] The Itinerary of Petachia, ed. E.N. Adler, Jewish Travellers, pp. 90-91. Arculf visited the ruins at Mamre about 700, and he identified it with old Hebron (T. Wright [ed.], Early Travels in Palestine [New York, 1968], p. 6). Fabri who came from Bethlehem to Hebron (1483) tells that before he reached Hebron, he came upon an olive grove, and he was told that here stood the old city of Hebron, and this name later came to cover the later houses which sprang up around the Cave of Machpelah (Ritter, The Comparative Geography of Palestine and the Sinaitic Peninsula, III, 300). This agrees with Benjamin's account about Abraham's house and the well at the north of Hebron.

[196] Ibn Jubayr also speaks of footprints impressed on holy stones around Damascus (Ibn Jubayr, p. 294). On Abraham's Oak, its history and its significance, see P.E.F. (1899), p. 39. Abraham's Oak is recorded also on the Medeba Map, Atlas of Israel (Jerusalem, 1970), 1/1.

[197] After describing the sepulchres of Hebron, the writer of Yihus ha-Avot (written in 1537) speaks of David's father's burial and of the graves of other Israelites there. Then he goes on to say that in the neighbourhood of the city are the oaks of Mamre, where Abraham pitched his tent, and the stone on which he sat during the circumcision (Genesis 8:9, 23-27). This stone was looked upon as a sacred memorial of the covenant with the Jews (Uri Ben Simeon, pp. 31-33). Samuel ben Samson, who visited the place in 1210, tells that it was venerated by the Arabs (Itinerary of R. Samuel ben Samson, ed. E.N.

Adler, Jewish Travellers, p. 104).

[198] The Itinerary of Petachia, ed. E. N. Adler, Jewish Travellers, p. 88.

[199] Ibid.

[200] See Benjamin's and Jacob b. Nathaniel's accounts, The Itinerary of Benjamin of Tudela, ed. M. N. Adler, p. 25; The Itinerary of Jacob ben Nathaniel ha-Cohen, ed. Grünhut, p. 12.

[201] Le Strange, Palestine under the Moslems, p. 299.

[202] R. Jacob, the Messenger of R. Jechiel of Paris, ed. E.N. Adler, Jewish Travellers, p. 120.

[203] Joachim, p. 75, n. 2.

[204] Ish Shalom, Christian Travels in the Holy Land, pp. 250-51.

[205] Estori ha-Parchi, pp. 221, 229, 299. Nahmanides also deals with the tomb's identification in his commentary on Genesis 35:16. For more details see Tosef, Sota 11:7; Breshit Raba 82:9; Joachim, p. 75.

[206] Le Strange, Palestine under the Moslems, p. 299.

[207] R. Gershom ben R. Asher from Scarmelo, p. 151; Jerem. 31:15.

[208] The Itinerary of Benjamin of Tudela, ed. M.N. Adler, p. 25.

[209] A full, detailed picture of Jerusalem, its past, meaning, archaeology, see Ritter, The Comparative Geography of Palestine and the Sinaitic Peninsula, IV, 1-212.

[210] N. Avigad, Ancient Tombs in Nahal Kidron (Jerusalem, 1954), p. 1

[211] The Itinerary of Benjamin of Tudela, ed. M.N. Adler, p. 23.

[212] Ibid. See also Mähl, pp. 20-21.

[213] Uri Ben Simeon states: "Infra, in valle Jeho-shaphat, est domus viventium (coemeterium) Israelis, ..." (Uri Ben Simeon, pp. 47-48).

[214] The Itinerary of Benjamin of Tudela, ed. M.N. Adler, p. 23.

[215] Avigad, pp. 139-41.

[216] The Itinerary of Jacob ben Nathaniel ha-Cohen, ed. E.N. Adler, Jewish Travellers, p. 99.

[217] Ish Shalom, Christian Travels in the Holy Land, p. 215; Avigad, p. 3.

[218] Wright, Early Travels in Palestine, p. 4. On the place of Jerusalem in the eyes of Medieval Christianity, see Mähl, pp. 11-16.

[219] The Christian tradition, reflected in Arculf's report, appears again in the crusading period. Sae-wulf, a pilgrim to the Holy Land in 1102, states: "That field is near the sepulchres of the Holy fa-ther, Simeon the Just and Joseph the foster father of our Lord. These two sepulchres are ancient structures, in the manner of towers, cut into the foot of the mountain itself" (Wright, Early Travels in Palestine, p. 42).

[220] Avigad, pp. 3, 37-78.

[221] The Itinerary of Benjamin of Tudela, ed. M.N. Adler, p. 23.

[222] Uri Ben Simeon, pp. 45-47.

[223] Avigad, p. 4.

[224] The Itinerary of Benjamin of Tudela, ed. M.N. Adler, p. 23.

[225] Prawer, "The Jews in the Latin Kingdom of Jerusalem," p. 78.

[226] The Itinerary of Jacob ben Nathaniel ha-Cohen, ed. E.N. Adler, Jewish Travellers, p. 99.

[227] The Jewish traveller, Meshullam b. Rabbi Menahem, states: "All who pass Absalom's monument... throw a stone on his grave,..." (Meshullam ben R. Menahem of Volterra, ed. E.N. Adler, Jewish Travellers, p. 192).

[228] Prawer, "The Jews in the Latin Kingdom of Jerusalem," p. 78, n. 28. See also Mähl, pp. 20-21.

[229] Avigad, p. 141. For more details, see Ritter, The Comparative Geography of Palestine and the Sinaitic Peninsula, IV, 172-76.

[230] The Itinerary of Petachia, ed. E.N. Adler, Jewish Travellers, pp. 88, 90.

[231] Ibid., p. 99.

[232] The Itinerary of Benjamin of Tudela, ed. M.N. Adler, pp. 23-24.

[233] R. Gershom ben R. Asher from Scarmelo, pp. 145-46. See also J. Morgenstern, "The Culting Setting of the 'Enthronement Psalms,'" HUC, XXXV (1964), 14-39.

[234] See II Samuel 15:30-32; I Kings 11:7.

[235] Isaac-Ezekiel Jehuda, "The Wailing Wall," Zion Measef, III (1929), 111, 114.

[236] R. Jacob, the Messenger of R. Jechiel of Paris, ed. E.N. Adler, Jewish Travellers, p. 117.

[237] The first to mention Huldah's tomb at the top of the Mount of Olives was the Jewish traveller, Estori ha-Parchi (Estori ha-Parchi, pp. 76, 101).

[238] The Letters of Obadian Da Bertinoro, ed. E. N. Adler, Jewish Travellers, p. 240. For details, see P.E.F. (1889), pp. 174-75; (1897), pp. 307-8.

[239] Wright, Early Travels in Palestine, p. 37.

[240] Ibid., p. 5.

[241] Ibid., pp. 41-42.

[242] See Ritter, The Comparative Geography of Palestine and the Sinaitic Peninsula, IV, 54.

[243] The Itinerary of Benjamin of Tudela, ed. M. N. Adler, p. 24.

[244] During the Middle Ages the legends ascribed to it many attributes. During the crusades, a Franciscan convent was built here (Ritter, The Comparative Geography of Palestine and the Sinaitic Peninsula, IV, 55; Wright, Early Travels in Palestine, pp. 36-37.

[245] The Itinerary of Benjamin of Tudela, ed. M.N. Adler, p. 24.

[246] This tradition was known in the Talmud (Ish Shalom, "Tradition of Graves in Palestine," p. 85). In the New Testament, it seems that King David's tomb was also known (Acts [2:29]).

[247] The Itinerary of Jacob ben Nathaniel ha-Cohen, ed. E.N. Adler, Jewish Travellers, p. 99.

[248] The Itinerary of Benjamin of Tudela, ed. M.N. Adler, p. 25.

[249] Ibid., pp. 24-25.

[250] Prawer, "The Jews in the Latin Kingdom of Jerusalem," pp. 81-82.

[251] "The omen terrified the entire city and was, as we believe, a portent of disaster...." (William

of Tyre, II, 162).

[252]Clearly all the traditions (biblical and post biblical) agree with the placement of the sepulchres within the walls of Jerusalem (Y. Yeivin, "Sepulchres of the Kings of the House of David," Journal of Near Eastern Studies, VII [1948], 39-40, 45). According to Ritter, there is no reason to doubt the burial place of David on Mount Zion (Ritter, The Comparative Geography of Palestine and Sinaitic Peninsula, IV, 56).

[253]P.E.F. (1881), pp. 94, 327; Yeivin, p. 40.

[254]R. Jacob, the Messenger of R. Jechiel of Paris, ed. E.N. Adler, Jewish Travellers, p. 118.

[255]Ibid., p. 132.

[256]Hirschberg, pp. 213, 220.

[257]Ibid., p. 215.

[258]Ish Shalom, "The Tradition of Graves in Palestine," p. 93.

[259]Le Strange, Palestine under the Moslems, pp. 299-300.

[260]RHC, HOcc. III, 293.

[261]Wright, Early Travels in Palestine, pp. 36-37.

[262]Palestine Pilgrims Text Society, XII, 43.

[263]Ibid., VII, Part I, 301-2.

[264]The Letters of Obadiah Da Bertinoro, ed. E.N. Adler, Jewish Travellers, p. 243. At the beginning of the sixteenth century, the author of Yihus ha-Avot mentions the royal sepulchres on Mount Zion and speaks of a very fine building over it (Uri Ben Simeon, p. 43). For more details, see P.E.F. (1874), p. 98; (1875), p. 102; (1879), p. 172; (1880), p. 167; (1884), pp. 77, 196; (1885), pp. 57, 61; (1895), pp. 263, 342.

[265] See the detailed description given by Ritter, _The Comparative Geography of Palestine and the Sinaitic Peninsula_, IV, 114-142. See also Meshullam's report as well as that of Bertinoro (_Jewish Travellers_, ed. E.N. Adler, pp. 191, 239; also the report of Wilhelm von Bondenselle, the German Dominican traveller (Ish Shalom, _Christian Travels in the Holy Land_, p. 227; R.E. Warren, "The Comparative Holiness of Mt. Zion and Moriah," _P.E.F._ [1869], pp. 76-88).

[266] _The Itinerary of Benjamin of Tudela_, ed. M. N. Adler, pp. 22-23.

[267] M. Swabe, "The Jews and the Temple Mount after the Conquest of Jerusalem by Omar," _Zion-Measef_, II (1927), 101.

[268] _The Itinerary of Petachia_, ed. E.N. Adler, _Jewish Travellers_, pp. 88-89.

[269] _Ibid._, p. 89. Jacob b. Nathaniel ha-Cohen mentions the "Temple and the Sanctuary" only by name without adding further details (_The Itinerary of Jacob ben Nathaniel ha-Cohen_, ed. Grünhut, p. 4).

[270] _Sifre_, Naso 1; _Zevahim_, 116b. See also Isaac Ezekiel, pp. 107-108.

[271] Vilnai, p. 71; Uri Ben Simeon, p. 41. See also Mähl, pp. 17, 19-20.

[272] _R. Jacob, the Messenger of R. Jechiel of Paris_, ed. E.N. Adler, _Jewish Travellers_, p. 119.

[273] See Saewulf's report (Wright, _Early Travels in Palestine_, pp. 39-40).

[274] _The Itinerary of Jacob ben Nathaniel ha-Cohen_, ed. E.N. Adler, _Jewish Travellers_, pp. 98-99.

[275] Exodus Rabba 2:2; Numbers Rabba 11:2; Uri Ben Simeon, p. 43; Ritter, _The Comparative Geo-_

graphy of Palestine and the Sinaitic Peninsula, IV, 51.

[276]Isaac Ezekiel, pp. 95-97, 102.

[277]The scroll of Ahima'as (11th century) speaks of a synagogue near the Western Wall (Ahima'as ben Paltiel, p. 47). However, it is not mentioned at all by Nahmanides in his detailed account of the temple site (M. Nahmanides, Kol Kitve Haramban [Writings], ed. D. Chavel, 2 vols. [Jerusalem, 1963], I, 424-32). Descriptions of the Western Wall are not given also in the report of Estori ha-Parchi (14th century); (Estori ha-Parchi, pp. 87-96, 410-11), nor in fifteenth century descriptions of Jerusalem. See Bertinoro's report, Jewish Travellers, ed. E.N. Adler, p. 240. As to Meshul-lam ben R. Menahem, see ibid., pp. 190-91.

[278]Joachim, pp. 44-45.

[279]The Itinerary of Benjamin of Tudela, ed. M. N. Adler, p. 26.

[280]Ibid. Ritter states that in the narratives of the pilgrims there is the greatest confusion regarding Shiloh. The people in the neighbourhood call it Nabi-Samwil, but the monks differ on this: some designate it as Shiloh and some as Ramah (Ritter, The Comparative Geography of Palestine and the Sinaitic Peninsula, III, 232).

[281]The Itinerary of Benjamin of Tudela, ed. M. N. Adler, p. 26.

[282]Ritter states that Nabi-Samwil is probably Mizpeh, and cannot be the city of Samuel the pro-phet (Ritter, The Comparative Geography of Pales-tine and the Sinaitic Peninsula, III, 235.

[283]See Survey of Western Palestine, III, 12; Joachim, p. 45. See also note 280 above.

[284]S. Assaf, "To the History of the Synagogue on Samuel's Tomb," BJPES, VI (1939), 142; S.H. Kuk,

"Note to the History of the Synagogue on Samuel's Tomb," BJPES, VI (1939), 143.

[285]Benjamin of Tudela, Sefer Masa'ot, ed. Asher, II, 95, n. 179.

[286]Meshullam Ben R. Menahem of Volterra, ed. E. N. Adler, Jewish Travellers, pp. 192-193.

[287]R. Gershom ben R. Asher from Scarmelo, p. 132; Uri Ben Simeon, p. 51.

[288]Meshullam Ben R. Menahem of Volterra, ed. E. N. Adler, Jewish Travellers, pp. 192-93; also Uri Ben Simeon, p. 51.

[289]The Itinerary of Benjamin of Tudela, ed. M. N. Adler, p. 21; Joshua 24:32. So does R. Gershom ben R. Asher, p. 115; also Uri Ben Simeon, p. 53.

[290]The Itinerary of Jacob ben Nathaniel ha-Cohen, ed. E.N. Adler, Jewish Travellers, pp. 96-97.

[291]The Itinerary of Benjamin of Tudela, ed. M. N. Adler, p. 20.

[292]Isaac ben Joseph ibn Chelo, The Roads from Jerusalem, ed. E.N. Adler, Jewish Travellers, p. 141. Of Jacob's well and Joseph's sepulchre, see Ritter, The Comparative Geography of Palestine and the Sinaitic Peninsula, IV, 317-20.

[293]The Itinerary of Jacob ben Nathaniel ha-Cohen, ed., E.N. Adler, Jewish Travellers, p. 96.

[294]The Itinerary of Benjamin of Tudela, ed. M. N. Adler, p. 28.

[295]The Itinerary of Jacob ben Nathaniel ha-Cohen, ed. E.N. Adler, Jewish Travellers, p. 93.

[296]Le Strange, Palestine under the Moslems, p. 402.

[297]Ibid., pp. 402-3; also Ritter, The Comparative Geography of Palestine and the Sinaitic Peninsula, III, 214.

[298]P.E.F. (1879), p. 87; (1876), 162; (1893), p. 255; (1881), p. 195, 212-14.

[299]The Itinerary of Petachia, ed. E.N. Adler, Jewish Travellers, p. 88.

[300]Ibid., pp. 90-91.

[301]Ibid., p. 91.

[302]The Itinerary of Jacob ben Nathaniel ha-Cohen, E.N. Adler, Jewish Travellers, p. 97.

[303]Ibid.

[304]Ibid., p. 92; Joachim, pp. 27, 88; Le Strange, Palestine under the Moslems, p. 447.

[305]The Itinerary of Benjamin of Tudela, ed. M.N. Adler, p. 28.

[306]The Itinerary of Petachia, ed. Benisch, p. 103, ns. 94-95; also Ritter, The Comparative Geography of Palestine and the Sinaitic Peninsula, IV, 376.

[307]The Itinerary of Benjamin of Tudela, ed. M.N. Adler, p. 34.

[308]Layard, Discoveries among the Ruins of Nineveh and Babylon, pp. 506-8.

[309]The Itinerary of Petachia, ed. E.N. Adler, Jewish Travellers, pp. 87-88.

[310]R. Gershom ben R. Asher from Scarmelo, p. 82; Uri Ben Simeon, p. 75.

[311]As to the exact location, see Ritter, The Comparative Geography of Palestine and the Sinaitic Peninsula, IV, 380, n. 2; Le Strange, Palestine

under the Moslems, p. 469; Joachim, p. 27, n. 11.
Ibn Jubayr speaks about a "Hill of Penitence" near
Mosul, on which Jonah stood and close by a blessed
spring named after him (Ibn Jubayr, p. 245).

[312]R. Jehiel, son of R. Solomon Heilperin, Seder
Hadorot (Warsaw, 1882), Part II, pp. 305-6; R. Gershom ben R. Asher from Scarmelo, p. 106.

[313]The Itinerary of Jacob ben Nathaniel ha-
Cohen, ed. E.N. Adler, Jewish Travellers, p. 97.

[314]Ibid., p. 78; The Itinerary of Petachia, ed.
Grünhut, p. 19.

[315]Ish Shalom, "Tradition of Graves in Palestine," pp. 79-98, 221-35, 351-58.

[316]The movement to visit holy places in the
Galilee gained momentum with the rise of Kabbalah.
Moses Cordovero (1522-1570) (I. Tishby, "Rabbi
Moses Cordovero as he appears in the treatise of
R. Mordekhai Dato," Safed Volume, ed. Itzhak Ben
Zwi and M. Benayahu, II [Jerusalem, 1963], 119-
166), and Isaac Luria (1534-1572) (D. Tamar, "Luria
and Vital as the Messiah Ben Joseph," Safed Volume,
II, 171) visited isolated villages, without contemporary Jewish inhabitants, but where Jews traditionally had resided. Followers of "Ari" habitually
visited the grave of Rabbi Simeon Bar Yohai (see the
following pages) and other graves of Tannaim and
Amoraim. Samuel Ben Hayyim Vital (1578-1678) (Tamar,
"Luria and Vital as the Messiah Ben Joseph," 174),
the greatest student of "Ari," reflects a deep knowledge of the Galilee topography (I. Ben Zwi, Palestine under the Ottoman Rule [Jerusalem, 1955], p.
189).

[317]The Itinerary of Benjamin of Tudela, ed. M.N.
Adler, p. 28.

[318]The Itinerary of Petachia, ed. E.N. Adler,
Jewish Travellers, p. 86; The Itinerary of Petachia,
ed. Grünhut, p. 29.

[319] R. Gershom ben R. Asher from Scarmelo, p. 77; R. Jehiel, Son of R. Solomon Heilperin, Part I, pp. 170-72.

[320] Ketuboth 103a.

[321] Estori ha-Parchi, p. 301.

[322] The Itinerary of Petachia, ed. E.N. Adler, Jewish Travellers, p. 86.

[323] The Itinerary of Benjamin of Tudela, ed. M.N. Adler, p. 28.

[324] R. Gershom ben R. Asher from Scarmelo, pp. 128-29, 131.

[325] The Itinerary of Jacob b. Nathaniel ha-Cohen, E.N. Adler, Jewish Travellers, p. 95; Joshua's grave is located also in the ancient Medeba Map (Atlas of Israel, Medeba Map 1/1). For details see P.E.F. (1878), p. 22; (1879), p. 193; (1877), p. 182; Joachim, pp. 40-41; Survey of Western Palestine, II, 378.

[326] Mount Gaash is mentioned in the Bible (Joshua 24:30) and it applied to a mountain in Mount Ephraim.

[327] The Itinerary of Petachia, ed. E.N. Adler, Jewish Travellers, p. 87.

[328] Nahum 1:4-6. Also Ibn Jubayr speaks of such footprints (Ibn Jubayr, p. 294).

[329] There is a tradition, however, which places Caleb's grave at Hebron (Joachim, p. 98).

[330] The Itinerary of Petachia, ed. E.N. Adler, Jewish Travellers, p. 87.

[331] Ibid., p. 94; The Itinerary of Jacob b. Nathaniel ha-Cohen, ed. Grünhut, p. 6.

[332] R. Jehiel, Son of R. Solomon Heilperin, Part II, pp. 109-11, 349-50; R. Gershom ben R. Asher

from Scarmelo, pp. 42-44.

[333]The Itinerary of Benjamin of Tudela, ed. M.N. Adler, p. 29. For more details, see P.E.F. (1877), p. 125.

[334]Itinerary of R. Samuel ben Samson, ed. E.N. Adler, Jewish Travellers, p. 108.

[335]Braslavsky, Studies in Our Country: Its Past and Remains, p. 342, n. 1.

[336]The Itinerary of Jacob b. Nathaniel ha-Cohen, ed. E.N. Adler, Jewish Travellers, p. 94.

[337]R. Gershom ben R. Asher from Scarmelo, pp. 44-48; R. Jehiel, Son of R. Solomon Heilperin, Part II, pp. 365-68.

[338]Koheleth Rabbah, 11.

[339]Itinerary of R. Samuel ben Samson, ed. E.N. Adler, Jewish Travellers, p. 108; R. Jehiel, Son of R. Solomon Heilperin, Part II, p. 367. The author of Yihus ha-Avot speaks also of a college there (Uri Ben Simeon, p. 69).

[340]The Itinerary of Jacob ben Nathaniel ha-Cohen and Itinerary of R. Samuel ben Samson, ed. E.N. Adler, Jewish Travellers, pp. 95, 108. A twentieth-century festival is held on Lag Be'Omer at the House of Study. The festival, "Hillula de Rabbi Simeon, ben Yohai" commemorates the death of the alleged author of the Zohar (Braslavsky, Studies in Our Country: Its Past and Remains, pp. 342-58; A. Ya'ari, "History of the Pilgrimage to Meron," Tarbiz, XXXI (1961), 78-79).

[341]The Itinerary of Benjamin of Tudela, ed. M.N. Adler, p. 28.

[342]R. Jehiel, Son of R. Solomon Heilperin, Part II, p. 199.

[343]On this scholar see R. Gershom ben Asher from

Scarmelo, pp. 102-4.

[344] The Itinerary of Jacob b. Nathaniel ha-Cohen, ed. E.N. Adler, Jewish Travellers, p. 95.

[345] A genizah fragment, written in the fourteenth century, lends credence to the custom of burying the dead near graves of famous personalities, often noted by our travellers who confirm coffins and casks of bones around the famous sites (Saadyana. Geniza Fragments of Writings of R. Saadya Gaon and Others, ed. S. Schechter, rpt. [Cambridge, 1969], pp. 80, 89).

[346] The Itinerary of Benjamin of Tudela, ed. M.N. Adler, p. 29. See Ritter, The Comparative Geography of Palestine and the Sinaitic Peninsula, II, 217.

[347] See R. Gershom ben R. Asher from Scarmelo, p. 12; Uri Ben Simeon, p. 67.

[348] Benjamin of Tudela, Sefer Masa'ot, ed. Asher, II, 109, n. 206.

[349] The Itinerary of Benjamin of Tudela, ed. M.N. Adler, p. 29.

[350] R. Gershom ben R. Asher from Scarmelo, p. 12; Uri Ben Simeon, p. 67.

[351] Ish Shalom, "Tradition of Graves in Palestine," p. 88.

[352] However, the placing of Miriam's well near Tiberias could also be a result of confusion between Kedesh Naphtali (in the north) and Kadesh Barnea (in the south) due to the similarity in names.

[353] Nitai is a Mishnaic sage (Abboth 1:6) through whom the chain of tradition links with succeeding generations.

[354] Estori ha-Parchi, p. 292.

[355] Ibid.

[356] Le Strange, Palestine under the Moslems, p. 406.

[357] For an excellent example of such various traditions concerning Jonah's tomb, see above and Joachim, pp. 23-28.

[358] Survey of Western Palestine, I, 233.

[359] As to the classification of the tombs and their architectural aspects, see Wilson, "Tombs in Palestine," P.E.F. (1869), pp. 66-71.

[360] Ibid., p. 66.

[361] See footnote 1 of this chapter.

CHAPTER VI

EXILE AND REDEMPTION IN THE BOOKS

OF THE TRAVELLERS

A great rise in messianic expectations and
hopes for redemption among medieval Jewry was caused
by the crusades.[1] People began to look for messianic signs in many historical events, and eschatological literature began to flourish. There were,
of course, many disappointments, as historical
events did not unfold as expected. Books with eschatological themes continued to be written; however, interpreting new historical events and seeing
new signs and hints, the hope for redemption never
ended.[2]

Characteristic of this period is the meeting
between the Karaite Solomon ha-Cohen and a Norman,[3]
probably named Johannes, in 1211 in Banias. The
latter had been moved by the persecutions the Jews
suffered and by Scripture, so that he finally adop-
ted Judaism between 1096 and 1102, and became known
as Obadiah the proselyte. Obadiah believed that
the messianic era was close at hand, and that the
Messiah would be a Jew. During his wanderings in
the east, Obadiah found himself in an atmosphere
filled with messianic expectations, and came into
contact with several different messianic movements.[4]

The sources collected by Dinur[5] serve as evidence that religious messianic ferment was felt
among Jews all over the Mediterranean world, and
even as far as Persia, as Benjamin testifies. The
appearance of false messiahs in different localities
reflects this religious mood. Around Constantinople
it was reported that Elijah, the precursor of the
Messiah, had been sighted, and the Jewish community
of Salonici underwent a period of repentance and
fasting.[6] It should be noted here that the Jewish
concept of the Messiah embodies a vast spectrum of
ideas which continually emerged throughout Jewish

267

history. Concepts such as "exile," "suffering,"
and "hope" must be understood in order to comprehend the messianic ideal.[7] For the Jews, history
was a continuous process of exile and redemption,
"a movement back to a lost Golden Age."[8] Man could
aid the process through doing penance and atoning
for his sins, as suffering was necessary to the
inner purification the Jew had to undergo if he expected to return to his land.[9]

    Twice in his Sefer ha-Qabbalah, the twelfth-
century Jewish chronicler Abraham ibn Daud indicates his intentions of relating a history of the
Second Jewish Kingdom, "because it serves as a
source of great consolation." It would "refute the
Sadducees, who claim that all of the consolatory
passages in the Bible were fulfilled for Israel in
the days of the Second Temple."[10] The importance
that this question held for ibn Daud may be seen
from the fact that he singled it out in his philo-
sophical work, Emunah Ramah.[11] In fact, the belief
in the return of the Jewish people from exile and
its recapture of ancient glory was central to rabbinic Judaism.[12] He shows that history was point-
ing to a new era of fulfillment, and that the present age was nearing its end.[13] Ibn Daud's history
ends the way it began, with the trust in a forthcoming divine consolation. What could that consolation be if not the advent of the Messiah and the
beginning of redemption?[14] In light of the persecutions suffered by Andalusian Jewry at the hands of
the Almohades, ibn Daud doubtless believed that
the time was ripe for redemption and that prophecies
were being fulfilled.[15] He felt that the Jews of
his day had endured all this and more.[16] Ibn Daud
predicted that the end would come in the year 1188-
89.[17] This date was also mentioned by his contemporary, Abraham bar Hiyya.[18] Mainmonides writes:
"There can be no doubt that these are the messianic
travails concerning which the sages invoked God
that they be spared seeing and experiencing them."[19]
Thus many believed that the Jew of the twelfth century was standing on the threshold of a new era.[20]
At no time in Jewish history after the second century was there such a flurry of messianic specula-

tion as there was in Andalusia in the eleventh and
twelfth centuries. Solomon ibn Gabriol, A. ibn
Ezra, ha-Levi, Bar Hiyya, and ibn Daud, in addition
to the many false messiahs, all show how important
messianism was in Jewish thought in that age.[21]

Before examining the role our travellers played
in this messianism, we must again refer to ha-Levi,
who had lived in Spain and was buried, according to
Benjamin, in Tiberias.[22] Ha-Levi dramatically
turned his back on Spain, and left for the Holy Land
where he intended to spend the rest of his life in
a way consistent with his new convictions. Ha-
Levi's poems reflect a deep disillusionment with
the political situation of the Jews, and some uncertainty about their future in Spain. He became more
and more convinced that a new home has to be found
if the Jews were to live a life free of humiliation.[23] From his book Kuzari it is clear that the
good life would be achieved only through the observance of the Torah, using Hebrew in everyday life,
and returning to the Holy Land.[24] What was at first
a religious conviction became a call for action.
"The stars of Spain were seductive substitutes for
the Cave of Machpelah and the sacred mount of Jerusalem, which in their ruins were more home to the
Jews than Cordova in its splendor."[25] The book of
Kuzari ends with the author stating his intent to
go to the Holy Land, to be the first to show a new
way of life, leading eventually to complete redemption.[26] Ha-Levi's emigration to the Holy Land,
therefore, was not undertaken for personal reasons,
as a means of atonement and as a pilgrimage.
Rather, his motives were idealistic in nature and
his immigration was therefore quite new and caused
much discussion and controversy.[27] He suggested
that Jews could begin the process of redemption by
actually living in the Holy Land.[28] Palestine,
then, occupied a central place in ha-Levi's plan of
redemption.

Against this background, we may now revert to
the twelfth-century travellers and see how the concepts of exile and redemption are reflected in
their accounts. It is clear from the itineraries

that the messianic expectations of the period had
a definite effect on the travellers.

The most important indication of this effect
is the place Palestine has in our travellers' accounts, for the Holy Land is given the most detailed
description in the itineraries. It is evident that
Benjamin of Tudela toured the Land extensively and
was familiar with its sites and holy places. His
description of Palestine is not only accurate, but
is also the longest and most detailed account that
we have for that time. The description of the Holy
Land is central to Benjamin's account as a whole,
and no other area receives the same treatment,
either in length, accuracy, or detail. The same is
true concerning Petachia. Besides Babylonia, only
Palestine occupies his attention so that he gives
longer descriptions, more references, and additional
details. As for Jacob b. Nathaniel ha-Cohen, the
Holy Land is the only area which his account covers.

Reading the accounts, we feel that the physical
atmosphere of Palestine formed much of Israel's
spiritual idealism, and the Land retained a powerful
hold over the people. Associated with the concepts
of Messiah and resurrection, Palestine became a matter of faith rather than geography. The descriptions of Palestine in the accounts reveal a very
special attitude, often sentimental in nature, that
our travellers had towards the Land. The enumeration of holy sites, even of stones and trees, shows
that merely walking in the Land aroused within the
travellers feelings and memories about the unique
place Palestine had in Jewish history. At the same
time it gave rise to a longing for a better future.
We cannot escape this thought in reading Petachia's
statement describing Jerusalem and the Temple
Mount:

> At Jerusalem there is a gate: its name is
> Gate of Mercy.... There is a tradition
> among the Jews that the Divine glory dis-
> appeared through this gate and through it
> would return. It is exactly opposite Mount
> Olivet.... His feet will stand that day on

Mount Olivet. They shall see distinctly
when the Eternal will return to Zion
through that gate.[29]

This paragraph reveals an association between the
Gate of Mercy and the idea of redemption. In addition, Mount Olivet is also strongly connected with
the same idea in the future, when the traveller
quotes from Zachariah (14:4) and Isaiah (52:7-8):
"His feet will stand that day on Mount Olivet."
The verse is part of the prophecies by Zachariah
and Isaiah concerning the messianic era and the day
of judgment when God will punish the nations who
inflicted miseries on His city. Following this day
of judgment, the prophet tells of a redeemed world
where even natural laws are changed. The city of
God becomes a universally recognized city, for God
Himself becomes universally accepted, and all of
the nations come to Jerusalem to worship Him.[30]

In Isaiah (Chapter 52) we again have a description of the restoration of the glory of God to Zion.
Jerusalem will be the Holy City and the redemption
will begin. The prophet then declares: "How beautiful upon the mountains are the feet of him who
brings glad tidings, announcing peace, bearing good
news, announcing salvation, and saying to Zion,
your God is King!" (Isaiah 52:7). We can feel the
pious traveller being engulfed with memories associated with prophecies of the redemption, memories
and which lead him to end with the statement: "They
shall see distinctly when the Eternal will return
to Zion through that Gate." The association between
the place and the messianic era is clear here, and
Petachia is confident that the "Eternal will return
to Zion." The very quote from Zachariah and Isaiah
cited by our traveller shows that he is conscious
of the redemption and that he himself expects that:
"they will see when the Eternal will return to
Zion." Who does he refer to when he says "they";
the Gentiles or the Jews? The author feels Petachia
refers to both. The Gentile world would realize
that they were wrong in treating the Jews badly, as
they would witness the restoration of Zion. The
Jews also would see that their expectations would

271

be fulfilled with the return of the Eternal to Zion.

This section of our traveller's account reflects the general mood of the generation which witnessed the crusades, showing both a reaction to the persecution in Europe and the religious ferment among the Jews who read in events messianic signs. Petachia is waiting with his generation for the messianic days. He cannot help but express his expectations while he is standing on the very spot, where, according to the prophets, messianic events are to take place.

The paragraph proves several other points. Zion occupies a prominent place in the redemption spoken about, as the "Eternal" will return to it. Palestine was important in the plan of redemption for Petachia too.

In addition, another interesting point, crucial to those times, is revealed by the paragraph. Petachia also relates that "one day the Gentiles wished to remove the rubbish and open the gate, but the whole land of Israel shook...." In an era that saw two major religions of the world each claim the Holy Land for itself and fight for its claim, the Jew, who believed that he was the true owner of the Land, stood by helplessly. Lacking the physical power that the Moslems and Christians had, the Jews stood aside and waited to see what would develop. Petachia's story of the disturbance of the Land shows the confidence that the Jews had that neither Christian nor Moslem could survive in the Holy Land, and that Palestine would accept only Jews as its inhabitants. An almost mystical relationship exists between the Jews and their Land, and the Land will accept no other nation, waiting for the Jews to return and resettle it. This concept of a mystical relationship between the Jews and the Holy Land was old and known among the Jews,[31] but the crusade era intensified it.

Petachia's statement almost reminds us of one made by Nahmanides in the middle of the thirteenth century. When he visited the Holy Land and saw it in ruins, Nahmanides said:

> It is a good sign...that our land does not
> accept our enemies. This also is a sound
> proof and promise to us, that you cannot
> find a country which is large and good and
> which was inhabited from time immemorial,
> and yet is desolate and in ruins. Because,
> once we left the land, it did not receive
> any nation or people, and everybody would
> try to settle it but were not successful.[32]

At the end of his commentary to the Pentateuch,
Nahmanides repeats this idea. In describing the
natural fertility of the Holy Land in contrast to
its desolation, he says:

> Today I saw in you [Holy Land] holiness,...
> I found in you a poor Jew and he is a dyer
> ...in his house assemble adults and child-
> ren [for prayer and study]..., a congrega-
> tion of poor and unfortunate people...and
> still the Land remains a Land of milk and
> honey...with all this, those who claim to
> love you have despised you...and from afar
> they [Christians and Moslems] mention you
> with pride as the Holy City saying: it
> has been given to us as an inheritance!
> And when they reach you...they flee as
> though running from a sword but no one
> pursues them: and there is much desola-
> tion in the fertile wide country...

and Nahmanides ends, "because they [Christians and
Moslems] are not deserving you and you are not
meant for them!"[33]

Thus Nahmanides saw in the failure of the crusaders to establish themselves in the Land a sign
that the Land was not promised to them. Although
the Land is obviously fertile, its desolation and
its destruction caused by the battles between Christians and Moslems indicate that neither side could
live permanently there. Nahmanides reflects a time
when few crusaders were willing to actually settle

in the Holy Land. Once they paid their pilgrimage, the crusaders hastily returned to Europe, although still claiming the Land from far off. The mystical relationship between the Jews and their Land is also reflected in the passage, and we are reminded of the thoughts of ha-Levi, set down in his _Kuzari_.[34]

This idea, that the crusaders could not establish themselves in a land promised to the Jews, can also be seen in the words of the Jewish chronicler Joseph ha-Cohen, who writes:

> And at the thirtieth of the month of May there was a large earthquake in the Orient ...a great part of Acre...fell and many died. The entire Tyre fell down.... Also a great part of Tripoli collapsed.... And there was a great famine in the land which did not give its yield in those days. And those that survived the famine the plague destroyed. And there was no hope to the uncircumcised in the Galilee...because Heaven fought them in order to force them to leave the land of Israel. Then God fulfilled his promise which He spoke unto Moses...saying: 'So devastated will I leave the land that your very enemies who come to live there will stand aghast at the sight of it.'[35]

Joseph ha-Cohen clearly expresses the thought that God fought against those contesting over the Holy Land, to fulfil his promise to Moses.[36]

That was the historical teaching of the failure of the crusades: the Land of Israel would not accept any nation except the Jews, to whom it had been promised. This, of course, convinced the Jews in the diaspora that redemption could become a reality. The exile would not last forever, and the Jews could continue to dream of a return to Zion. This hope and belief, which can be detected towards the end of the twelfth century with the demise of the crusade movement, became a strong part of Jewish thought in the century following.[37] We

274

have seen Nahmanides and Joseph ha-Cohen express it,
and Joseph Caspi also writes of it.[38] The latter
expresses the idea, that although the rule of the
crusaders over the Holy Land came to an end and the
Land was still not given to the Jews, the situation
was not hopeless. It is known, Caspi argues, that
many rulers may occupy the Holy Land, but their
rule is only temporary. God, who is the true owner
of all lands, is able to change the situation at
any time and return the Land to its rightful owners,
the Jews. God acts mysteriously and has many means
to carry out His plan of gathering the Jews in from
exile. There was no need to lose hope, for it is
within God's power to cause His people to return
and thus to start the redemption.[39]

It is interesting to note that Caspi states
that "no Christian can argue about this." In this
statement we can detect the theological arguments
which took place between the Christians and Jews
concerning the questions of exile, redemption[40] and
the destiny of the Holy Land. Caspi speaks here
with confidence, for the failure of the crusade
movement strengthened the position of the Jews who
claimed now more than before their rights of ownership of the Promised Land.

The twelfth-century Jew gradually developed
the idea that only the Jews could settle on the
Land. Petachia, by relating the story cited above,
shows himself as a member of a society which shared
the idea that Nahmanides expressed clearly later on,
when it was apparent that the crusaders would not
regain their power. Petachia ends the paragraph
with the statement that "Prayers are offered up
there" at the Mercy gate.[41] With this we can see
the pious traveller also offering his prayers,
prayers for the coming redemption of his people.

The paragraph we quoted from Petachia's Sivuv
is not the only place where he expresses his messianic hopes. Being in Mosul he reports:

...there was an astrologer whose name was
R. Solomon. There is among all the sages

275

in Nineveh, and the land of Assur, none as
expert in the planets as he. R. Petachia
asked him when Messiah would come. He replied, I have seen this often distinctly in
the planets. But Rabbi Judah the Pious
would not write it down lest he should be
suspected of being a believer in the words
of Rabbi Solomon.[42]

The enquiry of an astrologer about the Messianic
era proves in itself how anxious Petachia was to
learn of the redemption. The very concept of Messiah, with its rich content and its offer of hope,
had a deep impact on our traveller. The way he
phrased his question about "when Messiah would
come" shows that Petachia was aware of some of the
calculations which had set 1186-1188 as the appointed time of the start of the redemption. Only thus
can we understand our traveller's enquiries.

The astrologer replied that he had seen the
appointed time clearly and often in the planets.
This answer reveals that the astrologer himself was
expecting the coming of the Messiah. It is very
interesting that while the traveller forgot some of
the information on his way back home,[43] he was anxious to bring words of consolation back to his
people. The consolation was, of course, the answer
of the astrologer. R. Judah would not write it
down because it could stir the people into great
expectations, and disappointment could follow. The
researcher believes that R. Judah the Pious would
have written the message down had the date predicted been further off and there would have been no
fear of disappointment.[44]

It is clear that Jacob b. Nathaniel ha-Cohen
also has a strong attachment to the Holy Land. He
enumerates every holy site and grave he comes
across, and often relates traditions associated
with such places. His detailed list of grave shows
his own conviction of the holiness of the area, and
we can feel his enjoyment at walking from one holy
sepulchre to another. His descriptions are so
loving and emotional that we are not surprised to

find this statement at the end of the account:
"As I have been privileged to write about the Holy
Land, so may I be privileged to go there and die
there."[45] The Holy Land was seen by him, as it was
by many Jews, as the last station in life. It was
considered a privilege to be buried there, for not
many could arrange for such a burial. The most important point, however, lies in the fact that Jacob
expressed a wish "to go there and die there." He
not only wanted to be buried in Israel, but he actually wanted to die there. It was not unusual for
a Jew to die in the diaspora and be buried in
Israel, but Jacob wishes more than that. The author maintains that we can read in this phrase his
familiarity with the messianic expectations of the
time, and the calculations concerning the years
1186-1188. The traveller, being a pious Jew,[46]
could have been moved by these hopes and dreams and
might have prepared to go to settle in Palestine,
with the redemption date so near. It is impossible
to know whether Jacob had heard of ha-Levi's ideas,
but he most certainly heard the rumours of the
coming of the Messiah. Perhaps his pilgrimage and
visit to the graves of the Holy Land were a means
of atonement and preparation for the coming redemption. Interestingly, Jacob visited only holy sites
and graves, omitting any other details about the
Land. Do we have here an example of a pious Jew
preparing himself for the advent of the Messiah?

It is well known that many Jewish communities
at that time were caught in the messianic atmosphere, and some Jews actively were preparing themselves for the day to come. This shows the great
power of the crusade movement, in that it could
affect the Jewish people so deeply. Jacob b.
Nathaniel is a part of that excited society and
his pilgrimage reflects that stirring within the
individual. We should not, of course, forget the
impact that the calculations had on the people,
causing many to even emigrate to Palestine. Thus
the three hundred rabbis who emigrated from France
and England in 1211 to settle in the Holy Land were
motivated by the expectations that the redemption
would start in the middle of the thirteenth

century.[47] There is no reason not to consider that
Jacob made similar preparations based on the calculation of 1186-1188 as the projected date of the
Messiah's arrival. The researcher's impression is
that his pilgrimage was motivated by the messianic
atmosphere of his times.[48]

In his account Jacob also mentions those sites
in Jerusalem which are generally associated with
the messianic era and the redemption. These sites
include the Gate of Mercy, Mount Zion, Mount Olivet
and the Valley of Jehoshaphat. The investigator
believes that mentioning these sites in his time
had a special significance for the traveller and
aroused in him associations from the Bible and Jewish tradition. We have already seen that this was
the case with Petachia, but Jacob feels similar associations. Thus, when he reports of the waters of
Siloam and other large cisterns, and remarks that
the cisterns are not full, he is told that the
waters ran away and it is not known where the water
goes. "Thus said I, Jacob, to the Rabbis, 'This
is what our Lord the prophet Isaiah said' (Isaiah
30:9), 'His fire is in Zion and his furnace in Jerusalem.'"[49] Everything was associated with prophecies or biblical accounts, and it is clear that the
significance of the sites associated with redemption
and the Messiah was understood by Jacob as was only
natural in this period.

Finally, when Jacob reports of the Cave of Machpelah he states: "Once the monks made a small window therein and a strong wind came and killed them
all and they closed the window."[50] Do we not feel
that our traveller expresses the same idea found in
Petachia's Sivuv above? This is the notion that the
Holy Land and everything in it belong exclusively to
the Jews, and no one else can own it or do anything
successfully with it. The Gentiles could not make
even a small window in the wall of the Cave of Machpelah, for it is not theirs, as they cannot claim
ownership over the holy sites. This concept, which
emphasizes the mystical relationship between the
Holy Land and the Jewish people began to gain popularity in the crusade era and became stronger once

278

the crusaders began to falter.

Petachia's visit to the Holy Land could have been motivated by the same factors which motivated Jacob, namely the expectations of a messianic age and the desire to prepare for such an occurrence. It is amazing that Petachia's account is similar in several respects to the itinerary of Jacob, in that both enumerate holy places and sites and both emphasize stories and traditions associated with such places. This type of account reveals a certain emotional attachment on the part of the travellers to the Holy Land. The two pious German travellers, Petachia and Jacob, leave accounts which reflect the strong religious ferment of the time on the one hand, and Jewish expectations of redemption on the other.

Returning to Benjamin, we cannot ignore the fact that his account also reflects the spirit of the times and the traveller's familiarity with Jewish problems of the era. Certain statements in his account reveal his sensitivity to the situation. Reporting of the Jewish community of Lunel in Provence, he ends with the prayer: "may the Lord preserve them."[51] No doubt such a statement shows the traveller's familiarity with the situation of the Jews in Europe, as he prays for divine protection. The very fact that everywhere Benjamin goes he notes the political situation of the Jews proves again his awareness of the exile as a reality. He makes statements like this one concerning the Jews of Constantinople: "For their condition is very low, and there is much hatred against them.... So the Greeks hate the Jews, good and bad alike, and subject them to great oppression, and beat them in the streets.... Yet the Jews bear their lot with cheerfulness...."[52]

The following paragraph, which forms part of our traveller's report on the Jews in Arabia, also testifies to Benjamin's awareness of the Jewish world around him:

They give the tithe of all they possess...

279

to the recluses, who are the mourners of
Zion and Jerusalem, and who do not eat meat
nor taste wine, and sit clad in garments of
black. They dwell in caves or underground
houses, and fast each day with the exception of the Sabbaths and Festivals, and implore mercy of the Holy One, blessed be He,
on account of the exile of Israel, praying
that He may take pity upon them, and upon
all the Jews, for the sake of His great
Name....[53]

Here the exile becomes oppressive and omnipresent.
Significantly, these recluses implore the mercy of
God "on account of the exile of Israel," no matter
where they are dispersed. One can feel their awareness of the exile on the one hand, and their anti-
cipated redemption on the other. They pray that
God "may take pity on them, and upon all the Jews
...," reflecting the situation of the Jews everywhere awaiting the end of exile.

Furthermore, Benjamin could have been motivated to pay a visit to the Holy Land by the same
reasons which motivated the other twelfth-century
travellers. He could have been affected by the
messianic hopes of his time so as to want to make
his own personal pilgrimage. The messianic expectations of the time made a visit to the Land very
significant, for the Land was inextricably bound
up with the idea of a coming redemption. As a man
who grew up in a Spanish society, Benjamin was certainly aware of such ideas. Benjamin's account
proves that the traveller knew of ha-Levi,[54] so he
must have known of his feelings toward the Holy
Land, and of his subsequent emigration.

Thus, touring the Land was in itself an expression of the living memories of the past on the one
hand, and aspirations for future redemption on the
other. The mention of places in the Holy Land associated with redemption could not have been made
without memories of the past and present. Benjamin
mentions the Mercy Gate, Mount Olivet and the Valley
of Jehoshaphat, sites strongly associated with

redemption in both Jewish and non-Jewish traditions. That our traveller recognized the associations is clear from his description of the Valley of Jehoshaphat: "The Gate of Jehoshaphat leads to the Valley of Jehoshaphat, which is the gathering place of nations."[55] Being in the Valley of Jehoshaphat, the traveller remembered the prophecies of Ezekiel (20:35) and Joel (4:2), which saw the valley as the scene of the last judgment.[56] The association Benjamin makes between the site and the prophecy proves once again how conscious he is of the messianic hopes. Furthermore, before reporting on the valley, Benjamin speaks of the Temple Mount, where he says: "Jerusalem has four gates...and the gate of Gushpat, which is the gate of Jehoshaphat, facing our ancient Temple, now called Templum Domini."[57] Interesting is the contrast between the phrase "our ancient Temple" on the one hand, and the phrase "now called Templum Domini," describing the rule of the crusaders over the Holy Mount, which was once the site of the sanctuary and the Holy of Holies, also mentioned by our traveller.[58]

In speaking of the Gate of Mercy, he also mentions that "...thither come all the Jews to pray. ..."[59] These prayers would not, of course, be only personal in nature, but also would concern the state of the entire Jewish people, as the Jews would pray that the redemption be soon. It is impossible that our traveller, living in those difficult times, did not offer the same prayers in the Holy City.

Interestingly enough Benjamin shares with the other two travellers the notion that the Holy Land awaits its sons, and that no stranger can claim ownership of it. Benjamin, speaking of the Sepulchres of the House of David on Mount Zion, relates that the cave of the Sepulchres was found by two of the workers restoring the wall of a church on the mountain. Upon entering the cave, the two workers felt "a fierce wind come forth from the entrance of the cave and smote them.... And there came forth a wind like a man's voice, crying out: 'Arise and go forth from this place!'"[60] The two workers rushed in terror to report the incident to the Patriarch.

They were asked to accompany the Patriarch and return to the Cave, but they answered: "We will not
enter there, for the Lord doth not desire to show
it to any man."[61] The Patriarch gave orders that
the place be closed up and hidden from view.[62] Benjamin's point is clear. Non-Jews are not allowed
to enter the Sepulchres of the House of David.[63]
The incident reminds one of the failures of the
Gentiles to open a window in the Cave of Machpelah,
as related by Jacob b. Nathaniel, and the shaking
of the Land when an attempt was made to open the
Gate of Mercy, as told by Petachia. Again, no non-
Jew can remain permanently in the land promised to
the Jews.

     It has become clear by now that a strong reli-
gious polemic is reflected through our accounts.
This polemic comes to light very clearly when the
travellers report the Holy places in the Holy Land.
We can sense that the travellers argue against the
Christians who now rule the Land, but whose position is shaky. Even the Christians do not dare to
defile the Holy of Holies.[64] In the case of the
Cave of Machpelah it seems that Jews have certain
privileges which were not extended to Gentiles.
Petachia was allowed to enter the Cave and he was
told that Gentiles were not permitted to enter.[65]
Similar privileges were also extended to Petachia
at Jonah's tomb.[66] Benjamin relates that God would
fight those non-Jews who would try to enter the
royal sepulchres on Mount Zion.[67] In relation to
Rachel's tomb we hear from Petachia that one of the
stones of the tomb, after having been removed by
the Christians, miraculously reappeared in its former position.[68] In all these cases, the travellers
reflect a religious polemic against the Christian
world. Obviously, none but Jews have the legal
claim over the Holy Land, though this claim is only
theoretical. Certainly this polemic is another out-
growth of the atmosphere created by the crusades.[69]

     One of the most significant paragraphs in Ben-
jamin's account, reflecting the religious mood and
the messianic expectations of the age, occurs in a
section dealing with the Jews of Germany:

When the Lord will remember us in our exile,
and raise the horn of his anointed, then
everyone will say, 'I will lead the Jews and
I will gather them...' and when a wayfarer
comes they rejoice, and make a feast for
him, and say, 'Rejoice brethren, for the
help of the Lord comes in the twinkling of
an eye.' If we were not afraid that the
appointed time has not yet arrived nor been
reached, we would have gathered together,
but we dare not do so until the time for
song has arrived, and the voice of the
turtle-dove (is heard in the land), when
the messenger sill come and say continually,
'The Lord be exalted.' Meanwhile they send
missives one to the other, saying: 'Be ye
strong in the law of Moses, and do ye mourners for Zion and mourners for Jerusalem
entreat the Lord, and may the supplication
of those that wear the garments of mourning
be received through their merits.'[70]

We can feel the heightened emotions of the time and
the oppressive and humiliating reality of exile.
Yet, one more point is to be learned from this paragraph. We hear clearly that there was uncertainty
in the minds of the people as to the appointed time
when the redemption should start. It is stated
clearly that "if we were not afraid that the appointed time has not yet arrived...we would have
gathered together, but we dare not do so until the
time...has arrived...." In contrast with the communities of Spain and the East, where calculators
gave predictions of the end with some certainty, in
Germany the persecutions of the crusades and messianic disappointments led to the rise of the piety
movement.[71]

At this point it is worthwhile to describe
some of the characteristics of the piety movement
in order to see if there are any traces of it in
our travellers' accounts. We will thus be able to
better understand the overall themes of exile and
redemption.

Any talmudical scholarship which involved the mind but not the heart was not a satisfactory source of strength for many Jews. The sources which gave the individual the most strength in dealing with the hardships of the era were to be found in personal morality, belief, and piety. Thus there emerged a moralizing literature (mussar) designed for all Jews, the most popular of which was the Book of the Pious by Rabbi Judah Hasid of Regensburg.[72] The book itself was a collective effort, a product of three generations of scholars who lived in a territory of frequent persecutions from the beginning of the twelfth century until the beginning of the thirteenth century.[73] In the sphere of personal piety, though, fear of God and humility are preached, though extreme asceticism is not. Concepts of humility and repentance are the basic principles of the book's religious system. Thus we read in the book Rokeach:[74]

> The best crown is the crown of humility, the best sacrifice, a broken heart; the best virtue, bashfulness. A humble person is lowly in his own eyes, is modest, tender-hearted, and dispirited.... He forgives the one who talks evil of him; he speaks little and in a low voice:...when misfortune strikes, when he loses his children or immediate kin, he always bows to the justice of Providence. ... If in the days of persecution people arise against you, to force you to forsake your faith, you should sacrifice your life, as others have done. Do not complain when you see the prosperity and the merit of the wicked because God's ways lead to redemption, although His good deeds towards Jews at the moment are concealed from us.[75]

Echoes of the crusades may be heard in other recommendations given by the author of the Book of the Pious.[76] This was the moral code of the German Jews in this century. In addition, the poetry of the Franco-German Jews was filled with a spirit of martyrdom, and offered a psychology of resistance.[77]

284

Petachia and Jacob ben Nathaniel ha-Cohen show
some signs of having belonged to the piety movement
in Germany. Besides the fact that Petachia came
from the circle of Judah the Pious, who in fact
helped edit his Sivuv,[78] it is obvious that both he
and Jacob were pious, simple, and humble men. They
do not question very much and do not inquire at
great length. There seems to be a peaceful harmony
between them and their God. Thus, the morality and
way of life expounded in the Book of the Pious is
reflected in the itineraries of the two travellers.
Moreover, the Book of the Pious is a mixture of religious and ethical sayings and advice with naive
superstition. Sober wisdom shared space with fairy
tales about demons. The Jew, as seen through this
book, is harassed not only by human persecution,
but by an inner awareness and fear of sin.[79] Demon-
ology, as a matter of fact, is also quite marked in
the itineraries of Petachia and Jacob b. Nathaniel
ha-Cohen. With the emphasis in these accounts on
the traditions of the graves of the righteous, it
is to be expected that stories and legends, associated with the graves would be related.[80] It is
clear to any serious reader that he is in a world
of demons and spirits. As a matter of fact, Petachia relates how the Jews of Byzantium have the
power to put the dark forces at their service.[81]
Both travellers believe in the power of the spirits
of the deceased and accept the stories they hear as
fact.

The familiarity of our travellers with the
German piety movement is beyond doubt concerning
Petachia, and almost so in respect to Jacob ben
Nathaniel ha-Cohen. Viewing them as members of
this Hasidic movement, we may better understand
their view of the question of exile and redemption.
This also gives us a better understanding of the
description of Benjamin of German Jewry, in the
paragraph quoted above.

Though Judah the Pious affirms his belief in
the coming of the Redeemer, nevertheless, he dis-
courages messianic speculation and any sort of com-
putations.[82] There is thus a warning in the Book

285

of the Pious against such predictions, a practice
which he equates with sorcery. He threatens that
the spirits whose services were enlisted by a person for these ends will take revenge on the ques-
tioner for causing them futile exertion, and will
cause him to be exposed "to shame and ridicule before the whole world."[83] Apart from this general
hostility to magic and sorcery, one also senses
that Judah is worried about the despair that false
hopes may bring. This was the reason which caused
him to suppress the computation Petachia brought
back from the astrologer. Other passages[84] also
show how Judah and his school tried to tone down
the eschatological elements of Judaism.[85] Nevertheless, none of the German pietists ever gave up
hope in the coming of the Messiah, for such a belief was deeply entrenched in the mind of Medieval
Jewry. The Book of the Pious itself contains a
number of passages relating to the belief in the
ultimate advent of the Redeemer.[86]

In this chapter we have found that both Petachia and Jacob paid a very meaningful pilgrimage to
the Holy Land, reflecting the messianic spirit of
the times. As members of the German pietist movement, though, they did not speak freely of the advent of the Messiah. In spite of this, Petachia,
though close to one of the leaders of the movement,
could not restrain himself and inquired of an astrologer about the end of days. Thus, both men expected the Messiah in a quiet way, and in the mean-
time tried to lead humble and pious lives. The end
of the exile would be revealed by God at the proper
time, and the Germans were content to wait until it
came. This quiet patience, characteristic of the
pietist movement, is also revealed in the paragraph
cited above from Benjamin, when he speaks of German
Jewry. On the one hand we feel the expectations of
society for the end of days, but on the other we
see that the people realized that the time was not
yet ripe. Meanwhile, they tried to strengthen themselves by study and by leading a pious life. Our
accounts thus reveal the impact of the age of the
crusades in yet a different way, in the emergence
of a new way of life among German Jewry. This new

286

way of life emphasized piety and humility, and as
such the German pietist movement was the precursor
of the Kabbalistic movement which had its beginnings at that time.

A most fascinating segment of Benjamin's accounts as noted above concerns the legend of the
Ten Lost Tribes. This legend had a powerful psychological impact on the Jews of this period, for
it was very much related to the idea of redemption.
The Jewish people always thought that the redemption to come would bring about the return of the
Ten Tribes and their reunification with their
brothers. Consquently, many people throughout history have attempted to verify their existence and
discover their whereabouts.[87]

The Ten Tribes were exiled when the Kingdom of
Israel fell in 722 B.C.[88] and they apparently disappeared from the view of history. They remained,
however, very much alive in popular folklore, and
legends grew up about them.[89] For example, their
inability to return was explained by the fact that
they were exiled beyond the mysterious river Sambatyon.[90] This river spewed out sand and rocks
during the six days of the week, and the Tribes
were unable to cross it. The river was calm only
on the Sabbath, but then the laws of that day prevented its crossing.[91] It was therefore believed
that the Tribes would return only with the Messiah,[92] a belief found not only in Apocryphal books
but in New Testament writings as well.[93] The Rabbis in the Talmud identify the localities to which
the Ten Tribes were exiled according to the Bible.[94]
Talmudic passages which concern the Ten Tribes,
however, show that the Rabbis had no definite knowledge as to their location in their time. Later,
Khorasan was frequently mentioned as the dwelling-
place of the Ten Tribes.[95] A tradition was widespread until recent times that independent tribes
could be found there.[96]

Several things might have awakened in our
travellers the desire to learn about the Ten Tribes.
For one thing, Eldad ha-Dani, in a diary which be-

287

came well-known, claimed to have communicated with four of the Lost Tribes in Abyssinia.[97] Further-more, the legend of Prester John, which included tales of the Lost Tribes,[98] also probably encour-aged the travellers to search for them,[99] and Ben-jamin, at least, was aware of this legend.[100] The letter of Prester John was even translated into Hebrew[101] with some changes inserted reflecting a Jewish perspective. This shows the interest which surrounded the Lost Tribes at this time, which was a factor in motivating the travellers to search for them.

The era of the crusades was seen as the times of the wars of Gog and Magog,[102] which was to be followed by the return of the Ten Tribes as signi-fying the beginning of the redemption.[103] The travellers might have been at least partially moti-vated by the feeling that the return of the Lost Tribes and the redemption were not far in the fu-ture.[104] If we view the era as containing both a struggle between Islam and Christianity and a great deal of suffering for the Jews of Europe, we can see how this period was identified as one of cosmic importance.

In referring to the legend of the Ten Tribes, we may safely ignore Jacob ben Nathaniel ha-Cohen. The pious traveller was interested only in the Holy Land, far from the supposed location of the Lost Tribes, so the absence of any reference to the leg-end is understandable. On the other hand, it is surprising that Petachia makes little mention of the legend, since he visited Babylonia and wrote about Persia, the area where the Tribes were said to have settled. He does make several references to the Sambatyon. In the introduction to his itin-erary we read: "These are the travels undertaken by Rabbi Petachia...who travelled through many lands till he reached the river Sambatyon...."[105] This led Beazley to assume, mistakenly I believe, that Petachia's goal was to reach the Sambatyon, the dwelling place of the Ten Tribes. In addition, Petachia gives a geographical location for the river. The way the river is mentioned shows that

288

Petachia was aware of the direction in which the legend placed the Ten Tribes.[106] Even though Petachia makes no direct mention of the Lost Tribes, he does mention the Rechabites,[107] who became associated with the Ten Tribes: "Whilst at Baghdad he saw ambassadors from the Kings of Meshech, Magog is about ten days' journey thence. The land extends as far as the Mountains of Darkness. Beyond the Mountains of Darkness are the sons of Jonadab, son of Rechab."[108] Petachia thus shows that he had some knowledge of the legend of the Ten Tribes. Interestingly, he does not speak of strong, independent Jews when reporting about Persian Jews as Benjamin does. Rather, he tells of how the Jews there were oppressed.[109] Thus he was perhaps prevented from making any direct identifications of any contemporary Jews with the Ten Tribes, for he did not hear of any Jews who would even remotely resemble the Lost Tribes. This may account for the very few references to the legend.

After giving a description of Samarkand,[110] Benjamin reports according to a Rabbi Moses (for Benjamin himself never visited the area) as follows:

> Thence (from Tibet) it takes twenty-eight days to the mountains of Naisabur by the river Gozan. And there are men of Isreal in the land of Persia who say that in the mountains of Naisabur four of the tribes of Israel dwell, namely, the tribe of Dan, the tribe of Zebulun, the tribe of Asher, and the tribe of Naphtali, who were included in the first captivity of Shalmaneser, king of Assyria, as it is written (2 Kings XVIII:2): 'and he put them in Halah and in Habor by the river of Gozan and in the cities of the Medes.'[111]

It is important to note that Benjamin is careful to mention that his information is hearsay, and that[112] he himself makes no claim to have seen the Tribes. He continues by describing the area where the four Tribes were supposedly found:

289

The extent of their land is twenty days'
journey, and they have cities and large villages in the mountains: the river Gozan
forms the boundary on the one side. They
are not under the rule of the Gentiles, but
they have a prince of their own, whose name
is Rabbi Joseph Amarkala the Levite. There
are scholars among them, and they sow and
reap and go forth to war as far as the land
of Cush by way of the desert.[113]

The report stresses that the people are independent
and ruled by their own prince. Also, scholarship
is added to the theme of freedom, a common combination in the legend of the Lost Ten Tribes. An interesting passage in Benjamin's account concerns an
alliance between the four tribes and the Kofar-al-
Turak.[114] The King of Persia undertook a campaign
of revenge against the latter,[115] and, after a difficult march, he reached the mountains of Naisabur,
where Jews lived.

They came there on the Sabbath, and en-
camped in the gardens and plantations and
by the springs of water which are by the
side of the river Gozan. Now it was the
time of the ripening of the fruit, and they
ate and consumed everything. No man came
forth to them, but on the mountains they
saw cities and many towers. Then the King
commanded two of his servants to go and inquire of the people who lived in the mountains, and to cross the river either in
boats or by swimming. So they searched and
found a large bridge, on which there were
three towers, but the gate of the bridge
was locked. And on the other side of the
bridge was a great city. Then they shouted
in front of the bridge till a man came forth
and asked them what they wanted and who they
were. But they did not understand him till
an interpreter came who understood their
language. And when he asked them, they said,
'We are the servants of the King of Persia,
and we have come to ask who you are, and

290

whom you serve.' To which the other replied: 'We are Jews; we have no king and
no Gentile prince, but a Jewish prince
rules over us.' They then questioned him
with regard to the infidels, the sons of
Ghuz of the Kofar-al-Turak, and he answered: 'Truly they are in league with
us, and he who seeks to them harm seeks
our harm....' And on a certain day the
Jews asked him to join combat with them,
but he answered: 'I am not come to fight
you, but the Kofar-al-Turak, my enemy, and
if you fight against me I will be avenged
on you by killing all the Jews in my Empire. I know that you are stronger than
I am in this place.... Deal kindly with
me and do not fight against me,...and sell
me also the provisions which I require for
myself and my army.' The Jews then took
counsel together, and resolved to propi-
tiate the King on account of the Jews who
were in exile in his Empire. Then the King
entered their land with his army, and stayed
there fifteen days. And they showed him
much honour, and also sent a dispatch to
the Kofar-al-Turak their allies, reporting
the matter to them.[116]

This report presents several interesting details
concerning the Lost Tribes. First of all, the area
in which the Tribes dwelled seemed distant and mysterious. Benjamin emphasizes that it took a twenty-
day march to reach their settlement, and that they
were separated from Persia by a desert. This description introduces the reader to a legendary location. Other legendary elements include the fertile
land, the gardens, the plantations and the springs
of water "by the side of the river Gozan." A most
interesting detail concerns the Sabbath, the time
when the Persian king reached the settlement, as
"No man came forth to them." We can almost see the
Sambatyon, being peaceful on the Sabbath as a symbol of the separation between the Persians and the
Jews.[117] In addition, Benjamin gives an idyllic
picture of the Jewish settlement, including peace-

ful cities, villages, and the gate of the bridge.
The Jews also spoke a different language than did
the Persians,[118] again a legendary detail which
set these Jews apart from any others.

The central point of the description concerns
the answer of the Tribes to the question "...who
you are, and whom do you serve?" They replied:
"We are Jews; we have no king and no Gentile prince,
but a Jewish prince rules over us." We can sense
through this statement the pride and sense of freedom that the Jews had in asserting their independence from the Gentiles. These feelings of pride
are, of course, those of the reporter as well, for
he was a Jew living in exile. The medieval Jew,
constantly attacked as being a member of a weak
people and observing an ineffectual religion, must
have dreamt of strength and independence. This was
the meaning of the redemption for them. This episode also shows that the Jews could have physical
power. The mighty King of Persia did not want to
fight the Tribes, stating "I know that you are
stronger than I am in this place." Of course, the
Jews in exile, who never had any such strength,
found it flattering to hear of the existence of
these Tribes. Moreover, the Tribes were willing to
fight, but they reconsidered when they realized
other Jews might be hurt. The Tribes showed the
King honour for the sake of other Jews in the diaspora. Again, this reflects a fundamental issue of
Jewish life in the Middle Ages, when Jews felt
close and responsible for other Jews, no matter
where they were. This closeness contributed to the
survival of the Jewish nation in the diaspora.
Bearing all this in mind, we can see the contrast
between the Tribes on the one hand and the rest of
the Jews on the other. In fact, Benjamin's long
report came probably to stimulate Jewish pride and
to provide some consolation for less fortunate Jews.

Benjamin became very involved in his story and
perhaps might have been ready to set out himself in
search of the lost Jews, as he was living in a time
when rumours and legends about the return of the
Tribes enjoyed great popularity. In the very least

he wanted to confirm the stories that he heard.
At every place he went, he did not fail to mention
if any Jews there were free and independent. We
feel that the legend was much in his mind throughout his travels. One can sense his pride in the
political independence of the Jews of Arabia,[119]
and in the special emphasis he gives to repeated
mention of the Jewish Nasi,[120] describing him as
"of the seed of David."[121] In any event, there is
no mistaking the point that Benjamin's account gave
hope to the Jews and probably heightened messianic
expectations. If such Jews existed, especially if
they were descendents of or resembled the Lost
Tribes, then the messiah could not be far behind.
The Jews needed the legend to withstand the difficulties of the times.[122] From this point of view,
the revival of the legend may be considered by the
historians to be a true indication of the condition
of the Jewish spirit, which, though oppressed, always held onto its messianic hopes.[123]

The best example to reflect the messianic ferment of the time[124] and the collective psychological state of the Jewish community is Benjamin's
report of the story of David Alroy, the greatest
messianic episode of the period, that took place in
Persia. Our traveller reports:

> At this place (Amadia) there arose this
> day ten years ago, a man named David Alroy.
> ... He studied under Chisdai, the Head of
> the Captivity, and under the Head of the
> Academy Gaon Jacob, in the city of Baghdad,
> and he was well versed in the Law of Israel,
> in the Halachah, as well as in the Talmud,
> and in all the wisdom of the Mohammedans,
> also in secular literature and in the writ-
> ing of magicians and soothsayers. He con-
> ceived the idea of rebelling against the
> King of Persia, and of collecting the Jews
> who live in the mountains of Chafton to go
> forth and to fight against all the nations,
> and to march and capture Jerusalem. He
> showed signs by pretended miracles to the
> Jews, and said, 'The Holy One, blessed be

293

He, sent me to capture Jerusalem and to
free you from the yoke of the Gentiles.'
And the Jews believed in him and called
him their Messiah. When the King of Persia heard of it he sent for him to come
and speak with him. Alroy went to him
without fear, and he had audience of the
King, the latter asked him, 'Art thou the
King of the Jews?' He answered 'I am.'
Then the King was wrath, and commanded
that he should be seized and placed in the
prison of the King...in the city of Tabar-
istan....

At the end of three days, whilst the
King was sitting deliberating with his
Princes concerning the Jews who had re-
belled, David suddenly stood before them.
He had escaped from the prison without the
knowledge of any man. And when the King
saw him, he said to him, 'Who brought thee
hither, and who has released thee?' 'My
own wisdom and skill,' answered the other:
'for I am not afraid of thee, nor of any
of thy servants.' The King...loudly bade
his servants to seize him, but they answered, 'We cannot see any man, although
our ears hear him.' Then the King and all
his princes marvelled at his subtlety: but
he said to the King: 'I will go my way';
so he went forth. And the King went after
him.... Then Alroy took off his mantle and
spread it on the face of the water to cross
thereon...the servants of the King...said,
'There is no wizard like this in the whole
world.' That self-same day he went a journey of ten days to the city of Amadia by
the strength of the ineffable Name....

After that the King of Persia sent word
to the Emir Al-Muminin...at Baghdad, urging
him to warn the Head of the Exile, and the
Head of the Academy Gaon Jacob, to restrain
David Alroy from executing his designs. And
he threatened that he would otherwise slay
all the Jews in his Empire. Then all the

congregations of the land of Persia were in
great trouble. And the Head of the Captivity, and the Head of the Academy...sent to
Alroy, saying: 'The time of redemption is
not yet arrived: We have not yet seen the
signs thereof; for by strength shall no man
prevail. Now our mandate is, that thou
cease from these designs, or thou shalt surely be excommunicated from all Israel.' ...
Then...arose a king of the name of Sin-ed-
din, the king of Togarmim, and a vassal of
the King of Persia, who sent to the father
in law of David Alroy, and gave him a bride
of 10,000 gold pieces to slay Alroy in secret. So he went to Alroy's house, and slew
him whilst he was asleep on his bed. Thus
were his plans frustrated. Then the King
of Persia went forth against the Jews that
lived in the mountain: and they sent to the
Head of the Captivity to come to their assistance and to appease the King. He was eventually appeased by a gift of 100 talents of
gold, which they gave him, and the land was
at peace thereafter.[125]

The disturbances of this period led to the
rise of a military messiah, who sought to achieve
the restoration of the Jews and the capture of Jerusalem by fighting, rather than by miracles. The
goal of Alroy was to free the Jews from the yoke of
the Gentiles and to put an end to the exile. It is
important to note that at the centre of the redemption we find Jerusalem, representing the Holy Land.
It is also interesting that the Jews were ready to
follow Alroy and called him their Messiah. This is
evidence that the people were psychologically prepared for an emerging messianic movement. The miracles which David worked were characteristic of
medieval false-messiahs, and the report emphasizes
that Alroy was helped by the strength of the ineffable Name. Interestingly, the Jewish leaders
feared disappointment and persecution as a result
of this messianic movement, and therefore warned
Alroy that the time of redemption had not yet come.
The end of the story is again characteristic of the

failures of any Jewish messianic movement, as the false messiah was killed, the Jews had to pay tribute, and society returned to normal.

The episode of Alroy, long known by the brief hearsay report of Benjamin, attracted wide attention.[126] Fuller, though much distorted, is the hostile account given by Samau'al ibn Yahya al-Maghribi, who wrote The Silencing of the Jews and the Christians through Rational Arguments, a book whose primary purpose was to mock the Jews.[127] He cites the influence of David Alroy as an example of Jewish inferiority. From these often contradictory accounts, it appears that in the days of the Egyptian vizier Al-Afdhal (1120-21), one Solomon of Khazaria, along with his son Menahem sent letters to various Jewish communities announcing the ingathering of the exiles. Years later (1147) a similar thing happened, when the son Menahem or David Alroy or Al-Ruhi[128] assembled Jewish forces about himself. At first, it seems that the local Moslem commanders viewed this movement calmly. According to Baron,[129] it is probable that Alroy and the Jews of Amadia[130] both cooperated with the Moslems against the crusaders. It is also possible that Alroy, taking advantage of the confusion which followed Zengi's assassination (September 14, 1146), took possession of Amadia, whence he hoped to conquer Edessa and the Holy Land. He also sent messengers to many communities to lay the groundwork for his foray. Those messengers probably went beyond their orders and instructed the Baghdad Jews to assemble on their roofs on a certain night in order to be miraculously flown to Jerusalem.[131] The Exilarch and the Head of the Academy had no choice then but to threaten Alroy. At the same time the Persian Jews were threatened with severe persecution by the local authorities. Apparently David was assassinated. But the northern Jews continued to revere Alroy's memory,[132] and when Benjamin arrived there they still spoke enthusiastically of their "Messiah."[133]

The greatest difficulty comes in dating Alroy's movement. The movement seems to have extended

from about 1120 to 1147 and beyond, and it is the
final date which is most questionable.[134] Even-
Shemuel[135] expresses the view that the movement
continued far beyond the time of the second crusade. We thus have a much broader scene of the
messianic episode cited in Benjamin's report.

The period that began with the second crusade
(1147-48) witnessed a continuous struggle between
the crusaders and the Moslems, which eventually led
to the end of the crusaders' reign in the Holy Land
(1187). We have stated that at this time many Jews
were hoping that the messianic era was approaching.[136] Abraham bar Hiyya, who wrote his Megillat
ha-Megalleh about 1130, predicted that a conjunction of stars would occur in 1186 which would cause
calamities in the world. These troubles would last
for ten years, and in 1206 another conjunction would
occur, this time showing clear signs of the redemption.[137]

Behind the messianic movements of the time we
can detect then the calculations concerning the
end of the fifth millenium, and the impression the
struggle between Saladin and the crusaders made.[138]
Jews kept close watch on Saladin's campaigns, which
ended in 1187. A genizah document tells of a Jewish teacher who dreamt in 1187 that at the end of
that year the Egyptians would get a final victory
over the crusaders, and that in 1186 the redemption
would begin.[139] The messianic excitement grew
everywhere in the years beginning with the second
crusade.[140] The Moslem world urged Saladin to capture Jerusalem.[141] In the Christian world people
also expected a final war between Christians and
Moslems to begin.[142] The Jews in the Orient waited
enthusiastically for the war, which was associated
with the messianic calculations. Thus, people
were prepared for this conflict from the day Nur-
ed-din declared a holy war on the crusaders (1157).
It was at this time, argues Even Shemuel, that, in
Persia, an active messianic movement came to be
headed by David Alroy.[143] Alroy was in communications with the independent Jews who dwelled in the
mountains of Chafton in Kurdistan,[144] and he started

297

preparing them for the day when Jerusalem would be free of crusaders. Benjamin says that Alroy communicated with these Jews (in order) "to go forth and to fight against all the nations, and to march and capture Jerusalem." This is an historical point, which Benjamin relates concerning Alroy and his movement.

According to another source[145] the false messiah's name was not David Alroy but Menahem, surnamed Al-Ruhi.[146] As a young man of engaging appearance he gained influence with the governor of Amadia and attracted a considerable number of Jews of Persia. There is no doubt that David intended to go to the aid of Nur-ed-din against the crusaders, using the castle as his base. The source above states that the governor detected the conspiracy and had Alroy killed. Even Shemuel insists, though, that actually, Alroy was not killed then, but probably left the castle with his adherents and waited, hidden in the mountains, for a more appropriate time to make a move. Even Shemuel states that it is possible that Alroy was among those who pleaded with Saladin to hasten his attacks on the crusaders, and Alroy himself gathered Jews preparing to join Saladin in capturing Jerusalem.[147]

Using the Hebrew Apocalypse "Prayers of Rabbi Simeon Bar Yohay"[148] Even Shemuel states that at the end of 1179, Alroy's messianic movement experienced a renewal. These were the days of final preparation for the great forthcoming conflict between the Christians and Moslems, and the Jews decided to participate actively. Many capable fighters were under the leadership of Alroy, known in the new source as Abu Said ibn Daud, who declared himself only a precursor of the Messiah. As Alroy became stronger, the Jews and Arab tribes encouraged him to free his nation.[149] Alroy's fame[150] reached as far as Yemen, Egypt and North Africa. Everywhere preparations were being made, while Alroy's messengers hinted that Saladin was planning to give Jerusalem to the King Messiah once he captured it. They also published an epistle under Maimonides name,[151] urging the people to unify

behind Alroy because of his great scholarship.[152]
Furthermore, Maimonides supposedly sent his own
brother to Isfahan to confirm the rumours concerning the appearance of the forerunner of the Messiah.
A year and a half later his brother came back to report that the rumours were true.[153] The climax of
the epistle occurs at its conclusion, where it is
told that Saladin nominated Maimonides his minister
of finance[154] and announced his intention to capture Jerusalem and return it to the Jewish king.[155]
Thus, according to Even Shemuel, Alroy began his
career around 1160, appeared again in 1172, hid
seven years until 1179 and in the 1180's headed a
Jewish army ready to march on Palestine.[156] So the
forged letter would have been composed by one of
his followers.

It is quite easy to show that the epistle was
a forgery. Possibly Maimonides[157] tried to refute
the rumours in respect to the messianic movement
headed by Alroy in his <u>Iggeret Yemen</u>.[158] In a letter answering the inquiries of the scholars of
southern France,[159] Maimonides exposes the fallacies
of astrology and says:

> What has reached you in my name concerning
> the Messiah does not correspond to the
> facts: it was not in the East, in Ispahan:
> it was rather in Yemen that an individual
> arose...and proclaimed that he was a messen-
> ger come to prepare the way for the King
> Messiah and told them that the Messiah was
> in the land of Yemen.... I trembled for
> the Jews who were there, and composed some
> three or four tablets for them on the sub-
> ject of the Messiah and his signs.... If
> you heard that my letter has come to Fez,
> it is only because those remarks of mine
> that I sent to Yemen were copied and arrived
> in Fez.[160]

It is clear that the Yemenite Messiah was not David
Alroy, but Maimonides' statements do prove the existence of a false messiah in Persia. Maimonides
thought that a copy of his letter to Yemen arrived

in Fez, not realizing that another epistle had been written under his name,[161] speaking of Said b. Daudi,[162] either David Alroy, according to Even Shemuel, or another Messiah, according to other scholars mentioned, in Isfahan.[163]

To sum up this point we may say, in the author's opinion, that no matter which scholar is right, the years of the second crusade and the period immediately preceding 1187 reflect a great deal of messianic excitement among the Jews, particularly in the Moslem Orient. This is true whether the messianic movement reported by Benjamin began in 1120 and continued beyond the second crusade, or as Even Shemuel assumes, the movement extended to the end of the twelfth century and ended with the fall of the crusaders in the Holy Land. Thus, the report of the messianic movement by Benjamin reveals once again the hopes and the excitement shared by the traveller himself, and we can detect his disappointment in the movement's tragic end. The very fact that Benjamin mentions Alroy's episode reflects his own expectations and musings about the messianic signs.

Before leaving this subject, this is the proper place to raise one more question. We have noticed that in that same century ha-Levi, with whom Bemjamin was familiar, developed the idea of active redemption, meaning immigration to the Holy Land. Do our travellers share ha-Levi's concept of redemption, and had they been influenced by ha-Levi's own emigration?

We do not have any proof as to whether or not Jacob ben Nathaniel and Petachia were familiar with ha-Levi and his ideas. We have seen that Petachia inquired in Mosul of the coming of the Messiah, and, as a pious Jew, he accepted the traditional Jewish idea of redemption which recommended waiting for the Messiah to appear.[164] The same might be said of Jacob b. Nathaniel. Although we stated previously that Jacob expressed a wish "to go" to the Holy Land, at the same time we have no proof that he shared the active ideas of return raised by his

300

contemporary ha-Levi. Benjamin, who surely was
familiar with the poet-philosopher,[165] does not
give us any clues about his own reaction to ha-
Levi's ideas. Instead he reports of the Ten Lost
Tribes and occasionally hints of the "time" that
did not come.

It can safely be said that the twelfth-century
travellers were a part of the expectations of the
redemption in its traditional form. We have tried
to show that the Holy Land was the area of the most
importance in their travels, indicating a special
interest in it. This proves on the one hand that
they associated the Land with the redemption to
come, but on the other there is no proof that they
believed in taking part in an active redemption,
as advocated by ha-Levi.

Footnotes

[1]J. Mann, "Obadya, Prosélyte Normand Converti
au Judaisme, et sa Meguilla," R.E.J., LXXXIX (1930),
253; Mann, Texts and Studies in Jewish History and
Literature, I, 38-44; Mann, "A Second Supplement
to 'The Jews in Egypt and in Palestine under the
Fatimid Caliphs,'" p. 289; Dasberg, pp. 183-186.

[2]Y. Even Shemuel, Midreshay Geulah (Anthology
of Apocalyptic Midrashim), 2d ed. (Jerusalem, 1953-
54), the Introduction and the Interpretations.

[3]Mann, "Obadya, Prosélyte Normand Converti au
Judaisme, et sa Meguilla," p. 252.

[4]For a comprehensive study of the material relating to this interesting personality, see Mann,
ibid., pp. 245-59; Mann, Texts and Studies in Jewish History and Literature, I, 211; II, 42; S.D.
Goitein, "Obadyah, a Norman Proselyte," J.J.S., IV
(1953), 74, 84.

[5]Dinur, Israel in Diaspora (2)II, 231-89.

[6]The Karaites in Byzantium as well saw in the
events messianic signs (Ankori, "Studies in the
Messianic Doctrine of Yehuda Hadassi," pp. 192,
196, 197, 200; Mann, Texts and Studies in Jewish
History and Literature, I, 45; Mann, "The Messianic
Movements in the Time of the Early Crusades," XXIII,
255, n. 5).

[7]Werbalowsky, "Messianism in Jewish History,"
p. 30.

[8]Y. Baer, Galut (New York, 1947), p. 19.

[9]Y. Baer, "Israel and Exile in the Eyes of
Medieval Generations," Zion-Measef, VI (1934), 149.

[10]Abraham ibn Daud, Sefer Ha-Qabbalah, ed. S.D.
Cohen, pp. xxxv, 103; Abraham bar Hiyya shares ibn
Daud's ideas (Abraham Bar Hiyya, Hegyon Ha-Nephesch
Ha-Atzuvah, ed. G. Wigoder [Jerusalem, 1971], pp.
140, 145, 148.

[11]Abraham ibn Daud, Emuna Rama, ed. S. Weil
(Frankfurt 1852), p. 77.

[12]Moses Maimonides, Epistle to Yemen, ed. A.S.
Halkin (New York, 1952), p. xxvi; Silver, especially
Chapters II and III.

[13]Abraham ibn Daud, Sefer Ha-Qabbalah, ed. S.D.
Cohen, pp. 88-89, 213.

[14]Abraham bar Hiyya, Hegyon Ha-Nephesch Ha-
Atzuvah, p. 145; S. Schechter, Aspects of Rabbinic
Theology (New York, 1961), p. 97.

[15]Abraham ibn Daud, Sefer Ha-Qabbalah, ed. S.D.
Cohen, p. 219.

[16]Ibid., pp. 87, 96. In the twelfth century
the reality of "Exile" is reflected also in the
polemic literature of the time. Thus, Petrus Aba-
elardus, in his "Dialogus inter Philosophum, Ju-
daeum et Christianum," has the Jew give a horrible

picture of the "Exile" as Petrus himself saw it (Migne, CLXXVIII, 1617).

[17]Abraham ibn Daud, Sefer Ha-Qabbalah, ed. S.D. Cohen, p. 216.

[18]Abraham bar Hiyya, Sefer Megillat Ha-Megalleh, p. 108. On the system of Jewish Medieval writers to calculate the advent of Messiah, see A. Marx, "An Essay on the Year of Redemption," Hazofeh Le-Hochmat Israel, V (1921), 194-202.

[19]Twersky (ed.), A. Maimonides Reader, p. 438.

[20]See also Abraham bar Hiyya, Hegyon Ha-Nephesch Ha-Atzuvah, p. 140; J. Sarachek, The Doctrine of the Messiah in Medieval Jewish Literature (New York, 1968), pp. 118-20; Dasberg, pp. 183-185; Maimon B. Joseph, "The Letter of Consolation of Maimon b. Joseph," ed. and trans. L.M. Simmons, J.Q.R., II (1890), 62-101.

[21]Mann, "The Messianic Movements in the Time of the Early Crusades," XXIII, 243, 251; XXIV, 335-58; Baron, A Social and Religious History of the Jews, V, 138; Ankori, "Studies in the Messianic Doctrine of Yehuda Hadassi," p. 196; Silver, pp. 48, 74; Baer, "Israel and Exile in the Eyes of Medieval Generations," p. 160.

[22]The Itinerary of Benjamin of Tudela, ed. M.N. Adler, p. 29. See also Uri ben Simeon, p. 73.

[23]Baer, "Israel and Exile in the Eyes of Medieval Generations," p. 161; M. Peron, "Israel and Exile in Jehuda Halevi's Philosophy," Mahnayim, No. 80 (1963), p. 35.

[24]J. Guttman, Philosophies of Judaism, trans. D.W. Silverman (Philadelphia, 1964), pp. 120-123.

[25]Schirmann, The Hebrew Poetry in Spain and Provence, II, 488.

[26]Halevi, Book of Kuzari, pp. 258-259.

[27]B.Z. Dinur, "Halevi's Emigration to the Holy Land and the Messianic Ferment in His Days," Minha l'David (Jerusalem, 1935), pp. 158-59, 165; S.W. Baron, "Yehuda Halevi: An Answer to a Historical Challenge," Ancient and Medieval Jewish History (New Jersey, 1972), p. 139; for a different view see, G.D. Cohen, "Messianic Postures of Ashkenazim and Sephardim," Studies of the Leo Baek Institute (New York, 1967), pp. 138-139.

[28]Halevi, Book of Kuzari, pp. 86, 173, 185,259, 261.

[29]The Itinerary of Petachia, ed. E.N. Adler, Jewish Travellers, p. 90.

[30]See Zacharia 14:1-16. On the role of Jerusalem in the redemption see Mähl, pp. 11-26. The article speaks more from the Christian point of view. See especially pp. 14, 17, 20-21, 24-25.

[31]S.S. Cohen, "Palestine in Jewish Theology," HUCA, Jubilee Volume (1875-1925), pp. 171-209.

[32]Nahmanides commentary on Leviticus 26:32.

[33]Dinur, Israel in Diaspora (1)II, 445.

[34]See note 28 above.

[35]Joseph Ben R. Joshua ha-Kohen, Divre Hayamim (Amsterdam, 1733), pp. 33-34.

[36]Leviticus 26:32.

[37]This very significant idea is stated strongly once again by Nahmanides in the following section: "The fourth commandment that was incumbent upon us to occupy the Land which God the blessed be He gave to our forefather Abraham Isaac and Jacob, not to abandon the Land to other nations or to leave it desolate, as it was said to them, 'You shall inherit the Land and dwell there for to you have I given the Land for inheritance and you shall nourish the Land which I promised to your forefathers.'

And he specified through this commandment all of
the Land's borders...and the proof that this is a
Divine commandment can be seen from what God said
when He dealt with the spies, 'Arise and take possession as the Lord spoke to you, do not be afraid
and do not be hesitant...' and therefore we are not
permitted to let others possess it at any time....
We were commanded to come to this Land and to occupy the various provinces ("Medinoth") and to re-
establish our tribes.... Indeed we have been commanded to occupy (the Land) in every generation and
I say that the commandment which the sages emphasize so strongly, namely the inhabiting of the Land,
that they consider anyone who would leave the Land
of the dwelling there as an idolator.... We even
find in Midrash Sifre a story concerning R. Judah
ben Bethera, R. Matia ben Harasch, R. Hananiah ben
Ate, R. Joshua and R. Nathan who were departing
from the Land and reached Paltia when they suddenly
remembered the Land of Israel and they began to shed
tears and tore their clothing and then they began
to read this verse, 'and you shall inherit it and
dewll in it and you shall be strict in keeping it,'
and they said, 'to dwell in the Land of Israel is
equal to all the other commandments combined'" (Nahmanides, Sefer Hasagot Haramban Zal Sehsig 'Al
Rabenu Mose bar Maimon Zal Beminyan Hamitsvot, The
Fourth Commandment).

[38]Joseph Ben R. Aba Mari Caspi, Tam Hakesef, ed.
I.H. Last (London, 1913), pp. 43-45; see also Joseph
Kimhi, The Book of the Covenant, trans. F. Talmage
(Toronto, 1972), pp. 43-45, 49-53, and more espe-
cially, the commentary of his son David Kimhi on
Isaiah 52:1, 61:11, 64:9-10, 66:20; I Kings 11:39.

[39]Joseph Ben R. Aba Mari Caspi, p. 45.

[40]This theological argument is reflected well
in the twelfth century. The Christian writers repeat at this time the ideas of the Church Fathers,
especially those of St. Augustine, concerning the
destiny of the Jews. Thus Rupertus Tuitiensis (d.
1135) repeats the idea that Jews should be allowed
to live in humiliation and suffering until they

convert (Migne, CLXVII, 532). Petrus Cluniacensis, in his letter to the French king Louis VII (Migne, CLXXXIX, 367) relies on the famous verse in Psalms (59:12), which has been commented upon by Augustine (Migne, XLII, 261). In a more humane way, Bernard de Clairvaux speaks of the same idea, that Jews should be preserved as an evidence to the truth of Christianity (Migne, CLXXXII, 567). See note 69 below.

[41] The Itinerary of Petachia, ed. E.N. Adler, Jewish Travellers, p. 90.

[42] Ibid., pp. 68-69.

[43] See Chapter II, section 2 in the book.

[44] Could the reason Judah did not write the prophecy down be because he did not believe in astrology? See Cohen, "Messianic Postures of Ashkenzim and Sephardim,' pp. 143, 145-156.

[45] The Itinerary of Jacob ben Nathaniel ha-Cohen, ed. E.N. Adler, Jewish Travellers, p. 99.

[46] See Chapter II, section 3 in the book.

[47] See notes 56, 146 in Chapter V in the book.

[48] Werbalowsky writes: "...the phenomenon of smaller or larger groups of Jews leaving their countries of origin...to settle in the Holy Land was not infrequent.... But in point of fact many of these movements were inspired by messianic motives, though not necessarily by the belief that the Messiah had appeared and was calling his followers to leave the lands of exile and move to the Promised Land" (Werbalowsky, p. 40).

[49] The Itinerary of Jacob ben Nathaniel ha-Cohen, ed. E.N. Adler, Jewish Travellers, p. 99.

[50] Ibid., p. 98.

[51] The Itinerary of Benjamin of Tudela, ed. M.N.

Adler, p. 4.

[52]Ibid., p. 14.

[53]Ibid., p. 48.

[54]Ibid., p. 29. See note 165 below.

[55]The Itinerary of Benjamin of Tudela, ed. M.N. Adler, p. 23

[56]The Byzantine Karaite Hadassi emphasizes the valley in the context of the messianic days (Ankori, "Studies in the Messianic Doctrine of Yehuda Hadassi," p. 198). Joel's prophecy speaks of the day which will precede the restoration of Judah and Jerusalem to their former glory: "I will assemble all the nations and bring them down to the Valley of Jehoshaphat, and I will enter into judgment with them there on behalf of my people and my inheritance of Israel: Because they have scattered them among the nations, and divided my land" (Joel 4:1-3).

[57]The Itinerary of Benjamin of Tudela, ed. M.N. Adler, pp. 22-23.

[58]Ibid., p. 23.

[59]Ibid.

[60]Ibid., p. 24.

[61]Ibid., p. 25.

[62]Ibid.

[63]See Chapter V, section 2 in the book.

[64]The Itinerary of Petachia, ed. Grünhut, p. 33; The Itinerary of Benjamin of Tudela, ed. M.N. Adler, p. 23.

[65]The Itinerary of Petachia, ed. Grünhut, p. 34.

[66]Ibid., p. 31.

307

[67]The Itinerary of Benjamin of Tudela, ed. M.N. Adler, p. 24.

[68]The Itinerary of Petachia, ed. Grünhut, p. 32.

[69]It must be noted here that a strong religious anti-Christian and anti-Christianity polemic runs through the twelfth-century accounts. The best examples of this occur in the accounts about the Holy Land. However, it can also be detected in Benjamin's account of Rome (The Itinerary of Benjamin of Tudela, ed. M.N. Adler, pp. 6-8). In Rome Benjamin draws extensively from Josippon's classic book (see Bibliography), which contains an anti-Christian argument. We thus find that Benjamin refers to Titus who was punished by his own people for not conquering Jerusalem within two years. In the same Rome, God did not forsake His people; the glory of their past is present in the Temple vessels and in the legend of the weeping columns. Similarly, Sorrento, built by the son of Hadadezer when he fled in fear of David, the most famour Jewish warrior, and Joab, his famed general, and the mention of "a road under the mountain" built by Romulus, also in fear of David and Joab, indicate a particular form of Jewish nationalist spirit. This obvious apologetic and polemical spirit running through the travellogue is not accidental. It is a response to the impact of the crusades; the Jews felt despised and rejected. It must be remembered that ha-Levi wrote his famour Kuzari in the same period. The book was titled A Book to Defend a Despised Religion; its main objective was to defend "despised" Judaism. Also Joseph Kimhi, a twelfth-century Provencal Jewish scholar, wrote at this time (1150? 1160?) his Book of the Covenant, a strong anti-Christian polemic work in the popular dialogue form. This apologetic spirit and religious polemic, detected in Benjamin's description of Rome, takes on a clearer and more heightened expression when the twelfth-century traveller reaches the Holy Land and writes about places which had acquired sanctity for world Jewry. See The Itinerary of Petachia, ed. E.N. Adler, Jewish Travellers, pp. 79, 81, 84; The Itinerary of Peta-

<u>chia</u>, ed. Grünhut, pp. 19-20, 22-23, 27.

Funkenstein showed that in the twelfth century new patterns of anti-Jewish religious polemics developed in Western Europe. Added to the old forms, the religious polemics were intensified and led later to the attack against the Talmud (A. Funkenstein, "Changes in the Patterns of Christian Anti-Jewish Polemics in the 12th Century," <u>Zion</u> XXXIII [1968], 125-144). This was the most dangerous aspect of the Talmud trials in and after the thirteenth century. The new intensified religious polemic paved the way for further persecutions and expulsions. The ultimate purpose was the complete isolation of the Jews. See Chapter I, note 31 in the book. See also J. Trachtenberg, <u>The Devil and the Jews; The Medieval Conception of the Jews and Its Relation to Modern Anti-semitism</u> (New York, 1961), <u>et passim</u>.

[70]<u>The Itinerary of Benjamin of Tudela</u>, ed. M.N. Adler, p. 80. This paragraph, which is found in most printed editions, is believed by Adler, for reasons of style, to be a later interpolation (<u>The Itinerary of Benjamin of Tudela</u>, ed. M.N. Adler, p. 80, n. 1). My impression, however, as well as Dinur's (<u>Israel in Diaspora</u> [2] II, p. 282, n. 6) is that it would be wrong to assume this. However, if the paragraph quoted above could be proven to be an interpolation, then it could very well reflect what the people expected from our traveller's journey.

[71]See the excellent article by G.D. Cohen, "Messianic Postures of Ashkenazim and Sephardim," pp. 115-156.

[72]See Bibliography; also G. Scholem, "Jüdische Mystik in Westeuropa im 12. und 13. Jahrhundert," pp. 41, 43, 45.

[73]Rabbi Samuel Hasid, the father (1115-80), lived in Speyer, where his father's family had fled from Mainz during the first crusade. Samuel was involved with Aggadah and Midrash, as well as theosophy. He trained Judah, his son, in his methods

(<u>Sefer Hasidim</u>, Introduction). They believed that prayer preceded knowledge in Judaism, and that the sanctity of life as well as moral perfection were essential. They both tried to create the ideal of a <u>hasid</u> in their personal lives.

[74]The author, R. Eleazar (d. 1238) was a disciple of R. Judah the Pious.

[75]Eleazar Ben Judah of Worms, <u>Book of Rokeach</u> (Cremona, 1557), Introduction; M. Gudemann, <u>The Torah and the Life</u>, 3 vols. (Warsaw, 1897), <u>I</u>, 136-138. On Jewish mysticism in the West during the twelfth and thirteenth centuries, see G. Scholem, "Jüdische Mystik in Westeuropa im 12. und 13. Jahrhundert," pp. 37-54.

[76]Margalioth, pp. 201, 220, 221, 222, 436-437.

[77]G. Scholem, "Jüdische Mystik in Westeuropa im 12. und 13. Jahrhundert," p. 41; Dasberg, p. 185.

[78]See Chapter II, section 2 in the book.

[79]Medieval Jews and Gentiles lived in a world where spirits and ghosts appeared to be part of daily life. The community of Mayence, for example, believed a rumour that a congregation of ghosts was praying in the synagogue one night, and saw it as an omen of the tragedy of the first crusade. Baer brings several other instances where ghosts were said to have appeared, and maintains that this belief in ghosts came to Jewish folklore from the German (Baer, "The Religious Social Tendency of Sefer Hasidim," <u>Zion</u>, III [1937], 15). In Baer's essay, the impact of Christian pietistic concepts, propagated at that time especially by the Franciscans, is demonstrated. It was a temptation for man to try to enlist these spirits for his own purposes. Thus also folk mysticism went hand in hand with magic. So popular were these beliefs that even Judah the Pious had to warn his readers (Margalioth, p. 195 [206]).

[80]See Chapter V, section 2 in the book.

[81]The Itinerary of Petachia, ed. Grünhut, p. 36.

[82]Baron, A Social and Religious History of the Jews, VIII, 47.

[83]Margalioth, p. 195 (206).

[84]Ibid., pp. 193 (204), 195 (206).

[85]This has not been entirely controverted by Scholem's arguments (G. Scholem, Major Trends in Jewish Mysticism [New York, 1961], pp. 87-88).

[86]Margalioth, p. 189 (196).

[87]Newton, p. 11; The Letters of Obadiah Da Bertinoro, ed. E.N. Adler, Jewish Travellers, pp. 246-47; Saphir, I, 41; A. Neubauer, "Where Are the Ten Tribes?," J.Q.R., I (1889), 23. As a general rule, the Jews of the Middle Ages believed that the Lost Ten Tribes were settled in Arabia. The Khazars converted to Judaism in the eighth century, and thus they could not be mistaken for the Ten Tribes (D.M. Dunlop, The History of the Jewish Khazars [Princeton, 1954], pp. 89-115; 143-144). Nevertheless, in some accounts they were taken for the Lost Tribes (Eldad ha-Dani, ed. Epstein, pp. 22-29).

[88]II Kings 17:6 and 18:11.

[89]A. Godbey, The Lost Tribe Myth (North Carolina, 1930), pp. 15, 19; A.R. Anderson, Alexander's Gate: Gog and Magog and the Inclosed Nation (Cambridge, Mass., 1932), p. 58.

[90]The Sambatyon, a river which in its swift flow carries along stones and sand (or which consists solely of sand and stones, containing no water at all) so that no man may cross it; and which rests on the Sabbath, on which day it is either covered by a thick cloud or else by a sheath of flame, so that it may not be crossed; in some accounts it is not covered at all on the sabbath, and it is posssible to cross it on that day.

311

The first mention of the Sambatyon which we
have is in the Rabbinic literature where it is said
that part or all of the Ten Tribes, or the Benai
Moses are at or beyond the Sambatyon. Josephus (The
Jewish War, VII, V. 1) informs us that "Titus Cae-
sar...saw a river as he went along, of such a nature
as deserves to be recorded in history, it runs in
the middle between Arcea, belonging to Agrippa's
kingdom, and Raphanes. It hath somewhat very pecu-
liar in it; for when it runs its current is strong
and has plenty of water, after which its springs
fail for six days together, and leaves its channel
dry, as any one may see; after which it runs on the
seventh day as it did before, and as though it had
undergone no change at all: it hath also been observed to keep this order perpetually and exactly;
whence it is that they call it the Sabbatic river,
that name being taken from the sacred seventh day
of the Jews." One of these is probably the river
which Akiva had in mind when he told Turnus Rufus
that the Sambatyon proves that the Sabbath is the
true day of rest (Bereshit Raba, XI:6). It is however, evident that the other Rabbis who spoke of
the Tribes being beyond or at the Sambatyon had in
mind a river not in Judaea or Syria as was this one
which Josephus mentions and to which Akiva probably
refers, but at some distance from Palestine. This
is the implication which later commentators give to
Turnus Rufus' reply to Akiva (Bereshit Raba, XI:6).
The author feels mention should be made of
some opinions and statements concerning the Sambatyon which have not directly found a place in the
general discussion of the Ten Tribes, in which the
river is frequently referred. Abraham Yagel quotes
one of Maimonides' letters as follows: "This river
(Sambatyon) flows all the week days and rests on
the Sabbath. Indeed, in the time of my learned and
pious grandfather, a bottle was brought filled with
the sand of this river, which sand was in movement
the six days, and rested on the Sabbath. This is a
true fact, for more persons have seen it with their
own eyes" (Neubauer, "Where Are the Ten Tribes?",
411-12; A. Neubauer, Sammelband, III [Berlin, 1889],
39). Nahmanides on Deut. (XXXII:26) delivers himself of this opinion.

312

Our traveller, Petachia, says that in Yabneh there is a fountain which flows six days a week and on the Sabbath, not a drop of water is to be found in it (The Itinerary of Petachia, ed. Grünhut, p. 30). This may be the same stream as the one to which Josephus referred, for it is in the same region.

Christian records of the Middle Ages also made much of rivers and seas which, if not the Sambatyon itself, certainly possessed many of its properties. The letters of Prester John speak of the Sambatyon and of a great sea of sand, which is evidently the desert. The anonymous author of the "Itinerarium a Burdigala Hierusolem Usqus" maintains that the pool of Solomon dries up completely on the Sabbath (L. Ginzberg, The Legends of the Jews, 7 vols. [Philadelphia, 1911], VI, 407).

Many opinions have been expressed as to the source of the Sambatyon legend. See W. Max Müller, "An Egyptian Document for the History of Palestine," J.Q.R., IV (1912), 652, 654; Ginzberg, The Legends of the Jews, VI, 408. David Kaufman ("Le Sambation," R.E.J., XXII [1891], 285) propounds the theory that the legend of the Sambatyon concerned originally a river of sand and stones, as Eldad-ha-Dani has it, and that it was called נהר חול , a river of sand. The word חול , "sand" later was confused with its homonym, חל , "week day," and thus the river became one which flowed only on the six week days and not on the Sabbath. But as Ginzberg says, "this suggestion though rather ingenious, is for more than one reason quite untenable" (Ginzberg, The Legends of the Jews, VI, 408).

---

[91] Eldad ha-Dani, ed. Epstein, p. 13, n. 11; The Itinerary of Petachia, ed. Grünhut, p. 47, n. 174; Neubauer, "Where Are the Ten Tribes?", 20; A. Neubauer, La Géographie du Talmud (Amsterdam, 1965), p. 33.

[92] Neubauer, "Where Are the Ten Tribes?", 21.

[93] Acts 26:6.

[94] Neubauer, La Géographie du Talmud, p. 372.

[95] Judah b. Balam, at about the end of the eleventh century, stated, following M.J. Derenbourg's translation of his glosses to Isaiah ("Gloses d' Abou Zakariya ben Bilam sur Isaie," R.E.J., XVIII [1889], 74), "les dix tribus étaient dans le Khorasan, à חלח (Halah), חבור (Habor) et נהר גוזן (River Gozan) (II Kings 17:6), il paraît que חבור est le nom d'un fleuve du Khorasan appelé chaboras, et que נהר גוזן est un fleuve qui baigne la ville de Gazna, qui est aujourd'hui la capitale du Khorasan." The implication is that Judah believes that the Ten Tribes are still in the place he mentions (Fischel, "The Jews of Central Asia (Khorasan) in Medieval Hebrew and Islamic Literature," 35-36, 38-39; Rabinowitz, Jewish Merchants' Adventures, p. 51; Le Strange, The Lands of Eastern Caliphate, p. 424).

[96] E.N. Adler, Jews in Many Lands (London, 1905), p. 178; Benjamin of Tudela, Sefer Masa'ot, ed. Asher, II, 170-72, n. 311.

[97] Eldad ha-Dani, ed. Epstein, pp. 24-29.

[98] Neubauer, Sammelband, 14, 19.

[99] Baron, A Social and Religious History of the Jews, III, 205.

[100] Gustav Oppert, Der Presbyter Johannes in Sage und Geschichte (Berlin, 1870), pp. 17-18.

[101] Neubauer, "Where Are the Ten Tribes?", 188.

[102] The biblical passages dealing with Gog and Magog are: Genesis, 10:2, Ezekiel, Chapters 38 and 39, Revelation, 20:7-8; See also Wright, Human Nature in Geography, pp. 68-69; Anderson, Alexander's Gate; Gog and Magog and the Inclosed Nation, p. 61; G. Cary, The Medieval Alexander (Cambridge, Eng., 1956), p. 130.

[103] Toward the end of the eleventh century we have a rumour about the Ten Tribes, directly bound up with a Messianic movement. A letter which David Kaufman published ("A Hitherto Unknown Messianic

Movement among the Jews, Particularly Those of Germany and the Byzantine Empire," J.Q.R., X [1898], 139-51) apprises us of the fact that the Jews of Germany looked for the coming of the Messiah in the 256th lunar cycle, based on the word ר"נ"ו -256 in Jeremiah 31:7, which would end in the year 1104. Certain events which occurred at that time confirmed them in their view: the first crusade, which they interpreted to be the great world war between Gog and Magog which must precede the coming of the Messiah, and further a report that the Ten Tribes, behind the dark mountains, were preparing to unite with the other Jews to fight the common enemy, and redeem Israel. According to this report the dark mountains, situated near Germany, had all at once become lit up with great brilliancy, another sign of the end of the contemporary world order. It seems from the letter that a movement of German Jews had commenced toward the east in anticipation of the coming of the Ten Tribes. The belief in the Ten Tribes in Germany must have been strong for this report to have caused this mass movement. Signs and wonders were performed everywhere: Jews were given freedom, taxes were abolished, and other marked signs of favour were shown them. This is all the information that the letter gives us. We can realize the shock felt by the Jews when instead of the Ten Tribes, the crusaders appeared on the European scene. Abraham Yagel informs us of another occasion in Germany during the same period of the crusades when the Ten Tribes were also expected (Neubauer, Sammelband, 39). See also Dasberg, p. 184.

[104] H.Z. Hirshberg, "The Desire for Freedom in the Legends on the Ten Tribes," Mahnayim, LXXX (1963), 97, 98, 100; Ankori, "Studies in the Messianic Doctrine of Yehuda Hadassi," 196-97; Werbalowsky, p. 36.

[105] The Itinerary of Petachia, ed. Grünhut, p. 1.

[106] Ibid., p. 15; Beazley, II, 271.

[107] See Joseph ben Gorion, Josippon, ed. H. Hominer (Jerusalem, 1955-56), pp. 49-50.

[108]The Itinerary of Petachia, ed. Grünhut, p. 25.

[109]Ibid., p. 10.

[110]The Itinerary of Benjamin of Tudela, ed. M.N. Adler, p. 59.

[111]Ibid., p. 59. The British Museum text reads: "And he put them in Halah and in Habor and the mountains of Gozan and the mountains of the Medes" (The Itinerary of Benjamin of Tudela, ed. M.N. Adler, p. 59, n. 1). Nöldeke maintains that, according to II Kings XIX:12 and Isaiah XXXVII:12, there was a tract of land watered by the river Gozan, known by the name Gozanites which Scripture refers to (Neubauer, "Where Are the Ten Tribes?", 186.

[112]Concerning the rest of the Ten Tribes, R. Benjamin says that they may be found in Kurdistan and by the Zagros mountains (The Itinerary of Benjamin of Tudela, ed. M.N. Adler, p. 54).

[113]Ibid., p. 59.

[114]Ibid., pp. 60-62.

[115]See Benjamin's report, as far as it refers to Kofar-al-Turak (The Itinerary of Benjamin of Tudela, ed. M.N. Adler, pp. 60-61).

[116]Ibid.

[117]See n. 90 above.

[118]Eldad ha-Dani reported that they spoke Hebrew (Eldad ha-Dani, ed. Epstein, p. 24).

[119]One particular region which is important in Benjamin's account in respect to the Lost Tribes is Southern Arabia. A particular place in Arabia which is related to the legend of the Lost Tribes is Kheibar. See The Itinerary of Benjamin of Tudela, ed. M.N. Adler, pp. 47-50; Jewish Travellers, ed. E.N. Adler, p. 239; Graetz, Geschichte der Juden, III, 54; Neubauer, "Where Are the Ten Tribes?," 24; A.

Neubauer, "The Literature of the Jews in Yemen,"
J.Q.R., III (1891), 605-06, 607-08; Hirshberg, "The
Desire for Freedom in the Legends of the Ten Tribes,"
97-98, n. 3; A. Harkavy (ed.), Teshubot ha-Geonim
(Berlin, 1887), Part I, pp. 84, 94; E. Sapir, "Notes
on Judaeo-German Phonology," J.Q.R., VI (1916), 251,
259; J. Mann, "The Responsa of the Babylonian Geonim as a Source of Jewish History," J.Q.R., VII
(1917), 489; Mann, The Jews in Egypt and Palestine
under the Fatimid Caliphs, I, 118; J. Braslavsky,
"The Jewish Community of Chaibar," Zion, I (1935),
148, n. 1 and p. 174; also p. 175, n. 167; W. Bacher,
"An Alleged Old Source of the Jews of Yemen," J.Q.R.,
V (1893), 346; C.M. Doughty, Travels in Arabia
Deserta, 2 vols. (Cambridge, 1888), I, 127, 286; II,
129; S.Y. Rapaport, "About Independent Jews in Arabia and Kush till Today," Bikure ha-itim, IV (1824),
52, 53-54, 56-57; K. Ritter, Die Erdkunde im Verhältnis zur Natur und zur Geschichte des Menschen, 19
vols. (Berlin, 1832-59), XII, 570.

[120] The Itinerary of Benjamin of Tudela, ed. M.N.
Adler, pp. 47-48.

[121] See Chapter IV, section 1.

[122] Hirshberg emphasizes the important role played
by the legend of the Ten Tribes in strengthening the
desire of the Jews to continue to live as a separate
nation (Hirshberg, "The Desire for Freedom in the
Legends of the Ten Tribes," p. 100).

[123] G. Scholem, Sabbatai Sevi: The Mystical Messiah (1626-1676) (New Jersey, 1973), pp. 105, 261,
n. 173, 288; Werbalowsky, pp. 41-42.

[124] Marcus, The Jew in the Medieval World, p. 247;
Silver, p. 80.

[125] The Itinerary of Benjamin of Tudela, ed. M.N.
Adler, pp. 54-56.

[126] The accounts given by Ben Verga in Shevet
Jehudah (pp. 74-77) and by Joseph ha-Cohen, the
author of Emek Ha-Bakha (pp. 35-37) are evidently

317

based upon Benjamin's record. Part of Alroy's episode is brought by R. Joseph Sambary, published by A.E. Karkavy, Hadashim Gam Yeshanim (Jerusalem, 1970), pp. 47-49; however, it is slightly different from that of Benjamin.

[127]See the source, Marcus, The Jew in the Medieval World, pp. 247-50. Further information is available in a genizah fragment published by Mann, "Obadya le Prosélyte," R.E.J., LXXI (1920), 90.

[128]Both first names are equally messianic (Baron, A Social and Religious History of the Jews, V, 203).

[129]Ibid.

[130]A strategically located fortress northeast of Mosul whose inhabitants had known anti-Christian feelings.

[131]See footnote 127 above.

[132]Ibid.

[133]See N.A. Poliak's analysis, "David Alroy," Ha-Kinnus, I (Jerusalem, 1952), 404-06.

[134]Joseph ha-Cohen gives the date as 1163 (Emek Ha-Bakha, p. 35).

[135]Even Shemuel, p. 260.

[136]Mann, "A Second Supplement to 'The Jews in Egypt and in Palestine under the Fatimid Caliphs,'" p. 285; Mann, Texts and Studies in Jewish History and Literature, I, 38-44, 45, 458; Mann, "The Messianic Movements in the Time of the Early Crusades," XXIII, 243-61; XXIV, 335-38.

[137]Abraham bar Hiyya, Sefer Megillat Ha-Megalleh, p. 146.

[138]Mann, Texts and Studies in Jewish History and Literature, I, 458. Even Maimonides was affected by messianic hopes. S. Zeitlin expresses the opin-

ion that Maimonides wrote his law code, the Mish-neh Torah, as a constitution for the forthcoming Jewish state (Z. Zeitlin, Maimonides [New York, 1935], p. 85).

[139] Mann, Texts and Studies in Jewish History and Literature, I, 458.

[140] Ibid., 237; Ashtor-Strauss, "Saladin and the Jews," p. 319.

[141] Prawer, A History of the Latin Kingdom of Jerusalem, I, 527.

[142] Even Shemuel, p. 262, n. 25.

[143] Ibid., p. 259.

[144] See Chapter VI in the book.

[145] See the reference cited in note 127 above.

[146] Munk proves that he is identical with Alroy (The Itinerary of Benjamin of Tudela, ed. M.N. Adler, p. 56, n. 2).

[147] Even Shemuel, pp. 259-60.

[148] Ibid., pp. 268-86.

[149] Ibid., p. 260.

[150] Mann, Texts and Studies in Jewish History and Literature, I, 480.

[151] A. Neubauer, "Documents inédits," R.E.J., IV (1882), 173-79.

[152] This is how the epistle, in part, reads: "True, there is a man in Ispahan, by name 'Abu Said ben Daudi, and said that he is the military comman-der of the Messiah.... Many people, Jews and non-Jews, without number followed him.... He told them: 'The time of redemption is not yet arrived!' And he hid himself seven years.... In this year he showed

himself and many people, more than before, followed
him...then...Jews and the elders of Nebayot and
Kedar told him: 'Our master King Messiah of God!...
Command us to go to our brethren who dwell among
the nations....' He told them:...'The time is not
yet arrived...and I have been sent to prepare the
hearts of the Jews of suffer a few more years among
the nations; and I also commanded you not to reveal
the end, but keep it hidden!'" (ibid., pp. 174-75).

[153] Ibid., p. 175.

[154] Ibid., p. 178.

[155] Ibid., p. 176-77.

[156] However, various points argue against this
theory. Benjamin, who visited Babylonia in 1168,
reported that Alroy had risen ten years previously.
He does, though, mention in this connection the
prince of Mosul, Sin-ed-din, the brother of Nur-ed-
din, who died in 1149 (The Itinerary of Benjamin of
Tudela, ed. M.N. Adler, p. 33). Therefore, Ashtor
and Baron suggest that " עשׂר " be changed to
" עשׂרי ," i.e., twenty years previous (Ashtor-
Strauss, "Saladin and the Jews," p. 321, n. 57;
Baron, A Social and Religious History of the Jews,
V, 385, n. 69) and we thus arrive at the time of
the second crusade, which was assigned to the movement of Alroy by Mann (Texts and Studies in Jewish
History and Literature, I, 211, 480; Mann, "The
Messianic Movements in the Time of the Early Crusades," 347-48). It is hardly possible that the
same man headed a messianic movement forty years
later. Furthermore, there is a contradiction in
the geographical locations of the movement between
the sources. In the letter ascribed to Maimonides
the movement is in Isfahan, whereas according to
Benjamin and Yahya al-Maghribi, Alroy appeared in
the province of Mosul (Ashtor-Strauss, "Saladin and
the Jews," p. 321, n. 57). If Mann's opinion,
placing Alroy's episode at the time of the second
crusade is correct, it is also possible, then, to
assume that in Saladin's time it was not David Alroy who appeared, but his son, Menahem. This idea

320

is, in fact, recognized by Even Shemuel, p. 262, n. 27.

[157]It is well known that Maimonides objected to any calculation as to the time of Messiah (Marx, "An Essay on the Year of Redemption," p. 195).

[158]Twersky (ed.), A Maimonides Reader, p. 454.

[159]The letter of the rabbis to Maimonides brought in full by Marx, "The Correspondence between the Rabbis of Southern France and Maimonides about Astrology," HUCA, III (1926), 343-49; also see p. 357 there.

[160]Maimonides, "Letter on Astrology," ed. Twersky, A Maimonides Reader, pp. 472-73.

[161]Neubauer, "Documents inédits," pp. 173-79.

[162]Ibid., p. 175.

[163]Marx, "The Correspondence between the Rabbis of Southern France and Maimonides about Astrology," pp. 349, 356.

[164]See previous pages in this chapter in connection with the rise of the piety movement among the German Jews.

[165]Schirmann seeks to prove that ha-Levi was born not in Toledo, but in Tudela, Benjamin's own native city (H. Schirmann, "The Birthplace of Judah Halevi," Tarbiz, X [1939], p. 237).

CHAPTER VII

THE COMMERCIAL ASPECT IN THE BOOKS

OF THE TRAVELLERS

It is well known that Jews in the early Middle Ages up to the rise of the Italian city states were actively involved in local and world trade. Rabinowitz has shown in Jewish Merchants' Adventures that a certain Jewish group, the Rahdānites, were involved in the international trade of the early Middle Ages up to the tenth century.[1] Although the Jewish Rahdānites were prior to our travellers' period, their existence in world trade prompts us to examine whether Jews were still involved in international trade in the twelfth century. We begin this chapter with a general survey of the Mediterranean trade; then we show how that Mediterranean commerce is reflected within the travellers' accounts; and finally, we attempt to draw from the accounts and the Genizah records to reveal the part played by the Jews in that Mediterranean trade.

There was a revival of creative activity in various aspects of civilization in the twelfth century.[2] The expansion of Europe occurred in all directions, one of which was the movement of the crusades, the most influential of the time. The revival of trade and industry created a money economy which helped the kings to establish their power; for merchants and artisans, the era of the bourgeoisie was at hand.[3] To the Italian merchants, the crusades always appeared to offer economic opportunities.[4] During most of the twelfth century, the Italians had commercial quarters in a majority of the maritime cities of the Levant from which they carried on their trade. Those quarters became the centres of exchange for Oriental and European goods.

The Fatimid conquest of Egypt in July, 969,[5] marked the opening of the Genizah period which

ended in 1250, and was a time of significant changes
on the Mediterranean scene. The Moslem south lost
its naval superiority to the Christian north, and
on the African coast, the shift was from Tunisia toward Egypt and Byzantium.[6] Only the Fourth Crusade
in 1204 caused Byzantium to lose its position as a
Mediterranean power, and it was replaced by the Italian republics and the Normans.[7] Venice was the
only maritime power that lasted during all this time
(969-1250). It was a period of relatively free
trade and of growing economic activities,[8] and Europeans travelling on Genoese, Pisan and Gaetan ships
are mentioned throughout the Genizah papers, especially as traders, in both the eleventh and twelfth
centuries.[9] The European traders were not confined
to coastal towns. A letter sent from Alexandria to
old Cairo at the end of the eleventh century reads:

> Please take notice that no paper, cinnamon,
> or ginger are available in Alexandria. If
> you have any of the commodities, keep them,
> for the Rūm [here: Byzantine] are keen
> solely on them. All the Rūm are about to
> leave for old Cairo. They are only waiting
> for the arrival of two additional ships from
> Constantinople.[10]

In all the cases quoted by Goitein[11] we find the
Europeans as importers, though they did export goods
to the Moslem countries. Timber was a major export
from Europe to the Moslem area, coral was another.[12]
These exports, however, cheese being an exception,
were not handled by Jews.

The commercial life in the Mediterranean world
is reflected in the travellers' accounts, especially
that of Benjamin. His account details the commercial centres of the twelfth century including the
republics in Italy, the Byzantine capital, Constan-
tinope, and the Syro-Palestinian coast.

The Italian cities are the dominant commercial
centres. Travelling by ship from Marseilles to
Genoa, Benjamin considers the inner political life
of the northern communes, their division into strong

families fighting to control the city life.[13]   Significantly for our study, he perceives that the inhabitants of Genoa, "have command of the sea."
Moreover, "they build ships which they call galleys,
and make predatory attacks upon Edom and Ishmael,
and the land of Greece as far as Sicily, and they
bring back to Genoa spoils from all these places."[14]
Genoa, a powerful force felt by Moslems and Christians alike, was rising in its control of the sea
and was at constant war "with the men of Pisa" over
the domination of sea power. Pisa, Benjamin notes,
is about six miles from the sea and the river which
flows through the city "provides it with ingress
and egress for ships."[15]

     Although Venice and Florence were culturally,
politically and commercially significant, Benjamin
does not discuss them. He does mention Amalfi, a
significant commercial commune whose inhabitants
"are merchants engaged in trade...and buy everything for money."[16] They do not sow or reap, he
says; money rather than goods is used in their economic life. Here we have a clear reference to a
money economy in contrast to the feudal economy which
still persisted in Europe at that time. Benjamin
makes no reference to the town's turbulent history[17]
other than to describe its mountain fortress.[18] He
does note that merchants from Amalfi were present
in Alexandria.[19]

     Though he mentions Trani,[20] Messina,[21] and
Palermo[22] in Sicily, all flourishing and rich,[23] it
is obvious that Benjamin does not discuss all the
commercial city republics in Italy nor does he deal
exhaustively with the commercial significance of the
areas he does discuss. His account does reflect the
power and spreading authority of the northern city
republics and the prominence of Pisan and Genoese
merchants with regard to trade.

     It is clear from Benjamin's account that the
French Mediterranean ports were also affected by
the revival of trade at the time of the crusades.
A lively commercial life is pointed to in Monte-
pellier. In the twelfth century, this city was a

convenient clearing house for the trade between the
Holy Land and the Levant; the same is true with regard to Marseilles. Benjamin states of Montpellier:
"this is a place well situated for commerce...and
men come for business there from all quarters, from
Edom, Ishmael, the land of Algarve, Lombardy, the
dominion of Rome the Great, from all the land of
Egypt, Palestine, Greece, France, Asia and England."[24]
People of all nations are found there doing business
"through the medium of the Genoese and Pisans."[25]
However, of Marseilles Benjamin notes only that "it
is a very busy city upon the sea coast."[26]

    With regard to lands further east of Italy,
Egripos, the capital of Euboea, is mentioned as "a
large city upon the sea coast, where merchants come
from every quarter."[27] Armylo is another station
mentioned as a prominent place on the sea. However,
the most significant fact to be noticed here is Benjamin's statement that it is "inhabited by Venetians, Pisans, Genoese and all the merchants who
come there."[28] Once again we observe the Italian
merchants dominating the commercial life of the city.
As reflected by our accounts, Italy was the centre
of commerce with other cities planted on its east
and west on the southern European coast of the Mediterranean.

    Constantinople, the Byzantine capital, to which
Benjamin refers as "...a great town...the capital of
the whole land of Javan, which is called Greece,"[29]
was a second major commercial centre in the eastern
Mediterranean. Few cities have enjoyed such an excellent commercial location as did Constantinople;
and it was not surprising that for a long time it
was "a synonym for riches, a city of whose treasure
there was neither end nor measure."[30] However, the
eleventh century witnessed the initial decline of
Byzantine commerce.[31] The loss of a portion of Asia
Minor to the Seljuks, the seizure of Thebes and Corinth with the transport of its silk worms and weav-
ers to Italy (by Roger II in 1147) all contributed
to the disruption of the once prosperous economic
life.[32] Then the crusaders added the final blow by
altering the trade routes. Italian vessels now

carried cargo directly to the west from the crusading Syrian ports.

Although the Fourth Crusade would result in the eventual ruin of the Empire and the establishment of the Latin Kingdom,[33] when our traveller visited Constantinople he was still very impressed with the riches of the city.[34] He states "From every part of the Empire of Greece tribute is brought here every year and they fill strongholds with garments of silk, purple and gold. Like unto these storehouses and this wealth, there is nothing in the whole world to be found."[35] The Greek inhabitants are very rich, Benjamin notes, and they look like princes clothed in garments of silk with gold embroidery.[36] Benjamin continues in describing the commercial life in the city:

> All sorts of merchants come here from the land of Babylon, from the land of Shinar, from Persia, Media, and all the sovereignty of the land of Egypt, from the land of Canaan, and the Empire of Russia, from Hungaria, Patzinakia, Khazaria, and the land of Lombardy and Sepharad. It is a busy city, and merchants come to it from every country by sea or land and there is none like it in the world except Baghdad, the great city of Islam.[37]

It is interesting to note that Benjamin compares Constantinople with Baghdad. Each is a busy city and a commercial centre which attracted merchants from every country "by sea or land," a centre into which trade routes leading from the Far East, North, South, and West meet. He describes its trade accurately, though briefly. "The wealth and luxury of Constantinople," notes Gibbon, "demanded the productions of every climate.... Her situation invites the commerce of the world and in every period of her existence that commerce has been in the hands of foreigners."[38] Above all, Benjamin recalls the weakness of the Empire towards the end of the century when he states that their "natives are not warlike, but are as women who have no strength to fight."[39] This

effeminate trait of the Byzantines is also confirmed by others.[40]

   With the capture of Tyre in 1124[41] and fall of
Ascalon in 1153,[42] the entire Syro-Palestinian coast
enjoyed a period of economic prosperity. This prosperity is reflected by the fact that in the months
of the Passagium (the months of travel between Easter and late autumn) many ships were to be found in
the harbours. Documents regarding customs dues,
reflecting the scale of commerce, have been preserved.[43] Benjamin provides us with a good description of Tyre and its commercial significance in his
time. He states:

      ...New Tyre, which is a very fine city, with
      a harbour in its midst. At night time those
      that levy dues throw iron chains from tower
      to tower so that no man can go forth by boat
      or in any other way to rob the ships by night.
      There is no harbour like this in the whole
      world.... New Tyre is a busy place of com-
      merce, to which merchants flock from all quar-
      ters.[44]

The city impressed our traveller with its unique
harbour. Certainly, this in itself reflects the
commercial significance of the city. The security
precautions taken to protect the harbour during the
night reinforces our opinion of its commercial importance. Benjamin mentions special glassware and
sugar factories for which Tyre was renowned up to
1291 when the crusaders deserted the city.[45] Benjamin further notes that the fine Tyrian glassware
was prized in all countries,[46] and that "the sugar
was of high class." He also comments that "people
come from all lands to buy it."[47] Edrisi writes:
"Tyre is a handsome city...very fine glass and ear-
thenware are manufactured here...."[48] Benjamin's
account of Tyre as a commercial centre and elegant
city is further substantiated by William of Tyre's
account of that city in which this famous historian
was born.[49]

   Acre is also mentioned by Benjamin as "situated

327

by the Great Sea, it possesses a large harbour for all the pilgrims who come to Jerusalem by ship."[50] When Benjamin visitied it, its occupation was vital to the crusaders who preferred the sea route to the more dangerous land route.[51] Acre became the capital of the kingdom in July, 1187, after a loss of Jerusalem, and it was the last place to be abandoned by the crusaders.[52] The harbour was protected by its natural and man-made barriers.[53] Various twelfth century accounts of the city exist.[54] In 1185, Ibn Jubayr relates:

> Acre is the capital of the Frankish cities
> in Syria, the unloading place of ships
> reared aloft in the seas like mountains,
> and a port of call for all ships. In its
> greatness it resembles Constantinople. It
> is the focus of ships and caravans, and
> the meeting place of Christian merchants
> from all regions....[55]

Another maritime city on the Palestine coast specifically indicated by our traveller as having commercial importance is Ascalon. Benjamin reports that "New Ascalon is a large and fair place, and merchants come thither from all quarters, for it is situated on the frontier of Egypt."[56] Asher believes that Benjamin's style in describing Ascalon and his detailed reporting of its principal Jewish inhabitants indicates that Benjamin's visit to this city was motivated by commercial interests.[57]

Other maritime cities of secondary importance which are mentioned by Benjamin as lying on the Syro-Palestinian coast were Antioch,[58] Tripoli,[59] Sidon, Beirut,[60] Haifa,[61] and Jaffa.[62]

In Egypt we find mention of Alexandria, the famous commercial centre. Benjamin's description reflects both the importance of the city to Egypt and its Mediterranean trade life. First, he briefly reports the history of the city, its fine urban planning, its exquisite architecture and the academy of Aristotle as a centre of learning where "people from the whold world were wont to come

hither in order to study the wisdom of Aristotle.
..."[63] The streets are wide and straight and
"Alexander built it with great understanding."[64]
Continuing, he mentions the Pharos of Alexandria,
built for the merchants' benefit.[65] Benjamin's account of Alexandrian commerce and of the merchants
who engaged in trade in that city further substantiates his keen powers of observation. Alexandria
at this time was the most important centre for
Eastern commodities. Benjamin states:

> Alexandria is a commercial market for all
> nations. Merchants come thither from all
> Christian kingdoms: on the one side, from
> the land of Venetia and Lombardy, Tuscany,
> Apulia, Amalfi, Sicilia, Calabria, Romagna,
> Khazaria, Patzinakia, Hungaria, Bulgaria,
> Rukuvia [Ragusa?], Croatia, Slavonia, Rus-
> sia, Alamannia, Saxony, Danemark, Kurland,
> Ireland, Norway, Frisia, Scotia, Angleterre,
> Wales, Flanders, Hainault, Normandy, France,
> Poitiers, Anjou, Burgundy, Maurienne, Pro-
> vence, Genoa, Pisa, Gascony, Aragon, and
> Navarra, and towards the west under the sway
> of the Mohammedans, Andalusia, Algarve,
> Africa and the land of the Arabs; and on
> the other side India, Zawilah, Abyssinia,
> Lybia, El-Yemen, Shinar, Esh-Sham (Syria):
> also Javan, whose people are called the
> Greeks, and the Turks. And merchants of
> India bring thither all kinds of spices,
> and the merchants of Edom buy of them. And
> the city is a busy one and full of traffic.
> Each section has an inn of its own.[66]

This commercial exchange between Egypt and Europe,
described by Benjamin, is a significant fact in the
history of the time. The crusaders' efforts were
aimed against Egypt.[67] Nevertheless, this Asiatic
merchandise, "all kinds of spices," became a source
of great profit to the population. Thus, the Egyptian rulers never considered closing the ports to
the European merchants who paid duty on those commercial articles. Indeed, economic profits over-
came religious differences. The eagerness of the

Europeans to engage in this commercial exchange caused the Pope to pass prohibitive legislation, but these prohibitions were unsuccessful.[68] As noted accurately by Benjamin, Alexandria was a lively international trade centre, a busy city "and full of traffic." It is no wonder that the crusaders tried to control Egypt, with its wealth, as a key to insure the kingdom of Jerusalem.[69]

Thus, Benjamin's accounts reveal both the Mediterranean commerce and trade centres at that time. In the accounts we are aware of the ascendancy of the Italian maritime cities which dominated the commercial life of the area and brought about the ruin of the Byzantine Empire on account of their desire to contol that commercial centre in Constantinople. Scholars are in agreement that this struggle among Italian communes over trade privileges in the crusading maritime towns weakened in many ways the Latin Kingdom of Jerusalem.[70]

Benjamin and Petachia reflect trade centres and trade routes in other areas on the route to the Far East, both land and sea coast stations. We noted earlier that Benjamin observed Far Eastern merchants in Alexandria and Constantinople which is indicative of the commercial life between the Far East and the Mediterranean world. Among the land route trade centres, Benjamin mentions Damascus of which he remarks: "It is a place carrying on trade with all countries."[71] Benjamin's description of this city[72] is confirmed by the contemporary Edrisi.[73]

Baghdad was another world trade centre. Benjamin, in his description of the city,[74] compares its size and commercial significance with that of Constantinople.[75] Our traveller states "people come thither with merchandise from all lands" to Baghdad.[76] It is no wonder, since it was a centre to which land routes from the Far East, from the south—Persian Gulf, from the north and the west—the Mediterranean maritime cities, led.[77]

Of Ghaznah "the great city" Benjamin says, "it

330

is a city of commercial importance: People of all
countries and tongues come thither with their
wares."[78] Ghaznah, in all likelihood, served as a
commercial station for those merchants who were on
their way to the Far East or to the West. Benjamin
mentions other cities located on the trade route to
the Far East in which he reports the existence of
Jewish communities. However, he does not specify
whether the cities were commercially significant.[79]

Benjamin speaks of the island of Kish, a place
which in the Middle Ages, was strategically located
on the trade route from India to Europe.[80] He
states that the inhabitants "neither sow nor reap."

> The merchants who come from India and the
> islands encamp there with their wares. More-
> over, men from Shinar, El-Yemen and Persia,
> bring thither all sorts of silk, purple and
> flax, cotton, hemp, worked wool, wheat, bar-
> ley, millet, rye, and all sorts of food, and
> lentils of every description, and they trade
> with one another, whilst the men from India
> bring great quantities of spices thither.
> The islanders act as middlemen, and earn
> their livelihood thereby.[81]

Thus, it is brought to our attention that the inhabitants make their living as merchants and intermediaries. The significance of the island, therefore, is strictly commercial. Benjamin specifies
that the merchants coming from India bring great
quantities of spices, an item which subsequently is
brought into Alexandria and eventually invades the
European markets. The island was, therefore, in
Benjamin's time, a great trading centre for the exchange of merchandise from India, Central Asia and
Africa.[82] During the time between the decline of
Siraf and the rise of Ormuz,[83] Kish assumed great
importance as a trade centre and it was only after
the fall of Kish that Ormuz was able to take its
place.[84] Further confirmation of Kish's commercial
significance comes from Marco Polo, who mentions
Kish as a stopover point for travellers before they
again journey on the sea.[85] It seems that Benjamin

visited the island at its height. His description
of the trade here depicts the history of the commercial route with India.

Katifa also lies on the Persian Gulf, and is
mentioned by Benjamin with regard to the origin of
its pearls.[86] Benjamin's knowledge as to the formation of the pearls is incorrect.[87] Nevertheless,
Masudi, one of the earliest to describe the pearl
fisheries in the Persian Gulf, is in agreement with
Benjamin's account, as is Edrisi.[88] Although the
accounts clearly establish Katifa as a trading centre for pearls, it is Benjamin who informs us that
a Jewish official controls the pearl fishery owned
by the king.

Generally speaking, the Persian Gulf always
has been a sea highway between the ancient nations
of the world.[89] It was planted with trade stations,
and the coast fulfilled the role of a commercial
centre for the trade with the Far East. Benjamin
mentions Quilon "which is the beginning of the country of the sun worshippers."[90] During the early
Middle Ages, Quilon was a prominent seaport. Benjamin notes that the inhabitants are "all black in
colour."[91] Furthermore, he adds that they are hon-
est in their commercial dealings.[92] Business is
conducted at night during the summer in Quilon, "for
they have to turn night into day in consequence of
the great heat of the sun."[93] Benjamin also reports that pepper is found here and supplies us with
the following information:

> They plant the trees thereof in the fields.
> ... The trees are small, and the pepper is
> as white as snow. And when they have col-
> lected it, they place it in saucepans and
> pour boiling water over it, so that it may
> become strong. They then take it out of the
> water and dry it in the sun, and it turns
> black.[94]

In Benjamin's time, it was thought that white pepper
was another species, but Ritter[95] explains that after it soaks in water for eight to ten days, it

332

loses its black outer covering, thus becoming white pepper. Furthermore, Benjamin relates that in this part of the Far East, "calamus and ginger and many other kinds of spice are found."[96] As we stated before, Benjamin is aware of the fact that spices were transported from here to the Mediterranean ports and eventually to the West. Marco Polo's account categorically confirms Benjamin's description.

> ...The heat of the sun is so great there that it is scarcely to be endured.... The merchants from Manzi, and from Arabia and from the Levant come thither with their ships and merchandise and make great profit, both by what they import and by what they export.... Man and woman, they are all black....[97]

Moreover, the organization relating to the commercial transactions here is further confirmed by Edrisi.[98]

Up to this point, we have observed Benjamin's account as it reflects the trade activity in the Mediterranean—the commercial life in the maritime cities and the world trade centres—as well as his evidence of a more international aspect of trade existing during his time. One should now ask: were Jews involved in this trade, and if so, to what extent? Does Benjamin indicate such involvement, and do we have other proof to verify answers to this question? This question gains in importance if we remember that in the twelfth century the Italian city states assumed a significant trade role in the Mediterranean world and were on their way to control it. Under these circumstances, Jews could find it difficult to continue to play a major role in the trade of that time. Note, the author maintains, "to continue," since it is known that Jews had fulfilled this role in the world trade in the Middle Ages at least up to the tenth century.[99]

Under the Carolingians, the Jews enjoyed unprecedented freedom and it was in this period that they became the international traders. Pirenne points out the almost complete absence of merchants

333

other than Jews during the Carolingian period.
"Thus we seek in vain," he writes, 'for professional
merchants."[100] The Jews to whom he refers were the
Rahdānites, travelling merchants who still retained
a contact with the Orient.[101] Rabinowitz believes
that the rise of Islam gave them an unusual opportunity of which they took full advantage.[102] This
fact is also stated by Baron.[103] Heyd credits the
"great Jewish merchants whose role as intermediaries
between East and West was then so considerable."[104]
The existence of Jewish communities along the trade
route stations[105] made it easier for Jews to become
international traders. Day[106] notes three main
routes from Asia to Europe in the early Middle Ages
and Rabinowitz identifies them as those used by the
Jewish Rahdānites.[107] The activity of the Rahdānites came to an end probably in the tenth century,[108]
and soon the opening up of the trade routes followed
the crusades. Prior to the crusading movement, the
tenth century witnessed the rise of Venice to the
status of a new power in the Mediterranean trade.[109]
The Venetians, intermediaries in the trade between
Byzantium and the East, saw the Jews as dangerous
rivals and initiated steps to limit their activity.

     Despite the fact that the activity of the Rah-
dānites came to an end in the tenth century, the
Genizah documents indicate that in the twelfth century Jews continued to be involved in world trade.
It seems that Jews were occupying a decreasing role
in the Mediterranean world—becoming local traders
of secondary importance. Nevertheless, many of
them still remained international traders, journeying to the Far East in order to bring merchandise
to the Mediterranean ports. It is at these Mediterranean ports that other traders, principally those
of the Italian city states, assumed control, there-
by replacing the Jews. While most of the European
Jews were in a process of being pushed out of trade
to ultimately become moneylenders, the Oriental Jews
still occupied a significant trade role in our travellers' time. Even Rabinowitz states that only after the twelfth century did money lending and pawn
broking become a major occupation of the Jews.[110]

334

Before we refer to the Genizah records to il-
lustrate the above point, it is important to note
what light Benjamin's account throws upon this subject. When considering Montpellier as a commercial
city, Benjamin said of the Jews that they are rich
and charitable "who lend a helping hand to all that
come to them."[111] One may speculate; perhaps those
needing a helping hand are Jewish merchants, but no
such claim is made directly. As a matter of fact,
our traveller does not mention Jewish merchants in
the Mediterranean specifically except in Tyre:
"The Jews own seagoing vessels, and there are glass
makers amongst them who make that fine Tyrian glassware which is prized in all countries."[112] This
statement suggests that Jews in Tyre participated
in the Mediterranean trade and actually owned
ships.[113] It is plausible to assume that coopera-
tion existed between those Jews who owned the "sea-
going vessels" and those who made glassware.

On the island of Kish, Benjamin found 500
Jews[114] who, we may assume, were engaged in the
trade taking place on this island. Likewise, in
Katif, he found 5,000 Jews[115] who surely were traders—middlemen—or even more important officials
in the commercial sphere. One should recall that
this place was a pearl fishery owned by the King
of the country but "controlled by a Jewish official."

Benjamin refers to Aden and points out that
the place is on the route to India.[116] Ibn Batuta,
with regard to Aden, states: "Some rich merchants
reside here, and vessels from India occasionally
arrive."[117] Of prime significance is the fact that
Benjamin states that many of the Jews of Aden came
to Persia and Egypt.[118] If we consider Aden as a
trade centre, lying on the route to India, as Ibn
Batuta and Benjamin mention, then we can comprehend Benjamin's statement. Only as merchants and
for the purposes of trade would these inhabitants
travel, bringing their merchandise to trade centres
in Persia and probably to Baghdad in addition to
Alexandria and other trade centres in Egypt. Baron
believes that the Jewish traders of Iraq must have

335

played a significant role in this branch of commerce.[119]

Thus, the Egyptian Jewish merchant was supported by Jews, located in all the trade centres along the route to India, and sometimes even by his own relatives. There is no doubt that Egyptian Jewish merchants created some of those Jewish settlements. One must remember that trade with India prospered for a long time and often resulted in permanent settlements. Aden was the beginning point. There, in Aden, were the main stores, and from there, the merchants continued their journey to Ceylon and Malabar.[120] Some Jews settled for a long period of time in Aden, often travelling to Ceylon and India and returning to Aden with merchandise. Few returned to Cairo.[121]

One can now say that Benjamin's account reflects the reality that in the Mediterranean trade centres, Jews, as merchants played a decreasing role in trade. Nevertheless, Jews were still engaging in trade in the Persian Gulf locations on the route to India and their role in commerce was significant. The following genizah fragment, part of which is quoted here, is important for our subject. A Jew in India writes to his business correspondent in Cairo, probably early in the thirteenth century or even before.[122] He speaks in the third person:

> ...And...he is cheap
>   in his commercial transactions.
> He makes journeys from Malabar to Ceylon.
> But his goods are the whole year in Aden.
> Now it is his intention to make a change...
> If therefore, thou wilt wait until the
> time of his
>   removal that is good
> But if thou requirst thy goods then send
> A letter in thine own handwriting and he
> will hand
>   over the goods to him whom thou
> desirst...

> Five thousand Bahar as little thereof is to
>   be found in India.
> And he possesses none of it. There is also
>   but little Baspas in the market.
> And coryphyllum costs 40 per 10— I have
>   not voyaged to Aden this year.
> But still I had
> A little merchandise for thee which Sheikh
> Joseph Ibn Abulmana took with him.
> I wrote him a letter about it which he was
> to send you. Should he be in Egypt, may
> my master support him...[123]

The letter[124] proves the existence of Jewish merchants in the twelfth century journeying between
Egypt and India, with Aden on the Persian Gulf
assuming the role of a port of exchange. The writer of the letter points out that he did not voyage
to Aden this year, a comment which indicates previous visits. We are reminded here of Benjamin's
statement that Jews from Aden come to Egypt and
Persia. Moreover, the writer of the letter states
that he journeys from Malabar to Ceylon although
his goods are permanently in Aden, the port of exchange. Maimonides in the twelfth century corro-
borates the claim that Jewish merchants frequented
those areas[125] and another letter,[126] which had
been sent in 1153 from Aden to a person named in
the letter as Hillel ha-atar ben Nahman, "the pious
in Egypt" (Fustat), relating how a ship sank in the
India sea,[127] supplies additional evidence and indicates the dangers of the trade. The Genizah letters[128] point to a trade led by individual Jews and
one finds no Jewish guilds such as was the case in
Europe. That is why, the author believes, Benjamin
makes no mention of Jews on his list of nations
coming to Alexandria for the purpose of trade:[129]
there was no existence of a characteristic Jewish
trade as was the case in Pisa, Genoa, and Venice.[130]

Despite the high risks incurred in voyages to
India,[131] the India trade was "the backbone of inter-

national economy in the Middle Ages."[132] Numerous
Genizah documents relating to the India trade are
contained in the form of letters. The merchants
kept their records—for which Fustat served as a
terminus—in order to protect their rights. Usually, the first portion of such a letter confirms the
arrival of the merchandise or indicates their loss
(by shipwreck or attack by pirates). Next, a mention of the actions taken concerning the order given
by the addressee, would follow. The second portion
of the letter deals with the writer's own ship-
ments. Sometimes personal affairs would be discuss-
ed, often at great length.[133] Concluding the letters, there would be a list of presents accompanying
the merchandise ordered. This form is common in
letters exchanged between Aden and the Malabar
coast.[134] One group of Genizah documents associated with the India trade is composed of legal records. For example, on such a journey a merchant
did business for others, or was an agent often for
one or more investors. Accordingly, a deed of com-
menda, or "partnership according to Muslim Law"
would be drawn up. Upon his return home, the merchant would then write a statement regarding his
transactions in the interest of his partners and
deposit it with the local rabbinical or Moslem
court.[135]

The office of the "Trustee of the Merchants"
was of highest importance (Arabic, "Wakil," Hebrew,
"Peqid Hasoharim"). This office served as a kind
of head of the merchant group, about whose portion
the Genizah furnishes a plethora of information.
Information is given to us about the Wakils of Aden.
The position of "Trustee" was held by Hasan ben
Bundar close to the end of the eleventh century.
His son, Madmun who died in 1151, succeeded him in
heading Yemen Jewry. He was even given the title
of Nagid. Madmun was recognized both by the Exilarch and by the Nagid[136] of Egypt. He was the
"Trustee of all the lords of the seas and the desert," which Goitein interprets to mean that he was
engaged in agreements, in his client's interest,
with numerous rulers (or priates) who controlled
the Arabaian and Indian sea routes.[137] Goitein

338

believes that Madmun held a direct shipping line
between Aden and Ceylon. Furthermore, he encouraged Jewish goldsmiths to settle in Ceylon in order
to enhance his own business and to assume control
over that island.[138] There are numerous other persons prominent in the Genizah documents whom we
shall not mention.[139]

Benjamin's account, confirmed by the India Genizah papers, clearly reveal that during the twelfth
century, while the Europeans assumed naval supre-
macy, the Jewish role in the Mediterranean trade became limited.[140] Consequently, it is easy to comprehend why Jewish middle class merchants found the
commerce with the countries of the Indian Ocean more
promising. Benjamin's account, in addition to the
India Genizah documents, offers evidence for this.
Moreover, the crusades added a new dimension—religious hatred—which in essence prohibited the European Jews, especially in the Italian cities, from
assuming an important role in commerce. In Genoa,
Benjamin noted only two Jews and in Pisa, only 20.[141]
Nevertheless, it appears wrong to assume that there
was a complete elimination of the Jewish trade in
our period.[142] We must remember that the suffering
incurred by Oriental Jews was far less than that
incurred by European Jews. Furthermore, there is
still not enough evidence to indicate that the economic prohibitions imposed on Jews in the Italian
city states were carried out effectively. We must
note that Benjamin's account points out that Jews
were to be found in all the crusading coastal cities,
and settlements were uninterrupted from Europe to
India. There is some evidence which points to Jewish trade between Egyptian Jews and Byzantium[143]
and it can be assumed that a commercial route remained still unaffected by the rise of the Italian
city states. This line extended from Egypt to Spain,
especially Moslem Spain. Benjamin testifies that
in Barcelona trade ships from Egypt and Palestine
dropped anchor. Furthermore, the Responsa literature furnishes evidence as to the participation of
Jews in oil trade between Sevilla and Alexandria.[144]

With regard to the commercial life of the In-

dian trade, we must remember that in the period of
the crusades, the Indian spice trade flourished.[145]
There were two dominant trade routes: via the Persian Gulf, and via the Red Sea, the latter being
the better route.[146] The significance of Egypt on
this route remained the same in our period as it
was in ancient times. William of Tyre put it well
when he said that Egypt was the market of the two
worlds,[147] and Benjamin further substantiates
this.[148] The other trade route via the Persian
Gulf suffered on account of pirates, controlled by
the rulers of Kish.[149] Consequently, many preferred the land route from Baghdad to India, or via
Aden.[150] Thus, the route via the Red Sea, which
passed through Egypt, was in use more often. In
Aden, merchandise was transferred to light ships
due to shoals which made it difficult for large
ships carrying heavy merchandise to pass.[151] Thus,
the commercial trade in the Indian Ocean explains
why Benjamin found numerous Jews in Aden.

After the crusaders' conquest of the Holy Land,
the main commercial route from Aden through Kutz to
Cairo via the Nile and then to Alexandria evolved
because it became too dangerous to cross the Sinai
Peninsula.[152] This accounts for the rise of Jewish
settlements in Kutz and the flourishing Jewish communities along the Nile in Egypt as witnessed by
Benjamin.[153] From this point, we can conclude that
most of the spice trade passed through Egypt[154] and
thus the Egyptian Jews resided on the most important commercial route of our period. This explains
Benjamin's account which reflects a flourishing
Jewish life in Egypt and suggests that they were involved extensively in the Far East trade. The Egyptian Jews held an important role in commerce.[155]
Their competitors were the Moslems and the Indian
merchants.[156] It seems safe to say that the European merchants played almost no role in trade with
India.[157]

With regard to the Jewish role in commerce,
the material within Maimonides' Responsa is limited;[158] nevertheless, we can reconstruct the direction of this trading. We can note that voyages on

the route to India are mentioned in eight cases,[159] whereas only one voyage to Sicily in Europe is mentioned.[160] Many such queries concerning Indian trade are found in the Responsa by Maimonides' son, Abraham.[161] Thus, it seems clear that most of the Egyptian Jews traded with the East because of enormous supply and demand found in India and the rivalry of the Italian states in this region was quite unimportant.[162] It is significant to remember that Benjamin found most of the Egyptian Jews concentrated within the Delta cities, which were the commercial cities.[163] These Jews in Egypt engaged in Indian trade and had an effect on world trade. In addition to the Jewish settlements in Egypt, Jews had trade stations of such importance as those on the route to Ceylon as mentioned in Benjamin's itinerary. Among these stations were Aden, Kish, Katifa, Kandig, Ibrig and Ceylon. Thus, one may conclude that an increasing number of Jews were pushed out of the Mediterranean trade market on account of the rise of the European maritime powers. Benjamin's account substantiates this.

If on the one hand a serious limit of the number of Jews participating in the trade of the Mediterranean world can be clearly detected, on the other hand a growing number of Jews participating in the Indian trade can be observed. At the same time, the century in which Benjamin visited the Orient, was a transitional period because Jewish participation in Indian trade was only temporary since the appearance of Karīmīs (a powerful association which monopolized the trade with India, East Africa and the Far East, and made it difficult for individual merchants to participate in the Indian trade)[164] at the onset of the thirteenth century, when the Jews were forced eventually to become mainly local merchants.[165]

Historians rarely noticed the existence of trade with Eastern Europe during the period under discussion. Heyd states that there is a missing link in medieval economic history because of ignorance of Jewish trade in this period.[166] However, in the yet undeveloped areas of Eastern Europe, Jews

341

were still the main traders. From Germany and the
Byzantine Empire, Jews traded with Eastern Europe.
Regensburg, the dwelling place of our traveller,
Petachia, was a major centre of that trade, centred
especially in Kiev.[167] Baron[168] believes that Frederick Barbarossa had this role of Regensburg Jews
in mind when he renewed their old privileges in
1182.[169] The Polish people were not yet aware of
the value of their natural resources for which there
was a market in Silesia. Most of this trade was
carried on by Jewish merchants.[170]

In this year (1182) when restrictions on Jewish trade were characteristic elsewhere, the Jews
of Regensburg were given privileges by Frederick I,
"to buy and sell gold, silver and other things and
to exchange their possessions and wares and to receive profits, according to the old customs."[171]
In 1216, this was confirmed by Frederick II,[172] and
in 1230, Henry VII granted them even more privileges with regard to their possessions and their
jurisdiction.[173] These rights helped the Regensburg Jews to maintain their connections with the
East.[174]

The Regensburg-Kiev route was primarily used
by Jews.[175] R. Eleazar ben Isaac of Prague speaks
of the religious manners and customs of the small
Jewish communities which he came across in his
travels in Russia.[176] In 1171, a Jewish merchant
from Vladimir came to Cologne on business and was
arrested on a false charge.[177] Jews from Russia
can also be found in England at the twelfth century.[178] After the destruction of the Khazar
state[179] these trade routes became more dangerous,
but were revived at the time of the crusades. Benjamin's account testifies that in Constantinople
Russian merchants could be found among others,[180]
and ties between Russia and the Byzantine capital
are clearly shown by Vasiliev.[181]

An exceptional description of this route has
been left by Petachia. He journeyed from Prague to
Poland and from there to Kiev, then after six days
of travelling on the Dnieper, he reached the land

342

of Kedar.[182]   Petachia describes many of the customs he observed on his way in the East of Europe,[183] and his account is confirmed by that found
in East European sources.[184]   After eight days journey, our traveller reached a port where all those
who wished to board ships for distant lands gathered.[185]   Petachia does not mention the name of this
port, but says that it is located on the border of
Khazaria and surrounded by seventeen rivers.[186]
Brutzkus believes that this port is situated on the
Caucasus shore of the Kerch channel, near Kuban
Delta.[187]   At the time of Petachia's journey, it
came under Byzantine rule.

The slave trade was less important, especially
after the Christianization of Europe in the tenth
century.[188]   However, an ordinance (from about 1100)
which regulates the tariff at the toll barrier of
Rhenish Coblenz still reads that "Jews are to pay
four denarii for every salable slave."   This, according to Baron, was a meaningless repetition of
an earlier law.[189]   Interestingly, the slave trade
is not represented in the Genizah at all.[190]

From the end of the thirteenth century, the
percentage of Jews in international trade became
insignificant in Germany as a result of a series
of restrictions imposed against them.[191]   Subsequent to this, the whole trade with the East moved
in different routes: the Italian-Mediterranean in
the South and the Hanseatic in the North.

Footnotes

[1]The latest summary of this subject is to be
found in The World History of the Jewish People:
The Dark Ages, ed. C. Roth (Tel-Aviv, 1966), pp.
23 and 386, ns. 11 and 12.   However, Roth did not
notice the article by Cahen who believes that the
Rahdanites belonged to an earlier period (C. Cahen,
"Y a-t-il eu des Rahdanites," R.E.J., CXXIII [1964],
499-505).

[2]Clagett, Post, Reynolds, _Twelfth Century Europe and the Foundation of Modern Society_, pp. 189-207; Baron, _A Social and Religious History of the Jews_, IV, 149.

[3]Haskins, _The Renaissance of the 12th Century_, p. 62.

[4]E.J. Passant, "The Effects of the Crusades upon Western Europe," _C.M.H._, V, 327-30.

[5]William B. Stevenson, "Islam in Syria and Egypt," _C.M.H._, V, 274.

[6]S.D. Goitein, _Studies in Islamic History and Institutions_ (Leiden, 1968), pp. 308-28. The Genizah records of this period reflect the migration of the Maghrebi's (Westerners) to Egypt, a process which became clear in the beginning of the eleventh century and was still in existence around 1150 when the Normans and later the Almohades nearly devastated Tunisia (D. Corcos-Abulafia, "The Attitude of the Almohadic Rulers towards the Jews," _Zion_, XXXII [1967], 151, 156; Goitein, "Jewish Society and Institutions under Islam," _Journal of World History_, XI [1968], 174). It was these devastations which made final the changes in the trends of world trade: the shift of naval superiority from Tunisia toward Egypt.

[7]Goitein, _A Mediterranean Society_, I, 39.

[8]_Ibid._, pp. 29, 32.

[9]Corcos-Abulafia, pp. 149-50; Goitein, _ibid._, pp. 301-40. See also Ibn Jubayr, p. 325.

[10]Goitein, _A Mediterranean Society_, I, 44.

[11]_Ibid._

[12]_Ibid._, p. 46.

[13]_The Itinerary of Benjamin of Tudela_, ed. M.N. Adler, p. 5; C.W. Previté-Orton, "The Italian Cities

till c. 1200," _C.M.H._, V, 208-41, specifically 237, 240.

[14]_The Itinerary of Benjamin of Tudela_, ed. M.N. Adler, p. 5.

[15]_Ibid._

[16]_Ibid._, p. 9.

[17]Benjamin of Tudela, _Sefer Masa'ot_, ed. Asher, II, 31, n. 48. Also see Edrisi, II, 258.

[18]_The Itinerary of Benjamin of Tudela_, ed. M.N. Adler, pp. 8-9.

[19]_Ibid._, p. 76.

[20]_Ibid._, p. 9.

[21]_Ibid._, p. 78.

[22]_Ibid._

[23]Ibn Jubayr, pp. 338-340, 350. Also see Edrisi, II, 76-78, 81.

[24]_The Itinerary of Benjamin of Tudela_, ed. M.N. Adler, p. 3.

[25]_Ibid._

[26]_Ibid._, p. 5. Also see H. Pirenne, _Medieval Cities_ (Princeton, 1923), p. 92.

[27]_The Itinerary of Benjamin of Tudela_, ed. M.N. Adler, p. 10.

[28]_Ibid._, p. 11.

[29]_Ibid._

[30]Runciman, _Byzantine Civilization_, p. 130.

[31]William of Tyre, II, 461-67; Goitein, _A Medi-_

terranean Society, I, 39.

[32]F. Chalandon, "The Late Comneni," C.M.H., IV, 368.

[33]Joinville & Villehardouin, Chronicles of the Crusades, pp. 66-93.

[34]Ibid., p. 76. See Chapter IV, section 2 in the book.

[35]The Itinerary of Benjamin of Tudela, ed. M.N. Adler, p. 13.

[36]Ibid.

[37]Ibid., p. 12.

[38]Gibbon, III, 508-9.

[39]The Itinerary of Benjamin of Tudela, ed. M.N. Adler, p. 13.

[40]Ibn Jubayr, p. 355; Runciman, A History of the Crusades, II, 330; Sharf, p. 142.

[41]Runciman, A History of the Crusades, II, 168.

[42]Ibid., 338.

[43]Benvenisti, p. 77.

[44]The Itinerary of Benjamin of Tudela, ed. M.N. Adler, pp. 18-19.

[45]Prawer, A History of the Latin Kingdom of Jerusalem, II, 525-44.

[46]The Itinerary of Benjamin of Tudela, ed. M.N. Adler, p. 18.

[47]Ibid., p. 19.

[48]Le Strange, Palestine under the Moslems, p. 344.

[49]William of Tyre, II, 4-9.

[50]The Itinerary of Benjamin of Tudela, ed. M.N. Adler, p. 19.

[51]See Chapter IV, section 1 in the book.

[52]Prawer, A History of the Latin Kingdom of Jerusalem, II, 525-44; Runciman, A History of the Crusades, III, 387-423.

[53]Benvenisti, p. 78.

[54]Palestine Pilgrims Text Society, V, 11; Le Strange, Palestine under the Moslems, p. 330.

[55]Ibn Jubayr, p. 318.

[56]The Itinerary of Benjamin of Tudela, ed. M.N. Adler, p. 28. For a minute description of the city, see William of Tyre, II, 219-20.

[57]Benjamin of Tudela, Sefer Masa'ot, ed. Asher, II, 99, n. 187. See Chapter V, note 127 in the book.

[58]The Itinerary of Benjamin of Tudela, ed. M.N. Adler, p. 15.

[59]Ibid., p. 17.

[60]Ibid., p. 18.

[61]Ibid., p. 19.

[62]Ibid., p. 27; Le Strange, Palestine under the Moslems, pp. 346, 350, 375, 446,550-51.

[63]Ibid., pp. 74-75. This academy is mentioned also by Jacob b. Nathaniel ha-Cohen (The Itinerary of Jacob ben Nathaniel ha-Cohen, ed. Grünhut, p. 12).

[64]The Itinerary of Benjamin of Tudela, ed. M.N. Adler, p. 75.

[65]Ibid. The significance of this famous lighthouse is also noted by Jacob b. Nathaniel ha-Cohen
(The Itinerary of Jacob ben Nathaniel ha-Cohen, ed.
Grünhut, p. 12). Other observers also make note
of the lighthouse. William of Tyre states: "At
the end of that tongue rises a tower of marvellous
height called the Pharos" (William of Tyre, II, 336).
Ibn Jubayr states: "Description of it falls short,
the eyes fail to comprehend it, and words are in-
adequate...." (Ibn Jubayr, p. 33). Since the
coast was low, the lighthouse served an important
function.

[66]The Itinerary of Benjamin of Tudela, ed. M.N.
Adler, p. 76. Benjamin uses the term "Punduk"
(" פונדוק ") (ibid., [Hebrew], p. 69). See Ibn
Jubayr, pp. 30 and 368, n. 10.

[67]Runciman, A History of the Crusades, II, 362-
400.

[68]See Fourth Lateran Council decisions, Mansi,
XXII, 1058-67, especially 1066-67; Hefele, V, 1390-
96.

[69]With regard to its commercial significance
as an international trade centre, see William of
Tyre, II, 336. See also Ibn Jubayr's description,
pp. 32-35.

[70]Runciman, A History of the Crusades, II, 294;
Prawer, A History of the Latin Kingdom of Jerusalem,
II, 343-59.

[71]The Itinerary of Benjamin of Tudela, ed. M.N.
Adler, p. 30.

[72]Ibid., pp. 29-30.

[73]Le Strange, Palestine under the Moslems, pp.
237-40.

[74]The Itinerary of Benjamin of Tudela, ed. M.N.
Adler, pp. 35-42.

[75] Ibid., p. 12.

[76] Ibid., p. 42.

[77] G. Le Strange, Baghdad during the Abbasid Caliphate (Oxford, 1900), pp. 17, 46, 170, 225, 281.

[78] The Itinerary of Benjamin of. Tudela, ed. M.N. Adler, pp. 58-59.

[79] Ibid., pp. 57-59; Rabinowitz, Jewish Merchants' Adventures, pp. 50-51. See Chapter IV, note 533 in the book.

[80] S.D. Goitein, "Two Eyewitness Reports on an Expedition of the King of Kish (Qais) against Aden," Bulletin of the School of Oriental and African Studies, XVI (1954), 247.

[81] The Itinerary of Benjamin of Tudela, ed. M.N. Adler, pp. 62-63.

[82] P.M. Sykes, Ten Thousand Miles in Persia, or Eight Years in Iran (London, 1902), p. 58.

[83] Ritter, Die Erdkunde im Verhältnis zur Natur und zur Geschichte des Menschen, VIII, 772.

[84] Goitein, "Two Eyewitness Reports on an Expedition of the King of Kish (Qais) against Aden," p. 247.

[85] Marco Polo, I, 63; II, 340.

[86] The Itinerary of Benjamin of Tudela, ed. M.N. Adler, p. 63.

[87] J. Zeide, "On Medicine and Natural History in the Book of Travels of Rabbi Benjamin of Tudela," The Hebrew Medical Journal, XX (1953), 140-41.

[88] Abu'l-Hasan 'Ali Mas'udi, Meadows of Gold and Mines of Gems, trans. A. Sprenger (London, 1841), I, 344; Edrisi, I, 377; also see Ibn Jubayr, p. 64; Miles, II, 414-415.

[89]Sykes, Ten Thousand Miles in Persia, or Eight Years in Iran, p. 82; Goitein, "Two Eyewitness Reports on an Expedition of the King of Kish (Qais) against Aden," p. 247; Marco Polo, I, 83-84, 107-10, 110, n. 1.

[90]The Itinerary of Benjamin of Tudela, ed. M.N. Adler, p. 63.

[91]Ibid., p. 64.

[92]Ibid.

[93]Ibid.

[94]Ibid.

[95]Ritter, Die Erdkunde im Verhältnis zur Natur und zur Geschichte des Menschen, V, 615.

[96]The Itinerary of Benjamin of Tudela, ed. M.N. Adler, p. 64.

[97]Marco Polo, II, 375-76.

[98]Edrisi, I, 177.

[99]See note 1 in the present chapter of the book.

[100]See Ibn Khurradādbeh's report on the Rahdān-ites in Dinur, Israel in Diaspora (1)I, pp. 366-67.

[101]H. Pirenne, Mahomet et Charlemagne, 2d. ed. (Paris, 1937), pp. 123-26; H. Pirenne, An Economic and Social History of Medieval Europe (London, 1936), pp. 11-12. It has been restated by him in "Le Fin du Commerce des Syriens en Occident," Annuaire, II (Brussels, 1945), 677-87; C. Roth, "The Jews in the Middle Ages," C.M.H., VII, 644.

[102]This being proved in Chapter IX in Jewish Merchants' Adventures by Rabinowitz.

[103]Baron, A Social and Religious History of the Jews, I, 321-22.

[104]Heyd, Histoire du Commerce du Levant au Moyen Age, I, 77.

[105]See Chapter IV, section 4 and note 533 in the book.

[106]C. Day, A History of Commerce (New York, 1934), pp. 85-86.

[107]Rabinowitz, Jewish Merchants' Adventures, p. 152.

[108]Ibid., p. 169.

[109]J. Jacobs, Jewish Contributions to Civilization (Philadelphia, 1919), p. 199.

[110]Rabinowitz, Jewish Merchants' Adventures, p. 195.

[111]The Itinerary of Benjamin of Tudela, ed. M.N. Adler, p. 3.

[112]Ibid., p. 18.

[113]However, most scholars agree that Benjamin mentions this case as an exception rather than the rule (Strauss, "A Journey to India," p. 228, n. 42; Goitein, "Jewish Society and Institutions under Islam," p. 181 and 181, n. 29; Neustadt, "Contributions to the Economic History of the Jews in Egypt in the Middle Ages," p. 222). See also E.H. Byrne, Genoese Shipping in the Twelfth and Thirteenth Centuries (Cambridge, Mass., 1930), pp. 12-13.

[114]The Itinerary of Benjamin of Tudela, ed. M.N. Adler, p. 63.

[115]Ibid.

[116]Ibid., p. 67.

[117]Ibn Battuta, The Travels of Ibn Battuta, trans. and selec. H.A.R. Gibb (New York, 1929), pp. 109-10.

[118] The Itinerary of Benjamin of Tudela, ed. M.N. Adler, p. 67.

[119] Baron, A Social and Religious History of the Jews, IV, 175.

[120] Goitein, "Two Eyewitness Reports on an Expedition of the King of Kish (Qais) against Aden," p. 248.

[121] For an excellent example see R. Gottheil and W. Worell, Fragments from the Cairo Genizah in the Freer Collection (New York, 1927), pp. 44-56.

[122] Jewish Travellers, ed. E.N. Adler, p. 100.

[123] Ibid., pp. 100-1.

[124] A second document, a long family letter sent from Egypt to India, was published in Gottheil and Worell, pp. 44-56. A third genizah document was published by Braslavsky, "Jewish Trade between the Mediterranean and India in the Twelfth Century," Zion, VII-VIII (1940-43), 135-39, and dated 1149 in which the writer informs his brother, living in North Africa, that he, the writer, left India and reached Aden safely. The letter reflects the destruction of the Jewish life in North Africa. India Book collection of 330 letters relating to India trade is being prepared for publication by S.D. Goitein.

[125] Graetz, History of the Jews, III, 457; Goitein, "The Life of Maimonides in the Light of New Finds from the Cairo Geniza," pp. 29-30.

[126] Published by E. Strauss, "A Journey to India," pp. 217-31.

[127] Ibid., pp. 223, 225.

[128] In addition to the letters mentioned, we can point to two other letters dated 1134 and 1148 published by Strauss, "Of Economic Activity of Jews in

Moslem Countries during the Middle Ages," <u>Zion</u>, VII (1942), 145-51.

¹²⁹The Itinerary of Benjamin of Tudela, ed. M.N. Adler, p. 76.

¹³⁰Roth, "The Jews in the Middle Ages," p. 644; Previté-Orton, "The Italian Cities Till 1200," p. 239.

¹³¹A. Mez, The Renaissance of Islam, trans. S.K. Bukhsh and D.S. Margoliouth (London, 1937), p. 483.

¹³²Goitein, <u>Studies in Islamic History and Institutions</u>, pp. 329, 332; S.D. Goitein, "From the Mediterranean to India: Documents on the Trade to India, South and East Africa from the Eleventh and Twelfth Centuries," <u>Speculum</u>, XXIX (1954), 181, 186; Goitein, "Two Eyewitness Reports on an Expedition of the King of Kish (Qais) against Aden," p. 250.

¹³³See letters published in Goitein, "Two Eyewitness Reports on an Expedition of the King of Kish (Qais) against Aden," pp. 248-57.

¹³⁴Goitein, <u>Studies in Islamic History and Institutions</u>, p. 334.

¹³⁵Ibid., p. 335.

¹³⁶See Chapter IV, sections 3 and 4 in the book.

¹³⁷Goitein, "From the Mediterranean to India," p. 189.

¹³⁸Ibid., p. 191.

¹³⁹Goitein, <u>Studies in Islamic History and Institutions</u>, pp. 337-38; Goitein, "From the Mediterranean to India," pp. 191-95.

¹⁴⁰See Roth, "The Jews in the Middle Ages," p. 644.

¹⁴¹See Chapter IV, section 1 in the book.

142 Corcos-Abulafia, pp. 151, 157-58.

143 Mann, The Jews in Egypt and Palestine under the Fatimid Caliphs, II, 307.

144 Maimonides, Maimonidean Responsa, p. 364.

145 Heyd, I, 164.

146 Ibid.

147 William of Tyre, II, 336; Ibn Jubayr, pp. 35, 50, 53.

148 See p. 329 in the book.

149 Ibid.

150 Heyd, I, 166.

151 Ibid., p. 380. As to types of ships in the seas, see Mez, pp. 472-73.

152 Mez, p. 472.

153 See Chapter IV, section 3 in the book.

154 Heyd, I, 385.

155 See Chapter IV, section 3 in the book.

156 Heyd, I, 380; Mez, p. 450.

157 Goitein, Studies in Islamic History and Institutions, p. 350, n. 2; Heyd, I, 164, 167-170, 373; Mez, pp. 405, 399-400.

158 In the collection by Gottheil-Worell there is much information, for example pp. 1, 45, but mostly without specific date.

159 Maimonides, Maimonidean Responsa, pp. 22, 207, 243, 244, 247, 250, 299, 302.

160 Ibid., p. 250.

[161] Goitein, A Mediterranean Society, I, 437, n. 4.

[162] Goitein, "From the Mediterranean to India," p. 184; Strauss, "A Journey to India," p. 227.

[163] See Chapter IV, section 3 in the book.

[164] Goitein, Studies in Islamic History and Institutions, pp. 351-60.

[165] Goitein, A Mediterranean Society, I, 149.

[166] Heyd, II, 727.

[167] It is evident that the Jewish colony in Kiev played an important role. Jewish merchants were attracted there due to the city's commercial position (J. Brutzkus, "Trade with Eastern Europe, 800-1200," Economic History Review, XIII [1943], 31, 36; Dinur, Israel in Diaspora [2] II, 161).

[168] Baron, A Social and Religious History of the Jews, IV, 176, See also Pfaff, p. 206.

[169] Aronius, Regesten, No. 314.

[170] Abrahams, Jewish Life in the Middle Ages, p. 214.

[171] Aronius, Regesten, No. 314.

[172] Ibid., No. 403.

[173] Ibid., No. 448.

[174] Brutzkus, p. 35.

[175] Ibid., p. 36. See Chapter IV, section 1 in the book.

[176] Isaac ben Moses of Vienna, Or Zaruah, 4 vols., ed. H.J. Sapira (Zhitomir, 1862), I, 26; IV, 10.

[177] Neubauer-Stern, II, 71, 206.

[178] Jacobs, The Jews of Anjevin England, p. 73.

[179] Dunlop, The History of the Jewish Khazars, pp. 237-63.

[180] The Itinerary of Benjamin of Tudela, ed. M.N. Adler, p. 12.

[181] A. Vasiliev, "Economic Relations between Byzantium and Old Russia," Journal of Economic and Business History, IV (1931-32), 326, 328, 329.

[182] The Itinerary of Petachia, ed. Grünhut, p. 2.

[183] Ibid., pp. 2-3.

[184] Brutzkus, p. 39.

[185] The Itinerary of Petachia, ed. Grünhut, p. 3.

[186] Ibid.

[187] Brutzkus, p. 39. According to Brutzkus, Petachia's silence about the Jews of Prague, Poland and Russia is due to the fact that they were well known to Western Jewry (ibid., p. 40).

[188] S. Assaf, "Slavery and Slave Trade among the Jews during the Middle Ages," Zion, IV (1938), 91, 104.

[189] Baron, A Social and Religious History of the Jews, IV, 196; 336, n. 57.

[190] Goitein, A Mediterranean Society, I, 211; Abrahams, Jewish Life in the Middle Ages, pp. 112-117.

[191] Brutzkus, p. 41.

CHAPTER VIII

CONCLUSION

Our research has found that the twelfth-century
Jewish travellers were not a unique phenomenon in
Jewish history. Rather, they formed a link between
earlier and later Jewish travellers. The connection
goes beyond travelling to the very content and mess-
age of their itineraries. From this point of view,
Benjamin of Tudela, Petachia of Regensburg, and
Jacob ben Nathaniel ha-Cohen reflect continuity.

Although they form a link in a chain, the fact
remains that our twelfth-century Jewish travellers
seem to be a product of the times. Proper understanding of their itineraries is not possible without taking into consideration the crusades and their
impact upon contemporary Jews. The connection between the crusades and the travellers is examined in
its various aspects.

We have seen that our twelfth-century travellers embarked on their journeys with several goals
in mind. Among these were the desire to make a pilgrimage to the Holy Land, to communicate with other
Jewish communities, to satisfy their curiosity and
to see the "new world." The twelfth-century renaissance was an age in which the crusades served as a
cultural bridge between East and West.

The study of the itineraries of Benjamin and
Petachia provides no basis for the assumption that
they were motivated by the desire to investigate
the economic and political conditions of various regions to find a suitable asylum for European Jews.
Moreover, a more serious objection to this assumption stems from the findings of modern research
which show that although the crusades caused some
deterioration in the situation of twelfth-century
Jewry, a fundamental change in their condition did
not occur until the thirteenth century. During the
twelfth century Jews were protected by both church

357

and state. Hence, their condition remained generally favourable.

Another field in which this link has been detected is in the complicated subject of Exile and
Redemption. We have found that the reality of the
Exile is omnipresent in the itineraries. The awareness of persecutions and the relations between Jews
and Gentiles is clear. At the same time, the entire era of the crusades heightens Messianic expectations, creating an atmosphere of impending redemption in which rumours circulated of the approaching
reunification of the Ten Lost Tribes with their brethren. All these elements occupy a prominent place
in the twelfth-century Jewish itineraries. Although
it is not within the scope of this book to deal exhaustively with the legend of the Ten Lost Tribes,
it is dealt with briefly since it serves as consolation for Medieval Jewry. Nevertheless, the legend
is of such significance as a psychological stimulant
to Medieval Jewry that it deserves further research.
We have found that Benjamin emphasizes those characteristics of the legend which his contemporary Jewry
lack: physical power and political independence.
Consequently, the extensive reference to the Tribes
reflects the situation of twelfth-century Jews and
their aspirations for redemption.

The Redemption itself is expressed in a variety
of ways in the accounts: the story of the rise and
fall of a false Messiah, expectations of impending
Messianic days, and psychological preparations for
them. Petachia enquires of the time the Messiah is
expected and also reports of people beyond the Mountains of Darkness who are converting to Judaism.
The story of David Alroy, the false Messiah in the
Orient, is reported by Benjamin. From his account
of German Jewry, we have evidence of their eager
anticipation.

Above all, the concepts Exile and Redemption
find their expression in the account of the Holy
Land. It has been suggested that in the very reporting of the holy sites in the Land there may be
detected the travellers' attitude to it and their

own psychological state concerning the expected Redemption. The Holy Land occupies a prominent place
in these accounts and reflects the debate over it
between Jews and Gentiles. This is seen clearly in
the travelogue literature. A strongly religious
polemic has been detected through this and other
subjects. The holy sites are seen through Jewish
eyes—and more specifically through twelfth-century
Jewish eyes. The anger of the reporter against the
crusaders who then dominate the Holy Land may be
detected and at the same time, a hope and prayer
may be heard from the travellers concerning the future of the Land which is eventually to be returned
to the Jews.

It also has been suggested that the messianic
expectations which prevailed during the whole century, motivate Jews like Jacob b. Nathaniel to pay
a preparatory pilgrimage to the Holy Land in expectation of the day of judgment.

From another point of view, the study shows
that the twelfth century Jewish travellers' accounts
point to a transitional period in three various areas of concern: the place the Holy Land occupies
among the Jews, the various Jewish centres in the
world, and the role of Jews in world trade.

Our travellers visit the Holy Land on the eve
of the Moslem conquest of the crusaders. Soon the
Land is to come under Islamic rule. The failure of
the crusaders to establish a permanent kingdom there
makes a strong impact on Jewish thought. The Land
would not accept the Gentiles as it had been promised solely to the Jews, and the crusaders' conquest was only temporary. Thus, Jews are to be
found living in the Holy Land, and the accounts report the re-establishing of Jewish communities
there. Soon the trickle of immigration to the Holy
Land is to become a stream. Our travellers' accounts reveal the fact that Jews from the West already are to be found in various places in the Holy
Land. In the following century the new immigrants
become significant for the renewal and strengthening
of Jewish life there.

When the crusaders prove unable to strengthen their position there, a new thought takes hold among the Jews: to go there as a preliminary step for the coming redemption. Ha-Levi gives expression to this idea in his writings and in his decision to immigrate to the Holy Land.

With respect to the Jewish centres at that time, we are in a transitional period. First of all, our accounts show that Jews are spread over the known world. They are to be found in every country—from Babylonia and Persia to Arabia and India, and from North Africa up to the south of Russia. They are also to be found in Christian Europe—Spain, Italy, France, Germany, and the Greek islands. The most significant change which was to take place toward the end of the twelfth century and during the thirteenth century is the decline of the Jewish centres in Moslem countries and the rise of Jewish centres in Christian Europe to a leadership position both intellectually and numerically. The study has shown that in the time our twelfth-century travellers visited the Orient, it was assumed among Jews that the majority of their people were concentrated in the Moslem East. Our travellers indicate exaggerated numbers of Jews who were then allegedly in the Orient. Instead of the "tens" and "hundreds" reported to exist in the Jewish communities of Europe, we hear of "thousands" and "ten thousands" living in the Jewish communities in Babylonia and Persia. The large Jewish communities Benjamin finds in Narbonne, Lunel and Marseilles contain only 300 Jewish members each. The large Jewish communities in Italy numbered about 500. Only in Constantinople and Thebes Benjamin reports about 2,000 Jewish members; the medium communities number between 50-200 and most of the reported communities number less. On the contrary, in the Orient the picture reported is very different. Most of the communities number 2,000 Jewish members, and others, several thousand. Even if we assume that there are exaggerations here, we have to admit that our travellers are greatly impressed by the large Jewish communities they find in the Orient.

360

However, the decline starts among Oriental Jews towards the end of the twelfth century. In the second half of the thirteenth century there is a complete collapse of those Jewish centres. In the thirteenth century the Christian countries in Europe become the world Jewish centres.

We come now to the question of the Jewish role in world trade. Here, too, Benjamin's account reveals the ascendancy of the Italian city republics and the eventual end of the Jewish role in the Mediterranean trade, although it has yet to end completely. On the other hand, we are able, through Benjamin's account, to show that Jews continued, probably more than ever, to direct their mercantile enterprises in Indian trade. Though before a century would elapse, even in this Indian trade the Jewish merchants were to be replaced by the Kharimis traders.

Finally, we should admit that we have not in any way exhausted the importance of the materials provided for us by our three travellers. We have pointed out that there is an intensification of the hostility between Christian and Jew brought about by the crusades, and an increase in religious polemic on both sides. The polemic takes many forms, and we are able to show that nearly everything that happened to the crusaders in the Holy Land was interpreted in terms of Jewish idealism and aspirations. Thus, our travellers report the struggle over the holy places and the graves of the "heroes of the faith" which takes place, and the efforts to give significance to these sites in terms of Jewish or Christian interpretation. We also see how our travellers interpret the events in the Holy Land, both factual and apocryphal, when the crusaders fail to accomplish their goal, an interpretation growing out of the religious polemic, which sees all failure as an indication that the Land is ordained by God for the Jews alone.

Yet, while this struggle over the Holy Land goes on, it eventually spreads as well to other areas where Jews seek to maintain emotional, and,

at least from their point of view, historical ties
with the Holy Land through the identification of
objects and sites in their own diaspora towns with
objects and people related to the Holy Land. While
this requires a great deal of further study, and
would lead us far afield from our theme, it is interesting to note that both the Jews of Rome and of
Baghdad, for example, identify local objects with
the Temple in Jerusalem. In Baghdad, the gates to
the city are identified with the Temple gates, and
in Rome, two columns in the church of St. John
Lateran are identified with two columns from the
same Temple. A large number of other identifications are made.

     What makes this all so fascinating is that in
their struggle for identity, and in their resistance to persecution, the awareness of the role of
the Holy Land in their existence causes the Jews
to maintain an active relationship with their origins. If it means only identifying objects as
having come from the Holy Land, it at least keeps
the tradition and, during the twelfth century, the
hope of the return to the Holy Land alive. Though
living in the diaspora, and suffering from a sense
of rootlessness, they could feel at "home" because
a part of their Land is with them

     This sense of belonging to and identifying
with the Holy Land which plays a part in our travellers records, and in the reports of other writers
of this period, is being studied in an article which
the author is now preparing.

362

LIST OF ABBREVIATIONS

A.H.R.	American Historical Review
B.J.P.E.S.	Bulletin of the Jewish Palestine Exploration Society—English name of the Hebrew periodical known as: Yedi'ot ha-Hevra ha-Ivrit La-Hakirat Erez Yisrael Va-Attikoteha
B.S.O.A.S.	Bulletin of the School of Oriental and African Studies
C.M.H.	Cambridge Medieval History
C.E.H.	Cambridge Economic History
E.J.	Encyclopedia Judaica
Ex.	Exodus (Bible)
Ex.R.	Exodus Rabbah
Gen.	Genesis (Bible)
Gen.R.	Genesis Rabbah
H.E.	Hebrew Encyclopedia
H.U.C.A.	Hebrew Union College Annual
J.E.	Jewish Encyclopedia
J.Q.R.	Jewish Quarterly Review
J.S.S.	Jewish Social Studies
J.J.L.G.	Jahrbuch der juedish-literarischen Gesellschaft
J.J.S.	Journal of Jewish Studies
J.N.E.S.	Journal of Near Eastern Studies
J.R.A.S.	Journal of the Royal Asiatic Society
J.R.G.S.	Journal of Royal Geographical Society
M.G.W.J.	Monatsschrift für Geschichte und Wissenschaft des Judentums
P.E.F.	Palestine Exploration Fund
P.A.A.J.R.	Proceedings of the American Academy for Jewish Research
R.E.J.	Revue des études juives
R.H.C. H.Occ.	Recueil des Historiens des Croisades, Historiens Occidentaux
Sif.	Sifra
Z.D.M.G.	Zeitschrift der Deutschen Morgenländischen Gesellschaft

Z.F.H.B.	Zeitschrift für hebräische Bibliographie
Z.G.J.D.	Zeitschrift für die Geschichte der Juden in Deutschland

BIBLIOGRAPHY

I.   MANUSCRIPT

Benjamin ben Jonah of Tudela. The Itinerary of
     Rabbi Benjamin of Tudela, MS. Heb. $8^{O}2647$
     (formerly MS. Epstein, Vienna) and the copy
     included in the Yemenite MS. No. 20 of the
     Eylath Collection, both in the National and
     University Library, Jerusalem.

II. ORIGINAL SOURCES

Abraham Bar Hiyya. Sefer Megillat Ha-Megalleh.
     Ed. A. Poznanski. Berlin, 1924.

_____. Hegyon Ha-Nephesch Ha-Atzuvah. Ed. G.
     Wigoder. Jerusalem, 1971.

Abraham Ibn Daud. Emuna Rama. Ed. S. Weil. Frank-
     furt, 1852.

_____. Sefer Ha-Qabbalah. Ed. Gerson D. Cohen.
     Philadelphia, 1967.

Abraham Ibn Ezra. Commentary on the Bible (in
     various editions of the Hebrew Bible).

_____. Poetic Works. Ed. D. Kahana. Warsaw,
     1922.

Abraham Ibn Zacut. Sefer Yuchasin. Amsterdam,
     1717.

Abravanel, Don Isaac. Commentary to the books of
     the late prophets. Amsterdam, 1641.

Abū Mu'in Nāsir. Sefer Nameh: Nāsir-i-khorsau's
     Diary of a Journey Through Syria and Pales-
     tine in 1047 A.D. Trans. G. Le Strange.
     Palestine Pilgrims' Text Society. Vol. IV,
     London, 1893.

365

Abul Faraj (Bar Hebraeus). Chronography. 2 vols.
Vol. I ed. and trans. E.W. Budge. Oxford,
1932.

Acta Sanctorum.... Collecta, digesta, illustrata
a G. Henschenio et D. Papebrochio...ed.
noviss.,J. Carnandet. Paris and Rome, 1866.

Adler, E.N. "MS. of Haftaras of the Triennial
Cycle," J.Q.R., VIII (1895-96), 528-29.

Aescoly, A.Z. The Messianic Movements in Israel:
Sources and Documents on Messianism in Jewish
History. Jerusalem, 1956.

Agus, I.A. (ed.). R. Meir of Rothenburg, His Life
and His Works as Sources for the Religious,
Legal, and Social History of the Jews of Germany in the Thirteenth Century. 2 vols.
Philadelphia, 1947.

Aḥima'as ben Paltiel. The Chronicle of Aḥima'as.
Ed. B. Klar. Jerusalem, 1944.

Alkharizi, J. Tahkemoni. Ed. Y. Toporovski. Tel-
Aviv, 1952.

Aronius, J. Regesten zur Geschichte der Juden im
fränkischen und deutschen Reiche bis zum
Jahre 1273. Berlin, 1902.

Assaf, M. Safran shell Rishonim. Jerusalem, 1935,
pp. 129-82. (Containing extracts from the
Book of Customs by R. Asher from Lunel.)

_____. Sources and Research in the History of
Israel. Jerusalem, 1946.

Assaf, S. "Documents Concerning the History of
Jews in the Mediterranean Countries," Texts
and Studies in Jewish History. Jerusalem,
1946, Vol. I, pp. 130-42.

_____. "New Documents Concerning Jews in Pales-
tine and Egypt," Zion-Measef, III (1929), 112-
22.

Assaf, S. "New Documents on Proselites and a Mes-
     sianic Movement," Texts and Studies in Jewish
     History. Jerusalem, 1946, pp. 143-54.

_____. "New Material to the History of the
     Karaites in the Orient," Zion, I (1936), 208-
     51.

_____. "Relations between the Jews of Egypt
     and Aden in the 12th Century," B.J.P.E.S.,
     XII (1946), 116-19.

_____. "Sources for the History of the Jews in
     Spain," Texts and Studies in Jewish History.
     Jerusalem, 1946, Vol. I, 100-15.

_____. (ed.). "Collection of R. Samuel b. 'Ali
     Letters and of His Contemporaries," Tarbiz, I
     (1929-30), Book I, pp. 102-30; Book II, pp.
     43-84; Book III, pp. 15-80.

Baer, F. Die Juden im christlichen Spanien. 2
     vols. Berlin, 1929-1936.

Baronius, C. Annales Ecclesiastici a Christo Nato
     ad Annum 1198. Roma, 1588.

Ben Sasson, H.H. The Immigration to Israel during
     the Middle Ages. Jerusalem, 1962. (A collec-
     tion of documents.)

_____. (ed.). The Book of Old Victory. Jeru-
     salem, 1965.

Benjamin of Tudela. The Itinerary of Benjamin of
     Tudela. Ed. and trans. M.N. Adler, Oxford,
     1907.

_____. Sefer Masa'ot. Ed. and trans. A. Asher.
     2 vols. Berlin, 1840.

Berenfeld, S. (ed.). Book of Tears. 2 vols. Ber-
     lin, 1924-26.

Bibliotheca Geographorum Arabicorum. Ed. M.J.

Goeje. 8 vols. Leyden, 1874-94.

Bondy, G., and Dworský, F. (eds.). <u>Zur Geschichte</u>
<u>der Juden in Böhmen, Mähren und Schlesien von</u>
<u>906 bis 1620</u>. 2 vols. Prague, 1906.

Braslavsky, I. "Jewish Trade between the Mediterranean and India in the Twelfth Century,"
<u>Zion</u>, VII-VIII (1941-43), 135-39.

Carmoly, E. (ed.). <u>Itineraries de la terre sainte</u>
<u>des XIII à XVII siècles, traduits de l'Hébreu</u>
<u>et accompagnés de tables, de cartes, et d'</u>
<u>éclaircissements</u>. Bruxelles, 1847.

_____. <u>Mevaseret Zion</u>. A Collection of Let-
ters Concerning the Ten Tribes. Brussels,
1841.

Cowley, A.E. "Samaritana, I. Samaritan Dealings
with the Jews Based on Samaritan Fragments
from Cairo Geniza. II. An Alleged Copy of
the Samaritan Pentateuch," <u>J.Q.R.</u>, XVI (1904),
474-84.

David D'Beth Hillel. <u>The Travels of R. David D'</u>
<u>Beth Hillel</u>. Ed. W.J. Fischel. New York,
1973.

Davidson, I. (ed.). <u>Thesaurus of Medieval Hebrew</u>
<u>Poetry</u>. 4 vols. New York, 1924-33.

Derenbourg, M.J. "Gloses d'Abou Zakariya ben
Bilam sur Isaie," <u>R.E.J.</u>, XVIII (1889), 71-
82.

Dinur, B.Z. <u>Israel in Diaspora</u>. 5 vols., 2nd ed.
Tel-Aviv, 1961-65.

Edrisi, Abū Abdạllah Mohammad Bin Mohammed. <u>Géo-</u>
<u>graphie d'Edrisi</u>. Ed. and trans. P.A. Jau-
bert, <u>Recueil de Voyages et de Memoires</u>. 2
vols. Paris, 1836-1840.

Eisenstein, J.D. (ed.). <u>A Collection of Itinerar-</u>

ies by Jewish Travellers to Palestine, Syria,
Egypt and Other Countries. Tel-Aviv, 1969.

Eldad ha-Dani. Eldad ha-Dani. Ed. A. Epstein,
Pressburg, 1891.

Eleazar Ben Judah, of Worms. Book of Rokeach.
Cremona, 1557.

Estori ha-Parchi. Caftor va-pherach. Ed. A.M.
Luncz. Jerusalem, 1889-97.

Even Shemuel, Y. Midreshay Geulah (Anthology of
Apocalyptic Midrashim). 2nd ed. Jerusalem,
1953-54.

Farissol, A. An Epistle of the Ways of the World.
Prague, 1793.

Freehof, S.B. (ed.). A Treasury of Responsa.
Philadelphia, 1963.

Friedländer, M. "Ibn Ezra in England," Transac-
tions of the Jewish Historical Society of
England, II (1894-95), 61-75 (App. Sabbath
Epistle).

Fulcherius Carnotensis. Historia Hierosolymitana.
Ed. H. Hagenmeyer. Heidelberg, 1913.

R. Gershom ben R. Asher from Scarmelo. Sefer Yichus Hazzaddikim. Ed. A.M. Luncz. Jerusalem,
1896.

Gibb, H.A.R. The Damascus Chronicle of the Crusades. London, 1932.

Ginsbreg, L. Geonica. 2 vols. New York, 1909.

Goitein, S.D. "Contemporary Letters on the Capture of Jerusalem by the Crusaders," J.J.S.,
III (1952), 162-77. (The Arabic originals of
these letters, published in Zion, XVII [1952],
129-47.)

Goitein, S.D. "From the Mediterranean to India: Documents on the Trade to India, South and East Africa from the Eleventh and Twelfth Centuries," Speculum, XXIX (1954), 181-97.

_____. "Historical Evidence from the Pen of a Doctor and Liturgical Poet in Byzantium," Tarbiz, XXVII (1958), 528-35.

_____. "A Letter from Ascalon during Its Occupation by the Crusaders," Tarbiz, XXXI (1962), 287-90.

_____. "A Letter from Eretz Israel Dating to the Crusader Period," Yerushalayim. Review for Eretz Israel Research, II/V (1955), 54-70, 3 documents.

_____. "A Letter from Seleucia (Cilicia)," Speculum, XXXIX (1964), 298-303.

_____. "A Letter of Historical Importance from Seleuceia, Cilicia, Dated 21 July 1137," Tarbiz, XXVII (July 1958), 521-35.

_____. "Letters and Documents on the India Trade in Medieval Times," Islamic Culture, XXVII (1963), 188-205.

_____. (ed.). Letters of Medieval Jewish Traders. Princeton University, 1973.

_____. "The Life of Maimonides in the Light of New Finds from the Cairo Geniza," Peraqim, IV (New York, 1966), 29-42.

_____. "A New Autograph by Maimonides and a Letter to Him from His Sister Miriam," Tarbiz, XXXII (1962), 184-95.

_____. "New Sources on Eretz Israel in Crusader Days," Eretz Israel, IV (Jerusalem, 1956), 147-56.

_____. "New Sources on the Fate of the Jews in

the Time Jerusalem Was Conquered by the Crusaders," <u>Zion</u>, XVII (1952), 129-47.

_____. "Obadyah, a Norman Proselyte," (Apropos the discovery of a new fragment of his "scroll"). J.J.S., IV (1953), 74-84.

_____. "A Report on Messianic Troubles in Baghdad in 1120-1121," <u>J.Q.R.</u>, XLIII (1952), 57-76.

_____. "Two Eyewitness Reports on an Expedition of the King of Kish (Qais) against Aden," <u>Bulletin of the School of Oriental and African Studies</u>, XVI (1954), 247-57.

Goldziher, I. "Fragment d'une Lettre des Communautés du Caire à Celle d'Ascalon," <u>R.E.J.</u>, LV (1908), 58-59.

Gottheil, R.J.H. "A Cairo Synagogue Eleventh Century Document," <u>J.Q.R.</u>, XIX (1907), 467-539.

Gottheil, R. and Worell, W. (eds.) <u>Fragments from the Cairo Genizah in the Freer Collection</u>. New York, 1927.

Grayzel, S. <u>The Church and the Jews in the XIIIth Century</u>. New York, 1966.

Habermann, A. (ed.). <u>Book of Pogroms of Germany and France; Memoirs of Eye Witnesses of the Period of Crusades and Chosen Piyutim</u>. Jerusalem, 1945.

Hadassi, Yehudah Ben Elijah. <u>Eshkol Hakofer</u>. Gozlow, 1836.

Halevi, J. <u>Book of Kuzari</u>. Ed. H. Hirschfeld. New York, 1946.

Harkavy, A. "Fragment einer Apologie des Maimonidischen," <u>Zeitschrift für hebraeische Bibliographie</u>, II (Berlin, 1897), 125-128, 181-188.

Harkavy, A. (ed.). <u>Hadashim Gam Yeshanim</u> (Collection of Sources in Jewish History). Jerusalem, 1970.

_____. (ed.). <u>Teshubot ha-Geonim</u> (Geonic Responsa). 2 vols. Berlin, 1887.

Hefele, C.J., and Leclerq, H. <u>Histoire des Conciles d'après les documents originaux.</u> 9 vols. Paris, 1907-21.

Hildenfinger, P. "Documents relatifs aux Juifs d'Arles," <u>R.E.J.</u>, XLI (1900), 62-97; XLVII (1903), 221-242; XLVIII (1904), 48-81; 265-272.

Hirschfeld, H. "Arabic Portion of Cairo Genizah at Cambridge," <u>J.Q.R.</u>, XVI (1904), 575-76.

_____. "Some Judaeo-Arabic Legal Documents," <u>J.Q.R.</u>, XVI (1904), 408-13.

<u>The Holy Scriptures</u>. Philadelphia, 1917.

Ibn al-Qalānisī. <u>History of Damascus.</u> Ed. H.F. Amedroz (Leyden, 1908).

Ibn Battuta. <u>The Travels of Ibn Battuta.</u> Trans. and selec. H.A.R. Gibb. New York, 1929.

_____. <u>Voyages d'Ibn Batoutah.</u> Ed. C. Defrémery et Led B.R. Sanguinetti. Tomes 1-2. Paris, 1853. (French and Arabic Texts.)

Ibn Jubayr. <u>The Travels of Ibn Jubayr.</u> Trans. and ed. R.J.C. Broadhurst. London, 1952.

Ibn Khordâdbeh. "Kitâb Al-Masâlik Wa'l Mamâlik." Ed. M.J. De Goeje. <u>Bibliotheca Geographorum Arabicorum.</u> Vol. VI. Lugduni Batavorum, 1967.

Ibn Verga. <u>Shevet Jehudah.</u> Ed. A. Soḥat. Jerusalem, 1947.

Ibn Yihia, R. Gedaliah ben Don Joseph. _Chain of Tradition_. Venetia, 1587.

Isaac ben Moses of Vienna. _Or Zaruah_. Ed. H.J. Sapira. 4 vols. in 2. Zhitomir, 1862.

Ish Shalom, M. (ed.). _Christian Travels in the Holy Land_. Tel-Aviv, 1965.

Jacob ben Nathaniel ha-Cohen. _Travels of Jacob ben Nathaniel ha-Cohen_. Ed. L. Grünhut. Jerusalem, 1905.

Jacobs, Joseph. _Sources of Spanish-Jewish History_. London, 1894.

R. Jehiel, Son of R. Solomon Heilperin. _Seder Hadorot_. Warsaw, 1882. (Part I follows Parts 2 and 3.)

Jewish Travellers. Ed. E.N. Adler. New York, 1966.

Joinville & Villehardouin. _Chronicles of the Crusades_. Trans. M.R.B. Shaw. London, 1973.

Joseph ben Gorion— _Josippon_. Ed. H. Hominer. Jerusalem, 1955-56.

Joseph Ben R. Aba Mari Caspi. _Tam Hakesef_. Ed. I.H. Last. London, 1913.

Joseph Ben R. Joshua ha-Kohen. _Divre Hayamim_. Amsterdam, 1733.

_____. _Emek Ha-Bakha_ ("Valley of Tears"). Ed. M. Letteris. Vienna, 1852.

Judah b. Barzilai al-Barceloni. _Sepher ha'ittim_ (Book of Times). Ed. Jakob Schorr. Cracow, 1902-1903.

Kahn, S. "Documents inédits sur les Juifs de Montpellier au moyen âge," _R.E.J._, XIX (1889), 259-281; XXII (1891), 264-279; XXIII (1891), 261-278; XXVIII (1894), 118-141.

Kimhi, D. Commentary on the Bible, <u>Mikraot Gedolot</u>. 10 vols. Ed. Pardes. New York, 1951.

Kimhi, J. <u>The Book of the Covenant</u>. Ed. and trans. F. Talmage. Toronto, 1972.

Le Strange, G. <u>Palestine under the Moslems</u>. Beirut, 1965.

Levy, R. <u>The Astrological Works of Abraham ibn Ezra</u>. Baltimore, 1927.

Lewin, B.M. <u>Ozar Ha-Geonim</u>. 13 vols. Haifa-Jerusalem, 1928-43.

<u>Liber Assiri Salathielis, filii regis Jechoniae</u> (qui Ezra propheta, sive apocryphus liber Esdrae quartus dictus est). Ed. A. Kaminka. Tel-Aviv, 1936.

Lopez, R.S., and Raymond, I.W. <u>Medieval Trade in the Mediterranean World</u>. New York, 1955.

Maimon B. Joseph. "The Letter of Consolation of Maimon b. Joseph," ed. and trans. L.M. Simmons, <u>J.Q.R.</u>, II (1890), 62-101.

Maimonides, Moses. <u>Epistle to Yemen</u>. Ed. A.S. Halkin, New York, 1952.

_____. <u>Maimonidean Responsa</u>. Ed. A.H. Freimann. Jerusalem, 1934.

_____. "Maimonides' Treatise on Resurrection; The Original Arabic and S. Ibn Tibbon's Hebrew Translation and Glossary," ed. J. Finkel. <u>American Academy for Jewish Research. Proceedings</u>, IX (1939), 57-105. (Hebrew and Arabic Texts, 1-42.)

_____. <u>Kobez Teshubot Ha-Rambam We-Iggerotaw</u>. Ed. A. Lichtenberg. 2 vols. Leipzig, 1859. (Including Iggeret Teman, Iggeret Ha-Shemad.)

Mann, J. "An Answer from R. Samuel b. 'Ali, Gaon

of Baghdad," Hazofeh LeHochmat Yisrael, VI
(1922), 104-22.

_____. The Jews in Egypt and Palestine under
the Fatimid Caliphs. 2 vols. Oxford, 1920-22.
(Reissued in one volume by S.D. Goitein; New
York, 1970.)

_____. "Obadya, Prosélyte Normand converti au
Judaisme, et sa meguilla," R.E.J., LXXXIX
(1930), 245-59.

Mann, J. "A Second Supplement to 'The Jews in
Egypt and in Palestine under the Fatimid Caliphs,'" H.U.C.A., III (1926), 257-310.

_____. Texts and Studies in Jewish History and
Literature. Vol. 1, Cincinnati, 1931; Vol.
II, Philadelphia, 1935.

_____. "A Tract of an Early Karaite Settler in
Jerusalem," J.Q.R., XII (1921-22), 257-98.

Mansi, J.D., and others (eds.). Sacrorum conciliorum nova et amplissima collectio. 53 vols.
Florence, 1757— Paris, 1927.

Marco Polo. The Book of Ser Marco Polo, the Venetian, Concerning the Kingdoms and Marvels of
the East. Trans. and ed. with notes Henry
Yule. 2 vols. New York, 1926.

Marcus, J.R. The Jew in the Medieval World. Cincinnati, 1938.

Margalioth, R. (ed.). Sefer Hasidim. Jerusalem,
1972.

Marmardji, A.S. Textes géographiques arabes sur
la Palestine. Trans. en français. Paris,
1951.

Marmorstein, A. "Graves of Fathers," Zion Measef,
I (1926), 31-39.

Marx, A. "The Correspondence between the Rabbis
    of Southern France and Maimonides about Astro-
    logy," H.U.C.A., III (1926), 343-358.

Mas'udi, Abu'l-Hasan 'Ali. Meadows of Gold and
    Mines of Gems. Trans. A. Sprenger. Vol. I.
    London, 1841.

Meir ben Baruch of Rothenburg. Sha'are Teshuboth;
    Responsa of R. Meir ben Baruch of Rothenburg.
    Berlin, 1891-1892.

Meloh Hofnayim. Documents. Collected and ed. A.
    Geiger. Berlin, 1840.

Midrash Rabbah. Trans. under the editorship of
    Rabbi H. Freedman and Maurice Simon. 9 vols.
    and Index vol. London, 1951.

Migne, J.P. (ed.). Patrologiae curcus completus,
    Series latina. 221 vols. Paris, 1844-64.

Millgram, A.E. (ed.). An Anthology of Medieval
    Hebrew Literature. Philadelphia, 1935.

Mingana, D.D. (ed.). "A Charter of Protection
    Granted to the Nestorian Church in A.D. 1138
    by Muktafi II, Caliph of Baghdad," Bulletin
    of the John Rylands Library, X (Manchester,
    1926), 127-33.

Mirabilia Urbis Romae. Trans. F.M. Nichols. Lon-
    don, 1889.

Montague, R.J. Marvels of the East. A full repro-
    duction of the three known copies with intro-
    duction and notes. Oxford, 1929.

Mukaddasi, Al. Description of Syria Including
    Palestine. Vol. III: Palestine Pilgrims'
    Text Society. Trans. G. Le Strange from Ara-
    bic. London, 1886.

Müller, W.M. "An Egyptian Document for the History
    of Palestine," J.Q.R., IV (1912), 651-56.

Nahmanides, M. Kol Kitve Haramban (Writings). Ed. C.D. Chavel. 2 vols. Jerusalem, 1963.

_____. Sefer Hasagot Haramban Zal Sehsig 'Al Rabenu Mose bar Maimon Zal Beminyan Hamitsvot. Constantinople, 1510.

Nemoy, L. (ed.). "Al-Qirqisānī's Account of the Jewish Sect and of Christianity," H.U.C.A., VII (1930), 317-99.

Neubauer, A. "Documents inédits," R.E.J., IV (1882), 173-91 ("Document sur David Alroi," 188-91).

_____. "Egyptian Fragments," J.Q.R., VIII (1896), 541-51; IX (1897), 26-29.

_____. (ed.). Medieval Jewish Chronicles. 2 vols. Oxford, 1887-95.

_____. Sammelband. Vol. III. Kobez Al Yad— Collection of Hebrew documents from MSS. and rare books. Berlin, 1889. ("A Collection Concerning the Ten Tribes and Sons of Moses," pp. 9-74.)

_____. and Stern, M. (ed.). Quellen zur Geschichte der Juden in Deutschland. 2 vols. Berlin, 1892.

Otto of Freising. Chronica, sive historia de duabus civitatibus. Ed. A. Hofmeister. 2nd ed. Hannover and Leipzig, 1912.

Palestine Pilgrims' Text Society. 13 vols. London, 1892-97.

Petachia of Ratisbon. Sivuv ha-rav rabi Petachia.
1) Ed. and trans. A. Benisch. The Travels of Rabbi Petachia of Ratisbon. London, 1856.
2) Ed. L. Grünhut. Sivuv ha-rav rabi Petachia mi-Regensburg. Jerusalem, 1905.
3) Trans. and ed. E.N. Adler. Jewish Travellers. New York, 1966, pp. 64-91.

377

Pinkerton, J. Travels. 17 Vols. London, 1808-14.

Pinsker, S. Likkute Kadmoniyot (To the History of
     the Karaites and Their Literatures—Collection
     of Sources). 2 vols. Jerusalem, 1968.

Rankin, O.S. (ed.). Jewish Religious Polemic.
     Edinburgh, 1956.

Recueil des Historiens des Croisades, Historiens
     Occidentaux, 5 vols.; Historiens Orientaux,
     5 vols.; Documents Armeniens, 2 vols.; His-
     toriens Grecs, 2 vols. Paris, 1841-1906.

Röhricht, R. (ed.). Regesta Regni Hierosolymitani.
     Innsbruck, 1893-1904.

Saadiah b. Joseph al-Fayyumi. The Book of Beliefs
     and Opinions. Trans. S. Rosenblatt; ed. S.
     Landauer. New Haven, 1948.

Saadyana. Geniza Fragments of Writings of R. Saad-
     ya Gaon and Others. Ed. S. Schechter. 1903;
     rpt. Cambridge, 1969.

Saige, G. Les Juifs de Languedoc antérieurement
     au XIVe siècle. Paris, 1881.

Samau'al al-Maghribi. Ifham al-Yahud (Silencing
     the Jews). Ed. and trans. M. Perlmann. P.A.
     A.J.R., XXXII (1964), 33-104.

Saphir, J.E. Travels of Rabbi Jacob Saphir. 2
     vols. Mainz, 1847.

Sayings of the Fathers, Ed. and trans. J.H. Hertz.
     New York, 1945.

Schechter, S. "An Unknown Khazar Document," J.Q.R.,
     III (1911), 181-219.

Schirmann, H. The Hebrew Poetry in Spain and Prov-
     ence. 2 vols. Jerusalem, 1960.

Schlossinger, M. (ed.). The Ritual of Eldad ha-

Dani (Reconstructed and edited from Manuscripts and a Genizah Fragment with Notes, an
Introduction and an Appendix on the Eldad Legends). Leipzig, 1908.

Shahrastani, Al-. Book of Religious and Philoso-
phical Sects by I. Muhammad al-Shahrastani.
Ed. W. Cureton. London, 1846.

Starr, J. The Jews in the Byzantine Empire, 641-
1204. Athens, 1939.

Steinschneider, M. Die Geschichtsliteratur der
Juden. Frankfurt am Main, 1905.

Toviah Berabi Eliezer. Midrash Lekah Tov. Wilna,
1884.

Tritton, A.S., and Gibb, H.A.R. "The First and
Second Crusades from an Anonymous Syriac Chronicle," J.R.A.S. (1933), 69-101, 273-307.

Twersky, I. (ed.). A Maimonides Reader. New York,
1972.

Uri Ben Simeon. Yihus ha-Avot: Genealogia Patriarcharum, Prophetarum, Fustorum, Tannaorum,
Amoraorum, Super Quibus Pax, in Terra Israelis, & Extraeam. Ed. John Henricus Hottingerus, Cippi Hebraici. Heidelberg, 1659, pp. 27-
88.

Usamah ibn Munquidh. An Arab Syrian Gentleman and
Warrior in the Period of the Crusades: Mem-
oirs of Usamah ibn Munquidh. Trans. P.J. Hitti.
New York, 1929.

William of Tyre. History of Deeds Done Beyond the
Sea. 2 vols. Ed. E.A. Babcock and A.C. Krey.
New York, 1943.

Wright, T. (ed.). Early Travels in Palestine,
Translations of Medieval Books of Travel. New
York, 1968.

Wurtheimer, S.A. Ginze Yerusalayim (Collection of
Sources). Jerusalem, 1896.

Ya'ari, A. (ed.). Epistles from Palestine. Tel-

Aviv, 1942-43.

        . (ed.). <u>Travels to Palestine</u>. Tel-Aviv,
    1946.

Yisraeli, S. (ed.). <u>Chapters in the Thought of
    Israel</u> (Collection of Sources). Pardes Hana,
    1964.

III. <u>SECONDARY LITERATURE</u>

1. <u>Encyclopedias</u>

<u>Encyclopedia Britannica</u>. 11th ed. Vol. XXII. New
    York, 1911.

<u>Encyclopedia of Islam</u>. 1st ed. 4 vols. and supple-
    ment. Leiden, 1911-1938.

<u>Encyclopedia Judaica</u>. Vol. IV. Berlin, 1929.

<u>Encyclopedia Judaica</u>. 16 vols. Jerusalem, 1972.

<u>Encyclopedia of Religion and Ethics</u>. 12 vols. and
    Index vol. New York, 1955.

<u>Enzyklopaedie des Islam</u>. Vol. I. Leipzig, 1913.

<u>Hebrew Encyclopedia</u>. 22 vols. Jerusalem and Tel-
    Aviv, 1956.

<u>Jewish Encyclopedia</u>. 12 vols. New York and Lon-
    don, 1905.

<u>Shorter Encyclopedia of Islam</u>. Leiden, 1961.

2. <u>Books</u>

Abrahams, I. <u>Jewish Life in the Middle Ages</u>. New
    York, 1969.

Alder, E.N. <u>Jews in Many Lands</u>. London, 1905.

380

Agus, I. The Heroic Age of Franco-German Jewry.
    New York, 1969.

Altman, A. (ed.). Jewish Medieval and Renaissance
    Studies. Cambridge, Mass., 1967.

Anderson, A.R. Alexander's Gate: Gog and Magog
    and the Inclosed Nation. Cambridge, Mass.
    1932.

Ankori, Z. Karaites in Byzantium. New York, 1959.

_____, Binart, H., and Ben Sasson, H.H. Biblio-
    graphical Guide to the History of the Jews in
    the Middle Ages. Jerusalem, 1961.

Ashtor, E. See Strauss, E.

Assaf, M. History of the Arabs in Palestine. 2
    vols. Tel-Aviv, 1935.

Atlas of Israel. Jerusalem, 1970.

Avigad, N. Ancient Tombs in Nahal Kidron. Jerusa-
    lem, 1954.

Azemard, E. Etude sur les Israélites de Montpel-
    lier au moyen âge. Nîmes, 1924.

Bader, G. The Jewish Spiritual Heroes. 3 vols.
    New York, 1940.

Baer, Y. A History of the Jews in Christian Spain.
    2 vols. Philadelphia, 1961.

_____. Galut. New York, 1947.

_____. The Pogroms of 1096. Jerusalem, 1953.

Barber, B. Acculturation and Messianic Movements.
    Harvard University, 1941.

Baron, S.W. A Social and Religious History of the
    Jews. 8 vols. and index. Philadelphia, 1952-
    60. In progress.

Baron, S.W. The Jewish Community. 3 vols. Philadelphia, 1948.

Beazley, R. The Dawn of Modern Geography. 3 vols. London, 1897-1906.

Ben Jacob, A. A History of the Jews in Iraq from the End of the Geonic Period to the Present Time. Jerusalem, 1965.

Ben Zeeb, I. The Jews in Arabia. Jerusalem, 1957.

Ben Zwi, Y. Palestine under the Ottoman Rule. Jerusalem, 1955.

Benvenisti, M. The Crusaders in the Holy Land. Jerusalem, 1970.

Berman, V.L., et al. The Study of Judaism: Bibliographical Essays in Medieval Jewish Studies. Vol. 2, New York, 1976.

Blumenkranz, B. Juifs et Chrétiens dans le monde Occidental, 430-1096. Paris, 1960.

_____. Le Juif Medieval au Miroir de l'Art Chrétien. Paris, 1966.

Bourdrel, P. Histoire des Juifs en France. Paris, 1974.

Bousset, W. The Antichrist Legend. London, 1896.

Braslavsky, J. Studies in Our Country: Its Past and Remains. Tel-Aviv, 1954.

Brody, H. and Albrecht, K. The New Hebrew School of poets of the Spanish Arabian Epoch. London, 1906.

Bruhel, J. The Ten Tribes: Where Are They? London, 1880.

Bury, J.B. A History of the Later Roman Empire. 2 vols. London, 1923.

Byrne, E.H. *Genoese Shipping in the Twelfth and Thirteenth Centuries*. Cambridge, Mass., 1930.

Cambridge Economic History of Europe, 2 vols. Ed. J.H. Clapham and E. Power. Cambridge, 1941.

Cambridge Medieval History. Planned by J.B. Bury. 8 vols. Cambridge, 1911-36.

Carmoly, M. *Notice historique sur Benjamin de Tudèle; nouvelle édition suivie de l'examen géographique de ses voyages, par J. Lelewel*. Bruxelles et Leipzig, 1852.

Cary, G. *The Medieval Alexander*. Cambridge, England, 1956.

Charles, R.H. *Eschatology; Hebrew, Jewish and Christian*. London, 1889.

Chavel, B. *Ramban*. New York, 1960.

Chazan, R. *Medieval Jewry in Northern France*. Baltimore, 1973.

Clagett, M.; Post, G.; and Reynolds, R. *Twelfth Century Europe and the Foundations of Modern Society*. Madison, 1961.

Cohn, N. *The Pursuit of the Millenium*. New York, 1961.

Conder, C.R. *The Latin Kingdom of Jerusalem, 1099-1291*. London, 1897.

Cox, E.G. *A Reference Guide to the Literature of Travels*. 3 vols. The University of Washington, 1935.

Dan, J. *The Esoteric Theology of Ashkenazi Hasidism*. Jerusalem, 1968.

Dasberg, L. *Untersuchungen über die Entwertung des Judenstatus im 11. Jahrhundert*. Paris, 1965.

Day, C. A History of Commerce. New York, 1934.

De Bode, C.A.G. Travels in Arabistan and Luristan.
2 vols. London, 1845.

Doughty, C.M. Travels in Arabia Deserta. 2 vols.
Cambridge, 1888.

Dubnov, S.M. The History of the Jews. 5 vols.
New York, 1968.

Dunlop, D.M. The History of the Jewish Khazars.
Princeton, 1954.

Dupont, A. Les relations commerciales entre les
cités maritimes de Languedoc et les cités
mediterranéennes de'Espagne et d'Italie du
Xeme au XIIIeme siècles. Nîmes, 1942.

Elbogen, I., and Sterling, E. Die Geschichte der
Juden in Deutschland. Frankfurt, 1966.

Finkelstein, L. Jewish Self Government in the
Middle Ages. New York, 1924.

Fischel, W.J. Jews in the Economic and Political
Life of Medieval Islam. New York, 1969.

Galanté, A. Les Juifs de Constantinople sous
Byzance. Istanbul, 1940.

Gaster, M. The Samaritans. London, 1925.

Germania Judaica. Pt. 1 (to 1238), eds. I. Elbogen, et al.; Pt. 2 (to 1350), ed. Z. Avneri.
Tübingen: J.C.B. Mohr, 1963-1968.

Gibbon, E. The Decline and Fall of the Roman Empire. Ed. O. Smeaton. 3 vols. New York,
1932.

Ginsberg, H.L. Studies in Daniel. New York, 1948.

Ginsberg, L. The Legends of the Jews. 7 vols.
Philadelphia, 1911.

384

Godbey, A. The Lost Tribe Myth. North Carolina, 1930.

Goitein, S.D. Jews and Arabs throughout the Ages. New York, 1960.

_____. A Mediterranean Society; The Jewish Communities of the Arab World as Portrayed in the Documents of the Cairo Geniza. Berkeley and Los Angeles, 1967, Vol. I; Berkeley, Los Angeles, and London, 1971, Vol. II.

_____. Studies in Islamic History and Institutions. Leiden, 1968.

Graetz, H. Geschichte der Juden. 12 vols. Leipzig, 1866-1874.

_____. History of the Jews. 5 vols. Philadelphia. 1891-98.

Grant, A. The Nestorians; or the Lost Tribes. New York, 1841.

Greenstone, J.H. The Messiah Idea in Jewish History. Philadelphia, 1906.

Gregorovius, F. History of the City of Rome in the Middle Ages. Trans. A. Hamilton. London, 1894-1902.

Gross, H. Gallia Judaica: Dictionnaire géographique de la France d'après les sources rabbiniques. Paris, 1897.

Grousset, R. Histoire des croisades et du royaume franc de Jérusalem. 3 vols. Paris, 1934-36.

Gudemann, M. The Torah and the Life. 3 vols. Warsaw, 1897.

Guttman, J. Philosophies of Judaism. Trans. D.W. Silverman. Philadephia, 1964.

Ha-Cohen, R.M. The Cave of Machpelah. Israel, 1970.

Halberg, I. L'Extrême Orient dans la littérature
    et la cartographie de l'Occident des XII, XIV
    et XV siècles. Goteborg, 1907.

Haskins, C.H. The Renaissance of the 12th Century.
    New York, 1959.

Hennig, R. Terrae Incognitae. 4 vols. Leiden,
    1936.

Herzfeld, E.E. Archaeological History of Iran.
    London, 1935.

Heyd, W. Histoire du commerce du Levant au moyen
    âge. 2 vols. 2nd ed. Leipzig, 1936.

Hirshensohn, I.Z. Sheva Hochmot (subtitle, Geo-
    graphy in the Talmud). 2nd ed. London, 1912.

Hitti, P.K. History of the Arabs. 2nd ed. London,
    1940.

Husik, I. A History of Medieval Jewish Philosophy.
    Philadelphia, 1918.

Ish Shalom, M. Anthropological Investigation of
    Kivre Avot (Holy Tombs). Jerusalem, 1948.

Jacobs, J. Jewish Contributions to Civilization.
    Philadelphia, 1919.

_____. The Jews of Anjevin England. London,
    1893.

Joachim, J. Heiligengräber in Jesu Umwelt. Göttin-
    gen, 1958.

Katz, J. Exclusiveness and Tolerance. New York,
    1962.

Kayserling, M. Geschichte der Juden in Spanien und
    Pörtugal. Leipzig, 1867.

_____. Die Juden in Navarra. Berlin, 1861.

Kehimar, H.S. The History of the Bene Israel of India. Tel-Aviv, 1937.

Kimble, G.H.T. Geography in the Middle Ages. London, 1938.

Kisch, G. The Jews in Medieval Germany. Chicago, 1949.

Klein, S. (ed.). The Book of Yishuv. 2 vols. Jerusalem, 1938-39.

Klozner, J. The Messianic Idea in Judaism. 2nd ed. Jerusalem, 1927.

Kohler, K. Jewish Theology. New York, 1918.

Lammens, H. La Syrié, Précis Historique. 2 vols. Beyrouth, 1921.

Lane-Poole, S. A History of Egypt in the Middle Ages. London, 1968.

Latourette, K.S. History of the Expansion of Christianity. 7 vols. New York, 1937.

Layard, A.H. Discoveries among the Ruins of Nineveh and Babylon. New York, 1875.

_____. Early Adventures in Persia, Susiana, and Babylongia. 2 vols. New York, 1887.

_____. Nineveh and Its Remains. 2 vols. London, 1850.

Le Blanc, V. Les Voyages Fameux. Paris, 1658.

Lelewel, J. Géographie du Moyen Âge. Tomes I-V. Amsterdam, 1966. (Examen Géographique des Courses et de la Description de Benjamin de Tudèle. Tomes III-IV, pp. 37-75.)

Leslau, W. Falasha Anthology: The Black Jews of Ethiopia. New York, 1969.

387

Leslie, D.D. The Survival of the Chinese Jews:
     The Jewish Community of Kaifeng. Leiden,
     1972.

Le Strange, G. Baghdad During the Abbasid Cali-
     phate. Oxford, 1900.

_____. The Lands of Eastern Caliphate. Cam-
     bridge, 1905.

Luncz, A.M. (ed.). Jerusalem. Jahrbuch zur Beför-
     derung einer wissenschaftlich genauen Kenntnis
     des jetzigen und des alten Palästinas. Vol.
     II. Jerusalem, 1887.

Malter, H. Saadiah Gaon: His Life and Works.
     Philadelphia, 1921.

Mez, A. The Renaissance of Islam. Trans. S.K.
     Bukhsh and D.S. Margoliouth. London, 1937.

Milano, A. Storia degli ebrei in Italia. Turin,
     1963.

Miles, S.B. The Countries and Tribes of the Per-
     sian Gulf. 2 vols. London, 1919-20.

Monumenta Judaica: 2000 Jahre Geschichte und Kul-
     tur der Juden am Rhein. Ed. K. Schilling.
     2 vols. Cologne: 1963.

Moore, G.F. Judaism. 3 vols. Cambridge, 1927-30.

Munk, S. Palestine. Paris, 1845.

Munro, D.C., and others. Essays on the Crusades.
     Burlington, 1903.

Neubauer, A. La géographie du talmud. Amsterdam,
     1965.

Newman, A.A. The Jews in Spain. 2 vols. Phila-
     delphia, 1942.

Newman, L. Jewish Influence on Christian Reform

Movements. New York, 1925.

Newton, A.P. (ed.). Travels and Travellers of the Middle Ages. New York, 1930.

Niebuhr, C. Voyage en Arabie en d'autres pays circonvoisins. Tomes 1-2. Amsterdam, 1780.

Oesterly, W.O.E. The Evolution of the Messianic Idea. New York, 1909.

Olschki, L. Marco Polo's Asia. Baltimore, 1943.

_____. Marco Polo's Precursors. Baltimore, 1943.

Oppert, G. Der Presbyter Johannes in Sage und Geschichte. Berlin, 1870.

Ostrogorsky, G. History of the Byzantine State. Trans. J.M. Hussey. Oxford, 1956.

Palestine Exploration Fund, Quarterly Statements for years 1879-1886, 1874-1875, 1895-1897, 1869, 1889, London.

Parkes, J. The Conflict of the Church and the Synagogue. London, 1938.

_____. The Jew in the Medieval Community. London, 1938.

Perlman, S.M. The Jews of China. London, 1909.

Pieper, J. Scholasticism. New York, 1960.

Pirenne, H. An Economic and Social History of Medieval Europe. London, 1936.

_____. A History of Europe from the Invasions to the XVI Century. Trans. B. Miall. New York, 1939.

_____. Mahomet et Charlemagne. 2nd ed. Paris, 1937.

Pirenne, H. Medieval Cities. Princeton, 1923.

Polak, E. Persien: Das Land und seine Bewohner
("Persia" Its Land and Its Inhabitants").
2 vols. Leipzig, 1865.

Poliak, N.A. The Jewish Kingdom of the Khazars.
Tel-Aviv, 1943.

Port, C. Histoire du commerce maritime de Narbonne.
Paris, 1854.

Poznanski, S. Babylonische Geonim im nachgaonäischen Zeitalter. Berlin, 1914.

Prawer, J. A History of the Latin Kingdom of Jerusalem. 2 vols. Jerusalem, 1963.

Rabinowitz, L. Jewish Merchants' Adventures. London, 1948.

Rabinsohn, M. Le Messianisme dans La Talmud et les
Midrashim. Paris, 1907.

Régné, J. Étude sur la condition des Juifs de Narbonne du Ve aud XIVe siècles. Narbonne, 1912.

Richardson, H.G. The English Jewry under Angevin
Kings. London, 1960.

Ritter, K. The Comparative Geography of Palestine
and the Sinaitic Peninsula. Trans. (of the
Erdkknde von Asien) W.L. Gage. 4 vols. New
York, 1968.

_____. Die Erdkunde im Verhältnis zur Natur und
zur Geschichte des Menschen. 1st ed. Berlin,
1832-59. Vol. I—Afrika; Vols. 2-19—Asien;
Vols. 14-17—Sinai-Halbinsel, Palästina und
Syrien.

Röhricht, R. Bibliotheca Geographica Palaestinae.
Jerusalem, 1963.

Roth, C. The History of the Jews of Italy, Philadelphia, 1946.

Roth, C. (ed.). The World History of the Jewish People, the Dark Ages. Tel-Aviv, 1966.

Runciman, S. Byzantine Civilization. New York, 1955.

_____. A History of the Crusades. 3 vols. Cambridge, 1951-52.

Salmon, F.J., comp. Palestine of the Crusades: A Map of the Country. Jaffa, 1937. (Palestine Exploration Fund.)

Sapori, A. Le Marchand Italien au Moyen Âge. Paris, 1952.

Sarachek, J. The Doctrine of the Messiah in Medieval Jewish Literature. New York, 1968.

Schechter, S. Aspects of Rabbinic Theology. New York, 1961.

Schefansky, I. The Land of Israel in the Responsa Literature. Vol. I: "The Period of the First Gaons." Jerusalem, 1966.

Schipper, I. Toledot Ha-Halkalah Ha-Yehudit (Jewish Economic History). 2 vols. Tel-Aviv, 1935-36.

Schirmann, H. A History of Messianic Speculation in Israel. New York, 1927.

_____. The Poets of the Times of Abraham ibn Ezra and Jehuda Halevi. Jerusalem, 1956.

Schoeps, H.J. The Jewish-Christian Argument: A History of Theologies in Conflict. Trans. D. Green. New York, 1963.

Scholem, G. Sabbatai Sevi, The Mystical Messiah (1626-1676). New Jersey, 1973.

_____. Major Trends in Jewish Mysticism. 3rd rev. ed. New York, 1961.

Scholem, G. Some Chapters in the History of Cabbal-
    istic Literature. Jerusalem, 1931.

_____. The Messianic Idea in Judaism and other
    Essays on Jewish Spirituality. New York, 1971.

Schwarzfuchs, S. Supplément bibliographique: Addi-
    tions et corrections à l'ouvrage de H. Gross.
    Gallia Judaica. Amsterdam, 1969.

Sharf, A. Byzantine Jewry from Justinian to the
    Fourth Crusade. New York, 1971.

Shunami, S. Bibliography of Jewish Bibliography.
    Jerusalem, 1965.

Silver, A.H. A History of Messianic Speculation
    in Israel. New York, 1927.

Slessarev, V. Prester John. Minnesota, 1959.

Smith, A.L. Church and State in the Middle Ages.
    Oxford, 1913.

Socin, A. Palestine and Syria, Handbook for Tra-
    vellers. Ed. R.K. Baedeker. London, 1876.

Steinherz, S. (ed.). Die Juden in Prag. Prague,
    1927.

Stobbe, Otto. Die Juden in Deutschland während des
    Mittelalters. Amsterdam, 1968.

Strauss (Ashtor-Strauss), E. History of the Jews
    in Egypt and Syria under the Rule of the Mame-
    luks. 3 vols. Jerusalem, 1944-70.

_____. A History of the Jews in Moslem Spain.
    2 vols. Jerusalem, 1960-66.

Strauss, R. History of the Jews in Regensburg and
    Augsburg. Philadelphia, 1939.

_____. Die Juden im Königreich sizilien unter
    Normannen und Staufern. Heidelberg, 1910.

Survey of Western Palestine. Memoirs. 4 vols.
Ed. E.H. Palmer and W. Besant. London, 1881-
83.

Sykes, P.M. A History of Exploration. London,
1934.

_____. A History of Persia. 2 vols. London,
1930.

_____. Ten Thousand Miles in Persia, or Eight
Years in Iran. London, 1902.

Synan, E.A. The Popes and the Jews in the Middle
Ages. London, 1965.

Talmage, F. Disputation and Dialogue: A Reader
in the Jewish-Christian Encounter. New York,
1975.

Taylor, H.O. The Medieval Mind. 2 vols. London,
1925.

Thomsen, P. Loca Sancta. Halle an der Saale,
1907.

Thorndike, L. A History of Magic and Experimental
Science during the First Thirteen Centuries
of Our Era. 8 vols. New York, 1923-1958.

Trachtenberg, J. The Devil and the Jews: The Medieval Conception of the Jews and Its Relation
to Modern Antisemitism. New York, 1961.

Twersky, I. Rabad of Posquières: A Twelfth Century Talmudist. Cambridge, Mass., 1962.

Tydings, J.M. The Messiah of the Targums, Talmuds
and Rabbinical Writers. Louisville, 1912.

Urbach, A. The Tosafists. Jerusalem, 1957.

Vasiliev, A. History of the Byzantine Empire. 2
vols. Madison, 1958.

Wasserzug, D. The Messianic Idea. London, 1913.

White, W.C. Chinese Jews (A Compilation of Matters
    Relating to the Jews of K'ai-Fêng Fu). 2nd
    ed. New York, 1966.

Wilson, A.T. The Persian Gulf. Oxford, 1928.

Wright, J.K. The Geographical Lore of the Time of
    the Crusades. New York, 1965.

_____. Human Nature in Geography. Cambridge,
    Mass., 1966.

Ya'ari, A. Sheluhei Erez Yisrael (History of the
    Mission from Palestine to the Diaspora from
    the Time of the Destruction of the Second Tem-
    ple until the Beginning of the New Settle-
    ment). Jerusalem, 1951.

Yule, H. Cathay and the Way Thither. 4 vols. Lon-
    don, 1915.

Zeitlin, S. Maimonides. New York, 1935.

Zukerman, A.J. A Jewish Princedom in Feudal France
    768-900. New York and London, 1972.

3. Articles

Abrahams, I. "Sambary and Benjamin of Tudela,"
    J.Q.R., II (1890), 107.

Adler, E.N. "The Installation of the Egyptian
    Nagid," J.Q.R., IX (1897), 717-20.

_____. "The Jews in Southern Italy," J.Q.R.,
    XIV (1902), 111-15.

Adler, M.N. "Chinese Jews," J.Q.R., XIII (1901),
    18-41.

Aescoly, A.Z. "Some Comments on the History of
    Messianic Movements," Sinai, VI (1939), 80-82.

Albeck, S. "Rabbenu Tam's attitude to the Problems of his time," Zion, XIX (1954), 104-141.

Altmann, B. "Studies in Medieval German Jewish History," P.A.A.J.R., X (1940), 5-98.

Anderson, A.R. "Alexander at the Caspian Gates," Transactions of the American Philological Association, LIX (1928), 130-63.

Andreades, A.M. "The Economic Life of the Byzantine Empire," Byzantium. Ed. N.H. Baynes and H. St. L.B. Moss. Oxford, 1948, pp. 51-70.

_____. "The Jews in the Byzantine Empire," Economic History, III (1934-37), 1-23.

_____. "Sur Benjamin de Tudèle," Byzantinische Zeitschrift, XXX (1930), 458-61.

Ankori, Z. "The Correspondence of Tobias Ben Moses the Karaite of Constantinople," Essays of Jewish Life and Thought. New York, 1959, pp. 1-38.

_____. "Elijah Bashyachi: An Inquiry into His Traditions Concerning the Beginnings of Karaism in Byzantium," Tarbiz, XXV (1955-56), 183-201.

_____. "Some Aspects of Karaite Rabbinite Relations in Byzantium on the Eve of the First Crusade," P.A.A.J.R., XXIV (1955), 19-25; XXV (1956), 166-73.

Ankori, Z. "Studies in the Messianic Doctrine of Yehuda Hadassi," Tarbiz, XXX (1960-61), 186-208.

Arce Augustin. "El Sepulcro de David en un Texto de Benjamin de Tudela," Sefarad, XXIII (1963), 105-15.

Assaf, S. "About Jewish Activity in Moslem Countries during the Middle Ages, Especially in

Egypt and India," Zion, V (1939-40), 232-36.

_____. "An Ancient Synagogue in Damoha (Egypt)," Texts and Studies in Jewish History. Jerusalem, 1946, pp. 155-62.

_____. "Egyptian Jews in the Time of Maimonides," Moznaim, III (1935), 414-32.

_____. "From Egypt to Aden and India," Zion, IV (1938), 232-36.

_____. "New Movements of Proselytes and of Messianism," Zion, V (1939-40), 112-24.

_____. "Slavery and Slave Trade among the Jews during the Middle Ages," Zion, IV (1938), 91-125; V (1940), 271-280.

_____. "To the History of the Synagogue on Samuel's Tomb," B.J.P.E.S., VI (1939), 143-44.

Bacher, W. "An Alleged Old Source on the Jews of Yemen," J.Q.R., V (1893), 345-47.

_____. "Das Gaonat in Palästina und das Exilarchat in Aegypten," J.Q.R., XV (1908), 79-96.

Baer, Y. "Israel and Exile in the Eyes of Medieval Generations," Zion-Measef, VI (1934), 149-71.

_____. "The Political Situation of the Spanish Jews in the Age of Jehuda Halevi," Zion, I (1935-36), 6-23.

_____. "Rashi and the Historical Reality of His Time," Tarbiz, XX (1949), 320-32.

_____. "The Religious Social Tendency of Sefer Hasidim," Zion, III (1937), 1-50.

_____. "The Theory of the Natural Equality of Early Man According to Ashkenazi Hasidim," Zion, XXXII (1968), 129-36.

396

Bar-Adon, P. "Khaibaris of Jewish Origin," <u>B.J.P.</u>
    <u>E.S.</u>, VII (1946), 38-39.

Baron, S.W. "Yehuda Halevi: An Answer to a Histor-
    ical Challenge," <u>Ancient and Medieval Jewish</u>
    <u>History, Essays</u>. New Jersey, 1972. pp. 128-
    48.

_____. "The Historical Outlook of Maimonides,"
    <u>P.A.A.J.R.</u>, VI (1934-35), 5-114.

Ben Sasson, H.H. "Exile and Redemption through the
    Eyes of the Spanish Exiles," <u>I.F. Baer Jubilee</u>
    <u>Volume</u>. Jerusalem, 1960, pp. 216-27.

_____. "Jewish Medieval Chronography and Its
    Problems," <u>HaHistoryonim V'Askholot HaHistor-</u>
    <u>iah</u>. Jerusalem, 1963, pp. 29-49.

Ben Zvi, Y. "The Jews of Kheibar and Their Destiny,"
    <u>Knesset</u>, Book V. Tel-Aviv, 1940, pp. 281-302.

Benedict, B.S. "On the history of the Torah-center
    in Provence," <u>Tarbiz</u>, XXII (1951), 85-109.

Berger, A. "The Messianic Self-consciousness of
    Abraham Abulafia," <u>Essays on Jewish Life and</u>
    <u>Thought</u>. Presented in honor of S. Baron. Eds.
    J. Blau, <u>and others</u>. New York, 1959, pp. 55-
    61.

Berger, D. "The Attitude of St. Bernard of Clair-
    vaux Toward the Jews," <u>P.A.A.J.R.</u>, XL (1972),
    pp. 89-108.

Blumenkranz, B. "Les auteurs chrétiens latins du
    moyen âge sur les Juifs et le Judaisme," <u>R.E.</u>
    <u>J.</u>, CIX (1948), 3-67; CXI (1952), 5-61; CXIII
    (1954), 5-36; CXIV (1955), 37-90; CXVII (1958),
    5-58.

_____. "Quartiers juifs en France (XIIe, XIIIe,
    et XIVe siècles)," <u>Mélgnges de philosophie et</u>
    <u>de littérature juives</u>, III-V (1958-62), 77-86.

Borchardt, P.   "Der Reiseweg des Rabbi Benjamin von
    Tudela und des Rabbi Petachia aus Regensburg
    in Mesopotamien und Persien," J.J.L.G., XVI
    (1924), 137-62.

_____.   "The Sculpture in Front of the Lateran
    as Described by Benjamin of Tudela and Magis-
    ter Gregorius," Journal of Roman Studies, XXVI
    (1936), 68-70.

Bornstein, I.   "The Custom of Ordination and Its
    History," Hattekufah, IV (1919), 393-426.

Braslavsky, I.   "The Jewish Community of Chaibar,"
    Zion, I (1935), 148-84.

_____.   "The Jews of Khaibar in Palestine at the
    End of the Arab Period," B.J.P.E.S., VII (1940),
    78-84.

_____.   "To the History of the Synagogue on
    Samuel's Tomb," B.J.P.E.S., VII (1946), 40.

Brawer, A.Y.   "Jerusalem the Holy City," Mahnayim,
    No. 82 (1963), pp. 84-87.

Briggs, J.C.   "An Investigation of the Mount of
    Olives in the Judaeo Christian Tradition,"
    H.U.C.A., XXVIII (1957), 137-80.

Brutzkus, J.   "Trade with Eastern Europe, 800-1200,"
    Economic Historical Review, XIII (1943), 31-41.

Buchler, A.   "The Reading of the Law and Prophets
    in a Triennial Cycle," J.Q.R., V (1893), 420-
    68; VI (1894), 1-73.

Byrne, E.H.   "The Genoese Colonies in Syria," The
    Crusades and Other Historical Essays Presented
    to D.C. Munro. New York, 1928, pp. 139-82.

_____.   "Genoese Trade with Syria in the Twelfth
    Century," A.H.R., XXV (1919-20), 191-219.

Cahen, C.   "Y a-t-il eu des Rahdānites?" R.E.J.,

CXXIII (1964), 499-505.

Chalandon, F.   "The Later Commeni," C.M.H., IV,
    351-84.

Chazan, R.   "Jewish Settlement in Northern France,
    1096-1306," R.E.J., CXXVIII (1969), 41-65.

_____.   "The Bray Incident of 1192:   Realpolitik
    and Folk Slander," P.A.A.J.R., XXXVII (1969),
    1-18.

_____.   "The Blois Incident of 1171:   A Study in
    Jewish Intercommunal Organization," P.A.A.J.R.,
    XXXVI (1968), 13-31.

_____.   "A Twelfth Century of Communal History
    of Spires Jewry," R.E.J., CXXVIII (1969), 253-
    257.

Cohen, G.D.   "Messianic Postures of Ashkenazim and
    Sephardim," Studies of the Leo Baeck Institute.
    Ed. M. Kreitzberger. New York, 1967, pp. 115-
    156.

Cohen, S.S.   "Palestine in Jewish Theology," H.U.
    C.A. Jubilee Volume (1875-1925), 171-209.

Corcos-Abulafia, D.   "The Attitude of the Almohadic
    Rulers toward the Jews," Zion, XXXII (1968),
    137-60.

Cowley, A.E.   "Samaritan Dealings with Jews," J.Q.
    R., XVI (1904), 477-84.

Crémieux, A.   "Les Juifs de Marseilles au moyen âge,"
    R.E.J., XLVI (1903), 1-47; 246-268; XLVII (1903),
    62-86; 243-261.

Dalman, D.G.   "Der Pass von Michmas," Deutscher
    Palästina-Vereins Zeitschrift, XXVII (1904),
    161-73.

Dan, J.   "Rabbi Eleazar of Worms' Sefer Ha-Hakhma
    ("Book of Wisdom") and Its Significance for

the History of the Doctrines and Literature
of the Ashkenazic Hassidim," Zion, XXIX (1964),
168-81.

Dan, J. "The Vicissitudes in the Esoterism of the
German Hasidim," Studies in Mysticism and Religion Presented to G.G. Scholem. Jerusalem,
1967, pp. 87-100.

Denidas, M.A. "Leucas or Arta?" Ipeirotica Khronica, VI (1931), 23-28.

Denison, R. "Prester John and the Empire of Ethiopia," Travel and Travellers of the Middle Ages.
Ed. A.P. Newton. New York, 1926, pp. 174-78.

Deutsch, K.W. "Anti Semitic Ideas in the Middle
Ages," Journal of the History of Ideas, VI
(1945), 239-254.

Diehl, C. "The Fourth Crusade and the Latin Empire," C.M.H., IV., 415-31.

Dietrich, E.L. "Das Judentum im Zeitalter der Kreuzzüge," Saeculum, III (1952), 94-131.

Dinur, B.Z. "Halevi's Emigration to the Holy Land
and the Messianic Ferment in His Days," Minha
l'David. Jerusalem, 1935, pp. 157-82.

_____. "A Study of the History of the Jews in
Palestine during the First Crusade," Zion-
Measef, II (1927), 38-66.

Duncalf, F. "The Peasant's Crusade," A.H.R., XXVI
(1920-21), 440-53.

Edelmann, R. "Das 'Buch der Frommen' als Ausdruck
des volkstuemlichen Geistesleben der deutschen
Juden im Mittelalter," Miscellanea Mediaevalia
IV: Das Judentum im Mittelalter. Berlin,
1966, pp. 55-71.

Eliash, J. "New Information of Eleventh Century
Palestine," Sefunot, II (1958), 7-25.

400

Fischel, W.J.   "Azarbaijan in Jewish History,"
P.A.A.J.R., XXII (1953), 1-21.

_____.   "The History of Persian Jews during the
Sefevid Dynasty," Zion, II (1937), 273-94.

_____.   "Isfahan," The Joshua Starr Memorial
Volume, New York, 1953, pp. 111-28.

_____.   "The Jews of Central Asia (Khorasan) in
Medieval Hebrew and Islamic Literature," Historia Judaica VII (1945), 29-50.

_____.   "Kurdistan," J.S.S., VI (1944), 195-226.

_____.   "New Sources for the History of the Jew-
ish Diaspora in Asia in the 16th Century,"
J.Q.R., XL (1950), 379-99.

_____.   "The Region of the Persian Gulf and Its
Jewish Settlements in Islamic Times," Alexander Marx Jubilee Volume. New York, 1950, pp.
203-30.

Fischel, W.J.   "The 'Resh Galuta' in Arabic Literature," Magnes Anniversary Book. Jerusalem,
1938, pp. 181-87.

Frankel, Z.   "Galerie jüdischer Reisebeschreiber,"
M.G.W.J., Dresden, 1852, pp. 523, 541, 563-82.

Friedländer, M.   "Ibn Ezra in England," J.Q.R.,
VIII (1896), 140-54.

Funkenstein, A.   "Changes in the Patterns of Christian Anti-Jewish Polemics in the 12th Century,"
Zion, XXXIII (1968), 125-44.

Génicot, L.   "On the Evidence of Growth of Population in the West from the Eleventh to the
Thirteenth Century," Change in Medieval Society. Ed. S. Thrupp. New York, 1964, pp. 14-29.

Gil, M.   "The Radhanite Merchants and the Land of
Radhan," Journal of the Economic and Social

History of the Orient, XVII (1974), 299-328.

Goitein, S.D. "The Biography of Rabbi Judah Ha-
Levi in the Light of the Cairo Geniza Documents," Zion, XXVI (1960-61), 170-79.

_____. "Congregation Versus Community," J.Q.R.,
XLIV (1953-54), 291-304.

_____. "Jewish Society and Institutions under
Islam," Journal of World History, XI (1968),
170-84.

_____. "The Jews of Yemen between the Gaonate
of Egypt and the Exilarchate of Baghdad,"
Sinai, XXXIII (1952-53), 225-37.

_____. "The Last Phase of Yehuda Halevi's Life
in the Light of the Geniza Papers," Tarbiz,
XXIV (1954), 1-47.

_____. "The Local Jewish Community in the Light
of the Cairo Geniza Records," J.J.S., XII
(1961), 133-58.

_____. "The Mentality of the Middle Class in
Medieval Islam," Studies in Islamic History
and Institutions. Leiden, 1968, pp. 255-78.

_____. "Petitions to Fatimid Caliphs from the
Cairo Genizah," J.Q.R., XLV (1954-55), 30-38.

_____. "R. Jehudah Halevi in Spain in Light of
Genizah Writings," Tarbiz, XXIV (1952-55),
134-49.

_____. "The Sanctity of Palestine in Moslem
Piety," B.J.P.E.S., XII (1945-46), 120-27.

_____. "Slaves and Slavegirls in the Cairo
Geniza Records," Arabica, IX (1962), 1-20.

Golb, N. "New light on the persecution of French
Jews at the time of the Frist Crusade," P.A.
A.J.R., XXXIV (1966), 1-45.

402

Golb, N. "The Topography of the Jews of Medieval Egypt," Journal of Near Eastern Studies, XXIV (1956), 251-70.

Goldziher, I. "Bücherbesprechungen," Zeitschrift des Deutschen Palästina-Vereins, XXVIII (Leipzig, 1905), 151-54.

Goode, A.D. "The Exilarchate in the Eastern Caliphate, 637-1258," J.Q.R., XXXI (1940-41), 149-69.

Grayzel, S. "Pope Alexander III and the Jews," Salo W. Baron Jubilee Volume. 3 vols. Eds. S. Lieberman and A. Hyman. Jerusalem, 1974. Vol. II, pp. 555-572.

Gressman, H. "The Sources of Israel's Messianic Hope," American Journal of Theology, XVII (1913), 173-94.

Gross, H. "Notice sur Abba Mari de Lunel," R.E.J., IV (1882), 192-207.

_____. "Zur Geschichte der Juden in Arles," M.G.W.J., XXXI (1882), 465-471, 496-523.

Ha'alalel, D. "Ezra the Scribe in Moslem Tradition," Zion-Measef, V (1933), 214-17.

Halkin, A.S. "On the history of the Almohade persecution," The Joshua Starr Memorial Volume. New York, 1953. Pp. 101-110.

Haskins, C.H. "Further Notes on the Sicilian Translation of the Twelfth Century," Harvard Studies in Classical Philology, XXIII (1912), 155-66.

Hirschberg, J.W. "The Tombs of David and Solomon in Moslem Tradition," Eretz Israel: Publications of the Israel Exploration Society, III (1954), 213-20.

Hirshberg, H.Z. "The Desire for Freedom in the

Legends of the Ten Tribes," <u>Mahnayim</u>, No. 80
(1963), pp. 96-100.

Hoeniger, R.   "Zur Geschichte der Juden Deutsch-
lands im frühern Mittelalter," <u>Z.G.J.D.</u>, o.s.
I (1887), 65-97, 136-151.

Holmes, U.T.   "The Idea of a Twelfth Century Renaissance," <u>Speculum</u>, XXVI (1951), 643-51.

Hyamson, A.M.   "The Lost Tribes and the Influence
of the Search for Them on the Return of the
Jews to England," <u>J.Q.R.</u>, XV (1903), 640-76.

Isaac-Ezekiel-Jehuda.   "The Wailing Wall," <u>Zion-
Measef</u>, III (1929), 95-163.

Ish Shalom, M.   "Pilgrimage to Palestine during
the Middle Ages," <u>Ha'olam</u>, XLI (1931), 804-5.

_____.   "Traditions of Graves in Palestine,"
<u>Sinai</u>, VII (1940-41), 79-88, 221-35, 351-58.

Katz, S.   "Some Aspects of Economic Life in the
Byzantine Empire," <u>Pacific Historical Review</u>,
VII (1938), 27-39.

Kaufmann, D.   "A Hitherto Unknown Messianic Movement among the Jews, Particularly Those of
Germany and the Byzantine Empire," <u>J.Q.R.</u>, X
(1898), 139-51.

_____.   "A Rumour about the Ten Tribes in Pope
Martin V's Time," <u>J.Q.R.</u>, IV (1892), 503-8.

_____.   "Le Sambation," <u>R.E.J.</u>, XXII (1891),
285-87.

Kingsley, G.A.   "The Jews of the Extreme Eastern
Diaspora," <u>American Monthly Menorah</u>, V (1888),
10-19, 144-51.

Koebner, R.   "The Settlement and Colonisation of
Europe," <u>C.E.H.</u>, Cambridge, 1942, I, 1-89.

Krauss, S. "L'Émigration de 300 rabbins en Palestine en l'an 1211," R.E.J., LXXXII (1926), 333-352.

Kuk, S.H. "Note to the History of the Synagogue on Samuel's Tomb," B.J.P.E.S., VI (1939), 143-44.

_____. "R. Jechiel from Paris and Palestine," Zion-Measef, V (1933), 97-102.

Langmuir, G.I. "Judei Nostri and the Beginning of Capetian Legislation," Traditio, XVI (1960), 203-239.

Lebrecht, F. "Essay on the Caliphate of Baghdad during the Latter Half of the Twelfth Century," Benjamin of Tudela, Sefer Masa'ot. 2 vols. Ed. A. Asher. Berlin, 1840, II, 318-92.

Letts, M. "Prester John—Sources and Illustrations," Notes and Queries, CLXXXVIII (January-June, 1945), 178-80; 204-7; 246-48; 266-68; CLXXXIX (July-December, 1945), 4-7.

Lévi, I. "Les Juifs de France du milieu du IXe siècle aux croisades," R.E.J., LII (1906), 161-68.

Lewis, B. "An Apocalyptic Vision of Islamic History," Bulletin of the School of Oriental and African Studies, XIII (1949-51), 308-38.

Liebeschütz, H. "The Crusading Movement in Its Bearing on the Christian Attitude Towards Jewry," J.J.S., X (1959), 97-111.

Loeb, I. "La Controverse Religieuse entre les Chrétiens et les Juifs au Moyen Âge en France et en Espagne," Revue de l'Histoire des Religions, XVII (1888), 311-337; XVIII (1889), 133-156.

_____. "Polémistes chrétiens et juifs en France

et en Espagne," R.E.J., XVIII (1889), 43-70, 219-242.

Loewe, H.M.J. "The Seljuks," C.M.H., IV, 299-317.

Lopez, R.S. "Silk Industry in the Byzantine Empire," Speculum, XX (1945), 1-42.

Lynch, H.B. "Across Luristan to Ispahan," Royal Geographical Society. Proceedings, Sept. 1890, pp. 533-53.

Mähl, S. "Jerusalem in Mittelalterlicher Sicht," Die Welt als Geschichte, XXII (1962), 11-26.

Malter, H. "Shem Tob Ben Joseph Palquera," J.Q.R., I (1910), 151-81.

Mandelbaum, D.G. "The Jewish Way of Life in Cochin," J.S.S., I, No. 4 (1949), 423-60.

Mann, J. "Glanure de la Gueniza: 1. À Propos des Dix Tribes Perdues," R.E.J., LXII (1922), 148-54.

_____. "The Messianic Movements in the Time of the Early Crusades," Hattekufah, XXIII (1925), 243-61; XXIV (1928), 335-58.

_____. "Obadya le prosélyte," R.E.J., LXXI (1920), 89-93.

_____. "The Office of the Exilarchate in Babylonia and Its Branches at the End of the Period of the Gaonate," A Memorial Book to A. Poznanski. Jerusalem, 1969, pp. 18-32.

_____. "The Responsa of the Babylonian Geonim as a Source of Jewish History," J.Q.R., VII (1917), 457-90; VIII (1918), 339-66; IX (1919), 139-79.

Marcus, J.R. "Studies in the Chronicle of Ahīma 'atz," P.A.A.J.R., IV (1933-34), 85-91.

Marx, A. "The Correspondence between the Rabbis
of Southern France and Maimonides about Astrology," H.U.C.A., III (1926), 311-42.

_____. An Essay on the Year of Redemption,"
Hazofeh LeHochmat Israel, V (1921), 194-202.

Morgenstern, J. "The Culting Setting of the 'Enthronement Psalms,'" H.U.C.A., XXXV (1964),
14-39.

_____. "An Investigation of the Mount of Olives
in the Judaeo Christian Tradition," H.U.C.A.,
XXVIII (1957), 137-80.

Munk, M. "The Caraites of the Crimea," Jewish
Chronicle and Hebrew Observer, June 27, 1856,
p. 637. (Harvard University, Microfilm, NC
100.)

Munro, D.C. "The Speech of Pope Urban II at Clermont, 1095," A.H.R., XI (1905-6), 231-42.

Neubauer, A. "Eldad the Danite," J.Q.R., III
(1891), 541-44.

_____. "The Literature of the Jews in Yemen,"
J.Q.R., III (1891), 604-22.

_____. "Origin and Growth of the Nagid Dignity,"
J.Q.R., VIII (1896), 551-55.

_____. "Where Are the Ten Tribes?" J.Q.R., I.
(1889), 14-28, 95-114, 185-201, 408, 423.

Neustadt, D. "Contributions to the Economic History of the Jews in Egypt in the Middle Ages,"
Zion, II (1937), 216-55.

_____. "Some Problems Concerning the 'Negidut'
in Egypt during the Middle Ages," Zion, IV
(1938), 126-49.

Nowell, C.E. "The Historical Prester John," Speculum, XXVIII (1953), 435-45.

Nowell, C.E. "The Old Man of the Mountain," <u>Specu-</u>
<u>lum</u>, XXII (1947), 497-519.

Olschki, L. "Ponce de Leon's Fountain of Youth:
History of a Geographical Myth," <u>Hispanic-</u>
<u>American Historical Review</u>, XXI (1941), 361-
85.

Osborn, A.M. "Were the Ten Tribes of Israel Ever
Lost?" <u>Methodist Quarterly Review</u>, July 1885,
pp. 419-40.

Ostrogorsky, G. "Agrarian Conditions in the Byzantine Empire in the Middle Ages," <u>C.E.H.</u> Cambridge, Mass., 1942, I, 194-223.

Passant, E.J. "The Effects of the Crusades upon
Western Europe," <u>C.M.H.</u>, V, 320-33.

Perlman, M. "The Medieval Polemics between Islam
and Judaism," <u>Religion in a Religious Age</u>.
(Cambridge, Mass., 1974). Ed. S.D. Goitein,
pp. 103-129.

Peron, M. "Israel and Exile in R. Jehuda Halevi's
Philosophy," <u>Mahnayim</u>, No. 80 (1963), pp. 35-
37.

Pfaff, M. "Die soziale Stellung des Judentums in
der Auseinandersetzung zwischen Kaiser und
Kirche vom 3. bis zum 4. Laterankonzil (1179-
1215)," <u>Vierteljahrschrift für Sozial- und</u>
<u>Wirtschaftsgeschichte</u>, LII (1965), 168-206.

Pirenne, H. "La Fin du Commerce des Syriens en
Occident," <u>Annuaire, Institut de Philologie</u>
<u>d'Histoire Orientales et Slaves</u>, Brussels, II
(1945), 677-87.

Poliak, N.A. "David Alroy," <u>Ha-Kinnus, The World</u>
<u>Gathering for Jewish Studies</u>. I (Jerusalem,
1952), 404-6.

Postan, M. "The Trade of Medieval Europe; the

North," <u>C.E.H.</u> Cambridge, 1942, II, 119-257.

Poznanski, S. "The Beginnings of the Karaite Settlement in Jerusalem," <u>Jerusalem.</u> Ed. A.M.
Luncz, X (1913), 83-116.

_____. "The Establishers of Religious Sects in
Judaism," <u>Reshumoth</u>, I (Odessa, 1918), 207-16.

_____. "Mesvi-al-Okbari: Chef d'Une Secte
Juive au Dixième Siècle," <u>R.E.J.</u>, XXXIV (1897),
161-80.

Prawer, J. "The City and Duchy of Ascalon in the
Crusader Period," <u>Eretz Israel</u>, V (1958), 224-
38.

_____. "Jerusalem the Capital City of the Cru-
saders," <u>Yehudah Vi-Yerushalayim</u> (Israel Exploration Society). Jerusalem, 1957, pp. 90-
105.

_____. "Jewish Resettlement in Crusader Jerusa-
lem," <u>Ariel</u>, XIX (1967), 60-66.

_____. "The Jews in the Latin Kingdom of Jeru-
salem," <u>Zion</u>, XI (1945-46), 38-82.

_____. "The Vicissitudes of the Jewish and
Karaitic Quarter in Jerusalem during the Arabic Period, 640-1099," <u>Zion</u>, XII (1946-47),
136-48.

Previté-Orton, C.W. "The Italian Cities Till C.
1200," <u>C.M.H.</u>, V, 208-41.

Rabinowitz, L. "Eldad Ha-Dani and China," <u>J.Q.R.</u>,
XXXVI (1946), 231-38.

_____. "The Route of the Radanites," <u>J.Q.R.</u>,
XXXV (1944-45), 251-80.

Rapaport, S.Y. "About Independent Jews in Arabia
and Kush Till Today," <u>Bikure ha-itim</u>, IV

(1824), 51-77. (At Wayne State University the article has been wrongly catalogued under the year 1923.)

Rawlinson, M. "Notes on a March from Zoháb, at the Foot of Zagros, along the Mountains to Khúzistán (Susiana), and from Thence through the Province of Luristan to Kirmánscháh, in the Year 1836," J.R.G.S., IX (1839), 26-116.

Reifmann, J. "Comments on a Book: Eldad Hadani," Ha-Karmel, VIII (1870), 254, 262, 279-280, 286-87.

Rosenthal, J. "Anti-Christian Disputational Literature to the End of the Eighteenth Century," Areshet, II (1960), 130-179.

Ross, J.B. "A Study of the Twelfth Century Interest in the Antiquities of Rome," Medieval and Historiographical Essays in Honor of James Westfall Thompson. Ed. J.L. Cate and E.N. Anderson, Chicago, 1938.

Roth, C. "The Qualification of Jewish Physicians in the Middle Ages," Speculum, XXVIII (1953), 834-843.

_____. "Benjamin of Tudela: The Last Stage," Annuario di Studi Ebraici, Ed. Elio Toaff (1968-69), pp. 47-50.

_____. "European Jewry in the Dark Ages: A Revised Picture," H.U.C.A., XXIII, Part II (1950-51), 151-169.

_____. "The Jews in the Middle Ages," C.M.H., VII, 632-63.

_____. "On the History of the Jews in Cyprus," Sefer Zikaron le Yitzhak ben Tzvi. Jerusalem, 1954, pp. 285-99.

Rousset, P. "La conception de l'histoire à l'époque féodale," Mélanges d'histoire du moyen âge, dédiés à la mémoire de Louis Halphen. Paris, 1951, pp. 623-33.

Rushforth, McN. G. "Magister Gregorius de Mirabilibus Urbis Roma: A new description of Rome in the Twelfth Century," Journal of Roman Studies, IX (1919), 14-58.

Sapir, E. "Notes on Judaeo-German Phonology," J.Q.R., VI (1916), 231-66.

Sasson, S.D. "Iggeroth Paras We-Teman," Hazofeh, IX (1925), 209-31.

Scheiber, A. "Éléments fabuleux dans l'Eshkol Hakofer," R.E.J., CVIII (1948), 41-62.

Schiffmann, S. "Heinrich IV, und die Bischöfe in ihrem Verhalten zu den deutschen Juden zur Zeit des ersten Kreuzzüges," Zeitschrift für die Geschichte der Juden in Deutschland. III (1931), 39-58, 233-250.

Schirmann, H. "The Birthplace of Judah Halevi," Tarbiz, X (1939), 237-239.

_____. "The Life of Jehuda Ha-Levi," Tarbiz, IX (1936-38), 35-54.

Scholem, G. "Jüdische Mystik in Westeuropa im 12. und 13. Jahrhundert," Miscellanea Mediaevalia. IV: Das Judentum im Mittelalter. Berlin, 1966, pp. 37-54.

Schwarzfuchs, S. "De la condition des Juifs de France aux XIIe et XIIIe siècles," R.E.J., CXXV (1966), 226-229.

Setton, K.M. "On the Importance of Land Tenure and Agrarian Taxation in the Byzantine Empire from the Fourth Century to the Fourth Crusade." American Journal of Philology, LXXIV (1953), 225-59.

Shiel, J. "Notes on a Journey from Tabriz, through

Kurdistán, via Van, Bitlís, Sé'ert and Erbil,
to Suleimániyeh, in July and August, 1836,"
J.R.G.S., VIII (1838), 54-101.

Shulvass, M.A. "Crusades, Martyrdom, and the Mar-
ranos of Ashkenaz," Published in his Between
the Rhine and the Bosphorus: Studies and
Essays in European Jewish History. Chicago,
1964, pp. 1-14.

Shwarzboim, H. "The Messianic Movements of Alroy,
Molcho and Reubeni," Mahnayim, No. 81 (1963),
pp. 12-19.

Somogyi, J. "The Part of Islam in Oriental Trade."
Islamic Culture: The Hyderabad Quarterly Review, XXX (1956), 179-89.

Spiegel, S. "In Monte Dominus Videbitur: The Martyrs of Blois and the Early Accusations of
Ritual Murder," The Mordecai M. Kaplan Jubilee
Volume. New York, 1953. Hebrew Section, 267-
287.

Starr, J. "Contribution to the Life of Nahari ben
Nissim of Fustat," Zion, I (1935), 436-53.

Steinschneider, M. "Jüdische Schriften zur Geographie Palästinas," Jerusalem, ed. A.M. Luncz,
III (Jerusalem, 1889), 36-64.

Stevenson, W.B. "The First Crusade," C.M.H., V,
265-99.

_____. "Islam in Syria and Egypt," C.M.J., V,
242-64.

Strauss (Ashtor-Strauss), E. "A Journey to India,"
Zion, IV (1938), 217-41.

_____. "Of Economic Activity of Jews in Moslem
Countries during the Middle Ages," Zion, IV
(1939), 217-41; VII (1942), 140-55.

_____. "Prolegomena to the Medieval History of

Oriental Jewry," J.Q.R., L (1959), 55-68, 147-
66.

Strauss (Ashtor-Strauss), E. "Saladin and the
Jews," H.U.C.A., XXVII (1956), 305-26.

_____. "Some Features of the Jewish Communities
in Medieval Egypt," Zion, XXX (1965), 61-78,
128-57.

Sukenik, A.L. "Some Comments on Letters with Respect to Travels in Palestine from the Middle
Ages," Zion-Measef, II (1927), 108-11.

Sull, R.L. "Itinerario di Benjamino da Tudela,"
Vessilo Israelitico, XXXVI, No. 56 (1888),
56-58.

Swabe, M. "The Jews and the Temple Mount after the
Conquest of Jerusalem by Omar," Zion-Measef,
II (1927), 99-107.

Talmage, F. "Judaism on Christianity: Christianity on Judaism," The Study of Judaism. New
York, 1972, pp. 81-112.

_____. "R. David Kimhi as Polemicist," H.U.C.A.,
XXXVIII (1967), 213-235.

Tamar, D. "Luria and Vital as the Messiah Ben
Joseph," Safed Volume. II, eds. Itzhak Ben
Zwi and M. Benayahu. Jerusalem, 1963, 167-
177.

Täubler, E. "Urkundliche Beiträge zur Geschichte
der Juden in Deutschland im Mittelalter,"
Mitteilungen des Gesamtarchivs der deutschen
Juden. 4 (Berlin, 1913), 31-62.

Tishby, I. "Rabbi Moses Cordovero as he appears in
the treatise of R. Mordekhai Dato," Safed
Volume. II, eds. Itzhak Ben Zwi and M. Benayahu. Jerusalem, 1963, 119-166.

Tucci, R. "Di Benjamino di Tudela e il suo Viaggio,"

Societa geografica italiana: Bolletino, VII
(1941), 486-517.

Twersky, I.   "Aspects of the Social and Cultural
History of Provencal Jewry," Journal of World
History, XI (1968), 185-207.

Urbach, E.E.   "Études sur la Literature Polémique
au Moyen Âge," R.E.J., C (1935), 49-77.

Uspensky, F.   "Benjamin of Tudela's Notes on His
Journey," Annaly, III (1923), 5-20.

Vasiliev, A.   "Economic Relations between Byzantium
and Old Russia," Journal of Economic and Business History, IV (1931-32), 314-34.

Vilnai, Z.   "Eben Shetiya—The Foundation of the
World," Mahnayim, No. 84 (1963), p. 71.

Wacholder, B.Z.   "A History of Sabbatical Readings
of Scripture for the Triennial Cycle." Essays
on Jewish Chronology and Chronography (New
York, 1976), pp. 137-211.

Wallach, L.   "Yossipon and the Alexander Romance,"
J.Q.R., XXXVII (1947), 407-22.

Werbalowsky, R.J.Z.   "Messianism in Jewish History,"
Journal of World History, XI (1968), 30-46.

_____.   "Crises of Messianism," Judaism, VII
(1958), 106-20.

Worman, E.J.   "Notes on the Jews in Fustat from
Cambridge Genizah Documents," J.Q.R., XVIII
(1905), 1-39.

Ya'ari, A.   "History of the Pilgrimage to Meron,"
Tarbiz, XXXI (1961), 72-104.

_____.   "Messianic Movements in Yemen," Mahna-
yim, No. 81 (1963), pp. 46-57.

Yeivin, S. "Sepulchres of the Kings of the House of David," Journal of Near Eastern Studies, VII (1948), 30-45.

Zeide, J. "On Medicine and Natural History in the Book of Travels of Rabbi Benjamin of Tudela," The Hebrew Medical Journal, XX (1953), 137-41.

Zimmels, H.J. "Scholars and Scholarship in Byzantium and Italy," World History of the Jewish People. Ed. C. Roth. Tel-Aviv, 1966, pp. 175-88.

Zunz, L. "Essay on the Geographical Literature of the Jews from the Remotest Times to the Year 1841," Benjamin of Tudela, Sefer Masa'ot. Ed. A. Asher. 2 vols. Berlin, 1840, II, 230-317.

417

ABOUT THE AUTHOR

Dr. Yosef Levanon grew up in Jerusalem, Israel, where he attended the Hebrew University from which he earned his B.A. and M.A. degrees in Medieval European History. He later attended the McGill University of Montreal, Canada, for doctoral studies and held a professorial position in Judaic Studies at Oakland University in Rochester, Michigan.

Dr. Levanon has served as the Dean of the Midrasha— College of Jewish Studies in Detroit, Michigan from 1974 to 1978, and currently heads the Winnipeg Hebrew Schools, an elementary and Collegiate Day School System located in Winnipeg, Canada.